Russell Moore has, through a careful evaluation of the contribution of Carl F. H. Henry and others, provided a unique insight for evangelicals attempting to grasp and apply what it means to be a Kingdom Christian. Dr. Moore is one of the brightest minds working today in the arena of the relationship of Christ and the church and their relationship to the culture. Every serious Christian will profit through the reading of this book.

> —PAIGE PATTERSON
> President, Southwestern Baptist Theological Seminary

For far too long, evangelicals have waited for a serious study of the Kingdom of God and its political application. That book has now arrived, and *The Kingdom of Christ* will redefine the conversation about evangelicalism and politics. Russell Moore combines stellar historical and theological research with a keen understanding of cultural and political realities. This is a serious book about a very serious subject, and we are all in Dr. Moore's debt for this outstanding contribution. This is a landmark book by one of evangelicalism's finest minds.

> —R. ALBERT MOHLER, JR.
> President, The Southern Baptist Theological Seminary

A faithful heir of Carl F. H. Henry, Russell Moore not only reasserts a coherent Kingdom consensus around which evangelicals can gravitate, he also shows us a way forward in strength and unity. Anyone who cares about the future of evangelicalism will read this volume with both great interest and care.

> —C. BEN MITCHELL
> Associate Professor of Bioethics and Contemporary Culture,
> Trinity Evangelical Divinity School

Russell D. Moore's *The Kingdom of Christ* is at once an enlightening account of the merging theological vision of recent dispensational and covenant theologies, and a stirring call for a ⟨...⟩ ⟨...⟩ engagement based on this theological consensus. Her⟨...⟩ ⟨...⟩elical social activism meet in a riveting accou⟨...⟩ ⟨...⟩ we now are in the evangelicalism of the early ⟨...⟩ ⟨...⟩mplishment is nothing short of remarkable; ⟨...⟩ ⟨...⟩ as it is profound. As Christians called to "understand the times," we are granted enormous assistance through his careful scholarship and insight, and the church will only be strengthened as she embraces his call for a truly biblical and theologically responsible framework for sociopolitical engagement.

—BRUCE A. WARE
Professor of Christian Theology and Senior Associate Dean,
School of Theology, The Southern Baptist Theological Seminary

Moore's book challenges all evangelicals to find common agreement on one basis for political and social involvement: the Kingdom of God is already here but it is not yet fully here. Therefore it is right to seek to advance its influence in all areas of life, including government and society, but with the realization that these activities are never enough apart from primary focus on Christ as King. This is an informative, thought-provoking, and refreshing study that will have perspective-modifying implications for the way Christians understand their role in the world in this present age.

—WAYNE GRUDEM
Research Professor of Bible and Theology, Phoenix Seminary

The KINGDOM of CHRIST

THE NEW
EVANGELICAL
PERSPECTIVE

RUSSELL D. MOORE

CROSSWAY BOOKS

A DIVISION OF
GOOD NEWS PUBLISHERS
WHEATON, ILLINOIS

Library of Congress Cataloging-in-Publication Data
Moore, Russell, 1971-
 The kingdom of Christ : the new evangelical perspective / Russell D. Moore.
  p. cm.
 Includes bibliographical references and index.
 ISBN 1-58134-627-1 (rov : alk. paper)
  1. Kingdom of God. 2. Jesus Christ—Kingdom. 3. Christianity and politics—United States. 4. Evangelicalism—United States. 5. Theology, Doctrinal. I. Title.
BT94.M625 2004
231.7'2—dc22
               2004011548

BP		14	13	12	11	10	09	08	07	06	05	04
15	14	13	12	11	10	9	8	7	6	5	4	3	2	1

FOR MARIA

"The heart of her husband trusts in her"

(PROVERBS 31:11).

CONTENTS

ACKNOWLEDGMENTS

I wish to thank Marvin Padgett, Bill Deckard, and the editorial staff at Crossway Books for their commitment to this project and, more importantly, for maintaining a witness for historic Christianity in an era when Christian publishing houses face the perennial temptation to be something less than Christian. Without Bruce Ware this book would never be in print. He guided me as a faithful mentor through the doctoral dissertation from which this study emerged. He also encouraged and motivated me as a friend, colleague, adviser, and brother in Christ. I am indebted to him in ways he will never know until the consummation of the Kingdom of our Christ. Along with Professor Ware, the rest of my colleagues at The Southern Baptist Theological Seminary deserve my thanks and appreciation, especially President R. Albert Mohler, Jr.

I also wish to express appreciation to my research assistant, Jason Glas, and to my staff members, Beth Holmes, Leah Finn, Mary Sills, and Katie Law, for all of their help with this project. I am grateful to Christopher W. Cowan for his suggestions on the original manuscript of this book. A band of three brothers in ministry also encouraged me through this project as I have bounced off of the three of them ideas about this—and practically everything else. They are David Prince, pastor of Ashland Avenue Baptist Church in Lexington, Kentucky; Peter R. Schemm, Jr., professor of theology at Southeastern Baptist Theological Seminary in Wake Forest, North Carolina; and Randy Stinson, executive director of the Council on Biblical Manhood and Womanhood.

It is certainly not enough to say "thank you" to my beloved wife Maria. She is a Proverbs 31 woman—and if there were a Proverbs 32, she would be that as well. She is a constant reminder to me that the Kingdom of God is not a theory to be tested, but is instead "righteousness and peace and joy in the Holy Spirit" (Rom. 14:17). In the providence of God, since the beginning of this book project, I now have two more names to "acknowledge," and what precious names they are. In the summer of 2002, Maria and I adopted from a Russian orphanage our two sons, Benjamin Jacob and Timothy Russell. Our two little men have filled our home with the sounds of running feet and shrieking giggles, and I love them more than I ever knew it was possible to love.

But Benjamin and Timothy also have profoundly shaped—and reshaped—my theology of the Kingdom of God. Shortly after we arrived home with them, strangers would ask us a persistent question—"Are they brothers?" Turning to the Scriptures, I was startled to see that this was the question being answered repeatedly in the New Testament about a church made up of Jew and Gentile, slave and free, rich and poor—the question of whether sonship and brotherhood is about something more than genetic lines. With new eyes, I was impressed with the magnitude of the Bible's image of our adoption as sons into one common household of the Father (Rom. 8:14-29; Gal. 3:26-4:7). My investigations led me to reconsider some too easily drawn conclusions. I am thankful to my sons for making me a better theologian, but I am far more grateful to them for making me a better Christian. Repeating "Our Father" in the Lord's Prayer was too commonplace for me, until I knew the joy of seeing these two little faces looking up at me, hearing from their mouths the word "Daddy." Thanks to them, I have a foretaste of the Kingdom joy of joining my brother Jesus in saying the most radical and liberating words in all of Christian theology—"Abba Father" (Gal. 4:6). I look forward to teaching them about the Kingdom of Christ. But, even more than that, I look forward to joining them in it, when every foe is vanquished, and Christ is Lord indeed.

—Russell D. Moore
Easter, 2004

INTRODUCTION

The title of this book is, in some ways, awfully misleading. After all, there really is no "new" evangelical perspective about the Kingdom of God. What is true about the Kingdom of Jesus was, in one sense, "new" only when it was announced on the shores of Galilee, whispered in the catacombs of Rome, and shouted in the marketplaces of Ephesus. The Kingdom concept is a mystery older than the creation itself—a mystery that points to God's cosmic purpose to sum up the entire cosmos under the rule of one human King, Jesus of Nazareth (Eph. 1:10). What is "new" is that many evangelicals have stopped arguing about the Kingdom of God—and have started seeking after it.

From the very beginning of the contemporary evangelical movement, conservative Protestants have bickered and splintered over Kingdom questions. Is it future or present? Is it spiritual or material? Is it the church or the world—or neither or both? Is it to be found in evangelizing the lost or in reclaiming the culture? After a half-century of searching the Scriptures, however, a quiet consensus is emerging about the Kingdom of God—a consensus that offers possibilities for evangelical theology to correct some longstanding errors and missteps. To some degree, the Kingdom confusion among evangelicals was a byproduct of the theological health of the movement—it being protected from liberalism, after all, by the divergent streams of dispensationalism and covenant theology. Now, evangelicals have the opportunity to stop polarizing around the Kingdom question—marching off into partisan camps at war over the prophecy charts at the back of our Bibles.

This book takes a look at the Kingdom through the prism of evangelical political action, but that is not because the Kingdom is a tool to equip evangelicals for politics. It is not even because evangelical politics is all that important, in the larger scheme of things. Instead, it is because the failure of evangelical politics points us to something far more important that underlies it—the failure of evangelical theology. It was the capitulation to the political regime of Nazi Germany that convinced Karl Barth that "German Christianity" had forgotten Christ. In the same way, it was the "uneasy conscience" of a socially and politically disengaged fundamentalism that prompted theologian Carl Henry to question whether evangelicals had an adequate doctrine of the Kingdom of God.[1] For Henry and his colleagues, the problem was not that fundamentalists were apolitical—the problem was *why* they were apolitical. Their isolationism sprung from competing and unbiblical views of the Kingdom of God—views that would compromise their witness at almost every other point. And so evangelical political thought revealed the Kingdom crisis in evangelical theology. The same can be said of the theologically anemic (and often missiologically embarrassing) attempts at "Religious Right" and "Religious Left" activism since Henry's day. Could it be that evangelicals are seen as a political "constituency" because about all we have to offer the watching culture is politics? Could it be that the eclipse of Jesus in evangelical politics is a symptom of the eclipse of Jesus in evangelicalism itself?

This book calls evangelical Christians to shape our identity by our convictions about the Kingdom of God in Christ. The new perspective on the Kingdom of God can define evangelical theology along the lines of the central themes of the Old and New Testament canon. In the end, a renewed focus on the Kingdom is essential if evangelicals are ever going to grapple with the *evangel* of a crucified, resurrected, and enthroned Messiah. As such, American evangelicalism ought to become both more and less political. Evangelical theology will not serve an activist agenda to be an identity caucus in someone's political party. But evangelical theology will remind Christians that the call to Christ is not a call to "go to heaven when you die," but instead a call to be "joint-heirs" (KJV) with the Messiah who will inherit an all-encompassing Kingdom. This means that the most important political reality of all is not the local voter precinct or the White House reception room, but the creaky pews of the local congregation. A renewed Kingdom theology can remind evangelical churches that they are the rulers of the universe—but not yet (1 Cor. 6:3). This means that evangelicals can see the Kingdom of God as something more than the terminus point on the prophecy chart; something more than a crocheted sentiment hanging on the kitchen wall. It means that evangelicals can confront the Caesars of this age with a truth that once caused riots in the streets—there is "another king" (Acts 17:7). It means that we can remind ourselves that the only perspective on the Kingdom of Christ that matters ultimately is quite old. And that perspective has already been addressed over the waters of the Jordan and in the caverns of a garden tomb, and will be repeated once more before a watching cosmos: "Jesus is Lord" (Phil. 2:9-11).

LIST OF ABBREVIATIONS

BibSac	*Bibliotheca Sacra*
CSR	*Christian Scholar's Review*
GTJ	*Grace Theological Journal*
JBL	*Journal of Biblical Literature*
JETS	*Journal of the Evangelical Theological Society*
RevExp	*Review and Expositor*
TrinJ	*Trinity Journal*
SWJT	*Southwestern Journal of Theology*
WTJ	*Westminster Theological Journal*

1

An Uneasy Conscience in the Naked Public Square: Evangelical Theology and Evangelical Engagement

INTRODUCTION

"Modern conservatism owes much of its success to the aggressive political activity of evangelical Christian churches," observes commentator Russell Baker. "In Goldwater's era they stayed out of politics; now they crack whips."[1] Despite the exaggeration of this statement, it illustrates a key problem in constructing a basis for a theology of evangelical engagement. For much of the American news media, if not for large sectors of the American public as a whole, evangelical churches seem at times to be caricatured as not much more than Sunday morning distribution centers for Christian Coalition voter guides. The postwar evangelical project called for a vital presence of evangelicalism in the public square, but it did so in terms of a theologically cohesive foundation for cultural and political interpenetration. For the pioneers of contemporary evangelicalism, the political isolationism of conservative Protestantism was not problematic because it sidelined fundamentalists as a voting bloc; it was problematic because it pointed to underlying theological problems, centered on an inability to come to terms with the most central theme of Scripture—the Kingdom of God. And so, the task of evangelical engagement was about a recovery of Kingdom theology—not simply a mobilization of evangelical voters. In the years since World War II, however, the kind of theologically informed engagement envisioned by Carl Henry and the movement's other early theologians has not often been reflected in the most visible efforts at evangelical sociopolitical action. And, as with the fundamentalist isolationists before them, the failure of evangelical politics is often, at root, the failure of an evangelical theology of the Kingdom.

AMERICAN POLITICS AND EVANGELICAL ENGAGEMENT

The perception that evangelicalism is primarily a political movement is partially understandable since, for much of the nation, evangelicalism seemed to emerge *ex nihilo* in the mid-1970s, largely in relation to political happenings of the time, namely, the conversion of Republican Watergate felon Charles Colson and the very public evangelical identity of Democratic presidential candidate Jimmy Carter, with each announcing that he had been "born again."[2] Shortly thereafter, widespread publicity was given to the mass organizing of evangelicals and fundamentalists to oppose Carter on issues such as abortion rights, the Equal Rights Amendment, and the Panama Canal Treaty.[3] Since then, the evangelical presence on the national scene has been closely linked to evangelicals as a political constituency. Thus, the most widely disseminated analyses of American evangelicalism have seemed too often content to trace the movement in terms of the progression from Moral Majority to the Liberty Federation, from the Pat Robertson presidential campaign to the Christian Coalition. Even grassroots revivalist movements such as Promise Keepers are often considered part of an electoral constituency.[4]

Historians rightly identify the first visible rumblings of evangelical social engagement with Carl F. H. Henry's 1947 jeremiad, *The Uneasy Conscience of Modern Fundamentalism.*[5] Still, Henry could not have foreseen the way in which evangelicals would in fact lift their voices in the public square in the generation after *Uneasy Conscience*. After all, the National Association of Evangelicals of the 1940s and 50s deemed it necessary to plead for fairness for evangelicals on the public airwaves. With the onset of Moral Majority and other activist groups in the 1970s, 80s, and 90s, the mid-century urgings of Henry seemed dated, if not inconceivable, to a new generation of politically savvy evangelicals. The impetus to evangelical engagement included the emergence of an evangelical left, including an "Evangelicals for McGovern" organization formed to oppose Billy Graham's friend Richard Nixon in the 1972 presidential election.[6] While the evangelical sociopolitical left continued to exist throughout the rest of the century, most sectors of its influence seemed to drift away from any semblance of evangelical theological commitments.[7] Instead, the most vigorous evangelical forays into the sociopolitical arena have come from the right side of the cultural and political spectrum.

The most significant move toward evangelical engagement did not come through a reflection on the philosophical appeal of Henry or any other theologian. Instead, it came through the mobilization of the Christian right following the 1973 *Roe v. Wade* Supreme Court decision legalizing abortion, an act that served as the opening shot of the "culture wars." In 1976, the Jimmy

Carter campaign cleared the path for religious conservatives through Carter's self-disclosure of a new-birth experience, a disclosure that called for rigorous "spin control" from the campaign to convince the public that, among other things, Carter did not hear audible voices from God.[8] By the next election cycle, evangelical conservative activists would have a forum to question Republican primary candidates about their personal regeneration, or lack thereof.[9] By the end of the century, few eyebrows were raised when the Republican presidential frontrunner spoke in terms reminiscent of Jimmy Carter of "recommitting" his life to Jesus Christ through the ministry of Billy Graham.[10] The public discussions of evangelical piety were not limited to candidate autobiographies. Appeals to religious conservatives infused much of American political discussions, especially during the Reagan administration of the 1980s. After all, even Reagan's historic denunciation of the Soviet Union as an "evil empire," it must be remembered, was delivered before the National Association of Evangelicals. Even more remarkable, and relatively unnoticed, is the fact that this geopolitically significant statement was set in the context of Reagan's prayer that those behind the Iron Curtain might be born again, a comment that would have been unthinkable, even for Jimmy Carter, only a few years before.[11]

The emergence of politically active evangelicals, led by populist figures such as Jerry Falwell and Pat Robertson, received a mixed reception among their political cobelligerents. Conservative theorist Robert Nisbet denounced the evangelical conservatives as not conservative at all because they rooted their ideology in a theological underpinning, "a characteristic they share more with those Revolution-supporting clerics in France and England to whom Burke gave the labels of 'political theologians' and 'theological politicians,' not, obviously, liking either."[12] Most of the Republican conservative establishment, however, received the evangelical constituency as a key voting bloc, especially in the South and Midwest. One Jewish neo-conservative theorist, for example, wrote that most of his fellow Jewish conservatives, "however bemused they may be by styles of evangelical piety—a bemusement, I might add, shared by a number of non-evangelical Christians—still have no problem counting Christian conservatives as staunch cultural and political allies."[13]

The emergence of the Christian right, however, was not about crafting a united evangelical theology of sociopolitical engagement. Instead, evangelical political activists practically celebrated the fact that their entrance into the public arena was more of a forced conscription than a purposeful engagement.[14] Even many nonevangelicals, who shared some of the same cultural goals as the Christian right, supported the defensive nature of evangelical engagement.[15] As

Yale University law professor Stephen Carter notes, "The more that a nation chooses to secularize the principal contact points between government and people—not only the public schools, but little things, like names and numbers and symbols, and big things, like taxes and marriage and, ultimately, politics itself—the more it will persuade many religious people that a culture war has indeed been declared, and not by the Right."[16]

Thus, the political activism of twentieth-century evangelicals was not an essentially theological movement, even though many of the activists were reliant on the kind of worldview formulations provided by evangelicalism's theologians and philosophers.[17] Some of this had to do with an American public ignorant of and uninterested in the theological nuances of evangelical theology.[18] Much more had to do, however, with the motivations and public statements of the politicized evangelicals themselves. Evangelical political action, to begin with, often failed to see the larger social and political nature and the interrelationships of the issues over which they were so energized.[19] Moreover, the Christian right often deliberately sought to avoid theological commitments, for fear that they could not sustain the traditionalist coalition of evangelicals, Roman Catholics, conservative Jews, Mormons, and even right-leaning secularists. As Jerry Falwell explained, "Moral Majority is a political organization and is not based on theological considerations."[20] Similarly, the Christian Coalition's Ralph Reed contended, "This is not a vision exclusively for those who are evangelical or Roman Catholic or Greek Orthodox or Jewish. This vision makes room for people of all faiths—and for those with no faith at all."[21]

Even so, the lack of an overarching theology of evangelical engagement did not save the Christian right's political coalition, but instead unraveled it. The *ad hoc* nature of the religious right left evangelicals without the theoretical tools to evaluate political priorities *theologically*, and thus to articulate the issues in terms of an overarching evangelical worldview.[22] This further alienated some in the evangelical constituency, who began to wonder if evangelical political priorities were being negotiated according to the platform of the national Republican Party, rather than according to biblical revelation.[23] Moreover, at the century's end, evangelical optimism about their place in the "silent majority" of the American mainstream was replaced in many sectors by a sober pessimism that American culture was "slouching towards Gomorrah."[24] Religious conservatives would then broach the subject, not only of whether Christians should engage the public square but also of whether they could any longer support the American regime at all, or whether the American project was irreparably broken.[25]

EVANGELICAL THEOLOGY AND EVANGELICAL ENGAGEMENT

While the precise definition of evangelicalism may be hotly debated among evangelicals themselves, all sides agree that the term does not refer primarily to a voting bloc of the Democratic or Republican National Committees. This does not mean, however, that sociopolitical activism is incidental to evangelical identity. Evangelicalism, at least as originally conceived by the theologians at the helm of the postwar evangelical renaissance, is first of all a *theological* movement. Indeed, even the postwar call for sociopolitical engagement was cast in terms of a self-consciously theological agenda. As a result, the evangelical attempt to engage politically without attention to these prior questions of theological self-identity and underlying philosophy has served only to frustrate the kind of evangelical engagement envisioned by the movement's founding theologians.

Henry's *Uneasy Conscience*, after all, was not first of all a sociopolitical tract. Instead, it served in many ways to define theologically much of what it meant to be a "new evangelical," in contrast to the older fundamentalism.[26] Along with Ramm, Carnell, and others, Henry pressed the theological case for evangelicalism in terms of a vigorous engagement with nonevangelical thought.[27] As articulated by Henry and the early constellations of evangelical theology, such as Fuller Theological Seminary and the National Association of Evangelicals, evangelicalism would not differ with fundamentalism in the "fundamentals" of doctrinal conviction, but in the application of Christian truth claims onto all areas of human endeavor.[28] Henry's *Uneasy Conscience*, which set the stage for evangelical differentiation from isolationist American fundamentalism, sought to be what Harold J. Ockenga called in his foreword to the monograph "a healthy antidote to fundamentalist aloofness in a distraught world."[29] Thus, the call to sociopolitical engagement was not incidental to evangelical theological identity, but was at the forefront of it. Henry's *Uneasy Conscience*, and the movement it defined, sought to distinguish the postwar evangelical effort so that evangelical theologians, as one observer notes, "found themselves straddling the fence between two well-established positions: fundamentalist social detachment and the liberal Social Gospel."[30]

Such "straddling," however, is an inaccurate term if it carries the idea that Henry and his postwar colleagues sought to find a middle way between fundamentalism and the Social Gospel. The evangelicals charged the fundamentalists with misapplying their theological convictions, but they further charged the Social Gospel with having no explicit theology at all. "As Protestant liberalism lost a genuinely theological perspective, it substituted mainly a political program," Henry lamented.[31] The new evangelical theologians maintained that their agenda was far from a capitulation to the Social Gospel, but was instead the conservative antidote to it.[32] This was because, Henry argued, evangelicalism was a theology calling for engagement, not a program for engagement calling for a theology. The Social Gospel theologians, Henry claimed, "exalt the social issue above the theological, and prize the Christian religion mainly as a tool for justifying an independently determined course of social action."[33] Nonetheless, fundamentalism was also, in many ways, not theological enough for Henry and his cohorts, a fact that lay at the root of fundamentalist isolation, as the evangelicals saw it. Henry commended fundamentalists for their defense of the virgin birth, the deity of Christ, and so forth. This was not enough, he warned. "The norm by which liberal theology was gauged for soundness unhappily became the summary of fundamentalist doctrine," he wrote. "Complacency with fragmented doctrines meant increasing failure to comprehend the relationship of underlying theological principles."[34] This meant, Henry argued, that although conservative Christians could apply the biblical witness to evangelistic endeavors and certain basic doctrinal affirmations, "they have neglected the philosophical, scientific, social, and political problems that agitate our century," such that those seeking to find a theoretical structure for making metaphysical sense of the current situation were forced to find it in Marxism or Roman Catholicism.[35]

But doctrinal reductionism was merely a symptom of the crisis of fundamentalist isolation. The effort toward a "united evangelical action" in the public square was likewise hampered by the internal lack of cohesiveness within the American evangelical coalition itself. It is here, at the core of evangelical identity, that conservative Protestantism faced its crisis over the Kingdom of God. Despite the assertions that contemporary evangelicalism can be described best as a doctrinal "kaleidoscope" of various competing ideologies, a cursory glance at the postwar evangelical coalition will reveal less of a "kaleidoscope" than a river, fed by at least two very distinctly identified streams.[36] A vast array of historians has observed that the evangelical movement was strongly influenced by, as Sydney Ahlstrom puts it, a Reformed "denominational, seminary-oriented group" and "a Bible institute group with strong premillennial and dispensational interests" that were able to maintain an "uneasy alliance" against the common foe of modernism since dispensationalism gave the conservatives "a measure of interdenominational cohesion and esprit" while Reformed theology gave the movement "theological and historical prowess."[37] While some elements of this historiography are contested, the preeminence of these two streams in shaping contemporary evangelical theology is not in dispute.[38]

The Fundamentalist-Modernist controversy had provided a common enemy against which conservative Protestants, especially confessional

Calvinists and dispensational premillennialists, could coalesce in a common defense of orthodoxy. Henry, however, sought to serve in a role similar to that of William F. Buckley, Jr., in Buckley's successful attempt to create a "fusionist" postwar conservative political coalition between libertarians and traditionalists against the common threat of global communism and domestic liberalism.[39] The intellectual leaders of the fledgling evangelical movement after World War II recognized that a vast cooperative movement of conservative American Protestants would require more than tactical alliances against mainline liberalism on the left, obscurantist fundamentalism on the right, and a rising tide of secularism on the horizon. Henry's *Uneasy Conscience*, therefore, insisted that a socially and politically engaged evangelicalism could not penetrate society so long as the movement itself was saddled with internal theological skirmishes.[40] In this, Henry received the hearty agreement of other leaders such as Harold J. Ockenga and Edward J. Carnell.[41]

The skirmishes between Reformed and dispensational theologies were symptomatic of what Henry viewed as part of a larger trend of evangelical "navel-gazing."[42] This was, however, a real threat to evangelical theological cohesiveness, especially since the debates between the groups predated the postwar evangelical movement itself.[43] This lack of cohesion was even more important given that the bone of contention between evangelical covenantalists and evangelical dispensationalists was the concept Henry identified in *Uneasy Conscience* as most fundamental to an articulation of Christian sociopolitical engagement: the Kingdom of God.[44] Thus, the emerging evangelical movement could not dismiss the covenant/dispensational controversies over the Kingdom as mere quibbling over secondary matters, nor could these concerns be divorced from the rest of the doctrinal synthesis as though the differences were akin to the timing of the Rapture. Dispensationalists charged covenant theologians with shackling the biblical witness to a unitary understanding centered on the justification of individuals rather than on the larger cosmic purposes of God. Covenant theologians accused dispensationalists of denying the present reality of the Kingdom of Christ, divorcing the relevance of the Lord's Prayer and the Sermon on the Mount from this age, and with denigrating the centrality of the church by considering it a "parenthesis" in the plan of God. These Kingdom-oriented differences were multitudinous, and none of them could be resolved by an umbrella statement on last things appended to the conclusion of the National Association of Evangelicals statement of faith.

Despite some exhortations to the contrary, the evangelical movement's theologians seemed to realize that more than doctrinal détente was needed between these two groups if evangelicalism were ever to go beyond its

Kingdom paralysis toward a cohesive theology of evangelical engagement. Henry's *Uneasy Conscience* waded into the Kingdom debate as an incipient call for a new consensus, one that was a break from the Kingdom concept of classical dispensationalism and also from the spiritual understanding of many covenant theologians.[45] Henry was joined in this by the exegetical and biblical theological syntheses of George Eldon Ladd, who went even further in calling for a new evangelical vision of the Kingdom, usually riling both dispensational premillennialists and covenantal amillennialists in the process.[46]

Beyond the mere matter of a Kingdom "cold war" between these two streams of evangelical theology, however, was the fact that the differences on the Kingdom were directly correlated to various aspects of the evangelical sociopolitical task. The concept of the Kingdom was thus off-limits to the construction of an evangelical political theology, a situation that would paralyze any such effort since the problematic features of both fundamentalism and the Social Gospel in relation to the public square were directly related to Kingdom concepts. The incendiary debates about the Kingdom within conservative Christianity, particularly between dispensationalists and covenant theologians, had led, Henry argued, to a "growing reluctance to explicate the kingdom idea in fundamentalist preaching."[47] This aversion was so pronounced, he noted, that a fundamentalist spokesman had warned him to "stay away from the kingdom" when addressing the root of the uneasy conscience.[48]

Jettisoning such advice, however, Henry set forth his manifesto for sociopolitical engagement as, above all, a theological statement; more specifically, it was a plea for an evangelical Kingdom theology.[49] For Henry, such a Kingdom theology was urgent not only because of the theological fragmentation of evangelicals over the Kingdom question, but also because only a Kingdom theology could address the specific theological reasons behind fundamentalist disengagement:

> Contemporary evangelicalism needs (1) to reawaken the relevance of its redemptive message to the global predicament; (2) to stress the great evangelical agreements in a common world front; (3) to discard elements of its message which cut the nerve of world compassion as contradictory to the inherent genius of Christianity; (4) to restudy eschatological convictions for a proper perspective which will not unnecessarily dissipate evangelical strength in controversy over secondary positions, in a day when the significance of the primary insistences is international.[50]

The formation of such a Kingdom consensus was, however, easier proposed than accomplished, not only because of the internal theological Kingdom tensions within evangelicalism, but also because of the role of Kingdom theology in nonevangelical American Christianity. After all, a Kingdom consensus had indeed been achieved within the ranks of Protestant liberalism by the onset of the early twentieth century.[51] The integrative motif of the "Kingdom of God" proposed by mainline Protestant theologians was most vigorously opposed by dispensationalist and Reformed conservatives.[52] The ethical and anti-supernatural "Kingdom" offered by theologians such as Albrecht Ritschl, covenantalist biblical theologian Geerhardus Vos contended, gave liberals "an opportunity to remain within the circle of religion and yet have less of the obsession of God in religion."[53] Vos contrasted the definition "of God the Kingdom" in the theology of Jesus and the apostles with "the Kingdom (of God)" as offered by contemporary liberal theologians.[54]

KINGDOM THEOLOGY AND EVANGELICAL ENGAGEMENT

In the years since *Uneasy Conscience,* evangelical theology's "cold war" over the Kingdom has thawed dramatically. Remarkably, the move toward a consensus Kingdom theology has come most markedly not from the broad center of the evangelical coalition, as represented by Henry or Ladd, but from the rival streams of dispensationalism and covenant theology themselves. Progressive dispensationalists, led by theologians such as Craig Blaising, Darrell Bock, and Robert Saucy, have set forth a counterproposal to almost the entire spectrum of traditional dispensational thought.[55] With much less fanfare, but with equal significance, a group of covenant theologians, led by scholars such as Anthony Hoekema, Vern Poythress, Edmund Clowney, and Richard Gaffin, has also proposed significant doctrinal development within their tradition.[56] The move toward such development has been prompted by a Reformed theology dependent on the redemptive-historical emphasis of Geerhardus Vos.[57]

Interestingly, this growing consensus did not come through joint "manifestos," but through sustained theological reflection. The cooperative doctrinal endeavors between dispensationalists and covenantalists, especially through the Evangelical Theological Society's Dispensational Study Group, have resulted in what one dispensationalist scholar calls a spirit of "irenic yet earnest interaction" over the meaning of the Kingdom.[58] Nor has the consensus come through a doctrinal "cease-fire" in order to skirt the issue of the relationship of the Kingdom to the present mission of the people of God. Instead, it came as both traditions sought to relate their doctrinal distinctives to the overarching theme of the Kingdom of God as an integrative motif for their respective systems. Whatever the objections of critics in both traditions, progressive dispensationalists did not set out to "covenantalize" dispensational theology, nor did modified covenantalists set out to "dispensationalize" covenant theology. Rather, the coalescence with the other tradition on various disputed points seems almost coincidental in the scholarship of both groups.

Instead, at the forefront of the proposals within both traditions stands a more sweeping agenda—namely, an attempt to find a unifying center for their respective theologies in the overarching concept of the Kingdom of God. Progressive dispensationalists articulate the Kingdom as the central integrative motif of their system, citing this as a major distinction from earlier forms of dispensational theology.[59] In fact, the move toward a Kingdom theology even accounts for the name of the newer form of dispensationalism. It is called "progressive" not because it is more contemporary than other forms of dispensationalism but rather because in it "the dispensations *progress* by revealing different aspects of the final unified redemption," namely, the eschatological Kingdom of God.[60] At the same time, the modified covenantalists insist that their contention for the unity of the covenant of grace is expressed not primarily in a pre-temporal decree or in a static understanding of redemption, but rather through the unity of God's eschatological purposes to "restore and renew the human race and the cosmos" through the triumph of the eschatological Kingdom of God.[61] In this, the modified covenantalists reconfigure the emphases of the American Reformed tradition, while relating to a prominent theme in the Dutch Kuyperian stream of Reformed theology.[62]

The question of the place of this Kingdom consensus within evangelical theology is not isolated from the question of evangelical sociopolitical involvement. This is true, first of all, because it affects what Mark Noll identifies as the chief "apolitical impetus" of conservative Christianity's doctrinal streams, traditional dispensationalism and the southern Presbyterian concept of the "spirituality of the church."[63] The emergence of a Kingdom theology is criticized by both traditionalist covenant theologians and traditionalist dispensationalists for the sociopolitical ramifications such developments bring.[64] The move toward an evangelical Kingdom theology is not simply the construction of a broad, comprehensive center for evangelical theological reflection. As the Kingdom idea has been explored within evangelical theology, and within the sub-traditions of dispensationalism and covenantalism, specific points of contention have been addressed, especially in terms of the way in which the Kingdom concept relates to the consummation of all things, the salvation of the world, and the mission of the church. In so doing, this emerging Kingdom theology addresses the very same stumbling blocks to evangelical cultural engagement that were once identified as the roots of conservative Christianity's "uneasy conscience."

2

TOWARD A KINGDOM ESCHATOLOGY: THE KINGDOM AS ALREADY AND NOT YET

INTRODUCTION

There have been few issues more divisive among conservative American Protestants than that of eschatological timetables. The postwar evangelical theology led by Carl Henry recognized the lack of consensus among evangelicals on eschatology and the nature of the Kingdom of God to be at the root of fundamentalist isolation. So the call to evangelical engagement was a call to a reconsideration of the Kingdom. While the effort to move beyond the "uneasy conscience" sought to transcend the millennial debates of their fundamentalist forebears, it simultaneously recognized that eschatology could not be ignored in the construction of an evangelical sociopolitical ethic because eschatological presuppositions had driven Protestant political attitudes through both postmillennial optimism on the left and premillennial pessimism on the right. Since that time, however, evangelical theology has moved toward a Kingdom consensus around the concept of inaugurated eschatology, developments that are especially evident within the ranks of dispensationalism and covenant theology. This "already/not yet" Kingdom consensus carries with it, therefore, far-reaching implications for evangelical engagement in the public square.

ESCHATOLOGY AND THE THEOLOGICAL PROJECT OF POSTWAR EVANGELICALISM

It is not much of an overstatement to say that Carl F. H. Henry's *The Uneasy Conscience of Modern Fundamentalism* is first and foremost a tract on eschatology. Indeed, in the book's introduction itself, Harold J. Ockenga pointed out that the book grappled head-on with the foremost obstacle to evangelical social and political action—namely, the lack of a consensus on the nature of the

Kingdom. Some evangelicals recognized the "continuity" of the Kingdom, Ockenga complained, while some recognized the "breaks," leading to a "hopeless puzzle" for evangelical theology.[1] While other evangelical theologians, such as E. J. Carnell, attempted to critique the eschatological over-commitments of fundamentalism, Henry was the one theologian to address specifically and strategically the relationship between the Kingdom theology of fundamentalism and the fundamentalist withdrawal from the arena of social and political action.[2] The Kingdom issues raised by Henry, pointing evangelicals toward an incipient theology, would later be taken up by others, most notably George Eldon Ladd.

Postwar Evangelical Eschatology and The Uneasy Conscience

In his *Uneasy Conscience*, Henry tried to "triangulate" theologically between the Kingdom eschatologies of the Social Gospel left and the fundamentalist right. It would be a mistake to assume that Henry considered the two eschatological positions to be equal and opposite errors. Instead, he pointedly asserted that Protestant liberalism had more than a troubled conscience, but had in fact abandoned the gospel itself.[3] For Henry, the challenge for conservative Protestants was somehow to synthesize theologically the relationship between the biblical teachings on the "Kingdom then" of the future, visible reign of Christ and the "Kingdom now" of the present, spiritual reign of Christ. Until this matter could be theologically resolved, Henry believed, evangelical eschatology would remain kindling for the fires of a troubled social conscience. Surveying the contemporary eschatological options, Henry drew on a metaphor from the pages of the New Testament:

> The two thieves between whom Jesus was crucified might, without too wild an imagination, bear the labels of humanism and fundamentalism. The one on the left felt that Jesus had no momentous contribution to suffering humanity, while the one on the right was convinced of His saviourhood but wanted to be remembered in the indefinite future, when Jesus would come into His Kingdom.[4]

In the background of fundamentalist eschatological pronouncements stood the ghost of Walter Rauschenbusch. With a full ballast of "Kingdom now" rhetoric, for example, Rauschenbusch had called upon socialist organizers in the United States to welcome Christians into their ranks for the good of a common effort to "Christianize the social order."[5] Rauschenbusch applied the language of Christian eschatology, even of millennialism, to the no-small controversy within his own Northern Baptist ranks.[6] He redefined, however, the prophetic hope of a "millennium" to mean an imminent possibility of a Kingdom of social justice in the present age.[7] It was this view of the present reality of the Kingdom, Henry argued, that had led to the fundamentalist eschatological backlash that lay behind the "uneasy conscience." Fundamentalist political isolationism was, at least in one sense, an attempt to defend the future hope of the Kingdom from the anti-supernaturalism of the modernists. Henry may have warned evangelicals that they had overreacted, but he did not tell them their fears had been unfounded.[8] This was true especially in the area of eschatology.

For Henry, if an alternative to the Social Gospel were to be formulated, revelational theism would have to do it. In his *Uneasy Conscience* and elsewhere, Henry affirmed with earlier fundamentalists that the Social Gospel vision of a present Kingdom was little more than a continuation of the same anti-supernaturalistic presuppositions that had fueled both the left wing of the Fundamentalist-Modernist controversy and the larger secular Enlightenment opposition to Christian theism. He equated the eschatology of the Social Gospel with the Enlightenment idea of the inevitability of human progress, an idea intertwined with a naively optimistic, if not explicitly Pelagian, anthropology.[9] While thus perpetuating this anti-supernaturalist point of view, he argued, Enlightenment modernism and its Social Gospel colaborers had adopted a more fanatical devotion to an eschatological scheme than the most ardent Bible Conference organizers among the fundamentalists. "There has been more millennial fanaticism in modern anti-supernaturalistic theories than in contemporary evangelicalism," Henry wrote. "One of the curiosities of church history is that the naturalistic world-view, so hostile to the Christian notion of the kingdom, finally embraced zealously the idea of an immanent millennium."[10] Thus, Henry argued, Protestant modernism had attempted to baptize the Enlightenment idea of autonomous human progress by uniting it to a Christian eschatological vision of the Kingdom of God. Thereby, Protestant liberalism could equate "its strategy for abolishing social inequities" with "an immediate and forced bringing in of the kingdom."[11] Henry wondered how any such theological concept could be sustained after "the empirical happenings of two world wars, horrible in their toll of both life and security."[12]

Nonetheless, *Uneasy Conscience* pressed the claim that fundamentalists had overreacted as they tried to avoid the "tendency to identify the kingdom with any present social order, however modified in a democratic or communistic direction."[13] In so doing, however, the fundamentalists had strictly relegated the Kingdom to the age to come, thereby cutting off its relevance to contemporary sociopolitical concerns. Moreover, Henry complained, fundamentalism's pessimistic view of history informed by dispensationalist eschatology fueled an attitude of "protest against foredoomed failure."[14] Fundamentalism "in revolting against the Social Gospel seemed also to revolt against the Christian social imperative," he argued. "It was the failure of fundamentalism to work out a positive message within its own framework, and its tendency instead to take further refuge in a despairing view of world history that cut off the pertinence of evangelicalism to the modern global crisis."[15] The result, Henry concluded, was that "non-evangelical spokesmen" were left to pick up the task of sociopolitical reflection "in a non-redemptive context."[16] Henry did not level all of the blame for this otherworldly flight from the public square on fundamentalist dispensationalism, but he did suggest that dispensationalism carried a disproportionate share of the blame, in terms of both political engagement and personal ethics.[17]

Henry proposed that fundamentalists did not need to co-opt the Social Gospel vision of the Kingdom in order to answer the social and political dilemmas they faced. Instead, he argued that the postwar evangelical renaissance should capitalize on the theological strengths of both its premillennial and its amillennial eschatologies. He viewed both groups as the inheritors of the evangelical eschatological task following the dissipation of postmillennialism, even the more orthodox strands held by relatively evangelical theologians such as James Orr. Henry argued that evangelical eschatology had the responsibility to provide a biblical and theological alternative to the utopian visions of both evolutionary secularism and Protestant liberalism.[18] Thus, Henry's *Uneasy Conscience* did more than sound the alarm that fundamentalists had neglected "kingdom now" preaching. Henry also indicted fundamentalists for abandoning "kingdom then" preaching. It was not only that fundamentalists were too future-oriented to care about sociopolitical engagement, but also that, in the most important ways, they were not future-oriented enough. Henry focused the key reason for this "apprehension over *kingdom then* preaching" on what he considered to be the overheated zeal of the earlier generations of dispensationalist popularizers. It was true, Henry asserted, that World War II had demolished the postmillennial predictions of a "Christian century" of world peace and harmony. But the war had demolished just as surely the prophetic predictions of a revived Roman Empire, along with various efforts to identify the Antichrist on the world scene.[19]

In this, he aimed directly at the prophecy conference movement that had proven so integral to the fundamentalist coalition. Liberalism was wrong in its primary thrust, Henry argued, but,

On the other hand, fundamentalism has tended to take successive major crises as the last chapter of world history; repeatedly it has been preoccupied with "rescuing the furniture" on the mistaken assumption that "the house of humanity was totally destroyed." Fundamentalism was not wrong in assuming a final consummation of history, but rather in assuming that *this is it.*[20]

Such speculation, Henry concluded, had led to growing numbers of evangelicals "revolting against the prophetic detail of dispensational premillennialism" by "discarding premillennialism along with the detail, and shifting toward an amillennial position."[21] For Henry, this was not necessarily a hopeful sign. "The writer's own convictions are broadly premillennial, and he is not convinced that a discard of speculative accretions justifies an uncritical surrender of the whole premillennial structure," Henry wrote. "If the shift to amillennial grounds is made on firmer convictions, that is a different matter."[22] By the "broadness" of his premillennialism, Henry meant that he did not hold to the prophetic intricacies of dispensationalism, and that he did not deem a millennial view to be a test of evangelical authenticity, as did some of the earlier fundamentalists. Such "broadness" did not mean that he considered the matter irrelevant or peripheral to evangelical theology. He seemed to suggest openness to the amillennial position, if its proponents could convince him of its basis in the Scriptures. He was never convinced.[23]

What Henry did fear was an unwitting evangelical "gag order" on eschatological matters, in order to avoid the overstepping of the dispensationalist fundamentalists. Henry not only believed that a focus on future eschatological hope was a biblical mandate and an exegetical necessity, but he also believed that a healthy eschatological futurism was necessary to shield evangelicalism from the political paths already taken by the mainline denominations and by the larger culture. Henry thought, for instance, that the Social Gospel eschatology, for all its pretensions to being a prophetic critique, actually served to prop up the social and political status quo. "It was classic modernism, interestingly enough—with its notion of exaggerated divine immanence—that viewed the social orders as sacred or directly continuous with the Kingdom of God," Henry contended. "This has by no means been the view of evangelical Christianity."[24]

The eschatological futurism of evangelicalism, Henry continued, would ensure not only that existing structures were not given the uncritical imprimatur of the Kingdom of God, but also that Christianity would not succumb to the Constantinian temptation to Christianize forcibly any political order.[25] This commitment is seen to be especially relevant when one considers that the contemporary evangelical movement was seeking to assert its theological distinctives just as the United States of America had led an allied coalition through a world war against a dictator who claimed to be ushering in a "Third Reich" of Aryan utopia. Similarly, the postwar political atmosphere was charged with the escalating Cold War between the United States and a communist bloc committed to Karl Marx's utopian vision of a classless society.[26] Thus, Henry did not find it presumptuous to claim that the largely present-oriented eschatology of Protestant modernism was at least partially culpable for the Iron Curtain of communism falling across Europe and Asia following the Second World War.[27]

Postwar Evangelical Eschatology and the Kingdom Debate

Having diagnosed the eschatological impediments to a theology of evangelical engagement, Henry reassured evangelicals that his purpose in *Uneasy Conscience* was not "to project any new kingdom theory; exegetical novelty so late in church history may well be suspect."[28] It would seem, however, that a "new" (at least for American evangelicals) Kingdom theology was precisely what he was proposing. In calling on evangelicals to abandon the extremes of the Social Gospel and fundamentalist withdrawal, Henry simultaneously exhorted evangelical theology to underpin its eschatological convictions with a broader understanding of the Kingdom of God. He contrasted the Kingdom reticence of American evangelicals with the Kingdom exuberance of the apostolic witness of the New Testament. "The apostolic view of the kingdom should likewise be definitive for contemporary evangelicalism," Henry asserted. "There does not seem much apostolic apprehension over kingdom preaching."[29]

For Henry, this would mean that evangelicals would have to recognize the centrality of the Kingdom message to the New Testament, and adapt both their elaborate prophecy timetables and their reluctance to proclaim a present role for the Kingdom of God to it. This is because, Henry counseled, "no subject was more frequently on the lips of Jesus Christ than the kingdom."[30] Therefore, Henry maintained, evangelical theology must deal with the biblical data, which seems to indicate a Kingdom that has already been inaugurated and yet awaits a future consummation.[31] "No study of the kingdom teaching of Jesus is adequate unless it recognizes His implication both that the kingdom is here and that it is not here."[32]

For Henry, the biblical mandate for this type of inaugurated eschatology was far too great to be overcast by endless evangelical debates over the nature of the millennium or the timing of the rapture. It also carried with it inevitable implications for his call to sociopolitical engagement, starting with the fact that

Jesus both proclaimed the coming of His Kingdom and yet did not sanction a violent overthrow of the already existent ruling authorities. "The main difference between the kingdom of God *now* and the kingdom of God *then* is that the future kingdom will center all of its activities in the redemptive King because all government and dominion will be subjected to Him," he wrote. "This difference overshadows the question, however important, of whether the future kingdom involves an earthly reign or not."[33] Therefore, Henry contended, any effort to construct a theology of evangelical engagement would be in a very important sense tied to whether evangelicals could come to agreement on this kind of inaugurated eschatology.

He argued that an evangelical Kingdom theology must be "properly balanced" and therefore "two-pronged," with an "apostolic and an apocalyptic turn," meaning that it would be not "prophetically dogmatic" but "prophetically sensitive" and "socially alert."[34] Henry's concern for an "already/not yet" structure of evangelical eschatology could be seen in his 1971 "Jerusalem Conference on Biblical Prophecy," in which he assembled a virtual "who's who" of dispensationalist and covenant theologians in Israel for a discussion of evangelical differences on the meaning of the "last days."[35] In his address to the conference, Henry combined the "already" Kingdom emphasis of the covenant theologians with the "not yet" Kingdom expectancy of the dispensationalists, all within an explicit appeal to the kind of inaugurated eschatological framework already being discussed within New Testament theology by biblical scholars such as Oscar Cullmann.[36]

While Henry diagnosed the problem in *Uneasy Conscience,* George Eldon Ladd, a later addition to the Fuller Seminary faculty, began an exegetical and theological project related to this issue which he would pursue for the rest of his life.[37] Indeed, as Henry and other evangelicals further explored the meaning of inaugurated eschatology for evangelical theology, they were almost always either explicitly or implicitly in conversation with Ladd's work.[38]

Ladd, of course, was not the first to articulate an "already/not yet" concept of understanding biblical eschatology, nor did he claim such a distinction. In perhaps his most critical work on New Testament eschatology, *Jesus and the Kingdom: The Eschatology of Biblical Realism,* Ladd went to great lengths to establish his view of inaugurated eschatology within the context of the larger body of contemporary New Testament scholarship.[39] Having surveyed the fierce eschatological debates among nonevangelical twentieth-century biblical scholars, Ladd placed himself within what he considered to be a new consensus among New Testament scholars, perhaps most notably held by W. G. Kümmel, regarding a "synthesis of present and future in the understanding of the Kingdom of God."[40] From his very earliest writings, Ladd identified himself with Kümmel's position, even as he modified it.[41] Continuing the trajectory from Kümmel, argues biblical scholar Eldon Jay Epp, Ladd represented "a similarly moderating interpretation of Jesus' understanding of the kingdom of God."[42] Ladd furthermore linked his concept of inaugurated eschatology to the insights of Oscar Cullmann and Geerhardus Vos.[43]

This concept of the eschaton in terms of an "already/not yet" dualism, Ladd believed, made sense of the biblical data and solved the impasse between the arguments for consistent and realized eschatologies in the New Testament writings, especially in the teachings of Jesus.[44] Thus, it resolved the tension between the otherworldly "apocalyptic" interpretation of New Testament eschatology and the historically anchored "prophetic" interpretation, without seeking a refuge in Bultmann's eschatology of existential crisis.[45] Ladd's most focused work, however, was forged in response to eschatological questions within evangelical theology.[46] As such, Ladd's attempt to amass a Kingdom-oriented eschatology represented an explicit challenge to both the dispensationalist and Reformed traditions within the evangelical coalition. For Ladd, the crucial point for establishing an evangelical inaugurated eschatology was to come to a consensus on the present and future aspects of the reign of Jesus as messianic King.

In this, he found both the dispensationalist premillennialists and the covenantal amillennialists to be in error.[47] Against the debates between the dispensationalists and covenantalists on whether the reign of Christ was best to be understood as present within the life of the church or the heart of the believer, or future in the millennial Kingdom from a restored Davidic throne, Ladd posited his proposal: the Kingdom has arrived "already" in the person of Jesus and awaits a "not yet" consummation in the millennial Kingdom and in the eternal state.[48] For Ladd, this understanding of inaugurated eschatology represented more than simply a mediating approach between dispensationalism and covenantal amillennialism. It represented instead an attempt to forge a full-fledged evangelical theology of the Kingdom.

While dispensationalists severed the Kingdom from the present activity of the Messiah, Ladd argued, the amillennialists severed it from the goal of history by relegating the Kingdom to the arena of the human heart, the church, or the supra-temporal heavenly state. In Ladd's Kingdom theology, however, "the kingdom is seen to be a single concept, the rule of God, which manifests itself in a progressive way and in more than one realm. *It is God's saving will in action.*"[49] Thus, Ladd argued, evangelicals cannot minimize either aspect of the Kingdom of God as articulated by Jesus and echoed by His apostles.[50] In articulating the present nature of the Kingdom of Christ, Ladd was forced to spar with prevailing dispensationalist notions, many of which were rooted in the notes of *The Scofield Reference Bible* and in the systematic formulation of Lewis Sperry Chafer. For Ladd, as for Henry, this idea had profound implications for evangelical engagement.[51]

Ladd wrangled with dispensationalists such as Alva McClain, who made the case that the reign of the messianic Davidic King is not inaugurated until Jesus takes His place upon a throne in the Christocratic millennial Jerusalem.[52] "The theological confusion stems from a basic failure to understand the nature of Christ's mediatorial ministry; and this in turn derives from an unwillingness to accept the New Testament definition of the kingdom of God and to reinterpret the Old Testament in light of the New Testament definition," Ladd contended.[53] Dispensational theologians were quick to argue that Ladd's inaugurated eschatology was little more than a fatal concession to amillennialism. Dispensationalist John Walvoord, for example, dismissed Ladd's "already/not yet" proposal as a doomed attempt "to create a new type of eschatology which is a compromise between historic premillennialism and amillennialism."[54] He pointed to the endorsement of Ladd's scholarship by amillennial covenant theologians such as Roger Nicole as evidence of Ladd's weakening grip on the futurist Kingdom of premillennial doctrine.[55]

The key issue for Walvoord and others in the Dallas Seminary tradition was that Ladd's view of the eschatological Kingdom as in some way operative in the present age would necessarily mean the redefinition of the term. "While Ladd fully supports the concept that the kingdom has a future consummation, as do practically all orthodox scholars, what he attempts to ignore is that the kingdom is also theocratic and political and involves an actual reign of Christ on earth for one thousand years," Walvoord complained.[56] As late as 1974, Walvoord concluded of Ladd's *The Presence of the Future,* "One would judge by this volume that amillenarians can claim a new addition to their ranks."[57] While some dispensationalists, such as Walvoord, conceded that there was some sense in which the ascended Christ maintains "a spiritual rule of God in the hearts of those whom He has redeemed," such was not an admission to a present inauguration of the eschatological Kingdom.[58] Contra Ladd, dispensationalists maintained that the present age was an interregnum between the rejection of the Kingdom offered to Israel in the person of Christ and the establishment of the Kingdom at His return. J. Dwight Pentecost also affirmed a "spiritual kingdom" at work in the present epoch, but he associated it with a virtually different Kingdom, the universal sovereignty of God over the elect of all ages, rather than with the eschatological Kingdom of Christ.[59] Pentecost was representative of most of his dispensationalist contemporaries in arguing against Ladd's position regarding an inauguration of the messianic reign of Christ.[60]

With such being the case, Ladd argued that the dispensationalist understanding of Christ's role as Davidic King was the essential flaw in the "postponement" theory of the Kingdom. "It is difficult to see how Jesus could have offered to Israel the earthly Davidic Kingdom *without the glorious Davidic King* who was to reign in that kingdom," Ladd contended, contra the Dallas Seminary tradition. "The very fact that he did not come as the glorious King, but as the humble Savior, should be adequate evidence by itself to prove that his offer of the kingdom was not the outward, earthly kingdom, but one which corresponded to the form in which the King himself came among men."[61] Contrary to typical dispensationalist eschatology, Ladd maintained, the Davidic covenant of 2 Samuel 7 found an initial fulfillment in the ascension of Jesus following His resurrection from the dead. Thus, Ladd argued, Jesus is not waiting to assume the throne of David, but has already done so at His exaltation by God the Father. He pointed to the apostle Peter's sermon at Pentecost, tied so closely to the enthronement language of Psalm 110, as evidence for this claim. In continuity with the words of the enthronement psalm, the Father has placed His imprimatur on Jesus as, in the words of Acts 2:36, both Lord (absolute sovereign) and Christ (Davidic Messiah).[62]

Ladd therefore took issue with the prevailing dispensationalist theologies by suggesting that nowhere does Scripture demand that the inauguration of the Davidic covenant requires the literal seating of Jesus upon a literal structure in Jerusalem, thus demonstrating a basic hermeneutical difference between himself and his dispensationalist interlocutors. In light of the New Testament apostolic testimony, Ladd claimed, the Davidic throne has been transported from Jerusalem (Ps. 110:2) to heaven, where the Jewish Messiah has begun His reign as Davidic King as the fulfiller of the prophecies of 2 Samuel 7:13, 16; Isaiah 9:7; Jeremiah 33:17, 21; Psalm 132:11; and Psalm 110:2.[63] Peter's sermon does indeed involve a "radical reinterpretation" of the Old Testament promises regarding the messianic reign, Ladd conceded, if for no other reason than because Peter's sermon transfers the locus of the Davidic session from Zion to heaven. Even so, he argued, this reinterpretation is "no more so than the entire reinterpretation of God's redemptive plan by the early church."[64] Ladd argued that just such a reinterpretation of the Davidic reign of Christ is a biblical and theological necessity in light of Jesus' resurrection as the first stage of the eschatological resurrection of the righteous. If this is true, he suggested, "then the messianic age has begun and the messianic blessings have been given because the Messiah has already begun his reign."[65]

Such a divergence with dispensationalist evangelicalism signaled a difference in the significance of the millennium between Ladd's inaugurated eschatology and typical dispensationalist eschatology. For Ladd, the *Parousia* is not when Jesus assumes His reign but when this already existing reign as Son of David is revealed to a blinded cosmos. The visible millennial rule of Christ "will be the manifestation in history of the lordship and sovereignty which is his already."[66] Ladd agreed with the dispensationalists, however, that the kingly messianic purposes of Christ, as promised in the Davidic covenant, still await a future consummation in space-time history in which all things are made subject to Him and His enemies are made a footstool for His feet.

Unlike the dispensationalists, however, Ladd posited that this future reign must be understood in the "already/not yet" structure of redemptive history. Indeed, he argued, this kind of fulfillment-consummation tension is at the heart of the "eschatological kerygma" of New Testament theology.[67] The problem with the dispensationalists, Ladd asserted, was not that they held to a political aspect of the reign of Christ, but that they failed to see how the present, spiritual mediatorial work of Christ also stands in continuity with the Old Testament eschatological hope. "The New Testament does not make the reign of Christ one that is limited to Israel in the millennium," he wrote. "It is a spiritual reign in heaven which has already been inaugurated, and its primary purpose is to destroy Christ's spiritual enemies, the last of which is death."[68] Of Ladd's claim that Jesus' messianic reign as Davidic King was inaugurated at His ascension, dispensationalists such as Charles Feinberg were insistent: "That is not 'historic' premillennialism, but undiminished and recognizable amillennialism."[69]

These material and political facets of the future consummation of the Kingdom of Christ, however, put Ladd at odds with the amillennialism of much of the Reformed covenant tradition within the evangelical coalition. Reformed evangelicalism welcomed Ladd's emphasis on the present reality of the Kingdom because, as the *Westminster Theological Journal* noted, it brought "welcome evidence that American evangelicalism, which has been so long under the spell of modern dispensationalism, is now moving away from the dispensational view of the kingdom."[70] It was Ladd's view of the future consummation, however, that Reformed amillennialists likened to a "new postponement theory" similar to that of the dispensationalists because Ladd's future earthly consummation of the Kingdom denied the essentially spiritual nature of the Kingdom of God.[71]

In his debates with both dispensational premillennialists and covenantal amillennialists, Ladd insisted that what was at stake was not simply an outline of future events but the definition of the Kingdom of God itself. Ladd agreed with covenant theologian Louis Berkhof that if the Kingdom is defined as the millennial reign of Christ, then the premillennialists are "compelled by the logic of their system to deny the present existence of the Kingdom of God."[72] What he rejected, however, was the suggestion by Berkhof, O. T. Allis, and other covenant theologians that the Kingdom was "an entirely spiritual thing," consisting either of an Augustinian view of the rule of the church in the present era or of the view of disembodied souls reigning with Christ from heaven.[73]

Instead, Ladd insisted that evangelical theology must appropriate an eschatology that is Kingdom-oriented and thus able to explain the full biblical panorama of Kingdom teaching.

In order to do so, he maintained, evangelicals must construct a Christological view of the Kingdom and of the messianic mission of Jesus both in the present era and in the age to come.[74] For both Ladd and Henry, however, making such a proposal was quite different than seeing it achieved. With Reformed amillennialists insisting on a Kingdom that was essentially heavenly and spiritual and dispensationalist premillennialists insisting on a Kingdom that was essentially future and political, it was difficult for Ladd to see how the young evangelical movement could achieve the quixotic goal of a consensus eschatology of the Kingdom of God. As Henry warned, however, it was precisely this goal upon which the movement's hopes for a unified theology of sociopolitical engagement depended.

KINGDOM ESCHATOLOGY AND THE EMERGING EVANGELICAL CONSENSUS

Since the postwar era, the contested issue of evangelical eschatology has emerged as the focus of an evangelical rapprochement on the Kingdom of God. The gradual consensus developing within several significant quarters of American evangelicalism sees the eschatological Kingdom in terms of a tension between the "already" of initial fulfillment and the "not yet" of future consummation. "Recent theological discussions have been fruitful in that most scholars now agree that eschatology focuses primarily on the kingdom of God," observes Stanley Grenz. "They also speak of this kingdom as in some sense both a present and a future reality, so that ours is the time of the already and the not yet."[75] This development is seen in its heightening emphasis across the spectrum of contemporary evangelical theology, but especially within the closing gap between dispensational and covenant eschatologies. New Testament theologian Craig Blomberg hails central eschatological developments that "reflect a growing consensus among evangelicals, that are endorsed by not a few outside our circles, and that should be widely accepted and promoted, particularly in light of so much misinformation at the level of popular preaching, especially over radio and television."[76] While some recent evangelical scholarship seems to continue a very traditional model of eschatology as "last things," this new eschatological consensus is reflected increasingly in systematic projects that span the ideological fissures of contemporary evangelical theology. Both traditionalist conservatives and reformist innovators seek to understand biblical eschatology within a framework of "already/not yet" fulfillment.

Among traditionalist conservative evangelicalism, some attempts at an evangelical eschatology seem to betray very little influence of this kind of Kingdom-oriented inaugurated eschatology. Wayne Grudem's treatment of this doctrinal locus, for example, is remarkably similar to that of nineteenth-century Reformed theologian Charles Hodge in the way Grudem integrates eschatological concerns into his theological method.[77] Millard J. Erickson treats the topic of eschatology by covering extensively millennial and Rapture options, along with extended discourse on the Kingdom views of Schweitzer, Dodd, Bultmann, and Moltmann, while virtually ignoring inaugurated eschatology, except as it is reflected in progressive dispensationalism.[78] In his systematic treatment, Erickson goes so far as to label as "eschatomania" the scholarly consensus on the place of eschatology in the theological endeavor, a term he reserves also for popular apocalyptic entrepreneurs such as Hal Lindsey.[79] "In the view of those who follow this approach, however, the central subject of eschatology is not the future, but the idea that a new age has begun," Erickson notes. "Often the tension between the old and the new is emphasized; in fact, the phrase 'already, but not yet' has become a sort of slogan."[80]

Despite these reservations, the consensus on inaugurated eschatology exists throughout traditionalist conservative evangelical theology. Evangelical theologians Gordon R. Lewis and Bruce Demarest, for example, explicitly interact with the eschatological proposals of Kingdom-oriented scholars such as Ladd and Ridderbos. They outline an "already/not yet" view of the reign of Christ that is consistent with inaugurated eschatology, a doctrinal commitment they stress is of key importance to the biblical understanding of the Kingdom of God and of the present session of Christ.[81]

Perhaps the most striking appropriation of inaugurated eschatology within traditionalist evangelical ranks, however, is found in the later writings of Carl Henry.[82] Henry reflects his earlier eschatological concerns in *Uneasy Conscience* within his systematic treatment, *God, Revelation, and Authority.* The later Henry worries not so much about fundamentalist isolationism, but that liberation theologians may gain a foothold in the Third World because of the "constant danger facing evangelical theology" of "so idealizing the coming millennium that we lose a critical and formative role in the present sociocultural realm."[83] He sweeps away this objection to evangelicalism by affirming a clearly articulated inaugurated eschatology that fully reflects the Kingdom developments since Ladd's insistence on the New Testament "presence of the future."[84]

"The future is actually already at hand, and is unfolding within man's present earthly existence: the incarnation of Christ inaugurated God's kingdom, the resurrection of Christ publicly identified him as the future judge of the human race, and the present church age has initiated 'the last days' (Heb 1:3); the final consummation of all things is imminent," Henry maintains.[85] He further utilizes a Kingdom-oriented "already/not yet" eschatological framework to dismiss secularist/revisionist theodicies, as well as Jewish rejections of the messianic identity of Jesus on the basis of a seemingly postponed Kingdom.[86]

The left wing of contemporary evangelical theology has likewise embraced an inaugurated eschatology, with both initial fulfillment in the first advent of Jesus and a clearly defined consummation in the second. This is true even among the open theists, who represent arguably the most radical departure from traditional evangelical thought. Gregory Boyd, for example, appropriates inaugurated eschatology as a foundation of his "Trinitarian warfare worldview."[87] Boyd argues, in distinctly Ladd-like terms, for a Kingdom perspective on the miracles of Jesus and His post-resurrection enthronement, and on the tension between initial fulfillment and final consummation, even as he places the "already/not yet" schema of Kingdom fulfillment within an open view of God's relationship to the world and the demonic powers.[88] Thus, it would seem that Boyd has adopted much of the Kingdom-focused inaugurated eschatology of Ladd, as mediated through the spiritual warfare motifs of the third-wave charismatic appropriation of Kingdom theology.[89]

Likewise, reformist evangelical Stanley Grenz also articulates the growing consensus on inaugurated eschatology, often carefully outlining the doctrinal loci of Christian theology in decidedly eschatological terms with poles of initial fulfillment and future consummation.[90] Grenz notes that he reflects the "uneasy consensus" that the reign of Jesus is "inaugurated but not consummated."[91] "The consensus among New Testament scholars leads to the theological conclusion that the goal of history is both already present but also not yet here," Grenz concludes. "God has acted on our behalf, but the consummation of this divine intervention lies yet in the future."[92]

Throughout evangelical thought, these developments toward inaugurated eschatology have served, as theologian Bruce Ware has observed, as a vehicle for the diminishing of Kingdom skirmishes between American evangelicals, particularly in the covenantal Reformed and dispensationalist camps. "But what is heartening is that a basic eschatological framework established by inaugurated eschatology is now widely shared by these two theological traditions," Ware argues. "Our disagreements have more to do with the specific manner in which aspects of the already and not yet find their fulfillment than with fundamentally different schemes of eschatology viewed more holistically."[93]

Thus, it is important to note that this developing consensus within evangelical theology is more than simply a maneuver toward rapprochement on a controversial point of doctrine. It is precisely the kind of eschatological development envisioned by postwar theologians such as Henry and Ladd, recognizing both an "apocalyptic" future and a "prophetic" present for Christian eschatology. What is even more remarkable is the fact that these developments toward inaugurated eschatology have received their most thorough treatment in the theological scholarship of the formerly "warring camps" of evangelical dispensationalism and covenant theology.

Kingdom Eschatology and Dispensational Development

Perhaps the most significant moves toward a Kingdom-oriented eschatology have come within the dispensationalist contingent of contemporary American evangelicalism. Ware notes that the reaction of postwar dispensationalists to the "already/not yet" eschatological framework of Ladd most clearly illustrates the reasons why these developments are so important:

> Ladd's sharpest criticism came from some of his premillennial colleagues, whose dispensational commitments render it highly problematic to conceive of the *one* kingdom of God present now while its prophesied political, national, geographical and soteriological dimensions seem absent and hence unfulfilled. Given a dispensational framework in which God administers his relations with his people appropriate to the dispensation in which they live, talk of the presence of the kingdom, which kingdom has as its focus Messiah's physical and earthly reign over the redeemed nation of Israel, seems inappropriate and clearly at odds with a literal understanding of such messianic prophecy.[94]

The Kingdom as present reality. Postwar evangelical theologians such as Henry and Ladd were able to take aim at the wholly future Kingdom theory of dispensationalist eschatology precisely because it was not, relatively speaking, a moving target.[95] Ladd, therefore, was able to say that, among dispensationalists, "there will be found a basic agreement on the stages of the kingdom

as Dr. Chafer has traced them."[96] With the onset of progressive dispensationalism, such can no longer be said. Instead, progressive dispensationalist theologians have made a clear departure from Chafer's systematic formulation of
the relationship of the eschaton to the present epoch.

In its place, they have systematized an inaugurated eschatology with a
clear "already" facet that does not look all that different from that proposed
by Henry and constructed by Ladd. As a matter of fact, the appropriation of
an "already/not yet" framework of biblical eschatology by progressive dispensationalist theologians such as Darrell Bock, Craig Blaising, and Robert
Saucy has proven to be among the most remarked-upon venues in the analyses of dispensational development. Those outside the dispensationalist fold
have noticed the Ladd-like overtones of the newer dispensationalist inaugurationist eschatology.[97] These similarities to Ladd's "already/not yet" eschatology also have been noticed by traditionalist factions within the
dispensational tradition, often to no small controversy. After surveying the
adoption of inaugurated eschatology by progressive dispensationalists, traditionalist dispensationalist Stephen J. Nichols pronounces the system "already
Ladd/not yet dispensationalism."[98]

Progressive dispensationalism has veered sharply from the "wholly future"
Kingdom path of traditionalist dispensationalism, gradually defining and
defending the concept of an inaugurated reign of Christ that is in continuity
with the Old Testament covenants. Thus far, New Testament scholar Darrell
Bock has shouldered most of the responsibility for relating the "already" and
"not yet" aspects of this reign to the biblical messianic hope.[99] Bock concludes
that the Gospels, especially Luke–Acts, assume a fulfillment of Old Testament
messianic hope, which includes "national-political as well as spiritual
aspects."[100] With the coming of Jesus as Messiah, the Kingdom of God breaks
into the present era, as demonstrated by the healing and exorcism activities.[101]
Jesus does not completely initiate the Kingdom, however, until the coming of
the Spirit as the sign of the dawning eschaton and the inauguration of the new
covenant in Acts 2.[102] With the formation of the church as the gathered body
of the Messiah, Jesus asserts His regal authority as the seed of David through
the forgiveness of sins, Bock argues. "A king, indeed, shows his authority by
ruling a kingdom," Bock observes. "Jesus rules by saving and calling a new
community from all nations."[103]

Bock, in essential agreement with Blaising and other progressives, finds
in Acts 2 a clear explication of the "already" and "not yet" aspects of messianic Kingdom fulfillment. In this passage, Bock sees Peter's sermon as a tying
together of 2 Samuel 7, Psalm 16, and Psalm 110 into an apostolic assertion

that "Being seated on David's throne is linked to being seated at God's right hand."[104] This reality, the progressives argue, is reflected even in the Christological titles given to Jesus in the New Testament writings because "Jesus as Lord (Acts 2:30-36) and Jesus as Head (Eph. 1:19-23) are two ways to portray Jesus' ruling authority over the church" since both titles "are associated with imagery from Psalm 110:1, which is a regal (or royal) psalm."[105] Thus, Bock argues, in the person of Jesus, the "already" and "not yet" aspects of the Kingdom are complementary, not held in a conflicted or paradoxical tension.[106]

Such is not to say that this view of the present Kingdom activity of Christ is to be considered monolithic even within progressive dispensational ranks. One of the earliest pioneers of the progressive movement, Robert L. Saucy, disagrees with the thesis of Blaising and Bock, arguing instead that Jesus' fulfillment of Psalm 110 refers to messianic authority, but not to His function as Davidic King.[107] The extension of salvation benefits exists, Saucy contends, in the extension of redemption to the Gentiles because of Jesus' role as the promised messianic King of the entire earth, but does not manifest itself in a Davidic reign by Jesus over the church in the present age.[108] The present manifestation of the Kingdom, Saucy contends, comes not through the regal authority of the One ruling from David's throne, but through the persuasive power of word and Spirit.[109] Saucy's son, Mark Saucy, has articulated similar conclusions regarding this aspect of inaugurated Kingdom eschatology.[110] For the younger Saucy, the current messianic function of Christ is limited to the role of a salvific and interceding "Lord," not a conquering and ruling "King." Mark Saucy writes that, while he sees the exalted Son as "possessing the legitimacy and authority to rule from the Father's right hand," Jesus is "not exercising that authority," but instead "is passive and currently waiting for the promise" of Psalm 110.[111] The majority report among progressives, however, would seem to be that Jesus' current salvific activity is to be regarded not as something severed from His role as the fulfillment of Kingdom promise, as in traditional dispensationalism, but as an integral part of His identity as the anticipated Davidic ruler.[112]

In progressive dispensationalist eschatology, Jesus pictured His exorcisms as part of His messianic role, they note, and in the very same manner the forgiveness of sins necessitates rule and subjugation of such enemies as Satan and the fallen human nature. In His current salvific activity, as well as in His future coercive rule, Jesus exercises His authority as the "horn of salvation" from the house of David, as laid out in the birth announcements of Luke and Matthew. "Israel has a future hope of deliverance by the King who will rule over them (cf. Luke 1:31-35)," Bock observes. "But in his two volumes Luke's interest moved beyond Israel. People faced a battle with Satan and sin, a battle Jesus is winning as He brings people out of darkness and into light."[113] The use of Psalm 110:1 in Acts, Bock argues, vigorously presents Jesus' ruling function from God's side as the Davidic mediator of God's blessings. This ruling authority is exercised when His sovereignty over individual salvation is affirmed through religious rites such as baptism, which are performed "in His name."[114]

Such a viewpoint has profound ramifications for the older dispensationalist understanding that the cross and the formation of the church represent a "postponement" of Kingdom activity, at least in the Old Testament prophetic sense. Blaising and Bock, for example, argue that the messianic regal prophecies find their fulfillment in the very center of Jesus' salvific activity, the events leading to His sacrifice at Golgotha. The warning of 2 Samuel 7:14, that God would correct the sins of His Davidic ruler by striking Him with the rod, they contend, find their fulfillment in the synoptic accounts of Jesus being beaten with rods prior to His crucifixion. The Davidic heir does indeed bear the rod of God's wrath, though not for His own personal sin. Blaising and Bock see unmistakable Old Testament Kingdom imagery in Matthew's literary juxtaposition of Gentile soldiers beating the arrested Jesus with rods along with their mocking Him as "King of the Jews" and "Son of God," both titles consistent with Davidic covenantal Kingdom expectation.[115]

The Kingdom as future consummation. An affirmation of the "already" of Christ's messianic Kingdom does not mean that progressive dispensationalists have broken decisively with the "not yet" emphasis of the Niagara Bible Conferences and the *Scofield Reference Bible*. To the contrary, many progressive dispensationalist theologians have hailed the apocalyptic sensitivity of the early dispensationalists as one of the movement's greatest contributions to contemporary American evangelicalism. The apocalyptic, future-oriented perspective of the dispensationalist tradition rightly underscored, argues Darrell Bock, that "from Adam to the end, God is forging out a plan that will come to a triumphant resolution within the current progress of history."[116] Progressive dispensationalists, however, have offered a markedly different model for understanding the place of apocalyptic futurism in the role of Christian theology. This is especially apparent when one considers the progressive dispensationalist rejection of perhaps the most successful aspect of American dispensationalism, namely, the prophetic speculations of popular prophecy teachers ranging from the prewar Bible conferences to Hal Lindsey to Tim LaHaye.[117] Though many classical dispensationalists would disavow any connection between the more spectacular of these apocalyptic movements and the mainstream of dispensationalist thought, there are some indisputable doctrinal and institutional connections between the Dallas Seminary tradition and several attempts at tying current events to the prophetic timetable.[118]

The progressive dispensationalists, however, have sought from the very beginning to distance themselves from prophecy charts. In explaining the progressive dispensationalist movement to readers of *Christianity Today,* Darrell Bock, for example, complained that popular dispensationalist authors such as Lindsey often "succumbed to date setting or something very close to it."[119] By contrast, he explained, the new progressive dispensationalists are "more circumspect about identifying certain details in the prophetic calendar than some of their predecessors were" and are "less confident about the ability to lay out a detailed scenario for its contemporary fulfillment."[120] In their co-authored monograph on the subject, Bock and Blaising went even further, insisting that the "signs of the times" prophetic calendar watching of the popular dispensationalists actually undercut one of the dispensationalist distinctives that the pretribulational Rapture doctrine was intended to preserve: the imminent, anytime coming of Christ. Blaising thus argues that Lindsey's claims that current events are fulfilling the prophetic timeline represent a dispensationalist historicism, not the historic tradition of dispensationalist futurism.[121]

Of course, within the tradition of dispensationalist eschatology the apocalyptic hope has been expressed perhaps most clearly by its unwaveringly premillennial interpretation of Revelation 20 as being in continuity with the Old Testament covenant promises. This does not mean, however, that progressives simply reaffirm all the "not yet" aspects of the eschaton set forth by earlier generations of dispensationalists. Although the "already" of the Kingdom has undergone the most conspicuous development among dispensationalists, the "not yet" has been reconsidered as well. This is because the progressive dispensationalists do not equate the millennial reign of Christ with the Kingdom of God, as such. Instead, they see it as a particular manifestation of the Kingdom that stands in continuity with the progressive development of the Kingdom throughout the dispensations of redemptive history.[122] As Blaising and Bock argue, "The journey moves from its formation in promise to Israel and David to its culminating description in terms of millennium and then the new heaven and new earth."[123]

The most significant development on the future aspects of the eschaton, however, have come not in progressive dispensationalist understandings of the Millennium, per se, but in their treatment of the eternal state. Many progressives refuse to divide the Millennium and the eternal state into two separate redemptive epochs, but instead speak of them as two phases of the one final manifestation of the Kingdom, what Blaising and Bock call the "Zionic Dispensation."[124] In so doing, the progressives have found themselves charged by some traditionalist dispensationalists with starting down the path toward covenant premillennialism, if not amillennialism. Ryrie, for example, argues that seeing the Millennium as a first step in the eternal consummation does away with its unique dispensational status. It is no wonder, he argues, that modified covenantalists such as Vern Poythress find so much in common with the eschatological vision of the progressive dispensationalists.[125] Progressive dispensationalists have responded, however, that their understanding of the Millennium is still quite distinct from all covenantal systems because it retains a unique place for the fulfillment of geopolitical blessings to a reconstituted Israelite nation.[126]

In addition, many progressive dispensationalists contrast their eschatological vision with that of the classical dispensationalists, who, the progressives argue, see "the new earth in Platonic terms, as timelessness."[127] The Millennium, with all of its cosmic blessings, is an initial phase of this eternal Kingdom.

Kingdom Theology and Covenantal Development

The move toward an "already/not yet" framework of eschatology by evangelical theology's covenantal Reformed tradition was not as noticeable as the developments within dispensationalism. This is due, at least in part, to the less antagonistic reaction by the Reformed tradition to the broader evangelical call for an inaugurated eschatology in the postwar era. As Bruce Ware observes, the premillennialist Ladd found the strongest support for inaugurated eschatology "from members of the amillennial community, whose commitment to covenant theology allowed them to embrace more readily the notion of the one unified kingdom of God, present now in part while awaiting complete fulfillment in the age to come."[128] Nonetheless, the amillennial covenant tradition, like the dispensationalist tradition, has undergone a reconsideration of its eschatological framework in light of a growing commitment to the kind of "already/not yet" eschatology called for by Henry, Ladd, and others. In so doing, several significant theologians within the Reformed tradition have proposed models for better relating covenant eschatology in both its present and its future aspects to the overarching goal of the Kingdom of God.

The Kingdom as present reality. In the 1989 meeting between covenant theologian Vern Poythress and members of the Dispensational Study Group,

Robert Saucy concluded, after interaction with Poythress, that modified dispensationalists and modified covenantalists had come to substantial agreement on "a present initial stage fulfillment of the eschatological promises and a unified spiritual people of God."[129] Implied in this analysis is that dispensationalism had done most of the doctrinal revision. After all, if there was one thing that amillennialism (from Augustine to the present era) had maintained, it was a present manifestation of the Kingdom of God. This is especially true in terms of the covenantal kingship of Christ.

Within the canopy of contemporary American evangelical theology, amillennialism was most often articulated within the parameters of confessional, Reformed covenant theology. Consistent with the Westminster Confession of Faith and similar confessional statements, most confessional Reformed evangelicals have held that the relationship between the biblical covenants and the messianic reign of Christ is to be understood in the context of an overarching covenant of grace.[130] The Davidic covenant, then, would be a historical manifestation of this one covenant that spans redemptive epochs. Thus, Westminster Seminary theologian John R. Murray argued mid-century that the Davidic reign of Christ is to be understood as the guarantee of the security of the everlasting covenant of grace that is tied to Him. Murray argued that this kingly, covenantal rule of Christ is similar to the Noahic covenant in that the Davidic promise is presented in the Old Testament as another manifestation of God's "covenant of peace with His people," which is "an oath-bound and oath-certified assurance of irrevocable grace and promise."[131]

The Reformed tradition tended to emphasize the Kingdom of Christ in almost entirely present, spiritual terms, much to the chagrin of their premillennialist interlocutors. Covenant theologian Louis Berkhof argued that this present spiritual reality of Christ's reign is precisely what made the future-oriented Kingdom of premillennialism so untenable. If premillennialists were ever to argue for even an initial fulfillment of the promised reign of Christ from the Davidic throne, he argued, then the premillennialist's self-professed adherence to a "literal" interpretation of Scripture "goes by the board."[132] Thus, American evangelical amillennialists, such as Berkhof, emphasized the present kingship of Christ, and articulated this reign in decidedly spiritual and soteriological terms. "It is incumbent on Christ as the anointed King, to establish the kingdom of God, to govern it, and to protect it against all hostile forces," Berkhof contended. "He must do this in a world which is under the power of sin and is bent on thwarting all spiritual endeavors."[133]

Though evangelical covenantalists have always held to a present fulfillment of the kingship of Christ, this is not to say that contemporary developments within evangelical eschatology have left this area of covenantal theology unaffected. To the contrary, the shift toward a Kingdom-oriented eschatology has proven to have serious ramifications for the way in which some Reformed evangelicals articulate the initial fulfillment of the Kingdom rule of Christ. Anthony Hoekema has been a trailblazer in this regard, appropriating within Reformed theology the inaugurated eschatology of George Eldon Ladd and Herman Ridderbos. Explaining the tension between the "already" and the "not yet," Hoekema is careful not simply to speak of the present rule of Christ as a spiritual soteriological matter, but to set it within the broader context of a Kingdom purpose that is invading history in two stages. Distancing himself from the inordinately spiritual emphases of some of his American covenantalist forebears, Hoekema cites Ladd's definition of the Kingdom as meaning that "God is King and acts in history to bring history to a divinely directed goal," to make his case.[134]

Thus, for Hoekema, the present Davidic kingship of Christ must be understood as an eschatological activity, the first stage of the coming of the triumphant Kingdom. Hoekema's appropriation of inaugurated eschatology has proven to be a pioneering venture for American evangelical Reformed theology. As modified amillennialists within the Westminster Seminary tradition have attempted to place eschatology within the broader framework of the Kingdom, an "already/not yet" framework of biblical eschatology has grown in influence. As it has done with the dispensationalist tradition, this has led to an eschatologically focused understanding of the present reign of Jesus as Davidic King. Since, as noted above, no one in traditional Reformed theology was denying the presence of the Kingdom of Christ in this age, the emerging move toward a fully orbed inaugurated eschatology has impacted developing covenant theology in unique ways, consistent with Reformed theology's longstanding commitment to the present session of Christ as messianic King.

The inaugurated eschatology proposed by many modified covenantalists differs sharply from the traditional Reformed understanding of the final matters of Christian theology, often due to interaction with the broader fields of biblical scholarship. Perhaps most representative of this trend has been Westminster Seminary theologian Richard Gaffin, Jr.[135] As Gaffin notes,

> According to the traditional understanding, eschatology is a topic of dogmatic (systematic) theology, limited to those "last things" associated with and dating from the second coming of Christ, including the intermediate state following death. In the newer consensus, eschatology is expanded to include the state of affairs that has already begun with the work of Christ in what the New Testament calls "the fullness of time(s)" (Gal 4:4; Eph 1:10), "these last days"

(Heb 1:2), "at the end of the ages" (Heb 9:26). Involved also in this more recent understanding of eschatology are basic and decisive considerations already realized in the present identity and experience of the Christian, and so too in the present life and mission of the church.[136]

For Gaffin, this broader understanding of eschatology is a necessary corollary of "the renewed attention, beginning right at the close of the last century, to what, according to the synoptic gospels, is obviously the central theme of the proclamation of Jesus, namely, *the Kingdom of God.*"[137] This Kingdom perspective, Gaffin claims, mandates an "already/not yet" framework of the biblical material by maintaining the unity of canonical theology, a unity traditionally asserted by covenant theology that has been undermined unintentionally by covenant theology's traditional treatment of eschatology as "last things." The traditional view, Gaffin argues, "by emphasizing as it does the *distinction* between the first and second comings, giving rise to its systematic conception of eschatology, has lost sight of this unity and the way even in the New Testament, particularly the gospels, these two comings are mixed, so intermingled that the difficulty interpretation sometimes has in distinguishing them is well known."[138]

Thus, for Gaffin and likeminded Reformed theologians, the Kingdom present is not an exclusively soteriological matter pointing to an eschatological consummation. It is itself a manifestation of an initial fulfillment of the promised eschatological hope. "A global, elemental consideration, that comes from taking in the history of revelation in its organic wholeness, is the essentially unified eschatological hope of the Old Testament, a hope which, to generalize, has a single focus on the arrival of the Day of the Lord, inaugurated by the coming of the Messiah," Gaffin asserts. "From this perspective, the first and second comings, distinguished by us on the basis of the New Testament, are held together as two episodes of *one* (eschatological) coming."[139] With such being the case, Gaffin contends, an inaugurated eschatology is capable of "making clearer (what traditional Reformed theology has largely missed) the eschatological dimension of the Christian life and the present existence of the church, grounded in the fact that not only the justification but the regeneration/renewal already experienced by believers at the core of their being is nothing less than eschatological in nature (e.g., 'new creation,' 2 Cor 5:17; 'raised with Christ,' Eph 2:5-6)."[140]

As Vern Poythress has observed, this growing commitment among Reformed theologians to an explicitly eschatological understanding of the present reign of Christ may be seen in the reconsideration, led chiefly by Gaffin, of the eschatological meaning of the resurrection of Jesus.[141] In this, Gaffin points to the groundbreaking scholarship of Vos and Ridderbos as clearing the way for an eschatological understanding of the resurrection as essential to the "already/not yet" nature of the coming of the Kingdom.[142] For Gaffin, as for Hoekema and other inaugurationist covenantalists, the resurrection of Jesus is the preeminent "already" of the "already/not yet" Kingdom fulfillment "because in Christ's resurrection the history of redemption has reached its eschatological consummation."[143] With the resurrection seen as an eschatological Kingdom event, Gaffin asserts that passages such as 1 Corinthians 15 set forth an "already/not yet" eschatology in which the resurrected Christ is, in the apostle Paul's wording, "the first-fruits" of the end-time resurrection of the righteous.[144] It is significant, Gaffin argues, that Christ did not (actively) "rise," but that He (passively) "was raised" by the Father.[145] Thus, Jesus is raised as the head of a new humanity, and as messianic King over a new creation.[146] These developments represent a significant shift from traditional covenant theology by placing the resurrection of Jesus within the framework of the *historia salutis* as a decisively eschatological event.

Sinclair Ferguson likewise asserts that an eschatological view of the resurrection as the onset of the "already" of the Kingdom explains the Pauline conception of the "two ages":

> Older interpreters read Romans 1:3-4 within the matrix of classical patristic Christology as a statement of the two natures of Christ. But the contrast in view is not between the two natures but the two states of Christ, and more precisely between the two aeons of his existence: "according to the flesh" and "according to the Spirit"; his humiliation and his exaltation. His resurrection thus constitutes him messianic Son of God with power; in it he is adopted as the Man of the new age.[147]

Indeed, as Gaffin argues, the move toward a consensus on a Kingdom-focused eschatology requires the kind of resurrection emphasis he, Ferguson, and others within the Reformed tradition are articulating with increasing vigor.[148]

As developing Reformed theology has appropriated this eschatological view of the resurrection, it has emphasized the "already" of the "already/not yet" Kingdom in the present reality of the Holy Spirit. Anthony Hoekema points specifically to the outpouring of the Holy Spirit at Pentecost as an eschatological event in fulfillment of Old Testament prophecies regarding the last days of the messianic Kingdom.[149] For Hoekema, Pentecost perfectly demonstrates the importance of inaugurated eschatology for biblical theology because it means "that believers are already in the new age predicted by the Old Testament prophets, and are already enjoying the privileges and blessings of that age," but that "believers experience these eschatological blessings only in a provisional way, and look forward to a future consummation in the kingdom of God in which they shall enjoy these blessings to the full."[150] Thus, he argues, the presence of the Spirit "further illustrates this tension between what we already have and what we still anticipate."[151]

Some have observed a Reformed "revival of interest in the role of the Holy Spirit" as modified covenantalists relate pneumatology to larger questions of the resurrection of Christ and the onset of the Kingdom.[152] In this view, Pentecost is tied to the resurrection of Christ because it is the ascended Christ, exalted as the Davidic King, who is given the authority to pour out the Spirit, as exposited in the apostle Peter's sermon recorded in Acts 2. Ferguson suggests, "The coming of the Spirit is, therefore, the enthronement of Christ, just as the resurrection is the evidence of the efficacy of the death of Christ as atonement."[153]

Even in the discussion over the relationship between the Kingdom and the charismata, as in other areas, modified covenantalists such as Gaffin and Ferguson recognize that their understanding of the present Kingdom as an inbreaking of the eschaton is an expansion of Vos's incipient eschatology. It is by no means simply a continuation of Princeton fundamentalism.[154] This is because, Gaffin asserts, B. B. Warfield was unable to account for the uniquely eschatological nature of the Kingdom (especially the work of the Spirit) that pervades the New Testament, especially the Synoptic Gospels and the Pauline epistles.[155] Accordingly, modified covenantalists argue that the growing embrace by the heirs of Warfield of an inaugurationist understanding of the presence of the Kingdom is an advance toward a more biblical Kingdom theology.

The Kingdom as future consummation. Contra Ladd and the progressive dispensationalists, argue some within the Reformed evangelical tradition, this growing commitment to inaugurated eschatology actually shores up the covenantalist case for amillennialism. Vern Poythress, for example, argues that "certain features of inaugurated eschatology have opened doors toward greater friendliness on the part of amillennialists" to engagement on matters of eschatological concern.[156] He points with optimism to the amillennial appropriation of inaugurated eschatology in discussions of Revelation 20 by covenant theologians such as Meredith Kline and Gregory Beale.[157] Even so, Poythress contends, amillennialists must lead the way with serious revisions to their view of the future consummation, starting with a rejection of what Blaising calls a "spiritual vision" model of eschatology. In fact, Poythress argues that modified covenantalists are ready to concede many of the most contentious premillennial objections to the typical eschatological formulations of Reformed evangelicals. Their spiritual vision of eternity was less informed by the biblical vision of the Kingdom of Christ than by an ethereal, if not almost Platonic, hope for a temporal, heavenly existence.

Poythress argues that this stripe of Reformed eschatology has been challenged by covenant theology's interaction with biblical theology:

> Biblical theology has sensitized us to the character of inaugurated eschatology in the New Testament. In contrast to these twentieth century currents, amillennial thinking of previous centuries often let the fires of eschatological longing grow dim. Amillennialists sometimes spoke *only* of prophecy being fulfilled in the church, paying little attention to the consummate fulfillment of those prophecies in the new earth. In many circles people looked forward primarily to death and the intermediate state rather than to the Second Coming, the resurrection of the body, and the new heavens and the new earth, which are the primary focus of New Testament hope.[158]

With Poythress, modified covenantalist Michael Williams argues that this "spiritual vision" eschatology is firmly anchored in Augustine's role as "the father of Reformed eschatology."[159] Of Augustine, especially in his epochal *De Civitate Dei,* Williams observes, "He brought a Neoplatonic worldview to the consideration of eschatology, a worldview that has had long-lasting and unfortunate implications for Christian theology as a whole," but especially for the Reformed tradition.[160] Williams contends that the influence of Augustinian eschatology was not challenged by the early attempts at inaugurated eschatology by theologians such as Vos, but that Vos did "lay the groundwork for much of later Reformed revisionist thinking in eschatology," because Vos's "already/not yet" tension "was the starting point that allowed later thinkers such as Herman Ridderbos, Oscar Cullmann, Anthony Hoekema, and even the Baptist premillennialist George Ladd, to move beyond Augustinianism and toward a genuinely restorational eschatology."[161]

With such being the case, Poythress concludes, "Amillennialists today must try to be increasingly faithful to the biblical accent, and speak not only of a first stage of fulfillment in the life of Christ, the New Testament age and the church, but also of a second, consummate stage in the new heavens and new earth." Poythress contends that Anthony A. Hoekema's book *The Bible and the Future* "has set the pace in this area."[162] The groundbreaking nature of Hoekema's study certainly lends credence to Poythress's commendation of Hoekema's wide-ranging influence on modified covenantalism.

This is because Hoekema, and those within the Reformed tradition who follow his lead, break decisively with the "spiritual vision" model of eschatology. They do not see the ultimate hope of consummation either in the intermediate state or in a timelessly eternal heavenly existence. Instead, Hoekema and other modified covenantalists place the future consummation within a "new creation" model of fulfillment in the new earth. In this, they are in agreement not only with progressive dispensationalists but also with classical dispensationalists in finding the older amillennial view of prophetic promises to be biblically bankrupt.

Hoekema, for instance, agrees with John Walvoord's contention that "By no theological alchemy should these and countless other references to earth as the sphere of Christ's millennial reign be spiritualized to become the equivalent of heaven, the eternal state, or the church as amillenarians have done."[163] Hoekema responds,

> To the above we may reply that prophecies of this sort should not be interpreted as referring either to the church of the present time or to heaven, if by heaven is meant a realm somewhere off in space, far away from earth. Prophecies of this nature should be understood as descriptions—in figurative language, to be sure—of the new earth which God will bring into existence after Christ comes again—a new earth which will last, not just for a thousand years, but forever.[164]

Hoekema's adoption of a new creation model of the eschatological consummation is not wholly innovative, even within Reformed circles. Hoekema here draws from an incipient impulse within his Dutch Reformed tradition, especially the thought of Abraham Kuyper and Herman Bavinck.[165] Of Bavinck, for instance, William Dennison writes, "As he applied such an Aristotelian-Platonic teleological conception of history to the structure of biblical eschatology, Bavinck solidified the reformational picture of continuity between the creation and the new heaven and earth for his future neo-Calvinist companions in the twentieth century."[166]

For modified covenantalists, Hoekema's "new earth" model of future consummation corrects the crypto-Platonic aspects of the older model of amillennial eschatological hope, while reasserting the New Testament goal as the Kingdom, not heaven. It also seeks to address the premillennial argument that the picture of eschatology in the Old and New Testament Scriptures is earthly and material, not static and timeless in heaven or exclusively spiritual and ethical in the life of the church. In doing so, Poythress argues, the modified "new earth" eschatology "helps to bring the traditional millennial positions closer to one another," and thus may even serve to transcend the millennial impasse between covenantalists and dispensationalists and other evangelicals:

If all are able to agree that the new earth represents the most intensive fulfillment, arguments about fulfillments of a lesser scope will be seen to be less crucial. Moreover the emphasis on the new earth represents a definite, salutary
advance over all the traditional millennial positions. Most amillennialists, premillennialists, and postmillennialists alike have usually put their greatest
emphasis on fulfillment in the millennial period. They have then disagreed
among themselves over the character and date of the Millennium. This has
been particularly bad for amillennialists, because it leaves them with no
emphasis at all on a distinctively "earthy" character to fulfillment.
Dispensationalists have rightly objected to this kind of "spiritualization."[167]

Poythress further argues that the "new earth" envisioned by Hoekema and
other modified covenantalists "changes the scene entirely" because it is "very
much like the millennial earth as envisioned by premillennialists."[168] Therefore,
he observes, it may be a "comparatively minor dispute as to whether this renovation of earth, following the Second Coming, comes in one stage or two, that
is, in a one-thousand-year millennium followed by a fuller renewal or by total
renewal all at once."[169] Poythress, therefore, half-jokingly refers to the newer
modified covenantalists as "optimistic" premillennialists because what dispensationalists and other premillennialists call the Millennium "is even better
than they imagine" and "it goes on forever."[170]

KINGDOM ESCHATOLOGY AND EVANGELICAL ENGAGEMENT: AN EVALUATION

In the mid-twentieth century, C. S. Lewis remarked about the peculiar problem of relating a biblical eschatology to the social and political questions of any
era:

> We are afraid of the jeer about "pie in the sky," and of being told that we are
> trying to "escape" from the duty of making a happy world here and now into
> dreams of a happy world elsewhere. But either there is "pie in the sky" or there
> is not. If there is not, then Christianity is false, for this doctrine is woven into
> its whole fabric. If there is, then this truth, like any other, must be faced,
> whether it is useful at political meetings or no.[171]

The move toward an evangelical consensus on a Kingdom-oriented eschatology must be evaluated, first of all, in terms of biblical and theological coherence. Only then may evangelical theology probe its implications for social and
political activity. Nonetheless, the emerging evangelical consensus relating
eschatology to the Kingdom of God carries with it crucial implications both
for evangelical theology and for evangelical engagement. The developing

Kingdom eschatology, especially within dispensational and covenant theologies, actually answers many of the doctrinal stumbling blocks to united evangelical action in the public square first faced by the fledgling postwar evangelical movement.

Eschatology as a Theological Problem

During the heyday of the nuclear freeze movement, the First Baptist Church of Greenville, South Carolina, invited peace activist Sanford Gottlieb of the Committee for a SANE Nuclear Policy to address a gathering of local Christians on the issue of nuclear disarmament. According to historian David Stricklin, the first questioner of the session's question and answer period asked whether Gottlieb was a premillennialist or a postmillennialist. Stricklin quotes Furman University professor Albert Blackwell, who was present at the meeting: "Sanford Gottlieb is Jewish, and the look on his face indicated that he had no inkling of what his questioner was asking." Blackwell is quick to add, however, that others in the room knew exactly of what the questioner spoke, and why he asked it, since for many Christians these "are fighting words."[172]

The history of conservative American Protestantism has indeed borne out the contention that these are "fighting words." This is nowhere more evident than in the concerns of the postwar evangelical theologians over the eschatological divide within American fundamentalism. This is perhaps the most striking achievement of the developments in evangelical eschatology—namely, that one now can say there *is* an evangelical eschatology. This is true at least in regard to what all sides now agree are the central and defining aspects of Scripture's eschatological teaching. In a reaffirmation of the Protestant principle of *sola Scriptura,* covenantalists and dispensationalists have reexamined their respective systems in the light of biblical theology, and have come to strikingly similar conclusions. Thus, the topic of eschatology no longer serves to threaten the evangelical coalition, but actually may contribute to its doctrinal cohesion.

The developments toward a consensus on the nature of the Kingdom have proven some figures in the postwar evangelical movement, most notably E. J. Carnell, to be wrong in at least one important respect. First, evangelical theology could not come to a consensus by lessening the emphasis on eschatology as a matter irrelevant to the coalition. Instead, the consensus that has been constructed has been constructed through extended dialogue and discussion on matters of eschatological concern. Moreover, the consensus of the newer Kingdom-oriented eschatology is that eschatology is a central theme of biblical theology. The move toward a Kingdom eschatology does not repudiate the fundamentalist roots of evangelicalism, but in fact implicitly reasserts its roots in both historic Christian orthodoxy and twentieth-century American fundamentalism.

This is a crucial aspect of the developing consensus. There was a reason, after all, why the bodily and visible second coming of Christ was regarded as one of the five "fundamentals" to be defended from Protestant modernism.[173] This highlight on eschatology was far from a partisan sectarianism, but was instead a recognition that even the most minimal affirmations of orthodox Christian eschatology were under siege by the mainline denominational powers-that-be. And so, like the fundamentalist defense of the virginal conception of Jesus, this emphasis was a needed and almost entirely defensive move.[174] The fundamentalists were correct to note that the eschatological question was based in the more basic question of biblical authority and the reality of the supernatural. Harry Emerson Fosdick, for instance, acknowledged that the fundamentalists shared the New Testament understanding of the last things. Nonetheless, Fosdick simply dismissed the New Testament teaching on the eschaton as "the early Christian phrasing of hope" since no one "in the ancient world had ever thought, as we do, of development, progress, gradual change, as God's way of working out his will in human life and institutions."[175] Therefore, Fosdick was able to dismiss condescendingly the "literalist" eschatology as a resurgent pre-modern superstition that could be explained by the stressful geopolitical situation following the war in Europe.[176]

Moreover, it was not simply that Protestant liberals did not believe in orthodox eschatology. It was instead that they found it to be a danger to be rooted out and destroyed. University of Chicago Divinity School dean Shailer Mathews exhibits this attitude in a World War I–era tract, which includes conspiratorial-sounding rhetoric that sounds more akin to the later-twentieth-century anti-communist pamphlets than to a theological discussion. "Under the present abnormal war conditions Christian churches are being honeycombed by a movement liberally financed and widely organized *which threatens the spiritual and moral nature of Christianity,*" the editor's note warns. "It is the premillenarian propaganda."[177] The danger seen by Protestant liberalism was due to their commitment to an Enlightenment view of progress. Accordingly, the modernists tied their rejection of a physical coming of Christ to a definite counter-proposal in the evolutionary outworking of the Kingdom through the Social Gospel.[178] They therefore were able to see "eschatology" in the progress of human endeavor in music, painting, and architecture, such that the meaning of the "coming of Christ" would be "that, slowly it may be, but surely, his will and principles will be worked out by God's grace in human life and institutions, until 'he shall see the travail of his soul and be satisfied.'"[179]

The fundamentalists were right to see the bankruptcy of Protestant liberalism's redefined "eschatology" as part of a larger crisis in terms of biblical authority. The move toward a Kingdom eschatology in contemporary evangelical theology likewise offers an opportunity to relate eschatological concerns to the most basic commitments of Christian orthodoxy. Unlike the "eschatological theologies" of the contemporary Protestant left, the evangelical consensus maintains that the inauguration and consummation of the Kingdom has an ontological and metaphysical reality and is discovered through an authoritative divine revelation.[180] The very assertion that there is historic continuity between an executed first-century Jewish man and the goal of cosmic history is, by definition, a repudiation of the anti-supernaturalism of the contemporary inheritors of the Protestant liberal tradition.[181] As G. B. Caird correctly observes, "Eschatology is a defiant manifesto which declared, in the face of all realistic denial, that what is now held to be true in the purposes of God will become true in the experiences of His people and His world."[182] This "defiant manifesto," against the most pernicious historical hermeneutic of suspicion, encapsulates the best of the American fundamentalist tradition, a tradition that can be continued only to the extent that evangelical theology is willing to defend matters of eschatological import.

It is for this reason that evangelical theology alone is able to construct a coherent vision of biblical eschatology. Protestant liberal biblical scholars were correct to emphasize the eschatological nature and Kingdom centrality of Jesus' proclamation and the apostolic witness to it. Evangelical theology alone, however, has been able to echo this apostolic witness with intellectual integrity, precisely because only a supernaturalistic theology can include the same appeal to space-time history as the biblical writers themselves. The various attempts at an "eschatological" reading of the New Testament, from a historical-critical vantage point, have served to redirect eschatological concerns toward existential concerns, personal piety, social impulses, or personal ethics. Evangelical eschatology, however, can focus on the events of the biblical kerygma as determinative of New Testament eschatology. This means that evangelical eschatology can recognize that the Kingdom theme of the Old and New Testaments is not disconnected from history, but is anchored to a particular historical act— namely, the resurrection of the body of Jesus.[183]

Nonetheless, the postwar evangelical theologians were correct in their assessment that the fundamentalists had diverged from the central issues of the New Testament theology of the Kingdom, becoming bogged down in

internecine debates over issues such as the timing of the rapture and the tribulation period, aspects of eschatology arguably built more on theological infer-
ences than on the core of the biblical witness. Uniting around an "already/not
yet" model of Kingdom fulfillment does not automatically resolve eschatological debates within evangelical theology, a problem, after all, even for the
crowds applying (rightly, if in some aspects prematurely) the eschatology of
Davidic promise (Isaiah 62; Zechariah 9; Psalm 118) as Jesus entered Jerusalem
on a colt (Matt. 21:1-9). It is true that inaugurated eschatology, left undefined,
can mount such a consensus that it can become "a sort of slogan" within evangelical theology. This does not prove it wrong, however. Social theorist
Benjamin Barber observes that political conservatives and liberals both quote
Alexis de Tocqueville precisely because "he got so many things right."[184] The
same may be true for "already/not yet" eschatology. The newer consensus can
resolve the perennial evangelical eschatological confusion by integrating the
"last things" to an overall biblical picture of the Kingdom of God. Both dispensationalists and covenantalists have arrived at the centrality of the Kingdom
for understanding biblical eschatology, not primarily by understanding the centrality of the Kingdom motif in the biblical materials but by understanding the
centrality of Christ there. The eschaton then is to be understood as part of the
overall goal of the history of the cosmos—the universal acclaim of Jesus as
sovereign over the created order (Phil. 2:9-11) and the glorification of Jesus
through the salvation of the cosmos (Rom. 8:29).[185]

This is the key insight of inaugurated eschatology—namely, the fact that
its central biblical referent is not a golden age within history or the timing of
prophetic events, but instead is the One whom God has exalted as "both Lord
and Christ—this Jesus whom you crucified" (Acts 2:36). The "already" and
the "not yet" aspects of the Kingdom find their content in the identity and mission of Jesus as Messiah. This correctly locates the hinge of history as resting
on the incarnation, life, sacrificial death, resurrection, and ascension of Jesus
as the harbinger of the "last days" (Heb. 1:2), the "firstborn" of the eschatological resurrection of the righteous (Col. 1:18), and the Kingdom of God in
person. This Christocentric focus of inaugurated eschatology has necessitated
that the rival theological systems within the evangelical coalition revise some
of their more biblically problematic tenets, and jettison others. Most of these
eschatological revisions have come, not first of all over the timing of future
events, but over what biblically it means to speak of Jesus as "the anointed
One," the Christ. Thus, developments in both dispensationalism and covenant
theology have recognized that biblical eschatology cannot be severed from the
Christological fulfillment of the Old Testament covenants, which is, after all,

the predominant theme of the apostles and of Jesus Himself in explaining the meaning of the gospel.[186] With such being the case, this kind of inaugurated eschatology takes into account the crucial importance of passages such as 2 Samuel 7 for understanding the New Testament witness to the messianic Kingdom of Jesus.[187] This perspective shields evangelical theology from perceiving the present nature of the Kingdom as merely spiritual or existential, or as languishing in suspended animation until the eschaton. At the same time, these developments in evangelical eschatology remedy what theologian Adrio König has identified with precision as the "eclipse of Christ" in contemporary eschatology.[188]

These developments well reflect the biblical teaching on the epochal significance of the coming of Christ, especially in terms of His fulfillment of the Abrahamic and Davidic covenants, a fulfillment foreshadowed even in the praise accompanying His conception (Luke 1:32-33, 55, 68-75). This attention to the canonical meaning of the covenants helps to ensure that evangelical theology does not simply reach consensus that there is an "already" and a "not yet" to the Kingdom, but that it is able to agree on the meaning of the "Kingdom" itself. It does so by recognizing that inaugurated eschatology is a matter of Christology.

In so doing, the inaugurated eschatology of the New Testament makes sense of the decidedly eschatological nature of the resurrection and ascension of Jesus, events that the New Testament links explicitly to Jesus' messianic role as Davidic ruler. The newer consensus must not merely affirm the historicity of these events, but it must also emphasize the eschatological import for Jesus *as a human being*. Passages such as Romans 1:3-4 do not dismiss Jesus' ontological status as the eternal Son of God.[189] Evangelical Kingdom theology is not a return toward the ancient Christological heresy of adoptionism.[190] But these texts speak to more than the Chalcedonian definition. Instead, they specifically link Christ's resurrection to the covenant structure of the Old Testament. The shift in the ages seen in the New Testament relates Jesus' resurrection and ascension to the covenant Kingdom promises made generally to humanity in Adam (Gen. 3:15) and specifically to Israel through Abraham and David (Gen. 17:6; 2 Sam. 7:12-16). Jesus is resurrected and enthroned both as the obedient Son of Man (Dan. 7:13-14) and as the exalted Son of David (Acts 2:32-33) who has assumed His eschatological reign from His Father's right hand (Psalm 110; Acts 2:34; Rom. 1:3-4).[191] The resurrection and ascension of Jesus means that He is the "forerunner" or "pioneer" of the eschatological Kingdom of God (Heb. 1:10).

The newer consensus is right therefore to focus on the humanity of Jesus as the eschatological Man. One of Jesus' natures (the divine) is not ruling from heaven while the other (the human) awaits the eschaton.[192] Instead, evangelical eschatology must see the throne of David as an office, one from which Jesus has earned the right to rule. This is consistent with the requirements for obedience for the Davidic King found in the Old Testament. The Mosaic prophecy of the Israelite kingship asserts that the kingdom is contingent upon the king's obedience to the revealed will of Yahweh (Deut. 17:14-20). This is followed by the examples of the unfaithful ruling descendants of David who were swept away in their disobedience. It is further magnified in the Old Testament messianic theme that the Davidic King will love justice and truth, ruling righteously from the throne (e.g., Ps. 89:24-37). Moreover, Peter's use of Psalm 110 and 2 Samuel 7 in his Pentecost address clearly ties Jesus' reception of the Davidic covenant promises with the fact that the Father was pleased with Him (Acts 2:22-36). Thus, Jesus' exaltation as King through His resurrection from the dead and ascension to the right hand of the Father comes via what traditional Reformed theology has called the "active obedience" of Christ (Heb. 1:5-13; 5:7). It also comes via His "passive obedience" at Golgotha (Phil. 2:8-9; Heb. 10:12-13). Indeed, the exalted Jesus Himself announces in the Apocalypse that He "conquered and sat down with my Father on his throne" (Rev. 3:21, ESV).

This also presents evangelical eschatology with a more biblically focused understanding of the relationship between the inaugurated Kingdom of the resurrected Jesus and the dawning of the Spirit, a problem for both traditional dispensationalists and covenant theologians. The newer consensus offers just such a corrective attention to pneumatology. Ironically, this focus may well mean that the most enthusiastic scholarship in the area of evangelical pneumatology may come from the Dallas and Westminster traditions, the very ones who have held most tenaciously to the cessation of the sign gifts even as the rest of the evangelical coalition has grown more and more influenced by Pentecostalism and "third wave" charismatic ideas.[193] This is especially important given the way in which George Eldon Ladd's successors at Fuller Theological Seminary, most notably John Wimber and C. Peter Wagner, have appropriated his inaugurated eschatology for "power evangelism" and "signs and wonders" in the contemporary mission of the church.[194]

Contrary to the characterizations of covenant theology by traditional dispensationalists, the present spiritual benefits of the reign of Christ are not the "spiritualization" of Old Testament nationalistic texts. Traditionalist dispensationalist Charles Ryrie, for example, asks, "If Christ inaugurated His Davidic reign at His ascension, does it not seem incongruous that His first act as reigning Davidic king was the sending of the Holy Spirit (Acts 2:33), something not

included in the promises of the Davidic covenant?"[195] Contrary to such arguments, the nature of the "already" of the current reign from David's throne,
however, is informed by passages such as Isaiah 9:2, which describes the
Davidic son as a light to the nations. Repeated Old Testament texts speak of
the Davidic ruler as demonstrating justice and righteousness, which are then
defined by the prophets against the tyrannies of unjust and unrighteous mon-
archs. The Spirit of God is presented by the Old Testament prophets as resting
on the Davidic ruler who brings wisdom and understanding to the people (Isa.
11:2). This in turn is in continuity with the prophet Ezekiel, who presents the
Davidic ruler as not only exercising kingly authority over a flock but also mediating the cleansing work of the Spirit (Ezek. 36:22-32; 37:24-28).[196]

Moreover, the Gospel accounts of Jesus' authority over nature, sickness,
death, and the demonic powers do not simply verify His deity and indeed in
some cases do not do so precisely to demonstrate His role as the Spirit-anointed
Son of David (e.g., Matt. 12:18).[197] The Old Testament texts tie the anointing
of the Davidic King to God's approval (e.g., 1 Sam. 16:1) and God's presence
through His Spirit (e.g., 1 Sam. 16:13; Ps. 45:6-7). In the same way, Jesus is
anointed through the baptism of John, pronounced the Son of God by a voice
from heaven, and then, just as His father David, immediately sent in the power
of the Spirit to confront the enemy of His covenant God (Mark 1:9-12; Luke
3:21-4:14; 1 Samuel 17). The Old Testament furthermore speaks of the coming of the Spirit as accompanying the apocalyptic Day of the Lord (Isaiah 61;
Joel 2) and the resurrection from the dead (Ezek. 37:13-14). Jesus applies the
promise of the Spirit anointing of Isaiah 61 to Himself at the onset of His ministry (Luke 4:18-21). He then endures the apocalyptic judgment of God in His
own body, and initiates the last-days resurrection by being delivered from judgment three days later. Even Jesus' teaching that He will send the "living waters"
of the Spirit (John 7:38) is an implicitly eschatological statement. Not only does
the text indicate that this blessing of the Spirit is contingent upon the glorification of Jesus (John 7:39), but the statement itself points back to the "living
waters" theme of the Old Testament teaching on the eschatological Kingdom
(Zech. 14:8-9).[198] Likewise, the apostle Peter not only regards the outpouring
of the Spirit as an eschatological act of the enthroned messianic King (Acts
2:33), but he correlates the Spirit that "rests" on the Davidic heir with
Christians who share in His sufferings (1 Pet. 4:14).

This Kingdom understanding of the initial fulfillment of the eschaton
means much-needed correctives to both the dispensational and covenantal
wings of evangelical theology. For Charles Ryrie and other traditionalist critics of recent developments, the primary issue at stake is the present nature of

Christ's messianic session, especially in relation to the Old Testament covenants, particularly the Davidic covenant. Ryrie therefore asserts, "One of the major departures, if not *the* major one, of progressive dispensationalism from traditional dispensational and premillennial teaching is that Christ, already inaugurated as the Davidic king at his ascension, is now reigning in heaven on the throne of David."[199] It would appear that Ryrie is correct, although the early discussions within the Dispensational Study Group seemed to have relegated an inaugurated Davidic kingship to the periphery of the emerging movement.[200] Since then, however, the "already" aspect of the kingly rule of Christ has emerged as a central feature of progressive dispensational scholarship. While the new strain of dispensational thinking has called for a reconsideration of a variety of problematic issues, ranging from the law/gospel relationship to the work of the Spirit in redemptive history, nearly every eschatological question at issue is related to the "already" and "not yet" aspects of the reign of Christ.

The progressives are correct in their charge that older forms of dispensationalism often indeed were vulnerable to the charge of a practical "Nestorianism." Indeed, traditionalist dispensationalists not only seemed to sever the "thrones" of Jesus as Son of God and Son of David but also seemed to sever Jesus' "suffering servant" identity from His "messianic ruler" identity. The Christocentric vision of inaugurated eschatology is markedly different from Lewis Sperry Chafer, who doggedly opposed any suggestion of an inaugurated Davidic reign of Christ.[201] Difficulty comes, Chafer warned, "only for those who are determined to metamorphose a literal, earthly throne and kingdom into some vague and wholly imaginary spiritual idealism."[202] The newer Kingdom consensus, however, is able to explain the present-oriented Kingdom texts without diverting into "spiritual idealism," whereas traditionalist dispensationalists have no choice but to speak simply of a "spiritual" Kingdom of general sovereignty when discussing the "Kingdom of God" in the present era, if they can do so at all.

Chafer furthermore wrongly tied a bifurcated future hope to a bifurcated view of the person and work of Christ. "To Israel He is Messiah, Immanuel and King: to the church He is Lord, Head and Bridegroom," Chafer wrote. "The covenants and destinies of Israel are all earthly: the covenants and destinies of the church are all heavenly."[203] In this evangelical eschatological consensus Jesus is one Person, the Lord Jesus Christ, with one unified Kingdom purpose that spans the epochs of redemptive history, embraces the redeemed of all ages, and culminates in one unified Kingdom consummation.[204] This picture better reflects the New Testament emphasis on the unity of God's eschatological purposes, a unity that the apostle Paul roots in the redemptive work of Christ (Eph. 1:9-10; Col. 1:18-20). This means that the developing dispensational theology must not become *less* eschatological as it recognizes the more biblical reality of a present manifestation of the Kingdom. Instead, it is to become even *more* eschatological since eschatology is not to be thought of as (in the words of one end-times treatise) "things to come," but as an already-present reality that signals a yet-future consummation.[205]

At the same time, evangelical Reformed theology has at times failed to focus on the Christological and Kingdom orientation of pneumatology, in terms other than those narrowly limited to personal salvation and Trinitarian order. Though often overstating the case, traditional dispensationalists were right to note that the New Testament does emphasize the "newness" of the work of the Spirit, an emphasis actually safeguarded by a reforming dispensationalism that seeks to understand eschatology in terms of a canonical Kingdom theology.[206] The newer eschatological consensus, however, redirects Reformed theology toward a similar emphasis on the newness of the Spirit as an eschatological blessing tied to the resurrection and ascension of Jesus as King.[207] This point underscores much of the opposition the Kingdom-oriented covenant theologians face from their more traditional interlocutors.[208] The newer arguments of modified covenantalists thus sound quite similar, if not identical, to those of progressive dispensationalists.[209] Some Reformed theologians even do not hesitate to use the term "dispensational" to describe the once-for-all character of the coming of the Spirit at Pentecost.[210] This is a healthy development, especially when linked to Reformed development on the eschatological nature of the resurrection, a move in which the newer Reformed evangelicals are not saying less than their forebears, but are saying more.[211]

The Princeton wing of American fundamentalism could not be accused of ignoring the resurrection of Jesus, which was, after all, one of the "fundamentals."[212] The older tradition, however, tended to limit their emphasis to narrowly defined soteriological matters such as the resurrection as vindication of Jesus' deity or as necessary for the continued application of Jesus' atonement purchased at the cross.[213] Richard Gaffin is correct to see that Kingdom eschatology reverses an older tradition within Western theology, at least as old as Anselm, which concentrates the work of Christ most heavily on the benefits of His death, rather than on both His sacrificial death and His resurrection from the dead.[214] This is a welcome development, since the older Reformed tradition often seemed to follow a substitutionary model of the atonement with a less-emphasized, almost "moral influence" model of the resurrection.[215] By contrast, the newer consensus toward a Kingdom-oriented eschatology preserves the biblical emphasis that the Spirit is the Spirit poured out by Messiah in the last days. The new covenant blessing of the Spirit is permanent and universal among God's people in union with the resurrected Jesus, precisely because of the accomplished obedience of the Son of David who, unlike His predecessors, never need fear having the anointing of the Spirit taken from Him (1 Sam. 16:13-14; Ps. 51:11).

The newer consensus thereby synthesizes what is arguably the most biblical contribution of covenant theology on the present nature of the Kingdom with what is arguably the most biblical contribution of American dispensationalism—namely, the understanding that Scripture brims with an apocalyptic futurism.[216] The Kingdom consensus has come to agreement that the "not yet" of the Kingdom is of crucial theological significance, and that it does not refer to a heavenly existence but to a new creation. This more accurately reflects the biblical hope of a rule of Messiah in a new heaven and a new earth (2 Pet. 3:13; Rev. 21:1-4). It also understands that Scripture sees the relationship of believers to heaven as tied to the presence there of their King and Messiah, not as the place of their ultimate abode.[217] This contention bears the scrutiny of New Testament theology, especially the Pauline epistles, in which "heaven" seems to have a present, Christological referent (Eph. 1:3; 1:21; Phil. 3:20-21; Col. 1:5; 3:1-2; 1 Thess. 1:10) and thus is more emblematic of the "already" of the Kingdom than of the "not yet." This offers a healthy corrective to dispensationalism and covenant theology, as well as to the evangelical theological task as a whole.

Modified covenantalists are right to agree with the older dispensationalists in charging traditional covenant theology with holding to an Augustinian "spiritual vision" eschatology, with which it is impossible to reconcile the "earthy" feel of the prophetic promises, not only of the Old Testament but of the New as well.[218] The seemingly material aspects of the coming Kingdom, spoken of even in the Passover meal of Jesus with His disciples (Luke 22:15-16), were often neglected by earlier generations of Reformed theologians. Charles Hodge, for instance, contrasted a spiritual understanding of the Davidic reign of Christ with the "carnal" nature of premillennialism, which he dubbed a "Jewish doctrine" because of the "essential earthly character of the doctrine."[219] This view of the "not yet" reign of Christ is thus informed by the nature of the "already." A purely internal "spiritual" reign of Christ, articulated almost exclusively in terms of soteriology, is naturally related to the Reformed tradition's understanding not only of the eternal state but of the Millennium as well, which they usually set forth in terms of present spiritual realities.

Dispensationalists, however, are not exempt from this criticism as well. Because classical dispensationalists such as Scofield and Chafer so rigidly distinguished between Israel and the church, they set forth an eschatology in which the destiny of Israel as the "earthly" people of God was the renewed earth while the destiny of the Body of Christ as the "heavenly" people of God was heaven.[220] With the Jewish nation awaiting a Kingdom upon the earth and the church awaiting a heavenly Kingdom, it is little wonder that some progressive dispensationalists rightly conclude that the classical dispensational view of eschatology is ironically "amillennial," at least for the new covenant people of God.[221] This is perhaps the reason why dispensationalist eschatology has been directed historically toward a "spiritual vision" hope for heaven, with the emphasis on the "blessed hope" of a pretribulational rapture.[222] Thus, the developments within the dispensational tradition toward the Kingdom consensus mean that progressive dispensationalists are moving farther away from the spiritualized eternal state of traditional amillennialism, and are offering premillennialists an even *more* robustly articulated earthly future hope, one that includes both Israel and the church and that extends from the return of the Messiah through the Millennium and beyond.

Similarly, it is increasingly evident that covenant theologians were correct in their critique of traditional dispensational premillennialists as seeming to deny the eternality of the Kingdom promises. After all, dispensationalist premillennialists have often relegated the Kingdom promises to a thousand years of fulfillment in the Millennium, a position inconsistent with Old Testament passages such as Isaiah 9:7; 25:7-8; and 60:21; and New Testament passages such as Luke 1:32-33.[223] The appropriation of inaugurated eschatology, however, has answered this problem, as the Millennium is seen not as a separate dispensation from the eternal state, but as an initial phase of it.[224] George Ladd is correct to note that inaugurated eschatology's view of an initiated reign of Christ does not destroy premillennialism but rather supports its most central claim: "If then in the present age there is a real overlapping between the two ages so that while we live in the old age we experience the powers of the Age to Come, there should be no objection in principle to the idea that God in his redemptive purpose may yet have an age in which there is even further interaction between the powers of the new age and the present evil age."[225]

The key words in Ladd's explanation are, of course, "in principle." But, as the objections cited above against the "carnal" nature of the Millennium demonstrate, the "principle" of a millennial age was often what was at the heart of the dispute.[226] Now, even some doggedly amillennial covenant theologians suggest that the "bone of contention" has been overcome by the newer

Kingdom consensus regarding the hope of the new earth.[227] This does not resolve the problem, however, although it does clear the way for continued discussion. Henry and his fellow postwar evangelical leaders were correct to argue that the interpretation of Revelation 20 is a second-order issue, and therefore not a test of Christian orthodoxy or even of evangelical authenticity. This does not mean that it is not important. "The book of Revelation was written as a message from the ascended Lord, Jesus Christ, to the churches (1:1; 22:16)," Blaising rightly reminds evangelicals. "It should not be treated in a cavalier manner, but with respect."[228] The "new earth" by itself does not adequately explain texts such as Isaiah 65:17-25, which seem to conflate the "new heavens and the new earth" with an intermediate stage of the Kingdom in which death and rebellion are still present.[229] A premillennial Kingdom theology answers this problem by articulating the Millennium, not as a separate dispensation from the eternal state, but as an initial phase of it, even as the current reign of Christ over the church is an initial phase of His universal global dominion.[230]

This preserves the eternality of the Kingdom promises as well by abandoning the radical disjunction between "history" and "eternity." Kingdom eschatology should inform evangelical premillennialism that the Davidic reign of Christ need not terminate at the end of the Millennium, ushering in the "age of the Father's glory," as Ladd argued based on his interpretation of 1 Corinthians 15:28.[231] Instead, the Father's glory and the Father's sovereignty are reflected in the eschaton precisely through the eternal nature of the reign of the Son, whom the Father, after all, has chosen to rule as His appointed human vice-regent.[232] Furthermore, modified covenantal amillennialists are correct to note the biblical emphasis on the physicality of the "new earth," but they fail to note the equally biblical emphasis on the physicality of resurrection itself, especially in relation to the rule of regenerated and resurrected believers in Christ.[233] The "reign" that Christ promises to His believers, furthermore, is not a "spiritual" reign through the church. It is instead a coercive rule over the cosmos (Rev. 5:10), a reign that is impossible in either the "already" of the present age or the "not yet" of the final consummation. While amillennialists have pioneered the way for evangelical theology to understand the biblical witness to the present session of Christ at the right hand of the Father in fulfillment of Psalm 110, they have yet to demonstrate convincingly how He is presently exercising the kind of global worldwide dominion that is described in Davidic promise passages such as Psalm 72. If these passages are references to the reign of Christ over the new heavens and new earth (as Hoekema and other "new creation" covenantalists argue), they must explain more thoroughly from whence come the enemies over which the Davidic King will rule with a rod of iron (Ps. 2:9; 110:1-2; Rev. 2:26-27; 12:5; 19:15). It would seem therefore that a temporal millennial reign of Christ in the flow of this age's history is part of the messianic hope of Scripture.[234]

Eschatology as a Political Problem

An evangelical exploration of the present/future kingship of Christ is by its very nature a consideration of political theory since the social and political element is interwoven with biblical Christology. As Darrell Bock demonstrates, the Synoptic Gospel references to Jesus as the Davidic son display explicitly political and theocratic royal expectations in which a primary burden of the writings is "to show how the Davidic ruler comes to have such comprehensive authority over humans."[235] This is true especially when seen against the backdrop of the Old Testament witness to the political nature of the Davidic monarchy, beginning in the Mosaic allusions in the Pentateuch (Deut. 17:14-20), continued in the strikingly national terms of the covenant announced to David (2 Sam. 7:1-17; 1 Chron. 17:1-15), and repeatedly affirmed in the Psalms (especially Psalms 89, 110, and 132). The prophetic writings likewise speak in governmental, nationalistic terms when addressing the righteous reign of the Davidic throne (Isa. 9:6-7) who would inherit the "sure mercies of David" (Isa. 55:3, KJV), and whose rule would be affirmed by the anointing of the Spirit of Yahweh (Isa. 11:1-16). This messianic King is spoken of as protecting the people from their enemies (Ezek. 34:23-24; 37:24-26; Jer. 30:9). The reign of this monarch is presented in terms of political and moral righteousness (Deuteronomy 17; Psalm 72) and in terms of incontestable dominion (Ps. 89:25-27).

This political element of the biblical monarchial teaching has proven problematic for some interpreters of Scripture. Old Testament theologian Walter Eichrodt, for example, argues that the ancient Hebrews borrowed from the Canaanite understandings of the king as a "superhuman, semi-divine Being" in order to prop up the legitimacy of the Davidic dynasty and quell popular criticism.[236] Eichrodt points to such "borrowed" efforts at political stabilization in the motif of the adoption of the king as the son of the deity (Ps. 2:7), the description of the ruler's domain as global in its extent (Ps. 72:8), and the portrayal of the king as exalted to the right hand of the deity (Ps. 110:1).[237] These texts, however, are not ignored in the New Testament, but are explicitly related to the work of Jesus in His resurrection from the dead and ascension to the right hand of the Father, as seen clearly in, for example, the first chapter of the book of Hebrews.[238] From the very beginnings of the apostolic faith, the idea of a Kingdom of Christ has proven to be at least an incipient threat to the political powers-that-be. Throughout the Gospel accounts, from Herod's fear of political rivalry at the oracle of the birth of the heir of David (Matt. 2:1-12) to the Roman effort to put down a supposed political insurrection at His execution (Luke 23:1-25), political leaders are pictured as threatened by the political implications of Jesus' role as Davidic Messiah. Increasingly, evangelical eschatology is contending that these rulers' fears are well founded, if premature.

And yet, it is not simply the Kingdom theme that speaks to sociopolitical realities. It is also the way in which the Scripture speaks of the Kingdom as both present and future. Thus, Jesus confronts the political authorities in passages such as Matthew 26:63-64 by quoting the "not yet" messianic Kingdom references of Daniel 7 while submitting in the "already" to crucifixion, all the while maintaining that the political powers are temporal and derivative in authority. Jesus' words to "render unto Caesar" are almost immediately put to the test in the early church as Christ-appointed apostles are indicted for acting "contrary to the decrees of Caesar, saying that there is another king, Jesus" (Acts 17:7). Jesus speaks of the Kingdom "in your midst" (Luke 17:20-21), that it is given not only to Him but to His followers (Luke 22:29), while the apostle Paul mocks the Corinthian followers of Jesus for thinking themselves to be "kings" already (1 Cor. 4:8). The writer of Hebrews contrasts the "not yet" of all things in subjection to Christ with the "already" of His incarnation and atonement (Heb. 2:5-18). In grappling with these biblical realities, the task of constructing an evangelical theology of sociopolitical engagement has been greatly aided by a growing consensus that evangelical eschatology must focus first, not on the sound and fury of millennial meanings, but on the invasion of the eschatological, Davidic Kingdom into the present age, thus bringing the eschaton into the history of the world in the person of Jesus of Nazareth. By advocating an "already/not yet" model of this fulfillment, evangelical eschatology faces the challenge of integrating these interpretive issues into an understanding of how the present/future reign of Christ impacts contemporary problems of social and political concern.

The "already" nature of the Kingdom removes the chief obstacle of a fundamentalist withdrawal from politics and social action on the basis of a premillennialism that sees the Kingdom as wholly future. Was Henry correct about the sociopolitical implications of evangelical dispensationalism's rejection of any present reality for the Kingdom of God? While *Uneasy Conscience* arguably was the most forceful critique of the paralyzing effects of dispensationalist eschatology, Henry was neither the first nor the last to make this case. Historian George Marsden, for example, notes that twentieth-century funda-

mentalism was not wholly apolitical, pointing to the jingoistic political organizing and anti-communist activism of premillennial fundamentalists such as
Carl McIntire and Billy James Hargis as examples of the "paradox of super-
patriotic premillennialism" coming from those whose "attention was supposed
to be directed away from politics while waiting for the coming King."[239]
Marsden is correct in this assessment that the exceptions often proved the
problem. This is seen, for instance, in what commentator Rick Perlstein identifies as the "apparently defeatist" slogan of fundamentalist Bob Jones, Jr., in
support of 1964 Republican nominee Barry Goldwater: "Turn Back, America,
Turn Back: Only a Divine Miracle Can Save America Now."[240] Such comments, even as a political rallying point, reflected a long heritage of fundamentalist application of dispensational eschatology to the prospects of activism
within the social order.[241]

   Marsden rightly notes, however, that such examples do not negate the
politically paralyzing effects of fundamentalist eschatology, but rather confirm
it by spotlighting the "Manichean mentality" behind fundamentalism's awk-
ward forays into the public arena.[242] Historian Mark Noll concurs that some
fundamentalists in the 1930s and beyond plunged into protracted political
action, but much of this engagement was led by conspiracy theorists, often with
a decidedly anti-Semitic edge.[243] As Noll concludes, "If exceptions existed to
the general turn by evangelicals from political action, there were few, if any,
exceptions to the turn from political reflection."[244] Henry was therefore right
that any effort toward evangelical engagement must address theological—particularly eschatological—issues head-on.[245] While the future Kingdom of dispensationalist fundamentalism was used as an incentive for developing
personal ethics, it was used as an incentive to avoid the development of a social
ethic.[246] Thus, the question for the dispensationalist fundamentalists against
whom Henry was arguing was whether the coming Kingdom had anything to
say to a world situation that was counting down to Armageddon.

   Moreover, Henry was also correct to note that the Kingdom theology of
the dispensationally oriented fundamentalist bloc was further paralyzed politically by an obsession with tying current events to the apocalyptic prophetic
events of Scripture. Henry's lament, it would seem, had a solid historical basis.
World War II–era dispensationalists were rarely without voices attempting to
tie the tumultuous world situation to the pages of Daniel or the Apocalypse.
As Paul Boyer notes, many prophecy watchers found the Antichrist more often
in the person of Benito Mussolini than in Adolf Hitler, a fact that Boyer
attributes to Mussolini's rule from Rome along with his 1929 concordat with
the pope.[247] Boyer notes that many such dispensationalists would nuance their

speculations with a tinge of prophetic humility. He cites as an example dispensationalist leader Arno Gaebelein's careful, but nonetheless provocative, assessment of Mussolini: "Will this man, known for his ambition to be Europe's great dictator, develop into the final dictator? This is a question which only God can answer."[248] As historian Jon Stone argues, this prophetic speculation endowed premillennialist fundamentalist spokesmen with a degree of authority in proclaiming not only the meaning of Scripture but also the hidden meaning of history itself: "It seems, then, that long before the Swiss theologian Karl Barth urged Protestant ministers to preach with the Bible in one hand and the newspaper in the other, premillennial dispensationalists were reading the Bible as if it *were* the daily paper."[249]

Nonetheless, it is overly simplistic to lay fundamentalist sociopolitical isolation at the feet of dispensationalist eschatology. For example, in 1980, Carl Henry interviewed D. Martyn Lloyd-Jones, the renowned Calvinist pastor of London's Westminster Chapel, for *Christianity Today*. Lloyd-Jones dismissed Henry's inquiry about a distinctively Christian response to the economic situation. "Because man is a sinner, any human contrivance is doomed to fail; the only hope for the world is the return of Christ—nothing else," Lloyd-Jones responded. "It amazes me that evangelicals have suddenly taken such an interest in politics; to do so would have made sense 50 or 60 years ago, but such efforts now seem to me sheer folly for we are in a dissolving world."[250] Lloyd-Jones went on to offer a particularly eschatological reason for his political disengagement: "All my life I've opposed setting 'times and seasons,' but I feel increasingly that we may be in the last times."[251] This was based, Lloyd-Jones explained, on his belief that the Jewish occupation of the whole of Jerusalem since 1967 was a fulfillment of Luke 21:24, which speaks of Jerusalem under siege "until the time of the Gentiles be fulfilled." He joined this observation with his belief that the conversion of the Jewish people as prophesied in Romans 11 was taking place in contemporary Israel. There was, he concluded, "nothing but collapse" for Western civilization.[252]

Against Lloyd-Jones's pessimistic eschatology, Henry unleashed his *Uneasy Conscience* arguments for social and political engagement.[253] Lloyd-Jones, however, was not convinced, concluding, "It seems to me that our Lord's own emphasis was quite different, even opposed to this."[254] What is remarkable about this exchange is that it represents far more than an intercontinental dispute between two basically Reformed theologians over the role of Christians in politics. Instead, it represents a staunchly covenantal and amillennialist Lloyd-Jones offering exactly the same eschatological arguments against the Christian presence in the public square that Henry had first encountered from the largely premillennialist fundamentalists at the onset of the postwar evangelical movement.

Nor have the eschatological obstacles to evangelical engagement dissipated since then. Cal Thomas, an early participant in Moral Majority, for instance, now offers a distinctively pessimistic eschatological reason for disengaging from the political arena. "I do think our primary objective is not to tinker with the kingdom of this world," Thomas argues. "It's the same with my motel room: I don't like the wallpaper, but I didn't call an interior decorator to redecorate, because I'm only staying for one night."[255] The more pointed voices of evangelical postmillennialism, such as that of Gary North, thus charge evangelicalism with an ongoing commitment "to eschatological pessimism concerning the efforts of the church, in time on earth" resulting in an escapist and otherworldly "rapture fever," which looks for the Kingdom to come while ignoring the Kingdom mandate for the present age.[256] Evangelical engagement is impossible, North argues, because any "attempt to make Christianity socially relevant before the era of the millennium is inescapably the implicit abandonment of dispensational theology."[257] This is especially true, he argues, when the primary evangelical eschatological alternative is a Reformed amillennialism, which is even more pessimistic than dispensationalism since it "offers no hope for Christians in history, not even the Rapture."[258] Therefore, North asserts, the evangelical amillennialist is "basically a premillennialist without any earthly hope."[259] Evangelical theology thus faces the (often valid) criticisms of both liberation theologians on the left and theonomic theologians on the right that evangelical theology has been hijacked by an eschatology that ignores sociopolitical issues in an apocalyptic flight from the world.[260]

The developments toward an inaugurated eschatology can address just such critiques. Unlike the older fundamentalism, which tended to compare Christ's current Kingdom activity to David's anointed yet exiled status under Saul (1 Samuel 16—2 Samuel 1), the emerging evangelical eschatological consensus can call the church away from cultural withdrawal precisely because the throne of David is occupied and active even now. Thus, evangelicals can understand with the earliest Christian communities the political ramifications of a title too often taken for granted in the subculture of conservative American Christianity: the Lord Jesus Christ. An understanding of this initial fulfillment of the reign of Christ could spur evangelicalism to reexamine sociopolitical issues, not merely in the light of contemporaneous party platforms but in light of this "already" phase of the prophetic hope. Because an already exalted Davidic King rules the Christian community, evangelical theology has the mandate to scrutinize the features of current political relationships against the characteristics of the now-ruling messianic King, characteristics for which there stands an overwhelming canonical testimony. Because the Davidic ruler reigns *presently* with justice and wisdom (Ps. 72:1-2; Jer. 23:5), believers are given an authoritative standard by which they may condemn political tyranny and domestic abuse of power, even by those who claim evangelical identity. International human rights abuses may be resisted in light of the King who one day will exercise righteous diplomacy between the nations (Isa. 2:4).[261] Believers cannot have the option of inaction against judicial abuses since they are presently ruled by One whom the Scriptures describe as judging His subjects with fairness and equity.

Likewise, a people who are governed even now by a Davidic King of whom it is written, "with righteousness He will judge the poor" (Isa. 11:4), cannot ignore the political oppression of the underclass. The inaugurated Kingdom reign of Christ likewise holds implications for perhaps the first and most decisive test of the neo-evangelical movement's "uneasy conscience," namely, the church's response to what Pope John Paul II calls the "culture of death."[262] A view of Christ as having already initiated His Kingdom can speak to the implicit, as well as the explicit, objections that the proliferation of abortion rights and euthanasia are simply the inevitable signs of a darkening age. Evangelical Kingdom eschatology can recognize that the ultimate end of the mistreatment of the powerless will come when "all kings bow down before him, all nations serve him" (Ps. 72:11). Still, the initial fulfillment of the Kingdom spotlights the Kingdom *priorities* of the One of whom it is prophesied, "He will have compassion on the poor and needy, and the lives of the needy he will save. He will rescue their life from oppression and violence, and their blood will be precious in his sight" (Ps. 72:13-14). Because the initially realized Kingdom is governed by the Davidic heir who is described as an advocate "for the afflicted of the earth" (Isa. 11:4), evangelicals have the biblical impetus to plead for the life and liberty of the powerless in every stage of life.

The "not yet" phase of the Kingdom likewise transforms the social and political mandate of evangelical theology. While Henry and the postwar evangelical theologians warned that conservative American Christianity's fixation on apocalyptic futurism short-circuited any attempt at evangelical social and political engagement, others have maintained that fundamentalist eschatology was itself inherently political. Sociologist Sara Diamond, a culturally liberal critic of the Christian political right, disagrees with the conventional wisdom that evangelical eschatology has been subversive of political activity, even in its most dispensationalist forms of premillennialism. Even if millennial thinking is a distraction, she argues, a "good distraction can energize the faithful for the battles ahead."[263] She finds typical evangelical eschatology to be aglow with political overtones, especially in the popular belief in a pre-tribulational Rapture, which she says rhetorically magnifies the chasm between the "saved" and the "unsaved," "us" and "them," a chasm that cannot help but further a divisive and culturally destabilizing "culture war."[264] This is why, she argues, there is so much overlap between popular apocalyptic speculation and conservative political activism in the evangelical subculture; both are designed to keep group members distracted and thus satisfied with the sociopolitical status quo.[265]

It is precisely, however, such an uncritical support of the status quo that an emphasis on the yet future aspects of Kingdom fulfillment can counteract. In 1873 Friedrich Nietzsche observed, "The 'kingdom of Prussia' seems to have supplanted the 'kingdom of God.'"[266] This denial of any Constantinian identification of any secular social order with the eschatological Kingdom of God is perhaps one of the most valuable political contributions of evangelical premillennialism, a strength that the larger evangelical tradition would do well to absorb. With an insistence on a future Christocentric political Kingdom, evangelicals have maintained that all secular political orders are provisional and temporal, and thus cannot hold ultimate allegiance over the church. This means that evangelicals must develop a coherent message about how the secular kingdoms are to relate to the final Kingdom of God in Christ, taking into account passages such as Romans 13:1-7 and 1 Peter 2:13-17, while still recognizing that Caesar's dominion is temporary and limited in authority.[267] This "not yet" emphasis means therefore that evangelical Kingdom theology cannot identify any nation, including the United States of America, as above prophetic judgment. Thus, those evangelicals and Roman Catholics who have wondered aloud about whether judicial usurpation has rendered the United States government an "illegitimate regime" may well be in serious error in their conclusions but not in their theological basis for broaching the question.[268]

In this, evangelical eschatology does not undermine the foundations of democratic government, since governments are temporal realities created to serve a function for justice and order.[269] Indeed, an inaugurated eschatology actually supports the legitimacy of state functions in the "already" that would be unthinkable in the "not yet." Evangelicals may support the right of governments to execute criminals or to wage just wars precisely because the Kingdom is not yet wholly triumphant over this present evil age.[270] At the same time, a Kingdom-oriented eschatology avoids what Catholic political philosopher Robert Kraynak argues persuasively is the fundamental flaw of Christian attempts at political theory—namely, the tendency to baptize a Kantian notion of a "kingdom of ends" within the construct of classical liberal democracy as the goal of revealed religion.[271]

This refusal to equate any secular state with Kingdom fulfillment also applies to the current state of Israel, long a point of contention in evangelical eschatology.[272] The impact of dispensationalism on fundamentalism and evangelicalism has often resulted in an almost unqualified support for Israel, spurred on by popular apocalypticism among the evangelical grassroots constituency.[273] Believing that the nation's reestablishment in Palestine in 1948 was a fulfillment of Old Testament prophecies, many in the new Christian right political movement have translated their theological understanding into support for Israel as a key component of their political worldview.[274] Not surprisingly, Israeli governmental officials have welcomed such overtures on the part of evangelicals and fundamentalists.[275] Developments toward a Kingdom-oriented eschatology, however, do not give such a blanket endorsement of the present Israeli state, at least not on the basis of biblical prophecy.[276] This is because of the Christocentric nature of the messianic Kingdom, a theological contention covenant theologians have always maintained in relation to any future for the state of Israel.[277] "The modern Jewish state is not part of the messianic kingdom of Jesus Christ," contends Reformed theologian O. Palmer Robertson. "Although it may be affirmed that this particular civil government came into being under the sovereignty of the God of the Bible, it would be a denial of Jesus' affirmation that his kingdom is 'not of this world order' (John 18:36) to assert that this government is part of his messianic kingdom."[278]

What is remarkable is not that a covenant theologian would make such a statement, but that he would receive such hearty agreement across the evangelical theological spectrum by dispensationalists, and for precisely the same reasons—the necessity of Christ for the Kingdom. In fact, Craig Blaising has suggested that evangelical zeal for the reestablishment of Israel has clouded recognition of the present activity of the Davidic King as an agent of reconciliation and peace. He marvels that contemporary dispensationalists could overlook Israeli human rights abuses against the Palestinians when the biblical prophets explicitly condemned similar injustices.[279] This does not mean that evangelicalism erred by listening to its dispensational tradition regarding support for Israel. Indeed, it may be argued that, by equating the modern Jewish state with some prophetic fulfillment of the coming Kingdom, evangelicalism was not listening closely enough to dispensationalism. After all, dispensationalists have maintained that Israel is not only an ethnic category but also a religio-political body that is defined by its relationship to the Davidic monarchy. One cannot therefore christen a secular state as a recipient of the Abrahamic promise (as some popular dispensational teachers have been prone to do, citing Genesis 12:3) when that state does not recognize the promised Seed of Abraham and Son of David, through whom all the nations are to be blessed (Gal. 3:16). Dispensationalists should have been the ones reminding the rest of the evangelical coalition that the eschatological restoration of Israel is accomplished by the Messiah, not by the United Nations.[280]

A politically engaged evangelicalism would be in error if it sought to remedy these past errors by abandoning support for Israel.[281] American evangelicals should not expect their government to act as the Amorites and Canaanites with "hearts melted" at the thought of Israel's national presence on the global scene (Josh. 5:1-2), but neither should they overreact by canonizing the Palestinians as God's "new Israelites" held in bondage to a new (and rather ironically cast) "Pharaoh" of the Israeli state. Held to the standards of peace and justice defined by the activity of the messianic King, the tyrannies-in-waiting of Palestinian terrorist leaders should be repugnant to an eschatologically informed evangelical theology. Thus, current developments in evangelical theology probably will not alter evangelical support for Israel, but will ground such support in a quest for geopolitical stability and peace in the Middle East, not in the "Thus saith the Lord" of the prophecy charts.

Of course, the sociopolitical implications of conservative American Christianity's futurism did not end with support for Zionism. As noted above, Henry and the postwar evangelical theologians were right to fear that the prophetic speculation of popular apocalyptic Bible teachers would only destabilize the evangelical witness in the public square by equating various current events with prophetic fulfillment. This intersection between political positions and prophetic scenarios only increased in the decades following Henry's *Uneasy Conscience*.[282] The political implications of such speculations came into public discussion with the election of arguably the only dispensational premillennialist president of the United States, Ronald Reagan, who disturbed many theologians and political commentators with his references to "Armageddon," especially in reference to the Cold War nuclear tensions with the Soviet Union.[283] Historian Richard Kyle notes the political influence of popular evangelical apocalyptic speculation in Reagan's statement, "You know, I turn back to your ancient prophets and the Old Testament and the signs foretelling Armageddon and I find myself wondering if we're the generation that is going to see that come about."[284]

Of course, most of this fear of foreign policy by prophecy chart was wildly exaggerated.[285] After all, it is difficult to portray Reagan, who rarely attended church, as a dupe of any detailed system of evangelical doctrine.[286]

Furthermore, if Reagan was indeed hell-bent on fulfilling biblical prophecy through hastening Armageddon, he miserably failed his evangelical constituency, especially as his administration pursued policies that would lead to the demise of the Soviet "evil empire," or, as many popular evangelical prophecy speculators had identified it, "Gog and Magog."[287]

Even so, with a more carefully constructed theology of the "not yet" aspect of the Kingdom, the emerging evangelical consensus is adamant in its refusal to identify current events with sensational theories of the end of the age.[288] Both covenantalists and dispensationalists should be at the forefront of this awareness of the theological dangers of tying current political happenings to biblical prophecy, since these traditions would be the first among evangelicals to affirm that only prophetic authority can interpret prophetic fulfillment. And yet, previous generations of premillennialists and amillennialists (though especially premillennialists) acted remarkably similar to their Social Gospel postmillennialist interlocutors in identifying current political activities with the Kingdom program of God.[289] A perusal of cessationist articles of faith adopted by Westminster and Dallas seminaries might have chastened evangelicals that no continuing extra-biblical revelation existed upon which to base such speculations.

The "not yet" of Kingdom fulfillment has further import for evangelical engagement at one of its most contested points, even by Henry and the postwar evangelicals, namely, the political paralysis that can come with the "pessimism" of both premillennialism and amillennialism.[290] While the hopeless historical pessimism of the isolationist fundamentalists (and even of confessional evangelicals such as Martyn Lloyd-Jones) was indeed fatal to any theology of evangelical engagement, there was a certain sense in which eschatological "pessimism" was necessary to distinguish evangelical eschatology from that of Protestant liberalism.[291] The postwar evangelical movement was right to seek to transcend the narrow insistence on premillennialism as a boundary for fellowship by the early-twentieth-century fundamentalists. Nonetheless, evangelicals should not forget why the fundamentalists were so insistent at this point. It was because, among other reasons, the Social Gospel teachings of denominational liberals were insisting that a truly modern eschatology meant ushering in the Kingdom through social action, usually an appropriation of varying degrees of Marxist social thought, along with a robust affirmation of "Christian America."[292]

Premillennialism was not just a matter of prophetic timetables for many of these fundamentalists. It was a way of asserting the Christocentric nature of the Kingdom. It could not be "evolved" through historical processes, but could come only through the sovereign act of Christ Himself.[293] Thus, it was often inextricably linked to other debates over the necessity of regeneration and the exclusivity of the work of Christ.[294] This is not to say that premillennialism should be considered a basis for evangelical fellowship. It is to say only that the insistence on premillennial confessions of faith was quite often, at least in the beginning, less about undue narrowness than about preserving historic Christian orthodoxy, an orthodoxy that was imperiled by an evolutionary postmillennial model of the coming of the Kingdom. In many ways, then, the "pessimistic" eschatology of fundamentalism differed little from its "pessimistic" soteriology, which saw the cataclysmic intervention of the Spirit of Christ as the only hope for totally depraved individuals. In fact, as Carl Henry observed mid-century, the fundamentalist revolt against the Social Gospel was bolted to a biblical realism about the personal and historical strongholds of human depravity.[295] "Fed by a glamorized unregeneracy, the optimistic and utopian myths seem now to lack credibility, even if the activist protest movements of the 1960s temporarily revived them until disenchantment set in," Henry complains. "Marxist and Freudian analyses gained a hearing because they penetrated, however naively, to deeper roots of evil."[296] As Reinhold Niebuhr so emphatically expressed, even liberals eventually found bankrupt the "optimism" of liberal Protestantism, at both the personal and the societal level.[297]

So the much-derided "pessimism" of premillennialism in many ways served as a theological corrective to the arrogance of political triumphalism. As Stanley Grenz contends,

> As nineteenth-century American theological history so aptly demonstrates, left unbridled, optimism runs the risk of separating itself from its proper source and thereby degenerating into blind utopianism. The awareness of our role in cooperating with the God of history can easily lead to a sense that we are the determiners of our history. And the proclamation of the kingdom of God as the goal of historical activity can unfortunately be transformed into efforts to produce the kingdom of God within history. Consequently, in the midst of our confident acceptance of our mandate, we need to hear what the Spirit is saying to the churches through the pessimistic tone of premillennial eschatologies. Ultimately it is God, and not our feeble actions, who is the hope of the world.[298]

Similarly, the historical evidence seems to back up theologian Mark Saucy's contention that the dominant premillennialism of conservative American Protestantism helped to encourage "a healthy separation between the Kingdom's Already and its Not Yet which spares evangelical praxis from the snare" of such politicized mainline ecumenical bodies as the World Council of Churches.[299]

This is even more needed in the current climate, with theological alternatives such as theonomy on the right and liberation theology on the left championing an outworking of the Kingdom in the present age.[300] These concerns are, as noted above, not new at all. Westminster theologian Edmund Clowney, for example, forewarned that the abandonment of realist eschatology in the Presbyterian Church's proposed 1967 confessional revision promised a skewed view of Christian political action. The creed jettisons any mention of "a personal and visible return of the risen Lord Jesus Christ" and suggests that "the new heavens and new earth and kingdom of God are 'visions and images.'"[301] Thus, as Clowney pointed out, the creed encouraged social and political action, promising "a final triumph of God but [leaving] this triumph completely undefined."[302] These questions are not relevant to liberalism alone. There is on the evangelical right a very real temptation, as Richard Gaffin puts it, not only to a "millennial escapism," but also to a "quasi-theocratic utopianism."[303]

This is especially true given the fact that Kingdom eschatology is, by definition, an emphasis on the messianic role of Christ, precisely the emphasis some postwar evangelical theologians insisted was necessary for a theology of evangelical engagement. "Emphasis on the kingly office of Christ was never more needful than now," opined Henry in the political tumult of the 1960s. "For once God's righteous sovereignty becomes obscure, fallen man becomes skeptical that power can be morally employed."[304] Even so, a theology of evangelical engagement must increasingly contend with the notion that such an emphasis on the reign of Christ might lead to both theological and political imbalance. Mark Noll, for instance, argues that "the leaven of Lutheran cross-centeredness" must be added to the "lump of Calvinist kingly rule" to avoid a triumphalism of the cross in American political engagement.[305] Noll fears that the emphasis on the "already" nature of Christ's reign may be abused for political purposes, without the counterbalance of emphasis on Christ's passivity and suffering in the face of evil. He also fears an imbalanced emphasis here could lead to the appropriation of the "kingly" role by the church. Noll especially notes the inherent dangers of the kind of "Kingdom activity" of Abraham Kuyper in the turn-of-the-century Netherlands.[306] Here Noll is not without historical warrant for his uneasiness—a warrant that ranges from the reign of Constantine throughout the history of Christendom.

The developing Kingdom consensus on eschatology, however, anticipates and answers this problem by emphasizing, with Hebrews 2, that the present stage of the Kingdom is defined by the ascent of the suffering Messiah to

Golgotha, not by the descent of the new Jerusalem from the heavens. Thus, the "already" of the Kingdom is not defined by victorious evangelical political parties, but by periodic accomplishments punctuated with the sufferings of the people of God.[307] Similarly, contra all forms of dominion theology, this view of Kingdom activity helps to maintain the evangelical commitment to separation of church and state and religious liberty. A Kingdom eschatology can maintain that Christ will indeed rule over His enemies coercively while also keeping in healthy tension the New Testament emphasis that that day has not yet come (John 18:36). Rather the gospel comes now only in the persuasion of the sword of the Spirit, not with the coercion of the sword of steel.[308] "The mystery of the Kingdom is this: The Kingdom is here but not with irresistible power," Ladd counseled evangelicals. "The Kingdom of God has come, but it is not like a stone grinding an image to powder."[309]

The move toward a coherent eschatology of the Kingdom also addresses some of the failures of evangelical activism in the 1970s and beyond, failures that seemed often to stem from unrealistic expectations about the possibilities of political action, an optimism that was held, rather ironically, most often by premillennialists. In some instances, it would seem that conservative American evangelicalism went from the extreme of believing that no acts of public justice could be done in the present age to the opposite and equal extreme of seeming surprised that there was in fact no "moral majority" to coalesce around their ideas of civic righteousness. By expecting too much from political activity, evangelicals have seen figures such as Paul Weyrich move from direct-mail activism to fundamentalist isolationism in less than twenty years. Would not a more chastened and Kingdom-oriented view of the possibilities and limitations of political action have served the evangelical coalition well here, even as it would have done for the Social Gospel activists of the early twentieth century? Ironically, it is here that a comprehensive agenda of political engagement actually helps to maintain the "pessimism" inherent in evangelical apocalypticism, since politics is by its very nature an arena of compromise and negotiation, not of utopia-building. In this sense, it is not that the new Christian right was too political, but that, at times, it was not political enough.

An "already/not yet" Kingdom eschatology also empowers evangelical theology to address the twin threats of secular apocalypticism and utopianism. This is especially true in a philosophical environment that increasingly attempts to synthesize these seemingly contradictory themes.[310] Secular apocalypticism carries with it very real political implications, especially in the realm of environmental protection and energy policies. Evangelical engagement can and should work for environmental protection and peaceful coexistence among the world nuclear powers. But they can do so without succumbing to paralyzing scare tactics regarding an environmental Armageddon or nuclear holocaust, apocalyptic scenarios that bear a striking resemblance to some of the alarmist rhetoric of the Christian prophecy speculations, and often end with the same lack of credibility in the public square.[311] Evangelical theology can propose alternatives to this kind of outlook, without simply repackaging the faddish apocalyptic scenarios of secular culture within the context of Christianity.[312] A carefully detailed understanding of the "not yet" of biblical eschatology will remind evangelicals of the urgency of the task, without the panic of global destruction. "Man will not destroy himself from the face of the earth, nor will this planet become a cold lifeless star," George Eldon Ladd asserts. "The day is surely coming when the knowledge of God shall cover the earth as the waters cover the sea, when peace and righteousness shall prevail instead of war and evil."[313] A commitment to inaugurated eschatology within the broader context of Kingdom theology can only serve to bolster this assurance. Evangelicals who view the Spirit "already" in their midst as a guarantee that the now-reigning messianic ruler will consummate His promised "not yet" Kingdom may then engage the world powers with the assurance that the moon the psalmist deems a witness to the Davidic covenant (Ps. 89:36-37) will still be shining at the cosmic unveiling of the Son of David.

A commitment to Kingdom eschatology also serves to address the political problem of secular utopianism.[314] As political philosopher Eric Voegelin has pointed out, the most dangerous trends in human history have come through a neo-gnostic attempt at the "immanentization of the eschaton."[315] Voegelin traces this utopian temptation from the Kantian idea of progress toward a perfect existence in a cosmopolitan society to the "activist mysticism" of Karl Marx's Hegelian vision of a "final state of a classless realm of freedom" through "the revolution of the proletariat and the transformation of man into the communist superman."[316] Nor are these utopian visions limited to sweeping historical movements such as these. As Daniel Bell points out, the terrorism of the 1960s-era radical groups such as the "Weathermen" saw cells of individuals "living in the underground, for years, waiting for the revolutionary moment to arrive—again, a *parousia* promised by their eschatology."[317]

Although utopianism has driven both right- and left-wing ideological movements ranging from bolshevism to fascism, the utopian temptation has perhaps been most often identified, almost by definition, with the far left of the ideological spectrum, as historian Richard Ellis traces through American history.[318] This is because, Ellis contends, secular utopianism is pinned to a particular anthropology:

Human beings are naturally good, egalitarians typically believe, but are corrupted by bad institutions. Remake the institutions and we can reshape human nature. This strongly optimistic view of human nature and human potentiality is the motor that drives the utopian impulse of egalitarians. Without the optimistic conception of human nature, the emancipatory vision collapses.[319]

Evangelical eschatology has, of course, already met and evaluated a similarly idyllic link between human nature and human progress in the controversies over the Social Gospel postmillennialism of the twentieth-century Protestant left.[320]

Still, there is more that a Kingdom-oriented eschatology has to say to the various historical manifestations of secular utopianism. As social theorist Russell Jacoby argues, some form of utopianism has proven historically necessary to hold accountable the inadequacies of the status quo, such that "in an era of political resignation and fatigue the utopian spirit remains more necessary than ever."[321] A clearly developed evangelical theology of the "not yet" keeps such a historical vision at the forefront, while dismissing every secular attempt at utopia as, at best, a pretender to the throne. Thus, evangelicals can affirm, as did George Eldon Ladd, the conclusion of E. C. Gardner: "Christian eschatology means the end of all social and political utopias which expect to achieve a perfect pattern of peaceful society by human means and human strength."[322] Thus, a Kingdom-oriented, inaugurated eschatology can inform evangelicalism by reminding the movement that, as Carl Henry has counseled, all secularist and evolutionary models of utopian progress have "borrowed the biblical doctrine of the coming kingdom of God but cannibalized it."[323] Any theology of evangelical engagement needs such an emphasis so that future generations may recognize, as did Karl Barth and his theologian colleagues in the face of the Third Reich, these "cannibalized" Kingdom theologies when they rear their heads.[324]

At the same time, it tempers evangelical theology's temptation to "cannibalize" the Kingdom for its own ends. With the adoption of inaugurated eschatology, rooted in an overall commitment to a Kingdom-focused theology, evangelicalism has in many ways provided the foundation for the kind of "third way" ethic of sociopolitical engagement that Henry and others were seeking to define against mainline triumphalism and fundamentalist isolationism in the postwar era. In short, the commitment to an "already" of the Kingdom protects against an otherworldly flight from political and social responsibility while the "not yet" chastens the prospects of such activity. The inaugurated eschatological view of the Kingdom that has gained consensus thus addresses the concerns laid out by the postwar evangelical movement, especially in Henry's *Uneasy Conscience,* and provides a starting point for evangelical theological reflection on the relationship between the kingdoms of this temporal age and the eschatological Kingdom of God in Christ. Furthermore, this view of inaugurated eschatology has provided the foundation for reexamining some of the implications of two other points of theological and political controversy for the postwar evangelical movement, namely, the doctrines of salvation and the church.

3

TOWARD A KINGDOM SOTERIOLOGY: SALVATION AS HOLISTIC AND CHRISTOLOGICAL

INTRODUCTION

The Kingdom theology proposed by some in the postwar evangelical movement called for a broader, Kingdom-oriented understanding of soteriology, one that is able to tie personal regeneration to the broader cosmic purposes of God. A commitment to inaugurated eschatology and to the centrality of God's Kingdom purposes, it was argued, would necessitate a view of salvation that avoided the reductionistic soteriological pitfalls of both the Social Gospel and fundamentalist revivalism. As such, a clearly evangelical consensus on the meaning of salvation would inform the task of evangelical engagement and remove a persistent theological obstacle to evangelical presence in the public square. As with eschatology, this vision of an evangelical soteriological consensus has solidified in recent years, most visibly through the developments within dispensationalism and covenant theology. This move toward a Kingdom soteriology thus has far-reaching implications for the social and political task of contemporary evangelical theology.

SOTERIOLOGY AND THE THEOLOGICAL PROJECT OF POSTWAR EVANGELICALISM

"There was a time earlier in the Christian era when the evangelist's best ally was the theologian, whose forceful statements of the Christian revelation served to clarify the urgency of the task," Henry observed in the 1960s. "But today many theologians themselves need to be evangelized."[1] Henry's lament signifies the centrality of the doctrine of salvation for the postwar evangelical coalition, a centrality implied by the very designation "evangelical" and confirmed by the movement's coalescence around the evangelistic crusades of Billy

Graham.[2] The evangelical movement sought to define its vision of soteriology in terms of a rejection of Social Gospel liberalism and fundamentalist isolationism. In so doing, however, Henry and his allies recognized that their call for evangelical sociopolitical engagement would be resisted by a conservative American Protestantism skeptical that such engagement would turn evangelicals aside from their primary task: the personal regeneration of individuals. As with the matters of eschatology, Henry and those who followed him sought to articulate an essentially fundamentalist soteriology within the larger framework of the biblical emphasis on the Kingdom of God.

Postwar Evangelical Soteriology and The Uneasy Conscience

From the publication of Uneasy Conscience and throughout the formative years of postwar evangelicalism, Henry and his allies maintained that an evangelical concern for social and political structures is not, in fact, the first step toward Social Gospel modernism. "If evangelicals came to stress evangelism over social concern, it was because of liberalism's skepticism over supernatural redemptive dynamisms and its pursuit of the kingdom of God by sociological techniques only," Henry framed the debate in retrospect. "Hence a sharp and costly disjunction arose, whereby many evangelicals made the mistake of relying on evangelism alone to preserve world order and many liberals made the mistake of relying wholly on sociopolitical action to solve world problems."[3]

It thus would be a monumental inaccuracy to state that the postwar evangelical movement sought a mediating position between modernism and fundamentalism on the question of soteriology. The evangelical renaissance was not a referendum on the evangelism vs. social action flashpoints of the Fundamentalist-Modernist controversy.[4] The "uneasiness" that Henry would face from fundamentalists (including dispensationalists and covenantalists and others) on the question of the "Kingdom" debate grew largely out of the relationship between the Social Gospel's view of the Kingdom and its view of personal salvation. This was problematic for conservatives across the dispensationalist/covenantalist divide.[5] The politicized "Kingdom of God" bandied about by the denominational liberals seemed to be rooted in an embarrassment about the centrality of Christ and the purposes of redemption in orthodox Christianity. The Kingdom could not be about soteriology, because traditional soteriology carried with it such "pre-modern" themes as human depravity, Chalcedonian Christology, substitutionary atonement, forensic justification, and the need for a work of the Spirit in the human heart.[6]

With such being the case, fundamentalists were not outside the bounds of reason to be skittish about "Kingdom" proclamation, since the "Kingdom" so often meant the abandonment of personal salvation for civic improvement.[7] Nor were conservative Protestants alone in their charge that the prevailing "Kingdom" view threatened the proclamation of personal salvation as a growing neo-orthodox position put forth many of the same critiques.[8] Carl Henry was no exception to the antagonism toward Protestant liberalism's dismissal of the need for individual salvation through the new birth, emphasizing that his views of Social Gospel soteriology were precisely those of the last generation of fundamentalists, who he argued had offered valid critiques of the liberal movement, "perhaps by none more lucidly than by J. Gresham Machen."[9] At a meeting of the National Association of Evangelicals in the aftermath of the publication of *Uneasy Conscience,* Henry took pains to argue that "in contrast with the liberal social gospel the effective attack upon social problems could come only through an emphasis on what liberalism conceals—the substitutionary redemptive death of Christ for sinners."[10]

Reflecting on his manifesto fifty years later, Henry emphasized that *Uneasy Conscience* joined with the older fundamentalism in insisting that "the world crisis is fundamentally spiritual, not political and economic."[11] The new evangelical view of salvation did not confront the world "in order to make humans drool for material enhancement," he argued, "but rather to present humans with a spiritual dynamic that offers them new selfhood, moral power and incomparable hope," exactly the view of personal salvation maintained by Protestant orthodoxy.[12] With this commitment to a traditional, even "fundamentalist" view of personal regeneration, the new evangelical call to sociopolitical engagement could not have been further from that of the Social Gospel liberalism of the Protestant mainline, although elements in traditionalist fundamentalism were often more than willing to equate the two.[13] Still, Henry portrayed his call to engagement as a necessary effort not in spite of, but instead precisely because of the evangelistic initiatives of evangelicals such as Billy Graham.[14] To those conservative Christians who wished to jettison political engagement for an exclusive emphasis on personal piety and cooperative evangelism, Henry replied,

Perhaps, despite all that I have said, someone here is looking for a bomb shelter in which to propagate the evangelical faith. If so, let me propose a change on your reading list: retire your Bible to the Smithsonian Institute and get a copy of the Dead Sea Scrolls instead. The Essene caves are waiting for you. You won't have to worry about the world outside. You won't have to worry about neo-evangelicals. You won't have to worry about anything. And in A.D. 4000 some roving archaeologists from Mars may discover in those Judean hills that, during the great crisis of the twentieth century, Saint Kilroy slept here.[15]

So, for Henry, evangelical penetration of the culture with the message of personal regeneration necessarily entailed addressing the social and political crises of the time.[16] He argued that the conservative emphasis on personal evangelism to the exclusion of sociopolitical engagement isolated fundamentalism from the society it sought to evangelize.[17] It also, by seeming to put forth a gospel without a worldview, isolated fundamentalism from the stream of historic Protestant orthodoxy. Thus, the "apostolic gospel" stands in "futile resignation and submission to the triumphant Renaissance mood" while the "Christian social imperative is today in the hands of those who understand it in sub-Christian terms."[18]

Postwar Evangelical Soteriology and the Kingdom Debate

The evangelical dilemma over the relationship of redemption to sociopolitical engagement, however, was about more than the priorities given to personal regeneration and public justice. Instead, it was about differing understandings of the present and future realities of the Kingdom of God. As such, the question of relating evangelical soteriology to evangelical engagement was interrelated with the prior question of evangelical eschatology.

This was, Henry maintained, a problem of Kingdom definition. "The globe-changing passion of the modern reformers who operate without a biblical context is, from this vantage point, an ignoring of Jesus' insistence that 'all these things shall be added' only after man has sought first 'the kingdom of God and His righteousness'," Henry charged, citing Matthew 6:33. "Non-evangelicals tend to equate 'kingdom' and 'these things,' reflecting a blindness to the significance of the vicarious atonement of Christ."[19] Thus, Henry contended, the Social Gospel could not construct a biblical, Kingdom-oriented soteriology because of its Hegelian, evolutionary view of the Kingdom.[20] It likewise needed an optimistic view of humanity in order to justify the immanence of the Kingdom in the historical process.[21] Moreover, Protestant liberalism desperately sought to replace penal substitutionary atonement with social justice primarily because of the Social Gospel's prior eschatological commitments to a Kingdom without a Christ.[22]

Likewise, Henry found the fundamentalist dismissal of the relevance of social and political engagement as a hindrance to the priority of personal evangelism to be a similar issue of Kingdom definition. American conservative Protestantism's social and political isolationism reflected its essentially other-worldly view of the Kingdom of God, resulting in a view of salvation that concentrated almost solely on the rescue of souls from the imminent cataclysmic world judgment.[23] Henry was in essential agreement with this priority of personal evangelism because this soteriology sought to recognize the Christocentric nature of the biblical Kingdom of God.[24] Even so, Henry indicted the otherworldly soteriology of the fundamentalist right for failing to take into account the holistic fabric of the biblical portrayal of the messianic accomplishment of salvation. If personal salvation means a transfer into the Kingdom (present, future, or already/not yet), then the content of the Kingdom must inform the redemptive priorities of Christianity. Indeed, Henry noted, the very idea of the Kingdom of God, especially given its centrality in the gospel proclamation of Jesus, means that the Kingdom has "a social aspect, as well as an individual aspect," since "redemption is nothing if it is not an ethical redemption, and as such it comprehends more than the restoration of the individual to the image of God."[25]

For Henry, then, a Kingdom theology demanded that evangelicals understand the ramifications of the cosmic lordship of the ascended Christ. "The other temptation is to taper our proclamation of Jesus Christ solely to the message of individual redemption, the forgiveness of sins, and to conceal the fact that He is the King of truth and the Lord of life," Henry said, contrasting the fundamentalists with the modernists. "If it is objectionable to reduce the Gospel to a social ideology, it is no less objectionable to neglect and narrow the whole counsel of God by not affirming the lordship of Christ over the larger world of human learning and culture."[26]

Thus, salvation must be articulated in terms of the broader category of the Kingdom, since personal regeneration is about Kingdom advance—since, in the reign of Christ, God "has already impinged upon history in a supreme and decisive way through the incarnation and Christ's conquest over Satan," thereby pointing the cosmos "to a future superlative climax applying the consequences to the whole human race."[27] Evangelicals cannot fall into the crypto-gnostic trap of seeing the material world as intrinsically evil, a very real danger when fundamentalists combine an otherworldly soteriology with a rigidly legalistic personal morality.[28] This means that evangelicals must understand redemption to include a restoration to the creational imperatives of the cultural mandate of Genesis 1:27-28, a mandate that does not allow for a flight from public responsibilities.[29] It further means that Christianity is concerned that social structures conform to objective standards of justice, even as Christians seek the conversion of individuals.[30]

Henry further contended that a theology that ties redemption to Kingdom also means that evangelicals must keep the resurrection of the body, not the immortality of the soul, at the forefront of the doctrinal underpinnings of their soteriology. Unlike Greek philosophy and "Oriental speculation," Henry argued, evangelicals do not view flesh and matter as the seat of sin, but the whole person, a whole person who is redeemed in his or her totality by the salvific work of Christ.[31] This means that evangelicals must recognize that salvation covers the whole of human existence, thus implying that "Christian love is only half biblical when it deteriorates into a concern only for the souls of men and is indifferent to the needs of the body."[32]

Therefore, Henry argued, a truly evangelical soteriology will point beyond individual regeneration to the Kingdom of Christ for which the individual is born anew. It would take depravity seriously enough to condemn sin in both its personal and structural forms, as measured against the righteousness of the Kingdom. It would keep in mind the cosmic scope of the coming Kingdom, thereby witnessing to the coming lordship of Christ over every aspect of the created order. It would also recognize the "already" and "not yet" aspects of the inbreaking Kingdom, asserting the believer's responsibility to both ages.[33]

The relationship between the "already/not yet" eschaton and the redemption provided in Christ was explored more fully in the exegetical Kingdom theology of George Eldon Ladd. Like Henry, Ladd contended that the fundamentalist atomization of individual redemption apart from the holistic, cosmic aspects of the Kingdom purposes of Christ had impoverished the theological agenda of conservative American Protestantism. At the same time, Ladd, like Henry, believed that Protestant liberalism had cut itself off from Christianity itself by constructing a "Kingdom of God" social agenda without a Christological and soteriological focus. "The 'history' of the Kingdom of God is therefore the history of redemption, viewed from the aspect of God's sovereign and kingly power."[34] Therefore, the liberal Protestant sociopolitical construct of Kingdom realities was wholly antithetical to the Kingdom teachings of Jesus in the New Testament accounts.[35]

Thus, for Ladd, both the "already" and the "not yet" of the eschatological Kingdom were to be understood in terms of redemption.[36] The answer to relating the overarching Kingdom theme of Scripture to the gospel emphasis on personal redemption, Ladd argued, begins with an understanding of the centrality of Christ in the eschatological and soteriological purposes of God, a theme on which he claimed dependence on the work of Geerhardus Vos.[37] Ladd concluded that relating personal redemption to the Christocentric Kingdom purposes of God would broaden the pietistic concept of salvation inherited from fundamentalist revivalism. "The kingdom of God is therefore primarily a soteriological concept," he argued. "It is God acting in power and exercising his sovereignty for the defeat of Satan and the restoration of human society to its rightful place of willing subservience to the will of God."[38] For

Ladd, the fundamentalists were essentially correct about the nature of regeneration, unlike the Social Gospel liberals, but he nonetheless believed both had ignored the cosmic orientation of salvation—the left by morphing the Kingdom into ethical progress and the right by reducing salvation to personal flight from the world. "The Kingdom of God cannot be reduced to the reign of God within the individual soul or modernized in terms of personal existential confrontation or dissipated to an extra-worldly dream of blessed immortality," he argued. "The Kingdom of God means that God is King and acts in history to bring history to a divinely directed goal."[39]

The Christological nature of salvation is therefore, for Ladd, tied up in the warp and woof of canonical Kingdom teaching. This means that classical dispensationalism is wrong to sever personal salvation from Kingdom blessings by strictly segregating the "spiritual" salvation of the church from the "material" salvation of national Israel, Ladd maintained.[40] This dichotomy, for Ladd, tossed aside the Christological and Kingdom unity of the purposes of redemption. He also, however, found wanting the highly individualized and "spiritual" soteriology of traditional covenant theology, taking issue especially with the emphasis on the salvation of the individual "soul" articulated in the Kingdom theology of Reformed theologian Louis Berkhof.[41]

Instead, Ladd argued that the Kingdom motif of the Old and New Testaments set forth a view of salvation that was both personal and cosmic. The work of salvation does not mean a flight from the world, but means the redemption and restoration of the creation. Therefore, he contended,

> Salvation is not a matter that concerns only the destiny of the individual soul. It includes the entire course of human history and humankind as a whole. The coming of Christ is a definitive event for *all* people; it means either salvation or judgment. Furthermore, salvation is not merely an individual matter; it concerns the whole people of God, and it includes the transformation of the entire physical order.[42]

It is within this cosmic framework of salvation, Ladd asserted, that one is able to understand the biblical meaning of personal regeneration as the individual appropriation of the coming regeneration of the created order.[43] Since personal salvation is part of the coming of the eschatological Kingdom, Ladd believed, a holistic view of salvation must be emphasized, consistent with the holistic and soteriological nature of the Kingdom itself present in the person of Jesus. "Eternal life has to do with the total man," he asserted. "It concerns not only my soul but also my body."[44] Ladd argued that Jesus' earthly messianic ministry refuted any idea that redemption in this age is exclusively spiritual. He asserted that Jesus' healing miracles, for example, were not merely "physical" because they were connected with forgiveness of sin and granting of eternal life. The healings were "pledges of the life of the eschatological Kingdom that will finally mean immortality of the body."[45] Ladd concluded that the Kingdom therefore, and inferentially the proclamation of the church, "is concerned not only with people's souls but with the salvation of the whole person."[46]

KINGDOM SOTERIOLOGY AND THE EMERGING EVANGELICAL CONSENSUS

In the more than fifty years since Henry's jeremiad, evangelical theology has assembled a near consensus on the view that salvation is to be related to the broader picture of the Kingdom of God, and thus must be conceived from a holistic vantage point, not limited to the individualistic, pietistic, and other-worldly notions of much of earlier fundamentalist revivalism. This consensus soteriology in many cases has grown out of, and has been linked to, the grow-ing evangelical consensus on the inaugurated nature of eschatology. Like the eschatological consensus, it has been articulated both by traditionalist evan-gelicals on the right and by reformist evangelicals on the left of the ideological spectrum of the movement.

Among traditionalists, theologian Bruce Demarest has been among those who have called for a correlation between an orthodox soteriology and a devel-oped Kingdom theology, especially in light of the theological challenge of revi-sionist systems such as liberation theologies.[47] Demarest is one of a growing number of conservative evangelicals who have sought to ground a basically Reformed and self-consciously evangelical soteriology with a clear explanation that salvation encompasses more than just the souls of individuals. Instead, he argues, salvation, for the individual, means the restoration of the creation *imago Dei* and the onset of the eschatological Kingdom life to come.[48]

Millard Erickson has likewise sought to clarify the holistic and cosmic nature of salvation, especially as it relates to the orthodox doctrine of total depravity. For Erickson, as in the rest of the orthodox Christian tradition, sin and redemption are primarily about judicial guilt before God. Nonetheless, he argues, sin has cosmic and structural aspects that have too often been ignored by evangelicals.[49] An evangelical soteriology must take into account the holis-tic "kingdom of Satan" that must be routed in the purpose of redemption, he argues, by a primary focus on personal regeneration with a secondary focus on societal reform.[50] In this, Erickson resonates greatly with the arguments of the young Carl Henry.

The older Carl Henry has been at the forefront of conservative evangelicals in continuing to develop a Kingdom-oriented soteriology that would seek to explain salvation in terms of individuals and the cosmos, a concept that must be linked to the biblical concept of the Kingdom.[51] The overarching Kingdom unity of Scripture is in fact what explains the meaning of personal redemption, Henry argues. "God has much more in mind and at stake in nature than a backdrop for man's comfort and convenience, or even a stage for the drama of human salvation," he asserts. "His purpose includes redemption of the cosmos that man has implicated in the fall."[52] Thus, Henry argues, evangelicals cannot divorce personal salvation from its creational context, as a restoration of the rule of humanity in the image of God, or from its Christological focus on Jesus as the goal of creation.[53] Because the Kingdom is inherently Christological, Henry asserts, it is also tied inextricably to soteriology, especially when considered in light of the gospel narratives of the mission of Jesus.[54]

The left wing of evangelical theology has likewise sought to articulate a holistic and cosmic vision of salvation, often in terms quite similar to those offered by Henry and Ladd. Stanley Grenz, for instance, calls on evangelical soteriology to recognize that, while personal reconciliation between sinners and God is primary in the biblical doctrine of salvation, it does not exhaust the meaning of the salvation wrought in the atonement of Christ. Rather, he argues, Christian soteriology includes personal forgiveness of sins, the destruction of relational barriers between human beings, and the renovation of the cosmos.[55] With such being the case, he argues, soteriology must be seen in terms of God's eschatological purpose to restore creation, specifically through the person and work of Christ:

> The biblical writers also envision the reconciliation of humankind with the entire creation, including our physical environment which will experience the cessation of hostilities and the advent of peace. One day the animals will live in harmony with each other (Isa. 65:25), and the leaves of the trees will bring healing to the nations (Rev. 22:2). The christological center of the Bible leads us to conclude that this reconciliation will come as the effect of the work of Christ on behalf of the entire cosmos.[56]

Gregory Boyd, an even more revisionist evangelical "reformist," further argues that evangelical soteriology must take seriously the place of salvation in the Kingdom activity of God. For Boyd, this Kingdom soteriology expresses itself in what he calls a "Trinitarian warfare worldview" in which the Kingdom invades history through a cosmic struggle between God and powerful demonic forces.[57] Though radically differing with postwar evangelical theology on many issues, Boyd agrees with Henry and Ladd that salvation is related to the over-throw of satanic rule, that it is cosmic in its scope, that it is to be seen as the restoration of the created order (including human vicegerency over the earth), and that it is to be placed within the context of the inbreaking of the eschato-logical Kingdom in the person and work of Jesus as both the incarnate God and the head of a new humanity.[58]

Kingdom Soteriology and Dispensational Development

Evangelical historiography has at times seemed virtually to equate apocalyp-tic dispensationalism and popular fundamentalist revivalism. This correlation is not without abundant historical grounding. Although some—the Second Great Awakening's foremost revivalist Charles G. Finney, for instance—were advocates for neither dispensational premillennialism nor political disengage-ment, the later forms of fundamentalist revivalism into which the postwar evangelical movement was birthed often featured both.[59] Since Finney, virtu-ally all of the most prominent fundamentalist and evangelical populist revival-ists have embraced, to one degree or another, the basic framework of dispensational premillennialism. This tradition includes evangelists such as Dwight L. Moody, Billy Sunday, and Billy Graham, as well as the more politi-cized television evangelists of the late twentieth century.[60]

Dallas Seminary theologian Robert Pyne, a progressive dispensationalist, argues that the close tie between revivalism and dispensationalism contributed to the conflicted relationship between conservative Protestants and sociopo-litical engagement, primarily in terms of reaction to the theological emphases of the Social Gospel.[61] The essence of dispensationalist/revivalist facets of evangelicalism's "uneasy conscience" quite often is summed up in the oft-quoted premillennial cliché that believers are to be about manning the lifeboats, not polishing the brass on the sinking ship of a world careening toward the jaws of hell. The metaphor is perhaps most often associated with dispensationalist evangelist Dwight L. Moody, although it is certainly not unique to him, being used by, among others, C. I. Scofield.[62] While this state-ment may overstate the social action of individual dispensationalists, it does nonetheless demonstrate the link between a uniquely revivalist soteriology and a "pessimistic" eschatology.

Like Henry, the developing progressive dispensationalist movement has not repudiated the conversionist message of their fundamentalist dispensa-tionalist forebears. To the contrary, the developing theology has thus far com-mended the older forms of dispensationalism for preserving the priority of personal regeneration and individual evangelism, the gospel message that individuals must come under the saving refuge of the Messiah and unite with the people of God. Darrell Bock, for instance, credits dispensationalism for preserving the conversionist zeal of American evangelicalism in the aftermath of the Fundamentalist-Modernist controversy due to the dispensationalist tradition's crucial contribution to the parachurch movement and evangelistic movements and to the emphasis on all believers as ministers.[63] Nevertheless, progressive dispensationalists have begun the call for evangelicals to broaden the message of salvation beyond merely the emphasis on an otherworldly rescue of so many units of individual souls. They have done so by sketching a soteriology linked to the concept of the eschatological Kingdom, a doctrine of salvation that is Christocentric in focus, cosmic in scope, and holistic in nature.

Salvation as Christocentric. Because progressive dispensationalists consider soteriology within the overarching and unified Kingdom agenda of God in redemptive history, it has been necessary for them to explore the implications of the inherently Christological focus of redemption. This intentionally Christocentric soteriology has necessitated a comprehensive reinterpretation of several facets of dispensationalist soteriology, starting at the most essential aspect of the dispensationalist system itself, namely, the distinction between Israel and the church. Progressives have heeded the warnings of covenant theologians regarding the implications of Christology for soteriology.[64] This was indeed a difficulty for the older forms of dispensationalism, despite the reassurances by evangelical dispensationalists that they affirmed the centrality of Christ and the unity of the plan of salvation. Craig Blaising, for instance, attempts to defend Lewis Sperry Chafer as teaching the death of Christ as foundational to the salvation of both Israel and the church, but Blaising must nonetheless concede that Chafer "saw in the Bible two substantially different religions (Christianity and Judaism) which entailed different and opposed rules of life and different eternal destinies (heavenly vs. earthly)."[65] The difficulty for earlier dispensationalists such as Chafer and his successors might well have been the way in which they attempted to sever eschatology and soteriology. Chafer, for instance, contended that there "is no conflict between salvation and Kingdom [because the two] cover widely different fields of biblical doctrine."[66]

For progressive dispensationalists, however, the unified Kingdom purposes fulfilled in the one Messiah of both Israel and the nations necessitates that there is only one people of God and one unified plan of redemption.[67] "The unity of divine revelation, of the various dispensations, is found in the goal of history, the kingdom of God," argues Craig Blaising. "And since this kingdom is centered in the person and work of Jesus Christ, the dispensational unity of Scripture and of history is Christological as much as it is eschatological."[68]

Thus, Bruce Ware articulates a progressive dispensationalist view of the new covenant that swerves sharply both from the classical Chafer/Scofield view of two new covenants and from the modifications proposed by Charles Ryrie, precisely because of Ware's commitment to a common messianic salvation in Christ and thus entrance into a common messianic Kingdom.[69] The blessings of new covenant salvation, therefore, for both Israel and the church, are to be seen as the messianic provision of the Spirit-anointed Davidic King and so cannot be divided into two sharply segregated soteriological programs. This revision went beyond new covenant prophetic application, however, to the purpose of salvation itself, relating it specifically to the Kingdom of God in Christ.

For traditionalists such as Ryrie, this Christocentric soteriology is itself problematic as a departure from a dispensationalist distinctive—namely, the idea that the glory of God, not redemption, is central to God's purposes.[70] For traditionalists, the centrality of the glory of God, rather than of Christ or redemption, enabled the traditional dispensationalists to differentiate between "Kingdom" purposes (usually associated with Israel) and "salvation" purposes (usually associated with the individual regeneration of new covenant believers in the church age).[71] The Christocentric soteriology of the progressives then, traditionalists argue, is a blurring of soteriology with the Kingdom. Many traditionalists have charged progressive dispensationalism with abandoning a dispensationalist distinctive at precisely this point, by articulating soteriology from a Christological rather than a strictly theological standpoint.[72] This is because in this view, as traditionalist John Walvoord argues, a unified Kingdom theology bound together with soteriology is, by definition, the error of covenant theology.[73]

Progressives, however, have maintained that the Kingdom is, at least in one sense, soteriological, because the Kingdom is necessarily Christological. "Classical dispensationalism sought to organize Scripture around a soteriological dualism: a heavenly redemption yielding a heavenly people and an earthly redemption yielding an earthly people," note Blaising and Bock. "Although they united the classical dualism into a common salvation (either in 'heaven' or on 'the new earth'), revised dispensationalists remained strikingly anthropocentric in their reading of Scripture and their organization of theology."[74] Thus, Blaising and Bock argue, the Christological nature of redemption is the key to the various facets of salvific realities portrayed in Scripture in terms of spiritual, material, social, and political peace. It also, they argue, resolves the tension between the theocentric and messianic themes in the biblical Kingdom motif in the unity of the identity of Jesus.[75]

Salvation as cosmic. This Kingdom-oriented view of salvation, then, progressives contend, cannot be construed as a flight from the world, or as the salvaging of individuals from the condemnation of the material order. Instead, they posit, salvation in its broadest sense is to be understood as the redemption of the cosmos through the messianic accomplishment of Jesus. This redemption is not escape from creation but instead is a restoration of the created order that is accomplished in the "already/not yet" eschatological structure of the progressive unfolding of the Kingdom. For progressive dispensationalists, the very nature of salvation is understood differently precisely because the Christocentric understanding of a unified Kingdom purpose with one people of God rules out a "heavenly" destiny for the church as opposed to an "earthly" destiny for Israel, a concept so nettlesome that it has already seen several revisions in dispensationalist thought since the era of the *Scofield Bible.*[76] For progressives, the Kingdom purpose of Jesus does not allow for the kind of soteriological dichotomy offered by Chafer when he wrote of the person and work of Christ: "To Israel He is Messiah, Immanuel and King; to the church He is Lord, Head and Bridegroom. The covenants and destinies of Israel are all earthly; the covenants and destinies of the church are all heavenly."[77] Thus, for Chafer and for many of his theological successors, the hope of the church, ironically, was both amillennial and otherworldly.

While this kind of redemptive dualism has been rejected by the mainstream of evangelical dispensationalist eschatology, this does not mean that the tradition typically has spoken with one voice on the ultimate outcome of salvation.[78] For progressives, however, this line of thought affects more than eschatology, narrowly defined, but instead has direct implications for the Christian doctrine of salvation, including the nature of salvific hope.[79] More than this, however, it affects the very nature of salvation itself. The traditional dispensationalist view of salvation, Blaising argues, applies the cosmic aspects of salvation simply to the blessings of a restored Israel in a thousand-year millennium, not to the ultimate goal of salvation in the restoration of the entire created order in a new heavens and new earth.[80] Blaising argues that progressive dispensationalism has benefited directly from Ladd's construction of a "holistic premillennialism," which sees creation, salvation, and eschatology as interlinked in terms of the progressive outworking of the Kingdom. Ladd's constructive work on the goal of salvation as a *new earth,* in which the original goodness of creation is affirmed and restored, has "paved the way,"

Blaising argues, for dispensationalists to rethink the highly dualistic nature of their soteriology.[81]

Robert Saucy similarly contends that the growing theological consensus on the Kingdom of God as the goal of salvation and the theme of history necessitates a view of salvation that is cosmic in scope, encompassing the all-embracing nature of the Kingdom itself.[82] Saucy commends the work of modified amillennialists, such as Anthony Hoekema, in leading the way for a Kingdom vision of salvation that accounts for the entire scope of the Kingdom purposes of God in Christ, while maintaining the essentially spiritual nature of salvation. "What is meant by 'spiritual redemption,' however, can be ambiguous as this terminology can rightly encompass all of God's redeeming activity including human societal structures and finally the creation itself," Saucy observes. "Or it can be understood as more limited to the redemption summarized in the forgiveness of sins and the new life of the Spirit promised in the New Covenant."[83] While traditional covenant theology has affirmed the latter, more limited view of salvation, Saucy observes, the new Kingdom consensus offers an opportunity for both traditions to articulate the cosmic nature of salvation as creational restoration.[84] This view does not allow for an individualized, pietistic view of personal salvation, as in the extremes of some older forms of dispensational revivalism, but is set within the context of the inbreaking of the Kingdom and of the centrality of Christ as the focal point of redemption.[85]

Salvation as holistic. Craig Blaising argues that, from the progressive dispensationalist perspective, "The unity of Scripture is seen in the fact that there is one story of salvation—one creation, one redemption, and one holistic everlasting blessing for the redeemed."[86] Progressive dispensationalists distinguish themselves from many covenant theologians, who emphasize the essentially "spiritual" nature of the Kingdom, and therefore the essentially "spiritual" nature of redemption. At the same time, progressives distinguish themselves just as clearly from many older dispensationalists, who emphasized the "political" and "material" nature of the Kingdom, while emphasizing a primarily "spiritual" salvation for the church and a primarily physical and political salvation for national Israel. In the place of these two options, progressives favor a "holistic" view of salvation that is informed by the totality of their understanding of the Kingdom; in short, redemption that is individual and structural, present and future, spiritual and physical.

This holistic vision of salvation is informed by the understanding of salvation as Christological and cosmic. The ministry of Jesus, they argue, serves to confirm the holistic understanding of salvation portrayed in the Old

Testament prophetic writings, in which the "spiritual" blessings of the covenant promises are not contradictory of the "physical" or "national" blessings.[87] Jesus' metaphysical identity as the God of Israel and His covenant identity as Davidic Messiah (in its "already" and "not yet" aspects) both inform the holistic nature of Kingdom salvation:

> Both physical and spiritual blessings are given by Jesus. He makes atonement and forgives sins. He will give the Spirit, and He will raise the dead. He will bring peace to the earth and make it fruitful. He will give both joy and gladness. He, as both God and Davidic King, will shepherd His peoples with peace, security, and joy forever.[88]

It is precisely this holistic view of salvation that troubles some traditionalist dispensationalists about the progressives' efforts to link salvation to the Kingdom as a unifying center of systematic and biblical theology. Charles Ryrie, for instance, sees in this holistic understanding of salvation not only a confusion of the Kingdom with the church, but also the confusion of the spiritual and the secular. "Holistic redemption can easily lead to placing unbalanced, if not wrong, priorities on political action, social agendas, and improving the structures of society," he charges.[89] In this regard, Ryrie takes special notice of the progressives' use of the term "structural sin" as a reality to be confronted by evangelical theology.[90]

Not only is this Kingdom-oriented salvation, from the progressive dispensationalist vantage point, both spiritual and physical, but also it is national and political. In this, progressives maintain continuity with older generations of dispensationalists in asserting a future for a reconstituted Israel as a political body upon which the covenant God will lavish geopolitical promises He pledged to them in the Old Testament Scriptures. For progressives, the restoration of Israel as a nation is a crucial aspect of the "not yet" pole of inaugurated eschatology, but it is also pivotal to the construction of a new dispensationalist understanding of the relationship between the Kingdom and salvation. The future of Israel as a soteriological matter has long been ingrained in the fabric of dispensationalist theology. Lewis Sperry Chafer, for instance, included the "national salvation of Israel" as among the "things accomplished in [Christ's] sufferings and death" in his treatment of the work of Christ, right along with propitiation toward God and forgiveness of sins.[91] "The anticipation of such blessings for Israel is the theme of all the prophets, and such, indeed, is the salvation which awaits that people; but God is righteously free to act in behalf of sinners only on the ground of the fact that the Lamb of God has taken away their sins," Chafer argued, tracing the national elements of Old Testament and

New Testament promise for the people of Israel. "A major objective in the death of Christ is, therefore, the national salvation of Israel."[92]

For progressive dispensationalists, the future of Israel is even more to be understood as a soteriological matter, however, because it fits into a unified Kingdom theology in which every aspect of reality finds peace in the salvific, messianic mission of Jesus as Davidic King.[93] For progressives, holistic salvation does not mean that every aspect of Kingdom salvation is equally manifested in every redemptive epoch. It does mean, however, that redemption is not severed from the overall Kingdom program. In the restoration of national Israel, progressives maintain, not only does their theology maintain a national and political aspect as revealed in the promises to the nation, but the unity of the plan of redemption is also underscored, in contradistinction to some dispensationalist emphases of the past. As Robert Saucy argues, Scripture does speak of salvation in strikingly national and political terms, terms which are difficult to apply to the new covenant church as a multi-national Spirit body, and which are impossible to relegate to the eternal state.[94] Therefore, he contends in agreement with other progressives, Israel's future is more than a matter of prophetic fulfillment. It relates to the definition of messianic salvation itself, whether there remain structural and societal facets of the redemptive outworking of the Kingdom.[95] With this multifaceted view of salvation in terms of eschatological peace and reconciliation, progressive dispensationalists are thus able to integrate a unified Kingdom concept with a unified plan of salvation.[96]

Kingdom Soteriology and Covenantal Development

For the Reformed tradition within evangelicalism, there was far less radical revision needed in order to tie soteriology concerns to the conclusions of the emerging consensus on Kingdom theology. This is because covenant theology had maintained, by definition, a unified understanding of salvation and the basically redemptive center of God's Kingdom purposes. Beyond this, several strands of Reformed theology, most notably the Dutch Kuyperian tradition, had long stood for a cosmic, holistic understanding of soteriology.[97] The correlation between the Kingdom and a holistic view of salvation indeed has been essential to the Kuyperian stream within Reformed theology, as evidenced by Abraham Kuyper's perhaps most often quoted lecture, which came as he sought to convince his Calvinistic cohorts at Princeton Seminary that "Calvinism" is related to all of life and not simply to the salvation of the soul.[98] For Kuyper, salvation was not a matter of personal piety, and certainly not the escape from the created order, but rather a restoration and regeneration of the cosmos. Salvation was seen as the outcome of a cosmic war to reclaim the good creation for the glory of Christ. With this the case, Kuyper and the Kuyperian tradition have emphasized the Christocentric, cosmic, and holistic natures of redemption, along with the centrality of human vicegerency in the created order.[99] This is not to say that attempts at a Kingdom soteriology were limited to the Dutch tradition. Benjamin B. Warfield's postmillennial understanding of salvation likewise emphasized the cosmic and world-transforming nature of salvation in Christ. Indeed, Warfield argued that only the Christocentric salvation presented by Reformed theology, and not its Arminian and Amyraldian rivals, could do justice to the universal scope of salvation presented in Scripture.[100]

Nonetheless, as George Eldon Ladd complained in the postwar era, Reformed theology had often seemed to focus the concept of salvation narrowly on the redemption of individual souls.[101] For Reformed theologians such as O. T. Allis and Louis Berkhof, this came about, as Ladd noted, because of a fundamentally spiritual and otherworldly understanding of the meaning of the Kingdom. They did not sever salvation from the Kingdom, as did the dispensationalists, but they in many ways defined the Kingdom as spiritual salvation in this life and the spiritual vision of God in the heavenly life to come.[102] Thus, Louis Berkhof, arguably the most influential American Reformed theologian of the twentieth century, defined the kingly rule of Christ virtually exclusively in terms of individual, spiritual salvation.[103] Berkhof spoke for many in the Reformed tradition when he applied the essentially soteriological nature of the Kingdom to the Kingdom theologies of Social Gospel liberalism. Efforts at social and political reform were futile and unrelated to evangelical soteriology, Berkhof concluded, because the Kingdom of God is defined as "the rule of God established and acknowledged in the hearts of sinners."[104]

Like Henry, however, a newer generation of covenant theologians has recognized that the Scriptures did not seem to accord either with the hyper-individualized, otherworldly redemption of fundamentalism or with the politicized anti-gospel of the Protestant mainline. As Edmund Clowney argues, however, these are not the only options for evangelicals, especially for those anchored in the heritage of Reformed theology. Clowney concedes to arguments such as those of Henry that evangelicals have lagged behind liberals in addressing social concerns. "Yet it is not the case that orthodox theology presents only individual salvation and that contemporary secular theology has discovered social salvation," Clowney contends. "The biblical category that joins the salvation of the individual and of society is the category of the kingdom of God."[105]

With such being the case, the newer generation of covenant theologians has sought, like the progressive dispensationalists, to integrate more closely the doctrine of salvation with the emerging consensus on the nature and extent of the eschatological Kingdom. In a strikingly similar fashion to the developments within dispensationalism, this modified covenant theology has related individual salvation to the Kingdom of God by stressing the Christological, cosmic, and holistic nature of Kingdom soteriology. Modified covenant theology has thus maintained the priority of spiritual regeneration while noting that the goal of salvation is not about individual "souls" but instead about the restoration of the cosmos in Christ.

Salvation as Christocentric. As Robert Saucy has noted, the traditionalist dispensationalist charge that covenant theology was centered more on human redemption than on the glory of God has never held up against the reality of Reformed theology, which does in fact "clearly view the ultimate goal as the glorification of God, even as dispensationalists do."[106] Like the progressive dispensationalists, however, the modified covenantalists are carefully emphasizing the unity of the redemptive purposes of God not primarily in terms of either theology proper or anthropology, but instead in terms of Christology. Indeed, the Christocentric nature of salvation, some modified covenantalists argue, can only be seen in the kind of unified soteriology offered by covenant theology. Thus, Vern Poythress charges the older generations of dispensationalism with seeking to segregate the doctrine of salvation from the eschatological Kingdom of Christ.[107]

Modified covenantalists have sought to tie Kingdom theology to soteriology by reasserting the priority of union with Christ in human redemption. The adoption of believers comes through the declaration of Jesus as the messianic Son of God at His resurrection from the dead.[108] Thus, as Gaffin argues, the resurrection retains its Pauline centrality because the justification of believers hinges on the justification of Jesus as the righteousness of God and the propitiation for sins through His being raised by the Holy Spirit.[109] Pneumatology therefore is the key to linking the personal salvation of believers to the Kingdom purposes of God in Christ. Jesus, the messianic King, is exalted by virtue of His obedience to the law of God, even to death on the cross, and is therefore worthy to dispense the new covenant blessings of the Spirit.[110] The onset of the Spirit means the salvation of believers is ultimately about the purposes of God in glorifying Christ and establishing His Kingdom, not about transporting individual souls from earth to heaven. The age of the Spirit represents an epochal advance in the salvific Kingdom purposes of God, or, as

Sinclair Ferguson notes, "In the coming of Jesus, the Day of the Spirit had finally dawned."[111]

For modified covenantalists, the Christocentric nature of redemption is also seen in the relation between redemption and creation, especially in terms of Jesus' salvific function as the Second Adam, the head of a new humanity.[112] This is true especially in the growing number of Reformed theologians, led in recent years by Anthony Hoekema, who have sought to underscore the active obedience of Jesus in terms of His fulfillment of the cultural mandate given to Adam at creation. Hoekema, for instance, argues that salvation has been far too long removed in evangelical soteriology from the concept of the restoration of the *imago Dei,* along with its world-governing functions. Hoekema locates the restoration of the image in the work of Christ as the obedient human, as seen even in Jesus' rule over nature in the miracles of the gospel narratives.[113]

Thus, Westminster Seminary theologian Dan G. McCartney speaks for many in the modified covenantal stream when he argues that personal salvation cannot be understood apart from the unique role of humanity in the Kingdom purposes of God. It is significant, McCartney argues in continuity with Gaffin and Ferguson, that "Jesus received the kingdom as a human" since, before His incarnation, "the eternal Son was not a man, and thus did not rule as a man."[114] In this act of receiving sovereignty from God in the inauguration of the Kingdom of God, McCartney argues, the work of Christ is seen, not as an escape from creation, but as the restoration of it.[115] "The arrival of the reign of God is the reinstatement of the originally intended divine order for earth, with man properly situated as God's vicegerent," McCartney concludes.[116] In this, McCartney traces the salvific purposes of God from the patriarchal promise through the Davidic covenant to the preaching, exorcisms, and healings of Jesus to the pouring out of the Holy Spirit at Pentecost by the anointed Son of Man as the establishment of the Kingdom of God in saving power through the accomplishment of Christ. "Thus the kingdom of God and the kingdom of Christ are the same entity (Eph 5:5, 21), not only because Christ is God, for as God Christ has always reigned with the Father," McCartney asserts. "It is because Christ is now a *man,* and as a man rules as human vicegerent."[117]

Vern Poythress claims that McCartney's emphasis on Christ's restoration of the creational mandate in salvation has resonated with newer streams of Reformed theology because it stands in continuity with the Kingdom theology initially raised by Geerhardus Vos and developed through Gaffin and others, a theology that stresses the Christological nature of human redemption.[118] This is an especially important soteriological emphasis for the developing form of "new earth" amillennialism, he argues. "If Christ now rules as a man over the world according to Ephesians 1:20-21, He rules also as a Jew and as a son of David, because all other human rule on earth is derived from the fundamental Adamic rule," Poythress asserts. "All the promises are 'Yes' in Christ (2 Cor. 1:20), so all enjoyment of all blessings can come only in union with Christ, both for Jew and for Gentile, both now and in the future."[119] For Poythress, therefore, a key distinctive of the modified covenantalism is a new emphasis on the headship of Christ as both messianic King and Second Adam, resuming the human reign over the cosmos. This means that salvation, including its unity in the one people of God, is inherently Christocentric and Kingdom-oriented.[120]

Salvation as cosmic. This Christological vision of human salvation means that redemption cannot be construed as individualistic pietism. For many modified covenantalists, this lack of a Christocentric focus is precisely what led to the otherworldly nature of fundamentalist soteriology.[121] "The believer is changed from the ruin of the Adamic earthly creation to the life and sphere of Christ above the angels," writes Michael Williams of the exclusively "spiritual" understanding of redemption. "Salvation, then, is understood as release from this-worldly concern. It is flight from creation, flight from physicality."[122] With salvation as a restoration of the creational intention of the Kingdom of God, Hoekema contends, the scope of salvation does not end with the rescue of the individual soul from the world, but instead applies the cultural mandate to the development of a distinctively Christian world-and-life-view applicable to every area of human endeavor.[123]

This comprehensive view of salvation does not nullify, however, the centrality of personal regeneration. Instead, regeneration (along with justification, sanctification, adoption, and every other facet of individual redemption) is seen within the context of the Kingdom in inaugurated eschatology, as an inbreaking of the future restoration of the cosmos. Gaffin, for instance, challenges the presuppositions of those who hold that the Reformed view of depraved humanity, upon which the doctrine of regeneration is built, necessitates a pessimistic, creation-negating outlook on cultural endeavors.[124] Thus, for the modified covenantalist, personal regeneration is not simply personal at all but is the inclusion of the individual into the cosmic Kingdom purposes of God. Salvation is, as Michael Williams notes, "a foretaste of cosmic regeneration," as the Spirit of Christ creates in the human heart the same kind of new creation that will one day take place "with the eschatological renewal of the natural order" through the work of Christ.[125]

Salvation as holistic. If, in the newer emphases of evangelical covenant theology, redemption means creational restoration, then redemption is by definition a matter not limited to the individual "soul," but is instead holistic in its scope. This understanding is necessitated both by the cosmic extent of redemption and by the place of the resurrected body of Jesus in the Kingdom purposes of redemption, with both informed by the New Testament emphasis on the "already/not yet" tension of eschatological fulfillment. The resurrection body of the believer, Gaffin argues, is called "spiritual" in the Pauline corpus (1 Cor. 15:44), not because it is immaterial, "but because it embodies the fullest outworking, the ultimate outcome, of the work of the Holy Spirit in the believer, along with the renewal to be experienced by the entire creation."[126]

Thus, as Hoekema asserts, the "physical" and "material" aspects of existence cannot be overlooked in the mission of the church since human beings exist both in creation and in the eschaton "in a state of psychosomatic unity."[127] For Michael Williams, this commitment to a holistic view of redemption is a direct result of the Kingdom theology developed by theologians such as Herman Ridderbos, Anthony Hoekema, "and even the premillennialist George Ladd" as Reformed theologians have sought to move beyond a "verticalist" spiritual vision model of eschatology "to take real, significant strides toward a restorational eschatology."[128]

Along with the Kuyperian tradition of Reformed theology, the newer generation of evangelical covenantalists likewise emphasize the cultural and noetic effects of redemption, not simply the personal and spiritual outworking of Christianity in individual lives, a tradition adopted and modified in the postwar evangelical movement, especially by Henry.[129] This holistic vision of the relationship between creation and redemption is precisely what worries some in the American Reformed tradition about the modifications in covenant theology. Some, such as covenant theologian D. G. Hart, warn that the Kingdom theology called for by Henry and other neo-evangelical theologians is not consistent with the Westminster tradition of Reformed confessionalism, but instead represents a perilous "politicizing" of the gospel. Hart traces the "worldview Calvinism" mediated by the postwar evangelical movement through basically Reformed theologians such as Henry and Francis Schaeffer back to the culture-transformative Kingdom theology of Abraham Kuyper. For Hart, this Kuyperian "neo-Calvinist" tradition differs markedly from the heritage of J. Gresham Machen.[130] Hart calls on Reformed theology to turn back these trends toward a Kingdom-oriented view of the salvific work of Christ, especially in its attempt to forge a "Christian worldview" perspective in terms of social and political engagement. Instead, he argues, Reformed theology should concentrate a theology of redemption on an emphasis on individual justification and personal sanctification, rather than on the Kingdom of God, especially in its more Kuyperian interpretations.[131]

KINGDOM SOTERIOLOGY AND EVANGELICAL ENGAGEMENT: AN EVALUATION

Because evangelicalism is, by its very name, defined in terms of gospel, developments in evangelical soteriology are, by definition, relevant to the construction of an evangelical theology of sociopolitical engagement. Just as Henry called for an "already/not yet" model of the Kingdom of God that could transcend biblically the reductionistic debates that hinder the neo-evangelical hope for an engaged evangelical movement, he also led the way in calling for a full-orbed doctrine of salvation that concentrated the Christian focus on a world-and-life view that embraced all of life. This meant understanding redemption not in terms of a rescue of individuals out of the world, but in terms of a holistic view of redemption that sees individual conversion as the onset of God's cosmic Kingdom purposes. In the years since the postwar era, the developments within evangelical theology have offered just this kind of a comprehensive Kingdom soteriology, especially in the developments within covenant theology and dispensationalism. In so doing, these developments offer to remove some of the persistent soteriological obstacles to a theology of evangelical engagement while addressing some of the more pertinent Christian theological and philosophical underpinnings of social and political action.

Soteriology as a Theological Problem

Perhaps the most visible contribution of the Kingdom consensus is that it does indeed mark a substantive rapprochement on the question of soteriology. This is a marked advance from the days in which dispensationalist and covenantal evangelicals would accuse each other of proclaiming a "false gospel."[132] As discussions have progressed, the developing wings of the dispensationalist and covenant traditions have come now to what both recognize as a unified understanding of salvation.[133] This consensus goes beyond mere rapprochement, however. The effort to relate salvation to the Kingdom of God in Christ offers evangelical theology the opportunity to articulate salvation in a broad canonical and theological context from the vantage point of a unified Kingdom theology across the span of biblical revelation.[134]

In so doing, the emerging soteriological consensus serves to define "salvation" and "Kingdom" more clearly. New Testament scholar Norman Perrin was correct to argue that the Social Gospel had amputated soteriology from eschatology.[135] By defining "Kingdom" while doing away with the concept of eschatological judgment, Protestant liberalism swerved from the path of the biblical witness and historic Christian orthodoxy. At the same time, conservative American Protestantism, especially in its dispensationalist expression, amputated eschatology from soteriology, failing to see how "Kingdom" purposes and "salvation" purposes intersect in redemptive history.

A Kingdom-oriented soteriology remedies this problem by focusing the evangelical doctrine of salvation on a Christocentric vision of the Kingdom, informed by inaugurated eschatology. This has resolved the century-old debate between dispensationalists and covenant theologians about whether the glory of God or the redemption of the world was at the center of God's purposes for the created order. Dispensationalists, particularly, charged covenant theologians with ignoring the centrality of the glory of God, preferring to see salvation as the core of the biblical message.[136] This debate, however, was constructed on false premises, since in reality both traditions held to the glory of God as central.[137] They did, however, define the vehicle of God's self-glorification quite differently.

The newer consensus transcends this debate by coalescing around a more biblically resonant alternative. The glory of God, and not redemption *qua* redemption, is indeed at the heart of the purposes of God in creation, redemption, and consummation. Nonetheless, the New Testament does not present the glory of God as abstracted from the mission of Jesus, but instead presents it as finding its expression in His incarnation, atonement, and exaltation. The entire sweep of redemptive history therefore finds its goal in the glory of God *in Christ*.[138] Jesus therefore points to the glory of the Father, but affirms that "the Son of Man [is] glorified, and God is glorified in Him" (John 13:31). This means that the doxological and soteriological goals are not in conflict. Instead both find their purpose and fulfillment in Jesus' inheritance of the Kingdom. Thus, the apostle Paul ties the glory of God in the Philippian correspondence to Jesus' messianic role. God is glorified as His messianic vicegerent is recognized as the rightful Governor of the entire created universe (Phil. 2:7-11).[139] For this reason, the apostle Peter is able to speak of God's glory as focused particularly on the Kingdom inheritance of Jesus as Messiah (1 Pet. 4:11), a doxological theme that is in line with Old Testament messianic promise (Ps. 2:4-12; 110:1-7).

The New Testament then, especially in the Pauline epistles, fits human salvation not into a narrowly pietistic or "spiritual" framework, but as part of God's Kingdom purposes to renew the *imago Dei* by conforming believers "to the image of His Son, so that He would be the firstborn among many brethren" (Rom. 8:29). The New Testament then presents individual human salvation (in, for example, Eph. 1:3-14, which speaks of individual election to redemption in Christ) in strikingly cosmic and Christological terms, with human redemption seen as within "a view to an administration suitable to the fullness of the times, that is, the summing up of all things in Christ, things in the heavens and things on the earth" (Eph. 1:10). With this being the case, the purposes of soteriology are not disconnected from those of creation or consummation; all are focused on a full-orbed Christology.[140] Thus, the New Testament speaks of the enthronement of the resurrected Jesus, and his resultant lordship, in decidedly soteriological, as well as doxological, terms (Rom. 1:3; 10:9).

Salvation may then be seen in anthropocentric fashion, but only in consideration of one particular *anthropos,* the man Jesus who represents humanity as God-appointed Mediator between the fallen race and its Creator (1 Tim. 2:5). In this, the newer consensus picks up one of the neglected, but crucial, emphases of the older Reformed tradition, the centrality of Christ in the glorification of God. Thus, Princeton theologian Charles Hodge was right to argue that the installation of Christ as King is "not merely an unintended result, but the great end contemplated in the predestination of God's people" to salvation:

> That end is the glory and exaltation of Christ. The purpose of God in the salvation of men was not mainly that men should be holy and happy, but that through their holiness and happiness his glory, in the person of the Son, should be displayed, in the ages to come, to the principalities and powers. Christ, therefore, is the central point in the history of the universe. His glory, as the glory of God in the highest form of its manifestation, is the great end of creation and redemption.[141]

This Christological, Kingdom focus guards the New Testament emphasis on the glory of God in salvation, a glory that cannot be understood apart from the identity and mission of Christ in establishing His Kingdom. Jesus therefore speaks of the glorification of His disciples not simply in terms of a demonstration of God's justice and mercy, but in terms of a display of a glory that is specifically focused on Himself as their Redeemer (John 17:24). Thus, the Johannine Gospel opens with a testimony to the glory of the Father revealed in Christ (John 1:14). The messianic credentials of Christ are then defended in terms of the Father's glorification of Jesus (John 8:54), a glory that is seen in both the resurrection from the dead (John 11:40) and the crucifixion of Jesus in the place of sinners (John 12:28). This Christologically focused Kingdom soteriology therefore protects evangelical theology from a resurgent supralapsarianism that defines this glory theocentrically in terms of the supra-temporal glorification and reprobation of individuals.[142]

The newer soteriological consensus offers evangelical theology the opportunity to articulate salvation in terms of the specifically *messianic* work of Christ, a biblical theme too long neglected in conservative Protestant soteriology. The developments in dispensational and Reformed thought on the Christological implications of the cultural mandate, the *imago Dei,* and the inaugurated Kingship of Christ are a helpful starting point here. In the Genesis narrative, the primeval man is appointed, in Erich Sauer's description, "king of the earth," and thus is charged with subduing the created order and protecting it from evil.[143] The prophetic oracles of the Pentateuch regarding a future throne are couched within the context of protection from enemies (Gen. 49:8-10; Deut. 17:14-15), a concern repeated in the clamoring of the Israelite nation for a king "that we also may be like all the nations, that our king may judge us and go out before us and fight our battles" (1 Sam. 8:20).[144]

The kingship of Israel, with its Davidic line, is thus presented in terms of a Spirit-anointed king charged with subduing and defeating the enemies of the people of God (1 Sam. 8:19-20). Indeed, the removal of the Israelite kingship from Saul takes place precisely because Saul refuses to destroy utterly the enemies of Yahweh (1 Samuel 15), resulting in the loss of Saul's monarchy and the anointing of the Spirit of God, both transferred instead to the house of David (1 Sam. 16:1-3, 12-14). Indeed, as soon as David receives the anointing of oil by the prophet Samuel, he is anointed with the Spirit (1 Sam. 16:13), and immediately David as the "anointed one" leads the nation in the defeat of the Philistine attackers (1 Sam. 17:20-58), an activity that Saul recognizes as inherently kingly (1 Sam. 18:6-9). The definition of Jesus' messianic identity as the "anointed one," the bearer of the Spirit (Luke 4:18-19), is therefore set within this context of the anointed warrior-king.

This means that, contra dispensationalist traditionalism, there is no dichotomy between the "offer of the Kingdom" and the "forgiveness of sins," as though the forgiveness of sins can be anything other than a Kingdom act. Instead, in the Gospel of Luke, for example, messianic salvation is defined in terms of Jesus' promised Davidic kingship (1:32-33); the forgiveness of sins (1:50, 72, 77); the defeat of all enemies (1:51, 71); the crushing of political pretenders-to-the-throne (1:52); the provision of material blessings (1:53); the covenant restoration of national promises to Israel (1:54-55); the redemption of the Gentile nations (1:79; 2:32); and the monarchial anointing of the Spirit (4:18). In Jesus of Nazareth, therefore, salvation is a Kingdom activity whereby the Second Adam, the Son of David, displays His anointing by God and His faithful obedience to His mandate as King by protecting the created order, crushing the head of the ultimate enemy of the Kingdom, the Serpent (Gen. 3:15; Rom. 16:20; Rev. 12:9). The dispensing of the Spirit on those united to Him in faith is possible only because of union with the messianic King who is declared to be the Son of God (Gal. 4:4-7). It is this Christocentric focus of salvation that ties the salvation of human beings to the motif of the Kingdom of God and to the broader aspects of cosmic salvation. The defeat of Satan by the man Christ Jesus is pictured by the apostle John as the establishment of the Kingdom (Rev. 12:10; also John 12:31; Col. 2:15; Heb. 2:14-15; 1 John 3:8). The cosmic extent of salvation is seen as the Second Adam offers up to the Father a created order in which He has subdued every enemy (1 Cor. 15:24-26), and there is nothing unclean in the garden over which He rules (Rev. 21:1-8).

Thus, salvation is portrayed in the New Testament as more than simply the salvation of so many individual souls. Redemption is the transfer from the satanic kingdom to the eschatological Kingdom that God the Father has prepared for His Messiah (Col. 1:13), a transfer that is by definition a violent act of subduing "the god of this age" (2 Cor. 4:3-4, NIV) or "the prince of the power of the air" (Eph. 2:1-7). This means that evangelical theology must sort through the implications of the biblical warfare imagery of the advancement of the Kingdom, which is exactly the kind of redemption imagery called for by Ladd's Kingdom theology.[145] Evangelical Kingdom soteriology must avoid, however, the temptation of a metaphysical dualism. Conservative evangelicals must articulate salvation in terms of two warring kingdom authorities, while simultaneously evaluating the "warfare worldview" of reformist evangelicals such as Gregory Boyd and the "spiritual warfare" proposals of various charismatic groups issuing from, among other places, the post-Ladd Fuller Theological Seminary.[146] In this, Boyd and others have adopted a long-neglected biblical Kingdom theme that was jettisoned in earlier generations of American mainline Protestantism due to an anti-supernaturalist rejection of the reality of the demonic.[147] Nonetheless, the newer "warfare worldview" proposals fail to relate Christ's Kingdom activity as a warrior-king against the authorities of evil to His sovereignty over the cosmos, both of which are maintained in Scripture and in historic Christian orthodoxy.[148] They likewise ignore the fact that postwar evangelical theology maintained at least hints of a "warfare worldview" that was informed by an equally vigorous commitment to meticulous sovereignty.[149]

Even so, Boyd's work has helpful implications for a more biblical evangelical theology. In many ways, his warfare worldview is the culmination of post-conservative evangelicalism's attempt to break with the individualism of

American revivalism and the "flatness" of much evangelical biblical interpretation. In so doing, Boyd has identified perhaps the defining theme of canonical revelation—the triumph of Christ as divine-human warrior in the restoration of a fallen cosmos (Rev. 12:1-17).[150] This is a much-needed corrective to at least some of what Boyd identifies as a "blueprint" reading of redemptive history, which does indeed tend toward the bloodless and the abstract. It also puts the emphasis where Scripture does on the *telos* of the program of redemption—not on God's glory in the abstract, or on the justification of the individual sinner, but on the glory of God in the exaltation of Jesus as the triumphant Final Adam and mediatorial Warrior-King (Rom. 8:29; Eph. 1:10; Eph. 3:21; Col. 1:18). This return to a biblical understanding of Kingdom and warfare is perhaps why the best aspects of the warfare worldview (along with some of its unfortunate elements—such as God as divine risk-taker) are resonating with popular evangelical piety in such projects as John Eldredge's *Wild at Heart* books.[151] If this appropriation of the Kingdom warfare imagery present in Scripture and the Patristic tradition were magnified across the evangelical spectrum, the implications for the worship, evangelism, spirituality, cultural engagement, and internal structures of the churches could be monumental—and perhaps more significant than Henry and his generation's call for an evangelical renaissance in university education, philosophy, the sciences, and so forth. Catholic thinker Leon Podles is surely correct when he notes that the lack of emphasis on the cosmic warfare imagery of Scripture is one reason why much of both Catholic liturgy and Protestant revivalism has devolved into a saccharine sentimentality that tends to alienate men and rob worship of the gravity and awe that much of contemporary worship movements seek—and fail—to capture.[152] A significant advance in the evangelical theology of the Kingdom is possible if the rest of the movement is prompted by Boyd to think through the warfare implications of a Kingdom soteriology.

With the call for a reconsideration of this "warfare worldview" by some on the evangelical left, the conservative wing of evangelical theology would do well to reassert the historic Reformed confessional emphasis that the work of the Spirit in bringing sinners to salvation is not a matter of personal piety, but represents in fact the conquering of the kingdom of Satan (Mark 3:27; John 12:31-32; 2 Tim. 2:25-26). This kingly activity of Christ in conversion is a necessary corollary of the doctrine of effectual calling.[153] Effectual calling is a Kingdom act because it calls together a "flock" over which the Davidic shepherd rules (John 10:15-16; cf. Ezek. 37:24). Every conversion to faith in Christ represents a defeat of the principalities and powers by the sovereign Kingdom authority of the resurrected and exalted Christ (2 Cor. 10:4-5).

The newer emphases on the cosmic and holistic aspects of soteriology are derivative of the Christological focus of new covenant salvation, and are therefore welcome modifications to evangelical Kingdom theology. In relating the eschatological Kingdom to redemption, the emerging evangelical consensus is staking out a stance in a centuries-long dispute over whether (as Stanley Grenz poses the argument) to view human salvation primarily as "a total contradiction of human existence" or as "a continuation, albeit in a heightened manner, of what God inaugurated in the Garden of Eden."[154] With a unified Kingdom as the integrative motif of evangelical theology, creation and redemption are seen as part of one cosmic purpose, not set in antithesis to one another.[155] Thus, creation is not seen merely as a vehicle to the ends of God's ultimate purpose to manifest His mercy in redeeming elect souls and to manifest His justice in damning reprobate ones. The purposes of creation, redemption, and consummation are seen holistically as God's purpose to glorify Christ by fulfilling the Adamic creation mandate, the universal Noahic promise, the patriarchal covenants, and the Israelite monarchy in Him, thus exalting Jesus as preeminent over the entire cosmos as the agent of creation, the true *imago Dei*, the Davidic subjugator of all rival powers, the firstborn of the eschatological resurrection from the dead, and the atonement through whom final cosmic peace is found at last (Col. 1:15-23).

The newer developments in Kingdom theology offer the prospect of reminding evangelicals of what Francis Schaeffer contended at the onset of the "culture wars" regarding the message of salvation in Christ and the plight of contemporary human culture:

> This lostness is answered by the existence of a Creator. So Christianity does not begin with "accept Christ as Savior." Christianity begins with "In the beginning God created the heavens [the total of the cosmos] and the earth." That is the answer to the twentieth century and its lostness. At this point we are then ready to explain the second lostness (the original cause of all lostness) and the answer in the death of Christ.[156]

This creation-rooted and Kingdom-focused soteriology is a far more biblically resonant vision of salvation than the world-denying revivalism that neo-evangelicals such as Schaeffer and Henry sought to transcend in the postwar era.

It also places the intellectual task of theology into both a Kingdom and a redemptive context. Thus, for Henry, the cultural mandate and the creation intentions restored in redemption include a specific attention to the rational aspects of the *imago Dei* revealed in the Edenic order.[157] Thus, for Henry, a commitment to salvation in terms of the cultural mandate necessitates a commitment to a *Logos*-centered exploration of the meaning of Christian epistemology, especially in terms of human rational and moral capabilities, in order to correct a simplistic (and thereby dangerous) understanding of the cultural mandate. "If the forms of reason and morality do not in fact belong to the *imago Dei* but are environmentally derived, then no final reason can be given why dominion may not as legitimately be expressed in non-benevolent as in benevolent ways," Henry observes. "Indeed, precisely the Pharaoh-like dominion—man in the role of the 'trampler'—may be expected if man by creation is not bound by the criteria of logic and morality."[158] Henry's warning here is especially relevant as a "culturally engaged" evangelical theology seeks to interact with an increasingly anti-rationalist postmodern ethos.[159]

In articulating salvation within its Christocentric Kingdom orientation, evangelical Kingdom theology does not simply inform the prospect of a culturally engaged evangelicalism. In so doing, it also offers to correct the truncated view of human salvation that resulted not just in an evacuation from the public square but in a subtle shift in the definition of salvation itself. American revivalism unintentionally often articulated the message of the gospel in decidedly existential terms, often mirroring the error of Rudolf Bultmann in severing the relationship of the individual soul to God from the relationship of the world to its Creator.[160] This otherworldly revivalist message within the American evangelical subculture has in many instances had the long-term influence of translating salvation into a therapeutic model of personal self-actualization, exactly the converse of what was intended by the revivalism of twentieth-century fundamentalism.[161] "What God is doing in the world is thus contracted into what He is doing for us personally and privately," evangelical theologian (and critic of contemporary evangelicalism) David Wells complains. "The whole process turns God into a product and believers into customers."[162]

An evangelical soteriology focused on the cosmic purposes of the Kingdom guards against such a therapeutic internalization of personal salvation, while simultaneously guarding the spiritual and supernatural definition of redemption, contra the Christ-ignoring evolutionary and materialist notions of salvation offered by Protestant liberalism and its ideological descendants.[163] In a Kingdom-focused soteriology, George Eldon Ladd argued contra Bultmann, the present activity of the Kingdom of God is not reduced to solely a concern for individual decision.[164] In a Kingdom-oriented soteriology, personal regeneration is paramount, not because of an anthropocentric worldview, but because regeneration is tied to God's Christocentric purpose in saving the cosmos, a context presented by Jesus in the most familiar biblical treatment of regeneration, the discourse with Nicodemus (John 3:3-21).[165] The emphasis on the cosmic extent of salvation does not therefore negate the revivalist fundamentalist concern for the priority of personal regeneration. As Henry notes, a cosmic and holistic view of salvation actually guards the orthodox Protestant emphasis on personal regeneration through explicit faith in Christ in this interim era before the consummation of history: "Yahweh's promise of deliverance, His own glorification through His suffering servant, and the transformation of nature and history universally, are set in the eschatological context of a now soon approaching new age, a hope that centers in the coming Messiah and servant."[166] Thus, the Great Commission proclamation of personal faith in Christ for the forgiveness of sins is the vehicle for cosmic restoration and the ultimate salvation of the world.

The emerging consensus on the holistic nature of salvation likewise serves as a constructive development, particularly since both progressive dispensationalists and modified covenantalists along with their broader evangelical colleagues seem to define this holistic redemption in terms of the resurrection of Jesus. This is in notable contrast to Social Gospel concern for the body, a concern often almost wholly detached from the question of forgiveness of sins.[167] In Scripture, however, the resurrection of Jesus serves as a reminder that the work of Christ, consummated in His resurrection from the dead and exaltation at the right hand of the Father, completely reverses the Edenic curse in its personal, spiritual, physical, noetic, and cosmic aspects. As biblical scholar Andrew T. Lincoln notes,

> The resurrection and exaltation of Christ accomplish a new unity between heaven and earth, for Christ now has a heavenly body (1 Cor. 15:42ff), a body of glory (Phil. 3:21) and His humanity is now in heaven (Phil. 3:20f; Col. 3:1; Eph. 1:20ff; 6:9), and both serve as a pledge of the ultimate unity of the cosmos in Christ (Eph. 1:10).[168]

This understanding of redemption better fits with the canonical treatment of salvation. In the prophetic foreshadowing of new covenant redemption, salvation is seen as multifaceted, including spiritual, physical, bodily, social, relational, and political aspects of redemption (Ezek. 36:24-38; Jer. 31:31-36). These blessings are tied, however, to the coming of the promised consummation, manifested in the resurrection from the dead and the outpouring of the Spirit (Ezek. 37:12-14; 39:28-29). Jesus points to this holistic vision of Kingdom salvation by forgiving sins, casting out demons, and healing diseases by His authority as the Kingdom in person, the anointed King upon whom the

Spirit rests (Matt. 12:15-32; 15:29-31; Mark 1:21-39; Luke 4:18-19; 9:1-2; 11:20; 17:20; John 7:37-39).

The priority of personal regeneration is maintained precisely because salvation is seen, holistically, in terms of a bodily resurrection, the reversal of the Edenic curse, and the restoration of humanity as vicegerents of the created order. The work of the Spirit in regenerating the heart is not therefore seen as a purely "spiritual" matter. Instead, it is the uniting of the individual to the pioneer of salvation (Heb. 2:10), the One who is "justified" by God, has merited resurrection from the dead, and who therefore can claim the cosmos as His inheritance (Ps. 2:1-12; 45:6-17; Acts 2:22-36; 1 Cor. 15:21-28; Heb. 1:2; Rev. 1:4-6). Resurrection is seen as central to God's redemptive purposes because it is central to God's Kingdom purposes. Salvation is pictured, not in terms of escape from the world, but as restoring the human person's right to rule over the world (Matt. 19:28; Rev. 3:21). Thus, the writer of Hebrews pictures salvation in Christ in terms of the psalmist's paean to the place of humanity in the cultural mandate (Ps. 8:4-6; Heb. 2:5-9). Jesus claims the right to rule over the earth and to claim His Kingdom precisely because He has been raised from the dead (Rev. 1:18). Jesus' Davidic kingship is established by His resurrection from the dead (Rom. 1:3-4), as is His right to pour out the Spirit (Acts 2:32-33).[169]

The inheritance of the earth, therefore, is given to those who have been called forth from their graves by the Spirit who raised Jesus from the dead (Rom. 1:3-4), a Spirit granted in the "already" as a pledge of the inheritance of ruling the universe as a joint-heir with the resurrected Messiah (Eph. 1:14).[170] Thus, the apostle Paul pictures the indwelling of the Spirit and personal regeneration, not in terms of an otherworldly flight from creation, but as that which joins the believer to the resurrection of Christ (Rom. 8:11), thereby enabling the believer to share in His inheritance as ruler of the earth (8:17), in His bodily resurrection from the dead (8:23), and therefore in the restoration of the liberated cosmos to its intended governance, under the lordship of a crucified and resurrected divine/human King (8:20-22, 29).[171]

It is impossible, however, to relate salvation to the Kingdom without addressing fissures within contemporary evangelical theology over the definition of salvation. The first has to do with the growing reluctance, especially within the reformist wing of evangelical theology, to articulate salvation in terms of the necessity of explicit faith in Christ. The inclusivist position, which is held by theologians ranging from Clark Pinnock to John Sanders to Stanley Grenz, holds that salvation is universally available only through the atonement of Christ, but that this salvation may be appropriated through general revelation.[172] When, however, inclusivist evangelicals argue that the salvation of the unevangelized can come about in the same manner as that of the Old Testament believers, they ignore the Kingdom orientation of biblical soteriology. This problem is compounded when an otherwise conservative theologian such as Millard Erickson offers the possibility that "persons who come to belief in a single powerful God, who despair of any works-righteousness to please this holy God, and who throw themselves upon the mercy of this good God, would be accepted as were the Old Testament believers."[173] Erickson offers this possibility precisely because of the "sameness" he sees in Old and New Testament concepts of salvation. "Salvation has always been appropriated by faith (Gal. 3:6-9); this salvation rests on Christ's deliverance of us from the law (vv. 10-14, 19-29)," he writes. "Nothing has been changed in that respect."[174]

In a soteriology informed by inaugurated eschatology, however, a great deal has "changed in that respect." The New Testament writers speak of the salvation in Christ as the inbreaking of the eschaton, the arrival of the promised last days (Luke 2:26-32). Jesus Himself ties entrance into the eschatological Kingdom to a "looking" specifically at Him in faith (John 3:14-15). It is for this reason that the apostolic message, to Jews as well as to devout Gentile "God-fearers," was that the decisive, apocalyptic Day of the Lord had arrived in the identity and mission of Jesus of Nazareth (Acts 2:14-35), a turn of events that necessitated faith specifically in Him as Lord and Messiah (Acts 2:36-41). Thus, the apostle Peter proclaims with apocalyptic urgency to the Gentiles the necessity of explicit faith in Christ in continuity with the Old Testament promises of the eschaton (Acts 10:34-43). Likewise, the apostle Paul addresses the Athenian philosophers with the message that a soteriological shift has taken place in the resurrection of Jesus from the dead, meaning that God is "now declaring to men that all people everywhere should repent" because the eschatological judgment has been committed to the resurrected Jesus (Acts 17:30-31). Paul likewise points the Corinthians to the dawning of the "last days" opportunity for salvation from the Day of the Lord, a salvation He ties to explicit faith in the crucified and resurrected Jesus of Nazareth (2 Cor. 5:16–6:2).

The varying degrees of evangelical openness to inclusivist positions likewise do not do justice to the explicitly Christocentric nature of Kingdom soteriology. Evangelical inclusivists often seek to explain the salvation of those who do not respond to the proclamation of Christ in terms of the working of the Spirit. Clark Pinnock therefore argues that the "universality" of the Spirit's activity allows evangelicals "to be hopeful about people who have not yet acknowledged Jesus as Lord" since grace "is extant not only in Christian contexts but in every place where the Spirit is."[175] For Pinnock, the "truth of the Incarnation does not eclipse truth about the Spirit, who was at work before Christ and is present now where Christ is not named" since the "mission of the Son is not a threat to the mission of the Spirit, or vice versa."[176] Indeed, Pinnock rejects the *filioque* language of the Nicene Creed because it "promotes Christomonism," meaning that the phrase "diminishes the role of the Spirit and gives the impression that he has no mission of his own."[177] Indeed, Pinnock asserts that the mission of the Spirit is "prior to and geographically larger than the Son's," meaning that "the Spirit can be active where the Son is not named."[178] Amos Yong, a Pentecostal scholar, further develops Pinnock's pneumatocentric soteriology by challenging evangelical paradigms that "proceed from a christological starting point and are therefore closely intertwined with christological assumptions." What if instead, Yong asks, evangelical theology should begin "with pneumatology rather than Christology"?[179]

This is, of course, precisely the problem. In a Kingdom-oriented theology of redemptive history, the soteriological role of the Spirit means that He does not, in fact, have a "mission of His own." The Spirit is, as Richard Gaffin and Sinclair Ferguson have so effectively demonstrated, "the Spirit of Christ." Jesus Himself points to His bearing of the Spirit as a function of His messianic identity (Luke 4:18; 11:20; Acts 1:6-8), an understanding resonant with Old Testament Davidic hope (Isa. 11:2; 61:1-3). The apostolic preaching of Jesus as Messiah therefore pivots on His Davidic kingly activity in sending the Spirit to form sinners into a new eschatological Kingdom community (Acts 2:17, 32-36; 10:46-48; 15:7-9). Thus, Jesus picks up the messianic Kingdom expectation when He instructs His disciples, "the Spirit of truth who proceeds from the Father, He will testify about Me" (John 15:26). It is not unusual, therefore, that Jesus should say that the mission of the Spirit is to "glorify Me" (John 16:14), if in fact the goal of the redemptive Kingdom purposes of God is to see to it that Christ "will come to have first place in everything" (Col. 1:18). It is likewise not surprising that the apostle Paul should claim that salvation now comes in these last days to those who "confess with your mouth Jesus as Lord and believe in your heart that God raised Him from the dead," if in fact the eschatological goal of God's redemptive Kingdom program is that "every tongue will confess that Jesus Christ is Lord, to the glory of God the Father" (Phil. 2:11).

Evangelical inclusivism not only follows classical dispensationalism in severing redemptive history from the Christocentric purposes of God, it does so in a manner remarkably consistent with the "two peoples, two dispensations" emphases of the dispensationalist fundamentalists. Just as classical dispensationalists were forced to defend themselves from Reformed fundamentalists for teaching "two ways of salvation," many reformist evangelicals tend to sever God's relationship to Israel (with Jesus inheriting the role of Israel's mediator in the new covenant era) from God's purposes with the nations.[180] As did Scofield-type dispensationalism, post-conservative inclusivism fails to see the Kingdom's holistic consummation in the one-flesh relationship of the Messiah and his eschatological Bride (Eph. 5:32). Evangelical theology should reject this retrogression as vigorously as it rejected Scofield.

At the same time, a Kingdom-oriented soteriological consensus should drive evangelical theology back to its orthodox/fundamentalist roots on the questions of penal substitutionary atonement and forensic justification. These concepts are increasingly challenged within contemporary evangelical thought by those who wish, for instance, to replace penal substitutionary atonement with a "Christus Victor" model that sees the work of redemption in terms of Christ defeating the satanic powers rather than in terms of Christ bearing the wrath of God in the place of humanity.[181] Many of these proposals, such as that of Boyd, argue that this "Christus Victor" model is more appropriate to the Kingdom motif of Scripture, especially in light of the insights of inaugurated eschatology regarding the present kingship of Christ and in relation to a cosmic, holistic view of redemption. Boyd, for instance, argues that the classic Protestant penal substitutionary model of the atonement makes salvation anthropocentric and individualized.[182] Joel Green further argues that penal substitution removes the atonement "from the historical world in which we live and leaves it unconnected to personal or social reconciliation."[183]

These arguments, however, fail to demonstrate how either the New Testament's Kingdom-oriented view of salvation or its picture of cosmic warfare and holistic reconciliation is challenged by a view of the atonement that is pictured repeatedly in Scripture as both penal and substitutionary, in continuity with the Old Testament sacrificial system.[184] This is especially true when the biblical canon presents the cosmic bondage of the creation as contingent on human sin and guilt (Gen. 3:14-19; Rom. 8:19-23). The historic Protestant understanding of the cross as essentially propitiatory and substitutionary ironically serves as the only way to make sense of the cosmic implications of both redemption and the fall since, in both, the destiny of the created order is tied to the mandate given to the human vicegerents responsible for creation. Indeed, it is the only way to make sense of the "Christus Victor" model itself. Thus, the defeat of the powers of darkness in the crucifixion and resurrection of Jesus means that the ancient serpent is indeed defeated, but this defeat comes through reversing human slavery to sin and death (John 8:31-47; 12:31-33;

2 Tim. 2:25; Heb. 2:14-15) by bearing the punishment due to a humanity justly accused by the satanic powers (Col. 2:14-15; Rev. 12:10-12), and thereby restoring humanity as king of the cosmos in the person of the Second Adam (Rom. 5:12-21; 1 Cor. 15:21-28; Heb. 2:5-18).[185] Penal substitution as the central theme of the atonement is also necessary to maintain a "holistic" view of salvation. As the traditional Reformed understanding of total depravity underscores, the biblical definition of sin is not a gnostic matter of a pure spirit and an evil body. It is instead a condemnation of the whole person as a sinner, those who "lived in the lusts of our flesh, indulging the desires of the flesh and of the mind, and were by nature children of wrath" (Eph. 2:3).[186] The sinner is condemned for sin that works itself out through the whole person, resulting in an atonement that must reconcile the whole person to the Creator through Christ.

Thus, the "Christus Victor" outcome envisioned by the New Testament is, in fact, accomplished through a substitutionary atonement and a resurrection from the dead, acts that the New Testament links directly to the Davidic covenant fulfillment and Kingdom prerogatives of Jesus (2 Tim. 2:8-13; Rev. 5:5, 9-10). Similarly, contrary to the assertions of revisionists such as Green and Baker, the New Testament does not picture social reconciliation as being at odds with a penal, substitutionary atonement in which "Jesus came to save us from God."[187] Instead, the apostle Paul contends that human social reconciliation is a direct result of a prior reconciliation to God (Eph. 2:16-18), a reconciliation the apostle defines explicitly in terms of spiritual deadness and transgression of the commandments of God (Rom. 3:21-30; Eph. 2:1-15; Col. 1:20-21). Closely tied to this is the growing reluctance within evangelical theology to speak of the "courtroom language" of forensic justification.[188] And yet, neither the Old nor the New Testament conceives of a Kingdom without the very "legal" concepts of righteousness, judgment, and justification. The promise of the eschatological Davidic Kingdom in the Old Testament includes the promise that God will judge His people "between one sheep and another, between the rams and the male goats" (Ezek. 34:17-24). It is only the justified "sheep" of the pasture, Ezekiel writes, who will experience the "shepherding" of the Davidic King (Ezek. 34:23), a regal responsibility Jesus not only grants to Himself (Matt. 25:31-46), but explicitly ties to His assumption of the messianic throne (Matt. 25:31-32; see also 16:27-28).[189] It is not, therefore, that the move away from penal substitutionary atonement and forensic justification is a "doctrinal development" since the Fundamentalist-Modernist controversy, along the same lines as the move toward a Kingdom-oriented theology.[190] Instead, these developments actually compromise the Kingdom motif itself by ignoring the central biblical challenge to the kingship of humanity—the satanic

reign of death through sin and guilt.[191] It should come as little surprise, therefore, that, in seeking to redefine salvation in terms of other doctrinal commitments, some evangelical "reformers" are actually retreating to the long-ago
discarded positions once held by the dispensationalist fundamentalists of
yesteryear, such as the crucifixion as "Plan B" after the Jewish rejection of the
bona fide Kingdom offer.[192]

The emerging soteriological consensus likewise offers the opportunity to
address what is perhaps the remaining decisive cleavage between the dispensationalist and covenantal wings of evangelical theology—namely, the future
of Israel as a distinct political body among the other nations.[193] Modified
covenant theology argues against a restored Israelite nation on the basis of the
cosmic extent of redemption.[194] Progressive dispensationalists argue that
covenant theology's rejection of any future for Israel as a political body represents a "false dichotomy" in which salvation "must be either present or future,
either complete or not at all, either material or spiritual, either earthly or heavenly."[195] Dispensationalism here must address its own history, including
Chafer's unfortunate "two religions" articulation of the future of Israel, a formulation that at times, however unintended, did lead to the impression of what
Carl Henry rightly identifies as the unbiblical notion that Jesus and His disciples "contemplate a future restoration of Israel that is independent of his own
messianic role."[196]

This being said, progressive dispensationalists have moved toward answering the classic covenantal objection as to how one can distinguish between
national Israel and the nations, given Jesus' messianic status as simultaneously
the promised Israelite Messiah and the head of the one new humanity.[197] Their
view is not inconsistent with a holistic, cosmic salvation. Indeed, it would
appear that the more progressive strains of dispensationalism seek to share the
holistic soteriology of Ladd's Kingdom theology. Indeed, they claim to hold an
even more "holistic" salvation than Ladd because they see no biblical grounding to translate the Old Testament national/political promises into spiritual
blessings of the present age.[198] At the same time, the new dispensationalists
argue that salvific equality does not mean equality of roles, an understanding
shared by their conservative covenantal interlocutors on the question of
male/female relations.[199] After all, some progressives argue, salvific equality in
Christ does not rule out differing roles for national groups, even as Galatians
3:28 does not rule out complementary roles for men and women, who also
enjoy salvific equality in Christ.[200] But this argument falls short also, in that it
fails to distinguish between the creation order and the specific place of Israel
in redemptive history. After all, human beings are created male and female—

and that pronounced "good"—but are human beings created Jew and Gentile, from the beginning? The answer is obviously no, since the biblical storyline begins with one man and one woman—from whom all nations spring (Acts 17:26). The Galatians 3:28 text, when seen through the lens of male/female complementarity, actually undermines the dispensationalist argument at this point. For Paul, there is "no male or female," just as there is no "Jew or Greek." Why? It is because all Christians are, not "sons and daughters of God," but "sons of God." In accordance with the laws of biblical patriarchy, all Christians (male and female) receive a common inheritance because they are "in Christ," who is the Jewish royal firstborn son who receives all these blessings. Indeed Galatians 3:28 does not establish androgyny—or even egalitarian gender roles.[201] But it does speak to the key issue in the debate over the future of Israel, namely, who will inherit the promises made to the Israel of God?

It is here that the Christocentric focus of the emerging Kingdom soteriological consensus offers fruitful ground for further work on the future of Israel. Until this point, both dispensationalist and covenantal evangelicals discussed the issue as though it could be abstracted from the purposes of God in the true Israelite, Jesus of Nazareth. Both sides then miss the radically Christ-centered focus of the New Testament argument, especially in the Pauline epistles, that "all the promises of God find their Yes in him" (2 Cor. 1:20, ESV). Both sides miss the impact of the mystery Paul is unveiling when he argues against the Judaizers that the "seed of Abraham" who inherits the kingdom promises is not plural but singular (Gal. 3:16a). Indeed, Paul explicitly identifies the "offspring of Abraham"—the Israel of God—as Jesus of Nazareth (Gal. 3:16b). The dispensationalists are right that those who receive the promises to Israel do so because of ethnic identity and the boundaries of circumcision—but only because they are united to the only one for whom such things avail, Messiah Jesus. Covenant theologians are right that the Gentiles receive the promises made to Israel—but they receive them because they are considered by God to be "in Messiah." This is why Paul is able to refer to Gentile Christians as "the circumcision." They have the circumcision "of Christ" (Col. 2:11) because they are united with Him in His death and resurrection (Col. 2:12). This is why Paul is able to dismiss the tribal boundaries of circumcised and uncircumcised in the Colossian church. Not because circumcision is irrelevant, but because both groups now find their tribal identities in the Israelite of God, Jesus of Nazareth, so that, as Paul puts it, "Christ is all, and in all" (Col. 3:11, ESV).

It would seem that this is precisely the issue in the New Testament's insistence that the Gentiles have received "adoption as sons" (Rom. 8:14-23; Gal. 4:5-6; Eph. 1:5). The issue in this adoption for the apostle Paul is not simply relational (although it is that—the "Abba" cry to the Father). It is also an adoption that guarantees to the Gentiles an inheritance. They are now "heirs" of the promises of God made to the offspring of Abraham (Gal. 4:7). It is here that a blurring of the Scripture's Christocentric focus can lead to confusion. The "adoption" means that the Gentiles are *joint*-heirs—with the One who is the true Israel, the "firstborn" of God (Rom. 8:17, 29, KJV). It is not that God has "natural" sons—the Jews—and "adopted" sons—the Gentiles. Rather, both Jews and Gentiles find their identity in being conformed to the image of the Messiah, "in order that he might be the firstborn among many brothers" (Rom. 8:29, ESV). The "household" language of the New Testament cannot then be severed from the "political" nature of the promises to Israel since Yahweh is a "father" to Israel. If Gentiles find their identity in the Jewish son of the Most High, they are "sons of God," and thus "brothers" of the Jewish believers—receiving the exact same inheritance and thus welcomed into "the household of God," which means they are now "fellow citizens" with the Old Testament people of God (Eph. 2:19). The problem with the Gentiles in the old age, after all, is that they were "separate from Christ" (Eph. 2:12)—a separation that meant more than just spiritual hopelessness, but also alienation "from the commonwealth of Israel" and exclusion from the "covenants of promise" (Eph. 2:12-13). "But now," Paul argues, this has been remedied with the coming of the Kingdom—and it has been accomplished "in Christ Jesus" (Eph. 2:13).

Dispensationalists, even progressives, mistakenly speak of the millennial Israel as having a "mediatorial" role in dispensing the blessings of God to the nations. They are correct—except that Scripture presents this mediatorial role as belonging to Jesus (1 Tim. 2:5). Thus, the New Testament applies to Jesus language previously applied to the nation—the "firstborn" or the "son of God" (Ex. 4:22-23; Matt. 2:15). The first "Israel" himself, the patriarch Jacob, promises preeminence and rule to a tribe of Israel, Judah (Gen. 49:4, 9-12). The apostle Paul applies this language explicitly to Jesus (Col. 1:18). This emphasis is more than incidental or fragmentary. The identification of Jesus with Israel—as her king, her substitute, and her goal—is everywhere throughout the apostolic understanding of the Old Testament promise. When the apostles speak of "promises" being fulfilled (as in, for example, the sermon in Acts 13), they are not speaking of abstract heavenly comforts. They are speaking specifically of promises made to Abraham and the nation of Israel. The old covenant looked forward to the day when the nations would see the vindication of Israel, through Israel's resurrection from the dead and anointing with the Spirit (Ezek. 36:33-36). "My dwelling place will be with them, and I will be their God, and they shall be my people," Yahweh speaks through the prophet Ezekiel. "Then the nations will know that I am the LORD who sanctifies Israel, when my sanctuary is in their midst forever" (Ezek. 37:27-28, ESV). Israel, therefore, did not just long for a "Messiah." The Israelites longed for a Messiah who would reign over a messianic age, the day when the nations would come to Israel (Isa. 60:1-14), when the ends of the earth would be given as an inheritance to the Son of David (Ps. 2:8-9; 110:1-7). They were waiting for the resurrection of Israel, the marking out of Israel by the Spirit, the drawing of the nations to Israel. They were waiting, in short, for the Kingdom of God.

This is why the apostles inquire of the resurrected Jesus as to whether this was the time when He would "restore the kingdom to Israel" (Acts 1:6, ESV). Jesus answers their question by speaking of the power of the Spirit and the global task of the Great Commission (Acts 1:7-8). He was not changing the subject. He is the "Immanuel," the temple presence of God with the people (Matt. 1:23; John 1:14; 2:19-21). Israel is indeed raised from the dead, but there is only one empty tomb. All who will be raised from death must be raised "in Him" (Rom. 6:3-10). The nations are indeed drawn to Israel, but they are drawn not to a geographic temple but to an Israelite man who, when lifted up, draws all the peoples to Himself (Matt. 2:1-11; John 12:20, 32). Israel is indeed anointed with the messianic Spirit, but only one Israelite receives the Spirit—and pours the promise out then upon all who are "in Him." This is the reason Paul's polemic against Jew/Gentile divisions in the early church centered so often on pneumatology. Those, whether Jew or Gentile, who bear the Spirit show that they "belong to Him" (Rom. 8:9-11). They are "joint-heirs" with the Messiah (Rom. 8:17; Gal. 4:6). What do they inherit? They inherit the specific inheritance of Jesus—they are "in Him." And what does the resurrected Jesus inherit? The promises made to Abraham, Isaac, and Jacob (Acts 13:32-33). Thus, when dispensationalists speak of the "future" of Israel, they should speak of it in terms of the "future" of Jesus—a future He promises to share with His "friends" (John 15:14-15).

At the same time, covenant theologians speak too quickly of the church as "spiritually" replacing Israel. The covenantal land promises are posited too often as typological of the "spiritual" blessings of forgiveness of sins and eternal heavenly life.

Covenant theologians would do better to return to the Patristic eschatology of Justin Martyr who, in his apologetic polemics with Jewish objectors, claimed for the church continuity with Israel. And yet, as historian Oskar Skarsaune notes, he "does *not* say that the messianic expectation of the Jews is false, crude, unspiritual, etc. He does not say that the Jews are wrong in their ideas of the messianic age."[202] Instead, Justin identified all of the promises to Israel—both material and spiritual—as belonging to Jesus the Israelite—and therefore by legal inheritance to those who are united to Him as His "brothers" (John 20:17, ESV; Heb. 2:11, ESV). This is more resonant with the biblical text than the simple "replacement" language so often used by covenant theologians. God is not "replacing" one people with another. Instead, Israel begins with one man, Jacob the son of Abraham and Isaac; and Israel culminates in one man, Jesus the son of Abraham, Isaac and Jacob. Thus more needs to be said by covenant theologians than, in the words of one spokesman, "We believe the answer to 'What about the Jews?' is, 'Here we are.'"[203]

Instead, evangelicals should refocus the discussion to the identity of the believer in union with Christ—a union that means not only relationship but also inheritance. With salvation seen—in all of its aspects—as belonging first to the Messiah and only in Him to His people, the impasse over Israel's future is surmountable. There will still be disagreements about a possible mass conversion of the Jewish people at the eschaton. But this debate will center on the interpretation of New Testament passages such as Romans 9–11, meaning the argument over the future of Israel becomes once again more of a second-order eschatological dispute than an intractable argument over the very nature of salvation itself.[204]

Soteriology as a Political Problem

To see how the developments in evangelical soteriology may impact the task of evangelical sociopolitical action, one need only compare the relationship between evangelism and social action in contemporary evangelical Kingdom theology with that of its conservative Protestant roots. The mid-century evangelical subculture, even when advocating Christian civic activism, typically pitted evangelism against social and political engagement. Donald Grey Barnhouse, for instance, typified this approach, embodying simultaneously the constituencies of broad parachurch evangelicalism, dispensationalist revivalism, and Reformed confessionalism.[205] On the call for evangelical engagement, Barnhouse called for civic-minded Christians who are "aware of the true nature of the gospel" through "salvation for the individual sinner through the atoning work of Christ." After pointing to the dangers of the Social Gospel, Barnhouse reminded evangelicals that their goal is "to get men saved from sin so that the Holy Spirit, dwelling in the individual believer, can go on witnessing through the believer in the midst of a crooked and perverse nation, among whom we are to shine as lights in the world (Phil. 2:15)."[206] As contemporary evangelical Kingdom theology has sought to integrate the doctrine of redemption with the biblical theme of the Kingdom of God, it offers the opportunity to say more than this, while not saying anything less. A Kingdom-oriented soteriology answers many of the theological obstacles to sociopolitical engagement encountered by Henry and his neo-evangelical cohorts, while maintaining the evangelical commitment to the priority of individual regeneration and personal evangelism. Accordingly, the newer evangelical Kingdom consensus inevitably speaks theologically to a multitude of pressing social and political questions.

The newer developments in evangelical soteriology must first recognize that the perennial debates over evangelism and social action are not, first of all, about social action, or even about the Kingdom of God, but about the nature of the gospel and the very definition of salvation. Reformed theologian Edmund Clowney has rightly identified this problem in the oft-cited suggestion that "contemporary Christianity needs both Billy Graham's concern in saving souls and the World Council of Churches' interest in saving social structures."[207] However, Clowney correctly recognizes that "The problem with this patchwork solution is becoming increasingly evident" because "Billy Graham and the World Council theologians have very different views of salvation."[208] A call to evangelical engagement must therefore take into account the very different definitions of "salvation" bandied about not only in the hoary debates over the Social Gospel but in the much more recent interactions between evangelical and liberation theologians on this point.[209]

This divergence is never more evident than when the question of defining salvation is joined to the even more problematic question of defining the Kingdom of God. This Kingdom focus offers a foundation for a truly evangelical engagement because, unlike much of the early twentieth century's fundamentalist Protestantism, it portrays the Kingdom in terms broader than the call to individual decision so often predominant in American revivalism. As Henry lamented nearly fifty years after the publication of *Uneasy Conscience,* "Evangelical sermonizing often reaches its climax by interiorizing all doctrinal referents so that the appeal for personal decision obscures God's strong hand in external history and nature."[210] The Kingdom-oriented vision of redemption, however, like the Kingdom-oriented vision of inaugurated eschatology mitigates the temptation to bifurcate "spiritual" concerns from those of cultural and even cosmic significance. Just as an initially realized reign of Christ prevents evangelicals from forestalling all Kingdom activity to a future eschaton, a holistic view of redemption prevents evangelical theology from reducing the mission of Christianity to the rescue of individual souls from the world. It does this while simultaneously affirming the essentially soteric nature of the Kingdom itself.[211]

If redemption is the restoration of the creation order, not its repudiation, then evangelical theology must take seriously a creation mandate that values human culture as an aspect of human vicegerency over the earth (Gen. 1:26-30; 2:15; Ps. 8:4-8), a vicegerency fulfilled in the person and work of Christ (Heb. 2:5-9). A Kingdom-oriented salvation, which sees redemption as the restoration of the cultural mandate, will recognize the necessity of work for the fulfillment of human existence.[212] This is part and parcel of a biblical world-view understanding of salvation in which seemingly "mundane" aspects of life, such as labor and relationships, are to be transformed through calling, regeneration, and sanctification (2 Thess. 3:12; Eph. 5:22-6:9), to the extent that, in the Pauline teaching, the regenerate man who will not work is subject to the discipline of the church (1 Tim. 5:8). Evangelicals may disagree on the precise role of government in relief of poverty or on the necessity of a welfare state. Nonetheless, this view of Kingdom soteriology reminds evangelicals that human life reaches its creational goal not in cessation from activity, but in meaningful labor.[213]

Likewise, the emerging eschatological consensus has informed evangelical soteriology, and thereby the task of evangelical sociopolitical engagement, by reestablishing the place of the created order in the eschatological Kingdom purposes of God. In the emerging "new earth" understanding of the salvific transformation of the cosmos, human cultural endeavors are not simply temporal concerns, which will be consumed and forgotten in the static, timeless salvation enjoyed at the eschaton. Instead, creation is to be redeemed, albeit not by human effort, but by the cataclysmic coming of Christ, the Messiah, for whose inheritance the universe was created in the first place (Ps. 2:8; Isa. 49:6; John 1:3; Col. 1:16; Heb. 1:2). Furthermore, the New Testament seems to imply that some cultural human endeavors from within the stream of human history will be sanctified and will continue in the new order of the everlasting Kingdom of God (Rev. 21:26).[214] This idea should not be entirely foreign to evangelical theology, given the Scriptures' insistence that the effects of sanctification by the Spirit, purged of their impurities, will continue into the eschaton (1 Cor. 3:11-15).[215] Thus, sanctification and its outworking in the lives of the regenerate is not simply an "evidence" of regeneration, although it is certainly that. It is, as Paul teaches, the initial eschatological act of conforming the justified into the "image of His Son" (Rom. 8:29). In a very real sense, the identity of the human being, forged in the turbulence of this age's history, is of eschatological consequence, carried forth into the individual's eternal identity in the Kingdom of God.

At the same time, the apostle Paul can imply that the effects, even of the proclamation of unregenerate preachers, will continue into the age to come through the salvation of their hearers (Phil. 1:15-20). Moreover, the Old Testament speaks of the Spirit coming upon Bezalel of the tribe of Judah for the express purpose of "craftsmanship, to make artistic designs for work in gold, in silver, and in bronze, and in the cutting of stones for settings, and in the carving of wood, that he may work in all kinds of craftsmanship" (Ex. 31:1-5). If the Kingdom is concerned with the ultimate transformation of creation, society, and culture, then these things are certainly worthy of the concern of the regenerate church in the present epoch of redemption history.[216] This would mean that traditionalist conservatives, such as Russell Kirk, are correct that ultimately "culture" is more important than "politics."[217] After all, "culture" is a matter of the Adamic mandate that will continue into the eschaton, while the political structures will not continue into the eternal state but will be evaporated by the Kingdom of Christ (Dan. 2:44; Rev. 11:15).[218]

With this as a backdrop, evangelical theology is not forced to consider social and political engagement in terms of "spirit" versus "matter," or the task of personal evangelism as necessitating a withdrawal from the created order.[219] This grounding of soteriology is rooted in the creation purposes of God, as well as in the biblical eschatological *telos* of creation. The two come together in the bodily resurrection of Jesus from the dead, the decisive act of inaugurated eschatology that confirms the Kingdom purposes of God for the whole of humanity, body and soul, as well as for the whole of the created order. This informs the task of sociopolitical engagement because, as ethicist Oliver O'Donovan observes, the resurrection does away with any notion that Christian theology mandates a negation of the bodily and material aspects of created reality.[220]

Evangelical Kingdom theology thereby avoids the kind of isolationism Francis Schaeffer once denounced as responsible for evangelicalism's sluggishness in engaging the abortion debate prior to and immediately following the Supreme Court's 1973 *Roe v. Wade* decision, which codified the legal right to abortion in the United States. As Schaeffer saw it, evangelicals lagged behind Roman Catholics in condemning abortion rights, not just because of their political isolation, but because of their theology. Evangelicalism's collective yawn in the face of the abortion issue was, Schaeffer said, because of "the prison of their platonic spirituality," which failed to recognize that imperiled human life is not at the periphery of the Christian gospel.[221] The sociopolitical implications of the emerging evangelical consensus on redemption are illuminated by Schaeffer's contention that evangelical soteriology did not have the doctrinal resources to address the abortion issue. Schaeffer's analysis was verified, in the wake of *Roe,* in the public scrambling of American evangelicals, many of whom seemed to be asking, "What hath the revival tent to do with the abortion clinic?"

Christianity Today, for example, noted the court's legalization of abortion by blankly reporting that the decision "brought, as expected, immediate response from the nation's Roman Catholic leaders."[222] The issues were further crystallized as the magazine quoted Southern Baptist conservative patriarch W. A. Criswell, pastor of the First Baptist Church of Dallas, Texas, as affirming the *Roe* decision precisely because of his sharp distinction between soul and body: "I have always felt that it was only after a child was born and had life separate from its mother that it became an individual person, and it has always, therefore, seemed to me that what is best for the mother and for the future should be allowed."[223] While Criswell later took a pro-life stance on abortion rights, President Bill Clinton, over twenty years after Roe, only grew more dogged in his support of abortion rights, claiming that his views on abortion rights were the result of a very similar view of the relation of the body to the soul, which he attributes to a Southern Baptist pastor.[224]

By refusing to bifurcate the body from the soul, the Kingdom-oriented vision of a holistic soteriology articulated by, among others, progressive dispensationalists and modified covenantalists, might have well served an evangelical theology taken off-guard by *Roe*. By envisioning the mission of the Kingdom as encompassing concern for both body and soul, and by seeing Kingdom priorities as including both the justification of the wicked and justice for the innocent, evangelical theology might have been better prepared theologically for the cultural upheaval that led to the debate over abortion rights.[225] This holistic interrelationship between the Kingdom and salvation would also serve as an impetus for evangelical theology to engage vigorously other matters of life, which are growing as reproductive and human cloning technologies proliferate. Ironically, the application of a holistic understanding of redemption in the post-*Roe* era has come most conspicuously from the evangelical right-flank, chiefly on the abortion issue.[226]

A Kingdom-oriented, holistic vision of soteriology would necessitate church-based social ministry as well as personal evangelism in a ministry to the whole person, but social ministry is not enough. Evangelicals must also address the cultural and political undercurrents that threaten the lives of individuals and the societal order itself. Evangelical theology might, for example, respond to the burgeoning gay rights movement by equipping congregations simultaneously to proclaim the biblical warning that unrepentant homosexuals will not inherit the Kingdom of God (1 Cor. 6:9) while demonstrating the merciful nature of that Kingdom by maintaining AIDS hospice care and rigorous discipleship programs for homosexuals who come to faith in Christ through the ministry of the church. At the same time, evangelicals must engage the sociopolitical forces that support and accelerate the understanding of the family as a social construct that can be defined by society on an almost *ad hoc* basis. A holistic understanding of salvation would likewise mean that evangelical theology must view pornography as more than a matter of individualistic "personal sin." Instead, evangelical theology could agree in part with certain sectors of feminist thought that the lucrative pornography industry destroys societal order and degrades women by seeing their bodies as objects for mass consumption.[227]

The eschatologically informed cosmic understanding of salvation as a Kingdom activity likewise informs the relationship between evangelical theology and environmental policy.[228] Evangelical Kingdom theology can posit environmental stewardship as a distinctively Christian endeavor, given the restoration of human vicegerency in the person and work of Christ. This understanding is contrary to much of the ideology of contemporary environmental movements, which tend to posit humanity as an almost parasitic presence on the earth, rather than the intended sovereign over it.[229] Furthermore, the understanding of salvation as restoration of creation negates the conception that the earth is irrelevant to the Kingdom purposes of God by demonstrating the place of the creation in the establishment of the Kingdom, from the original creation through the Noahic covenant (Gen. 9:8-17) to the final regeneration of the cosmos (Col. 1:20).[230] This view still maintains the limitations of environmental action because of the theological understanding that ultimately the destiny of the earth is tied to the more basic problem of human sin and guilt.[231]

Furthermore, a holistic view of redemption necessitates the cultivation of a vigorous worldview theology. In the emerging Kingdom theology of the evangelical consensus, salvation as a matter of the "heart" is not reduced to social justice (as in Social Gospel liberalism), nor is it a matter of personal ethical piety as in other forms of Protestant liberalism. Neither is it, however, the pietistic world-denying "heart" religion, disconnected from matters of public justice and order, as in some forms of conservative revivalism. Instead, as Kuyperian theologian Henry Van Til reminds evangelicals, "Since religion is rooted in the heart, it is therefore totalitarian in nature," meaning that it claims every aspect of the life of the Christian community, including the tasks of cultural, social, and political engagement.[232] This resonates with the biblical picture of the "heart," not as a matter of individual inward piety, but as the whole direction of personal existence (Deut. 4:29; 1 Sam. 16:7; Jer. 17:9; Matt. 15:19).[233] Thus, redemption means that worldview-construction is inherently a part of the mission of the church, a task that invariably addresses social and

political questions of human existence. Thus, as Carl Henry asserts of the biblical redemptive mandate for evangelical theology, "The Christian world-life
view embraced heaven and earth from creation to end time and enlisted a fellowship of redeemed and regenerate humans in a salvific mission of interper-
sonal and public duty and functioning as a channel of God's love and of social
justice."[234]

Perhaps the most important contribution of evangelical Kingdom soteriology to evangelical sociopolitical engagement, however, is the fact that it
maintains the priority of the redemption of sinners. The evangelical Kingdom
consensus does not leave the meaning "holistic" salvation undefined, which is
not at all an insignificant matter, given the definitional confusion over such
"holism," and the extent of redemptive benefits to the "whole person" and
social structures in the present era. This is especially important since evangelicalism's political left wing has been quite vocal in calling for a "holistic" view
of salvation.[235] The lessons of the Social Gospel should teach evangelical theologians, however, how easily the rhetoric of "holistic" soteriology can lead to
a minimization of the proclamation of personal regeneration and justification
through faith.[236] As Robert Saucy has warned persuasively, any theology of the
Kingdom that does not "understand salvation today as involving priority of
personal spiritual regeneration" is in peril of moving toward the political theologies of the Protestant left.[237] Saucy would seem to be correct in noting that
the dispensational tradition reminds evangelicalism that the presence of the
Kingdom differs in its aspects from epoch to epoch, with this interim era
between the advents of the Messiah seeing the Kingdom most active in the present age through the calling of unbelievers to salvation in Christ. This understanding would seem to find more than adequate biblical grounding, since, as
noted above, the New Testament speaks of a very real "dispensational" shift
to the last days with the coming of Christ, a shift that focuses attention on an
urgent proclamation for sinners to seek refuge in Christ (Acts 17:30-31; Rom.
3:25-26; 2 Cor. 6:1-3).

While evangelical Kingdom theology has helpfully critiqued many of the
more individualistic, decisionistic elements of American revivalism by relating
salvation to the Kingdom of God, evangelical theology must not lose the invig-
orating contribution of revivalism to American Protestantism, namely, the
emphasis on personal, individual appropriation of redemption.[238] Whatever
the methodological flaws and differences of the various English and American
revival movements, the evangelistic thrust of the nineteenth century did spur
the church on to social and political engagement without sacrificing the priority of personal regeneration. "The Wesley and Whitefield revivals were tremen-

dous in calling for individual salvation, and thousands upon thousands were saved," notes Francis Schaeffer. "Yet even secular historians acknowledge that it was the social results coming out of the Wesley revival that saved England from its own form of the French Revolution."[239]

The importance of the priority of personal regeneration for sociopolitical engagement is demonstrated in the ministry of the man who, arguably, embodied the "uneasy conscience of modern fundamentalism," Billy Graham. As Graham biographer William Martin notes, Graham, like other conservative evangelicals of his day, made numerous public statements eschewing social action, usually relating his political discomfort to his pessimistic dispensational eschatology and the priority of evangelism over social reform, and yet he was surprisingly progressive on the question of race.[240] It may be argued that Graham insisted on the desegregation of his southern crusades, not because of an elaborate political theory, but because of his theology of the indiscriminate offer of personal salvation. Before Graham could articulate the fact that segregation was socially unjust, he could recognize that it was serving as a stumbling block to the proclamation of the gospel to unbelieving individuals of various races and economic classes.[241] This rebellion against the social status quo based on the hope for the salvation of all who believe, without partiality, resonates with similar reasoning used by first-century Jewish Christians as they faced the question of social intercourse with Gentiles, a situation which also resulted in social reconciliation based on the reception of the same message of personal redemption.[242] As Henry applied the message to the context of racial reconciliation in twentieth-century America, "Because it champions the redemptive realities inherent in the Christian religion, evangelical Christianity will vindicate the judgment that the Negro is not only politically an equal but also spiritually a brother."[243]

As has been noted above, individual regeneration is not the sum of the message of the lordship of Christ; and, after all, Billy Graham's racial progressiveness was unusual among southern clergymen. Even so, the sound commitment to evangelistic fervor among American evangelicals, when combined with a serious call to reflective biblical engagement on matters such as racial reconciliation, can bolster the commitment to a just social order.[244] The priority of personal regeneration does not mean an internalized, individualistic pietism, nor does it mean maintaining a sharp division between evangelism and social action. It does, however, mean that evangelical theology, especially as it is informed by the growing consensus on the Kingdom of God, must remember that personal regeneration is by definition "holistic," in that it holds forth the salvation of the whole person through the resurrection of the body in Christ

(Matt. 10:28) and that it achieves social reconciliation, justice, and community in the "already" aspect of the Kingdom of God as a guarantee of the coming cosmic setting of all things in order in Christ.

Furthermore, contemporary evangelical theology must recognize that attention to the doctrinal content of soteriology is the first priority in any effort at a pan-evangelical witness in the social and political arenas. As Henry argued in the 1960s, a reprioritization or redefinition of the evangelistic message of Christian theology skews the very nature of Christian public witness because the evangelical gospel of a forensic justification based on the alien righteousness and substitutionary sacrifice of Christ maintains the centrality of justice in the order of the universe.[245] Henry's point is bolstered in light of the impact of a Social Gospel Protestant liberalism that sought to redefine both the atonement and public philosophy in terms of the centrality of love rather than the centrality of justice.[246]

In examining the philosophically troublesome "love ethic" of American liberalism, Henry rightly tied the sociopolitical difficulties to prior soteriological concessions:

> To misstate the biblical view of the equal status of righteousness and love in God's being brings only continuing problems in dogmatics. Redemption soon loses its voluntary character as divine election and becomes an inevitable if not necessary divine provision. Discussion of Christ's death and atonement in modernism is uncomfortable in the presence of such themes as satisfaction and propitiation. Future punishment of the wicked is revised to conform to benevolent rather than punitive motivations, and hell is emptied of its terrors by man-made theories of universal salvation. The state is no longer dedicated to justice and order, encouraging and enforcing human rights and responsibilities under God, but is benevolently bent toward people's socio-economic wants.[247]

Evangelical efforts at sociopolitical engagement must employ systematic theology to evaluate increasing calls to prioritize love over justice in Christian soteriology through the minimization of forensic justification, through the rejection of eternal eschatological retribution for the unrighteous, or through a paradigm shift from "courtroom" to "family room" imagery in the proclamation of the evangelical message of salvation.[248] A decisive stance on these issues, as Henry warned mid-century, will be the key to keeping evangelical engagement both evangelical and engaged.[249]

The key to understanding the kind of Kingdom-oriented salvation articulated by the emerging evangelical consensus is a developed Christology that takes into account the unity of Christ's person and work along with an eschatology that sees both a present and a future element to the reign of Christ. Thus, evangelical theology has grappled with, and come to some consensus on the relationship between salvation and the Kingdom, and the relationship of both to the social and political task of the regenerate community. Because Christ is simultaneously the covenant God who pledged to create a people for Himself and the anointed ruler of that people, the Messiah offers a salvation that cannot be truncated into bare spiritual blessings in one dispensation or mere political authority in another. Therefore, although the church does not yet wield political authority over the nations, it must recognize that the redemption it offers has a social and political element that is intrinsically tied to the gospel itself. Matters of sociopolitical engagement cannot therefore be dismissed or reformulated as "unspiritual" or irrelevant to present Kingdom activity. If the Kingdom is to be understood as having a present reality, and that reality is essentially soteriological, then the Kingdom agenda of evangelical theology must focus on the biblical fulcrum of these eschatological, salvific blessings: the church.

4

TOWARD A KINGDOM ECCLESIOLOGY: THE CHURCH AS KINGDOM COMMUNITY

INTRODUCTION

"One of the most important questions you can ask theologians is where they go to church," ethicist Stanley Hauerwas has observed.[1] Bound up with this comment is a larger question on the place of ecclesiology in Christian theology. The problem of the role of the church in the public square is not a new one, but was one of the challenges faced by the postwar evangelical movement's call for evangelical social and political engagement. The issue was complicated, however, by a fundamental tension over the theological definition of the church itself, much less its role in the world. This tension was nowhere more clearly seen than in the divergence over ecclesiology in the rival dispensational and covenant systems within the infant evangelical movement. In the years since the postwar era, however, evangelical theology has sought to articulate a clearly defined ecclesiology. In this project, contemporary evangelical theology has laid out a doctrine of the church integrated with the emerging consensus on the nature of the Kingdom of God in Christ. Evangelical theology has emerged with a near consensus on the relationship between the Kingdom and the church, along with remarkably similar concepts of how the church should relate to the world in the present era. These developments toward a Kingdom ecclesiology are especially crucial for the task of evangelical sociopolitical engagement, given the importance of ecclesiology in the debates over the public role of the church in distinguishing the evangelical call to engagement from both isolationist fundamentalism and socially active Protestant liberalism.

ECCLESIOLOGY AND THE THEOLOGICAL PROJECT
OF POSTWAR EVANGELICALISM

The difficulty of the postwar evangelical movement in tying a doctrine of the church to a Kingdom-oriented theology of sociopolitical engagement was of critical concern to Carl Henry and his colaborers in the cause of defining evangelical identity. The difficulty in achieving this objective is seen in the very nature of the movement itself, both in terms of its popular front manifested in the Billy Graham crusades and in its more scholarly front manifested in Fuller Theological Seminary.[2] It is far from difficult to see the origins of such a "free enterprise" view of the church, especially when consideration is given to the doctrinal continuity between the older fundamentalism and the new evangelicalism. After all, the denominational structures of the mainline churches were, by mid-century, almost without exception in the hands of the modernists, a fact that gains further precedence when it is noted that the dispensationalist Dallas Seminary, the Reformed confessional Westminster Seminary, and the broadly evangelical Fuller Seminary were all non-denominational parachurch entities formed to circumnavigate the liberalizing forces within the existing church structures.[3] Significantly, it was within this atmosphere of parachurch cooperation that the evangelical discussion of the church took place.

Postwar Evangelical Ecclesiology and The Uneasy Conscience

Henry and others in the movement recognized that a sustainable theology of evangelical engagement could not be achieved without some form of consensus on the church. The new evangelical concern over the doctrine of the church was inextricably linked to related soteriological concerns. It was not simply that the denominational church structures had neglected preaching the gospel of individual salvation that galled conservative Protestants. It was also that the liberals had succeeded in turning the denominations into the equivalent of political action committees, addressing a laundry list of social and political issues.[4] The problem with the Social Gospel ecclesiology, Henry concluded, was the same anti-supernaturalism that destroyed its soteriology; Protestant liberalism had replaced a regenerate church over which the resurrected Messiah ruled as Head with a largely unregenerate visible church.[5] Henry thereby tied the liberal Protestant view of the church and political action directly to a theologically problematic view of salvation, a "neo-Protestant view" that "substitutes the notion of corporate salvation for individual salvation."[6] Thus, even while maintaining the need for individual action in the public square, Henry maintained that the endless political pronouncements of the churches were an affront to the purpose of the church. "The Church as a corporate body has no spiritual mandate to sponsor economic, social, and political programs," he argued in the midst of the omni-political 1960s. "Nowhere does the New Testament authorize the Church to endorse specific legislative proposals as part of its ecclesiastical mission in the world."[7] In so doing, Henry pointed out the irony of church officials proclaiming the certitudes of redemption with less and less certainty while simultaneously making sociopolitical statements that seemed to come with their own self-attesting authority. "Is it not incredible that some churchmen, whose critical views of the Bible rest on the premise that in ancient times the Spirit's inspiration did not correct erroneous scientific concepts, should seriously espouse the theory that in modern times the Spirit provides denominational leaders with the details of a divine science of economics?" he asked.[8]

At the same time, Henry denied that this position was inconsistent with his call for evangelicals to move beyond the "uneasy conscience" toward a holistic view of redemption and responsibility toward society. "We do not support the position that the Christian's only concern is the saving of men's souls and that, for the rest, he may abandon the world to the power of evil," he wrote. "Nor do we deny the Church's scriptural right through the pulpit and through its synods, assemblies and councils to emphasize the divinely revealed principles of a social order and to speak out publicly against the great moral evils that arise in community life."[9] Still, finding an alternative to the politicized churchmanship of the Protestant left was increasingly difficult for a trans-denominational evangelical movement. Evangelicals across the United States did indeed have an identity, Henry editorialized in *Christianity Today*, because their "common ground is belief in biblical authority and in individual spiritual regeneration as being of the very essence of Christianity."[10] Nonetheless, he warned, this common ground was "crisscrossed by many fences" since evangelicals "differ not only on secondary issues but also on ecclesiology, the role of the Church in society, politics, and cultural mores."[11]

From Henry's vantage point, a retarded ecclesiology was an inheritance from fundamentalism, a vestige that evangelicals needed to address if they were to emerge from "Amish evangelicalism" and provide an alternative to the Protestant mainline. In short, the lack of a coherent evangelical ecclesiology meant the lack of a cohesive evangelical movement.[12] Long after the postwar era, Henry reflected that "the Jesus movement, the Chicago Declaration of young evangelicals, independent fundamentalist churches and even the so-called evangelical establishment, no less than the ecumenical movement which promoted structural church unity, all suffer a basic lack, namely, a public identity as a 'people,' a conspicuously unified body of regenerate believers."[13] With

Henry, certain segments of the evangelical conscience were also a bit uneasy about its lack of a coherent understanding of ecclesiology. Almost from the very beginning of the movement, some evangelicals worried that the parachurch nature of evangelicalism represented a problematic individualism that reflected the culture of mid-century America more than the revealed imperatives of the first-century apostolic mandate.[14]

Postwar Evangelical Ecclesiology and the Kingdom Debate

In calling evangelicals to a more theologically workable understanding of the role of the church in social and political engagement, Henry and his postwar evangelical colleagues faced the titanic task of more than simply resolving internecine differences over baptism, church government, and other ecclesiological issues, as daunting as that project alone would have been. Instead, postwar evangelical theology had to confront the question of the relationship between the church and the Kingdom of God in order to differentiate their view of evangelical engagement from that of the Social Gospel, and to guard against the isolationism of fundamentalism.

Henry argued that a Kingdom theology of evangelical engagement was made necessary by the way in which the relationship between church and Kingdom was delineated both on the left and on the right of the spectrum of American Protestantism. This was especially true given the low view of the church assigned by the Social Gospel, in which the primary focus was not the regenerate community but "the Kingdom." Henry complained that this definition of the Kingdom could not help but lead to politicized church structures because the "universalistic view that the social order is to be considered as a direct anticipation of the Kingdom of God, whose cosmic rescue and redemption is held to embrace the totality of mankind, regards Christians as the vanguard of a New Society to be achieved through politico-economic dynamisms."[15] Thus, Henry concluded, conservative Protestantism's lack of an ecclesiological counter-proposal had left the theological landscape with two politically problematic alternatives: Roman Catholicism and Protestant liberalism.[16] An evangelical alternative, however, was rendered almost impossible by the evangelical debate over the nature of the Kingdom. Henry especially fingered the dispensational stream of fundamentalist theology at this point. The construction of an evangelical theology of the role of the church in the world was hindered, Henry concluded, since dispensational ecclesiology virtually severed the New Testament *ekklesia* from the Kingdom purposes. This was the result, he explained, of the dispensationalist "postponement theory" in which Jesus' Davidic reign is rejected by the nation of Israel at His first advent. "As a consequence, the divine plan during this church age is concerned, it is said, only with 'calling out' believers," Henry noted. "This theory has gained wide support in the north during the past two generations; many persons automatically identify if [sic] not only with all premillennialism, but with all fundamentalism."[17] Nonetheless, Henry was not therefore resigned to a Reformed position that would see the Kingdom simply in terms of the spiritual blessings offered through the church.[18] In the place of these two options, he called for an evangelical ecclesiological appropriation of inaugurated eschatology. In terms of an evangelical doctrine of the church, he argued, the teachings of Jesus must be highlighted "both that the kingdom is here, and that it is not here."[19]

For Henry, the doctrine of the church is the fulcrum in which eschatology and soteriology meet in the Kingdom purposes of God. Thus, a Kingdom-oriented ecclesiology would be essential to the development of a theology of evangelical engagement. Therefore, the doctrine of the church must be understood biblically in terms of the redemptive progress of the Kingdom and the inaugurated reign of Christ over the regenerate community.[20] Only a Kingdom-oriented ecclesiology, he argued, could rescue Christianity from the unbiblical and unbalanced futurism he called them to discard.[21]

For Henry, the debates over the church were really part of the ongoing debates over the Kingdom and the role of the reign of Christ in the present era. Protestant liberalism's ecclesiology then "still subordinates the person of Jesus to the Kingdom-idea" in locating the Kingdom "in Jesus' work and teaching, not in His person" while others saw the restoration of the Israeli state as the coming of the Kingdom.[22] By calling for an evangelical ecclesiology, Henry and the postwar theologians thereby seemed to recognize that the problem was not that Protestant liberalism had too high a view of the church, but rather that it had too low a view, a concern borne out by the Social Gospel theologians' tendency to pit "the Kingdom" against the church.[23]

For Henry, however, the inauguration of the Kingdom in the current era meant that the "closest approximation of the Kingdom of God today is the Church, the body of regenerate believers that owns the crucified and risen Redeemer as its Head."[24] The relationship between the church and the Kingdom prevents either the politicization of the church or its withdrawal from the sociopolitical order. The Kingdom orientation, Henry argued, reclaimed ecclesiology as central to evangelical Christianity, thereby rescuing it from the notion that "the isolated local church, out of effective contact with the larger Christian fellowship, or that the isolated believer, maintaining his personal devotions in independence of the local church, is ethically self-sufficient."[25] This individualism, he asserted, infected earlier forms of fundamentalism with "the secular accentuation of individual life," resulting in the tendency to settle "ethical questions by a short-shrift legalism."[26] A theology of evangelical engagement, he concluded, could not start from bare individuals, but instead from "the moral perspective of an organic fellowship within which all walls of partition are demolished."[27] If the church is a sign of the coming Kingdom, Henry argued, the mission of the church's prayerful focus "must include within its scope Russian totalitarianism, Indian poverty, Korean suffering, American greed; it embraces the hospitals, the factories, the service clubs, the prisons, and the brothels."[28]

As a sign of the eschatological Kingdom, governed even now by the ascended Christ, Henry maintained, the church does not have the right to take over the reins of government, but it does have the responsibility to testify to the righteous justice of the Kingdom.[29] Indeed, he noted, the church is to model before the watching world the reality of the inaugurated Kingdom of Christ. The church as focus of Christ's reign in this age, Henry asserted, is what maintains the distinction between the church and the world.[30] The politics of the Kingdom enter the present era through the visible demonstration by the church of what it means to live under the eschatological reign of Christ by being a New Society called to "mirror in microcosm" the messianic rule in the new heavens and new earth.[31] This stance therefore cannot be fit into the theological/political categories of fundamentalist withdrawal, Social Gospel triumphalism, or Niebuhrian realism.[32]

This concern for the development of an evangelical theology of the relation between Kingdom and church was exegetically and theologically developed in the Kingdom theology of George Eldon Ladd. Ladd argued that an evangelical Kingdom ecclesiology would have to distinguish itself from several historic understandings of the church/Kingdom relationship.[33] The sociological interpretation, Ladd observed, sees the Kingdom as "the ideal social order to be achieved on earth by the church," a viewpoint represented by the postmillennialism of both old Princeton orthodoxy and the Social Gospel.[34] Ladd dismissed this view as assigning to the church an unbiblical role: "Evil will be overcome only by the supernatural advent of Christ to establish his Kingdom."[35] At the same time, however, Ladd turned his fire toward inadequate evangelical models of the relationship between the church and the Kingdom. Many in the Reformed tradition were unbiblical, he argued, in seeming to equate the Kingdom with the church, a position he traces from Augustine through the Reformers to several contemporary proponents of covenant theology, including biblical theologian Geerhardus Vos.[36] He likewise dismissed the "eschatological interpretation," with its cleavage between church and Kingdom, a position Ladd argued was conceived in the patristic era and continues in the consistent eschatology of Albert Schweitzer and, within evangelicalism, in dispensational theology.[37] Ladd was particularly energized against the dispensational understanding that posited a "parenthesis" between the present age of the church and the future age of the Kingdom.[38]

In the place of the prevailing covenant and dispensational models, Ladd offered a view of the church and the Kingdom based on his view of the "already/not yet" manifestation of the Kingdom in Christ, a vantage point that "finds the fundamental meaning of the Kingdom of God not in the church nor in an eschatological order nor in an earthly social order but in the rule of God himself."[39] This view, he contended, takes in the best features of the Reformed and dispensational approaches while allowing for the New Testament emphasis on ecclesiology:

> The Kingdom of God necessarily involves the church. The church is the people of the Kingdom, those who have accepted the redemptive rule of God. The rule of a King must have a people, and the church consists of those who have received the Kingdom of God (Mark 10:15), i.e., who have bowed before God's rule in Christ, and have been brought thereby into that sphere of life over which Christ reigns. They have been delivered from the powers of darkness and transferred into the Kingdom of Christ (Col. 1:13). They know the blessings of God's rule which are righteousness and peace and joy (Rom. 14:17). In addition, they are those destined to enter in its eschatological consummation.[40]

Even so, Ladd refused to identify the Kingdom with the church, but instead contended that the church exists as the instrument or agency of the Kingdom since it possesses the power of the keys of the Kingdom and the preaching of the gospel of the coming age.[41] "The Church therefore is not the Kingdom of God," he wrote. "God's Kingdom creates the Church and works in the world through the Church."[42] Ladd compared the church to first-century apocalyptic sects, such as that at Qumran, because it exists as "an eschatological community and a witness by word and deed to the sure victory of God's Kingdom."[43] As such, Ladd argued, "the church is an eschatological community not only because it witnesses to God's future victory but because its mission is to display the life of the eschatological Kingdom in the present evil age."[44] This means, Ladd concluded, that the church must preserve its distinction from the world without withdrawing: "As long as the church lives with a vital sense of an eschatological character and destiny, it will continue to be the church and not a part of the world."[45] The role of the church in the present age is therefore to serve as an instrument and custodian of the Kingdom in the midst of the kingdoms of this present epoch.[46] "It is therefore the church's duty to display in an evil age of self-seeking, pride, and animosity the life and fellowship of the Kingdom of God and of the Age to Come," Ladd concluded. "This display of Kingdom life is an essential element in the witness of the church to the Kingdom of God."[47]

KINGDOM ECCLESIOLOGY AND THE EMERGING EVANGELICAL CONSENSUS

In 1959, *Christianity Today* polled twenty-five of what it considered to be the world's leading theologians, a sampling that ranged from Paul Tillich to Cornelius Van Til, with the question, "What is the most vital issue facing contemporary Christianity?" Karl Barth responded with the question of the relationship between the church and the political powers. "How do you explain the fact that the large Christian bodies cannot pronounce a definite *yes* or *no* on the matter of atom warfare?" he asked. "What significance has this fact: (a) in regard to the Church's own message; (b) in regard to the world around her (the Church)?"[48] Evangelical E. J. Carnell of the still-fledgling Fuller Seminary, however, provided a much more basic concern, arguing that the doctrine of the church itself was the neglected issue that most needed to be addressed by Christian theology.[49]

In the years since, evangelical theology has provided renewed attention to this neglected doctrinal locus. As with the loci of eschatology and soteriology, evangelical theology would seem to have amassed a consensus on what was once perhaps one of the most troubling dissensions in the evangelical coalition, the relationship between the visible church and the Kingdom of God. As with the other two doctrinal focal points, this consensus seems at many levels to span the ideological fault-lines of contemporary evangelical theology as representatives of both the traditionalist conservative and reformist progressive wings of evangelical theology are moving toward a common understanding of the Kingdom orientation of the doctrine of the church.

On the conservative end of the evangelical spectrum, the effort toward a Kingdom ecclesiology is seen explicitly in the later, systematic writings of Carl Henry.[50] Henry's later work sketches out an incipient ecclesiology, though it seems to be constructed largely as a series of *ad hoc* responses to specific issues troubling the evangelical movement and its interaction with rival cognitive systems. Whereas Henry's early statements on the church seemed to focus on the political relationships of the church contra the claims of politicized ecumenicalism, the later, more systematic treatment does so contra the claims of liberation theology and other revolutionary movements. Henry self-consciously develops his ecclesiology within the context of his commitments to inaugurated eschatology and holistic soteriology. "When Christianity discusses the new society it speaks not of some intangible future reality whose specific features it cannot as yet identify, but of the regenerate church called to live by the standards of the coming King and which in some respects already approximates the kingdom of God in present history," Henry asserts.[51] Therefore, he concludes, a distinctively evangelical view of the church emerges from a prior commitment to Kingdom theology.[52] With such being the case, Henry emphasizes that neither personal redemption nor inaugurated eschatology can be understood without a concept of the church as an initial manifestation of the Kingdom of God, the focus of the "already" of the Kingdom in the present age.[53]

Henry warns therefore against politicizing the church in the manner of the ecumenical left because such efforts give false assurance to the unregenerate world that it can obtain salvation by "Christian" legislation. Nonetheless, believers who make up the church have citizenship in "two realms" and therefore possess "express political duties on the earth" that they must "pursue more vigorously than does unregenerate humanity."[54] Thus, for Henry, the fact that the church is an "approximation" of the eschatological Kingdom defines Christian political activity. The church *qua* church must engage the social and political structures because the church must counter the flawed assumptions of the world. Therefore, the eschatological community must "expound the factuality of the kingdom in its Edenic forfeiture, in its prophetic promise, in its Christological manifestation, in its apostolic proclamation, and in its ongoing conflict with alien powers that the risen Lord perpetuates through the regenerate society that he directs as commander-in-chief."[55]

The idea of the church as an eschatological community of the Kingdom is likewise developed within the reformist wing of evangelical theology, primarily through the writings of Stanley Grenz. Castigating the "parachurchicity" of contemporary evangelicalism, Grenz warns that evangelical theology "must recapture a credible ecclesiology," criticizing the individualistic emphases of conservative evangelical theologians such as Wayne Grudem and Millard Erickson.[56] Grenz and Henry, however, are not that far apart on their conception that the church must be understood within the Kingdom context of both inaugurated eschatology and cosmic soteriology.[57]

Like Henry, Grenz emphasizes the role of the regenerate church as an initial manifestation of the Kingdom, which exists as a sign to the outside power structures of what the mediatorial reign of Christ ultimately will come to be. For Grenz, therefore, this Kingdom orientation is necessary to understand what he means by the centrality of the "community of God" for the project of systematic theology. Likewise, the church as the present manifestation of the Kingdom community is necessary to inform the "already" and the "not yet" of the Christian eschaton.[58] The church is thus a realized aspect of the Kingdom program to the degree that the gathered community is "a sign of God's reign."[59]

For Grenz, like Henry, this focus on the church as Kingdom community is likewise informed by a holistic vision of salvation. The church is the model of the reconciliation and redemption that extends to every aspect of created existence.[60] This means, he argues, that since the future consummation of the Kingdom, as well as its present salvific inbreaking, are experienced in community, the church is "more than a collection of saved individuals who band together for the task of winning the lost" but is instead "the community of salvation."[61] As such, a renewed ecclesiology is essential to the attempt at an evangelical Kingdom theology.

As with eschatology and soteriology, the remarkable consensus within evangelical ranks on the Kingdom orientation of ecclesiology is perhaps best seen in the developments within the dispensational and covenantal traditions. Both streams of evangelical theology have seemed to recognize the respective obstacles to a coherent ecclesiology that they have contributed to the evangelical subculture. In so doing, both streams have sought to recover a more biblically informed vision of the church as regenerate community by exploring more fully how the church fits within the broader picture of a theology of the Kingdom of God in Christ. For both traditions this project has meant a reconception of the place of ecclesiology and the corporate nature of salvation in their respective systems. It has also meant a move toward rapprochement on the once thorny issue of ecclesiology.

Kingdom Ecclesiology and Dispensational Development

A unique understanding of the relationship between the church and the Kingdom is part of the very fabric of American evangelical dispensationalism. As dispensationalist theologian John Feinberg has noted, "the belief that the church is a distinctive organism" beginning with the inauguration of the new covenant is a distinctive of the system's view of the discontinuity between the Old and New Testaments.[62] This is borne out in the grassroots appeals of the evangelical dispensationalist popularizers as well as in the historic polemics over the "newness" of the church between dispensationalist and covenant theologians.[63] The newer generation of dispensational theologians would seem to offer a qualified endorsement of some of the contributions of traditionalist forms of dispensationalism to evangelical ecclesiology. Craig Blaising, for instance, hails Chafer's emphasis on the invisible church (an emphasis fueled, it might be argued, by Chafer's view of the coming apostasy of the visible church) as a forerunner of the postwar evangelical movement, insofar as it was "an encouragement of evangelical cooperative ministries which is based on the reality of the universal body of Christ."[64] Darrell Bock likewise hails the older forms of dispensationalism for fostering an emphasis on the priesthood of believers and the gifts of the Holy Spirit, an emphasis he claims contributed to the parachurch ministry structure of the contemporary evangelical movement.[65]

In many other ways, however, dispensational theology has recognized that its ecclesiology has had several problematic features. As many observers of American evangelicalism have noted, these features were woven in with dispensationalism's eschatological commitments and were widespread in their influence on the larger evangelical movement.[66] Many contemporary dispensational theologians have pointed to studies such as that of non-dispensationalist Michael Williams, who calls on dispensationalists to recognize that outside theologians such as Millard Erickson have accurately characterized a systemic flaw in dispensational theology, namely, the diminished role of the church.[67] Williams points to the inordinately "otherworldly strain" of C. I. Scofield's and Lewis Sperry Chafer's conception of Christians as "heavenly citizens" who are merely passing through the created order on their way to eschatological bliss.[68] Citing Chafer's conception of the church as a "missionary society" created to train witnesses for Christ, Williams sees the root of dispensationalism's weak ecclesiology in an eschatological grid that anticipates an apostate institutional church in the last days. With such being the case, dispensationalists have been forced to locate the primary work of the Holy Spirit within the individual, not within the believing community.[69] Ironically, Williams concludes that such individualism actually led to the encroaching secularism it was designed to protect against, since the dispensational believer could isolate himself from social, political, and educational concerns while living life "as if the gospel did not even exist."[70]

Progressives have faced the charge from more traditionalist dispensationalists that their ecclesiology abandons the *sine qua non* of the church as a distinct entity from Israel. And yet, the progressives have maintained the uniqueness of the church as a new covenant Spirit-body.[71] Nonetheless, the progressives have dramatically altered the understanding of the church in relation to the Kingdom, with a concept of the church as a "functional outpost" or "sneak preview" of the coming Kingdom. Because the church has been knit together by the Messiah Himself, and because it has received in inaugurated form the new covenant blessings He dispenses, the church is the focal point of the current regal activity of Christ. With such an understanding, many progressive dispensationalists propose that the church is to be a "workshop of Kingdom righteousness" in which the nature of the eschatological reign of Christ is revealed through its internal ministry, its external pronouncements, and even by its very makeup as a multinational Spirit-created entity.[72] As a matter of fact, some have suggested that the idea of the church as an initial manifestation of the Kingdom is "much more widely accepted" than the concept of an inaugurated Davidic kingship upon which it (arguably) rests.[73] This understanding of the church as Kingdom community comes with the progressive dispensational view of pneumatology as tied to the resurrection and ascension of Christ. Thus, Blaising and Bock do not simply relate the church to the Kingdom, but actually *define* the church in terms of the Kingdom.[74]

This concept is developed within progressive dispensationalism chiefly by Bock, who has called evangelical theology to transcend both the radical discontinuity of traditional dispensationalism and the radical continuity of traditional covenant theology in the understanding of Kingdom and church.[75] Thus, this reality informs the tension between the "already" and "not yet" aspects of the Davidic reign of Christ.[76] With this being the case, the dispensational relationship between the church and the world is more clearly defined in terms of the progress of the Kingdom. Because the church is the locus of Kingdom activity, Bock argues, progressive dispensational theology may contribute a sixth option to the five relationships between Christ and culture outlined by H. Richard Niebuhr.[77] In the place of these, Bock offers "Christ as the transformer of His community as a model for other cultures."[78] Since the church is the one visible manifestation of the invisible reign of the Davidic ruler who will one day exercise indisputable sovereignty over all peoples, Bock argues that the church must be able to say to the world through its efforts at social compassion and reconciliation across racial, economic, and gender lines, "if you want to see God and the promise of his powerful, transforming rule, look at what he is doing among us."[79] Blaising argues therefore that the church is "a revelation of the kingdom of God" and "an inaugurated manifestation of a holistic redemption" while at the same time qualifying the specific political nature of the church.[80]

Both progressive dispensationalists and their traditionalist critics recognize that this construct of a relation between church and Kingdom represents a shift in dispensationalist starting points toward sociopolitical engagement. Charles Ryrie believes this political element highlights exactly the fears more traditional dispensationalists have about the Kingdom-oriented ecclesiology of the progressives because "promoting kingdom righteousness in the present time is not the mandate of the church."[81] Progressive Robert Pyne argues instead that the progressive understanding of the church as an initial expression of the Kingdom of God closes "a theological loophole for those whose understanding of social ethics had been thrown out of balance by sin, controversy, and culture."[82] He further notes that the very effort to construct a serious ecclesiology has political ramifications because it counters the lingering effects of the reality that dispensationalism itself "was born as a separatist movement with a natural isolation from (and distrust of) existing social and ecclesiastical structures."[83]

Kingdom Ecclesiology and Covenantal Development

Twentieth-century Reformed theologian Louis Berkhof complained that, despite the centrality of the Reformation debates over ecclesiology, the American Reformed theological tradition had neglected the doctrine of the church.[84] While Berkhof's analysis is not without error, covenant theology has exhibited considerable ambiguity on the specific problem of relating the church to the Kingdom of God.[85] This in turn is related to the already-discussed tensions within Reformed theology over the nature of the Kingdom and the nature of salvation. George Eldon Ladd's complaint that American Reformed theology promoted an ecclesiological definition of the Kingdom would seem to find ample support, not only in the nineteenth-century Reformed tradition but also in the seminal writings of Geerhardus Vos.[86] In due time, the developments within Reformed evangelicalism seem to have listened to critiques such as that of Ladd, answering them by applying the developing Kingdom consensus to the doctrine of the church.[87] With such being the case, the Reformed ecclesiological development has been hinged to development on other doctrinal questions.

Edmund Clowney argued as early as the 1960s that confusion about the role of the church in relation to the Kingdom had led to the theologically slipshod politicization of Protestant denominations. This, he argued, was a direct result of a separation between soteriology and ecclesiology. The United Presbyterian Church's proposed 1967 revision to its confession of faith, Clowney argued, saw the mission of the church almost exclusively in terms of "social renewal" precisely because it believed the salvific goal of the Kingdom was the universal brotherhood of humanity under the Fatherhood of God.[88] Clowney maintained that the proposed confession not only merged the Kingdom with the church, but it also merged the church with the state, denying the state the "power of the sword" and charging the church with "establishing in the world the discipline of the house of God."[89] Against this view, Clowney, then president of Westminster Seminary, did not simply assert the "spirituality of the church," segregating the church off from political concerns. Nor did he spiritualize the Kingdom into an equation with the church. Instead, Clowney appropriated a Ladd-like Kingdom theology, which maintained both the "already/not yet" understanding of eschatology and a holistic vision of soteriology, to the mission of the church. This is to be understood, Clowney argued, by understanding the current form of the Kingdom in terms of Christ's present reign over the church and His fulfillment of the cultural mandate.[90]

Since this time, major work has been done within the modified covenantal stream in attempting to relate ecclesiology to a robust Kingdom theology. Covenant theologians have sought to emphasize the "newness" of the church as it is related to the exaltation of Jesus as ascended King, and heir of creation, even while maintaining the unity of the people of God and the church's identity as the "new Israel" of God.[91] The very existence of the church, argues Gaffin, means that the resurrected Jesus has received the inheritance of the Kingdom from the Father. "The Spirit, then, is the 'vicar' of Christ," Gaffin argues, pointing to the formation of the church at Pentecost. "As 'the Spirit of truth,' he has no agenda of his own; his role in the church is basically self-effacing and Christ enhancing, so much so that his presence in the church is, vicariously, the presence of the ascended Jesus."[92] Poythress likewise maintains that the dispensational and covenantal views on the church as a new work of the Spirit in continuity with the unity of the Old Testament people of God are not that divergent after all.[93] The newness of the new covenant church in relation to the Spirit demonstrates the doctrinal development here, as some traditional covenant theologians have accused modified covenantalists of adopting dispensationalist elements in both pneumatology and ecclesiology.[94]

Modified covenantalists further conclude that a Kingdom perspective on the church rules out the atomistic individualism inherent in evangelical theology, including at times within the Reformed confessional tradition. Gaffin, for instance, writes,

> There has been an undeniable and persistent tendency to isolate the work of the Spirit and eschatological realities from each other. This has happened as part of a larger tendency to divorce the present life of the Church from its future. Typically the work of the Spirit has been viewed individualistically as a matter of what God is doing in "my" life, in the inner life of the believer, without any particular reference or connection to God's eschatological purposes.[95]

Seeing the church as the focal point of the Spirit's present activity, and thus as the community of the Kingdom, Gaffin argues, means that the church is to see the community of faith as "of one piece with God's great work of restoring the entire creation, begun in sending his Son 'in the fullness of time' (Gal 4:4) and to be consummated at his return."[96]

Michael Williams concurs that the kind of "new creation" eschatology proposed by the modified covenantalists necessitates an emphasis, not just on soteriology, but on ecclesiology in contrast to the way in which "modern evangelicals miss the cosmic, earthly, and bodily reality of the promise of the future because our eschatological vision is more informed by the self-absorption and individualism of Western culture than it is by the biblical proclamation of the resurrection of the body and the restoration of creation."[97] Because the cosmic Kingdom salvation of which the church testifies is communal, Vern Poythress argues, "we ought not to vaporize or overly individualize the kind of fulfillment of Old Testament promises that we experience in union with Jesus Christ" since the Messiah is "Lord of the *community* of God's people, not simply Lord of the individual soul."[98]

With the church seen as the locus of present Kingdom activity, some modified covenantalists are even more emphatic in dismissing the traditionalist dispensationalist notion that the church is a "parenthesis" in the plan of God. Nonetheless, it also means that Reformed theology cannot consider redemption and the church as two sharply different categories. Anthony Hoekema, for instance, argues from Matthew 16:18-19 that "the church is not a kind of parenthesis or interlude awaiting [Jesus'] return to establish his kingdom, but that the church is the chief agency of the kingdom, since the keys of the kingdom are given to it (that is, to Peter as the representative of the church)."[99] This means, Hoekema argues, especially in light of the eschatological ecclesiology of Ephesians, that Reformed theology must stress "the centrality of the church in the redemptive purpose of God."[100]

Thus, modified covenantalists distinguish their view of the sociopolitical relationships of the church from those of Protestant liberalism, liberation theologies, theonomy, and the "spirituality of the church" tradition of southern Presbyterianism. For Gaffin, this Kingdom-oriented ecclesiology excludes both cultural triumphalism and isolationist surrender, both of which have served as perennial temptations for Reformed theology.[101] The key for Gaffin, contra theonomy, is that the cultural mandate is being fulfilled by the church as Kingdom community, a church "in the wilderness" of suffering. Thus, the church is ruled by the eschatological King, but is not yet ruling with Him.

Among the modified covenantalists, no one has been more forthright about the possibilities of Kingdom ecclesiology in defining the social and political responsibilities of the church than Edmund Clowney. Clowney argues that the church "as the community of Christ's kingdom on earth is a theo-political order," and therefore serves as "the heavenly *polis* on earth" as a colony of heaven in the present age.[102] As such, the church is not isolated from the state, but witnesses to the righteous demands of the Kingdom of God. Even so, Clowney contends, the spiritual nature of the church transforms its political objectives and methodologies.[103] With such being the case, Clowney argues, the church is not simply "an association for conducting public worship" but instead mirrors before the world the "politics of the Kingdom," the eschatological demands of corporate righteousness and justice.[104] The church anticipates the Kingdom, he asserts, by maintaining its unique distinction from the state since "Christ does not give the keys of the kingdom to Caesar, nor the sword to Peter before the parousia."[105] This is further seen, Clowney contends, in the way in which the family is restored to its creational intent within the structures of the church "in a way that the state, an institution made necessary by the fall, is not."[106]

KINGDOM ECCLESIOLOGY AND EVANGELICAL ENGAGEMENT: AN EVALUATION

The ecclesiological debates faced by the evangelical movement as Henry launched his call to sociopolitical engagement have largely been answered by developments within the movement's theological project. Evangelical theology seems to have reached a consensus about the relationship between the inaugurated Kingdom and the church. It is imperative that this consensus be examined to see whether it promises the kind of theological coherence promised by theologians across the spectrum of evangelical life. Furthermore, this call to a Kingdom ecclesiology carries with it implications for evangelical engagement, as Kingdom theology is focused on the very real social and political structures and stances of communities of faith.

Ecclesiology as a Theological Problem

This development addresses a longstanding area of pressing concern in contemporary evangelical theology, especially in light of the perennial struggles between dispensationalists, covenant theologians, and others within the evangelical coalition on the matter of the church. A move toward a Kingdom consensus in evangelical theology cannot avoid ecclesiology, since the church has been in many ways ground zero in the evangelical skirmishes over the Kingdom. The developments in evangelical Kingdom theology at this point, especially within the dispensationalist and covenant traditions, represent a real doctrinal advance toward a coherent and distinctively evangelical theology of the Kingdom. With such being the case, the ecclesiological developments here are largely spun off from the conceptual development of the Kingdom idea itself. A "parenthesis" understanding of the church is unworkable, even in a dispensationalist context, once a framework of inaugurated eschatology is embraced; on this much traditionalist dispensationalists are indeed correct. A starkly "spiritual" equation of the church with the Kingdom is impossible, even in the most Augustinian of Reformed communions, once "new creation" eschatology and a holistic vision of cosmic salvation are embraced.

Therefore, these developments mean that, in many ways, a real consensus has been reached among the divergent evangelical theological traditions, at least on the broader themes of Kingdom and church. Both dispensationalists and covenantalists, along with the mainstream of evangelical theology, now affirm that the church maintains some continuity with Israel as the people of God. The various sides of the Kingdom divide accept that the church is, at least in some sense, a new stage in the progress of redemption, brought about by the eschatological nature of the coming of Christ. They affirm that the church is not to be equated with the Kingdom, while also maintaining that the regenerate Body is an initial manifestation of the Kingdom. They agree that the church is the focal point in the present age of the inaugurated reign of Christ as Davidic Messiah. In so doing, evangelicals of the divergent traditions have confronted the theologically problematic areas of their respective systems, arriving at an ecclesiology that makes better sense of the theological assertions of the biblical texts on the nature of the church.

In evaluating this development, it would seem necessary to affirm that historic covenant theology has been correct in maintaining not only the presence of the Kingdom in the present age, but also some essential continuity between the Kingdom and the church in the biblical outworking of redemptive history. If one concedes that the New Testament concept of the church is as an eschatological reality, it is impossible to conceive of the church without reference to the Kingdom. This makes better sense of, for example, the way in which Jesus uses explicit Kingdom language in reference to the internal polity and external proclamation of the church (Matt. 16:18-19; 18:15-20). Thus, the apostle Paul is able to speak of "the God who calls you into His own kingdom and glory," not in terms merely of an eschatological glorification, but in terms of the present congregational activity of the church at Thessalonica (1 Thess. 2:10-14). The New Testament speaks of the church, not in terms of a "parenthesis" in the Kingdom program, but as those "upon whom the ends of the ages have come" (1 Cor. 10:11). Likewise, the New Testament never severs personal regeneration from membership in the church. Both individual regeneration (John 3:3) and the establishment of the church (Col. 1:3-14) are presented in terms of Kingdom realities. The initial fulfillment of Davidic promise at Pentecost meant not only a pneumatological dynamic in personal regeneration, although it certainly meant that (Acts 2:37-40). It also meant the simultaneous submission of the crowds to the membership and ordinances of the church (Acts 2:41-47). Thus, the Pauline writings pay special attention to the headship of Christ over the church in the present age (Eph. 1:22; 4:15; 5:23; Col. 1:18), a reality that is presented with both eschatological and soteriological ramifications.

It is here, however, that the Reformed tradition benefits from the older dispensationalism's equally biblical emphasis on the "newness" of the church as a dispensational advance. The dispensationalists were correct to maintain that the church in the New Testament is not simply a continuation, however quantitatively enhanced, of the *qahal* of the old covenant. Instead, the church is presented in the New Testament in decidedly eschatological terms, especially in reference to the initial fulfillment of the new covenant promise that the eschatological people of God "will all know Me from the least of them to the greatest of them" (Jer. 31:34). There is no Israelite Mission Board in the Old Testament, despite the conversion of a Rahab here and a Uriah there. The streaming of the nations to Israel is an eschatological hope—a hope the New Testament ties to the unity between the resurrected Jesus and His body, the church. Thus, the New Testament ecclesiology is inexplicable without an understanding of the Old Testament concept of the messianic Kingdom. When Jesus and the apostles use language of "flock" or "vineyard" or "household" for the church, they are not creating metaphors but reaching back to prophetic writings that promised a last days' restoration of Israel.

Progressive dispensationalism modifies this understanding of the "newness" of the church, but it nonetheless salvages those aspects that seem most resonant with New Testament theology. Thus, the newer Kingdom-oriented ecclesiology can speak of the church as an eschatological activity precisely because it is *not* a parenthesis. The new covenant community exhibits what the Old Testament prophetic writings consider the eschatological realities of the outpouring of the Spirit (Ezek. 36:24-28) and the rule of the Son of David over a submissive people of God (Ezek. 34:23). This makes sense of the way in which the apostle Peter relates the formation of the new Spirit-body as an epochal advance, one that at least partially fulfills the apocalyptic oracles of the end of the age (Acts 2:17-21; Joel 2:28-32). The apostolic message at the same time relates the formation of the church to the enthronement of the Messiah (Acts 2:22-36; Ps. 16:8-11; 110:1). For Peter, both of these fulfillments receive their immediate application within the membership of the church community (Acts 2:41-47). The newer consensus is not troubled therefore by the Kingdom implications of James's application of the Davidic covenant to the life of the church, including the almost mundane problem of Jewish-Gentile racial and theological skirmishes within the visible gatherings of the communities of Christians (Acts 15:12-21). James relates the initial fulfillment of the covenant, not to a visible shaking up of the world order, but to the "spiritual" matter of reconciliation within the church, a reconciliation that both Acts and the Pauline corpus consider to be of eschatological import precisely because of Messiah's pouring out of the Spirit onto the church (Acts 10:34–11:18; Eph. 2:11–3:11).

Thus, the emerging Kingdom ecclesiology fuses covenant theology's understanding of the church in continuity with Israel with dispensationalism's understanding of the church as a new manifestation of grace. Seeing the church through the prism of the Scripture's Christocentric focus, there is no room for a "parenthesis" church or any notion of "two peoples of God." As with the doctrine of salvation, this tension is resolved not by arguing for the "replacement" of a Jewish nation with a largely Gentile church, but by centering on the head/body relationship between the church and Jesus, the true Israelite. The New Testament does appropriate Old Testament Israelite language for the church, but it does so by seeing the church and her Messiah as an organic whole—not by seeing one group of people "replacing" another. Thus, the "newness" of the church is seen in the triumph of Christ—not as an interruption in salvation history. Israel is a barren and fruitless vineyard (Ezek. 19:10-14), precisely because she lacks the rule of the anointed messianic King (Ezek. 19:14). This thorn-infested vineyard of the Israelite nation is a theodicy issue—since the vineyard keeper sees His field yielding "wild grapes" (Isa. 5:1-7). And yet, in language resonant with the Genesis cultural mandate, there is always the prophetic promise that Israel would one day "blossom and put forth shoots and fill the whole world with fruit" (Isa. 27:6, ESV). The vineyard/fruitfulness language is applied to the church in the New Testament, but only because the eschatological community members are "branches" of the "true vine"—Jesus, the remnant of Israel (John 15:1-17). The church blossoms and bears fruit, but only through union with the Spirit-anointed Messiah of Israel (Isa. 11:1; Gal. 5:22-23). The same is true of the Old Testament motif of the Shepherd and His flock—kingly imagery of a ruler over a political body—specifically the house of Israel under the monarchy of the Davidic King (Jer. 23:1-8; Ezek. 34:11-24;

Mic. 2:12). Thus, when Jesus gathers "other sheep" into "one flock" with "one shepherd" (John 10:16), He is establishing *both* the newness of the church in redemptive history and the continuity of the church with Old Testament Israel. After all, the gathering of the "flock" in the Old Testament promises is the gathering together of Israel as a unified nation (Jer. 3:15-20; 31:10-11), but it is the *last days* gathering of the nation as a regenerate people. When the nation is restored, gathered into the one flock, it is then that they are "sons" of God, that they receive their inheritance and call God "Father" (Jer. 3:19).

Equally as evocative is the New Testament imagery of the church as "Bride of Christ." This language is not created out of nothing, but draws on the Old Testament's imagery of Yahweh and Israel as bride and bridegroom. And yet the Old Testament prophets charge Israel with adultery; she is a faithless wife (Ezek. 16:1-58; Jer. 3:20), who breaks God's covenant "though I was their husband" (Jer. 31:32, ESV).[107] The Old Testament prophetic hope maintains with equal clarity, however, that Yahweh's eschatological purpose is a faithful, purified Bride (Jer. 31:33-34)—a promise the New Testament identifies as the "one-flesh union" between Jesus and His church (Eph. 5:22-32). The day is coming, Yahweh promises, when Israel will "call me 'My Husband,' and no longer will you call me 'My Baal'" (Hos. 2:16, ESV). This day is linked with the cleansing of Israel from idolatry and the inclusion of those who were "not my people" into the Kingdom of Israel's God (Hos. 2:17-23). Moreover, the bridal imagery in the prophets is explicitly tied to father/son and shepherd/flock imagery regarding the relationship between Yahweh and Israel. Thus, the New Testament can claim that the "mystery" to which the creation ordinance of marriage points is the eschatological headship of Jesus over His church—a relationship that pictures both continuity and discontinuity with Old Testament Israel.

Ironically, while both dispensationalists and covenantalists are moving toward each other, a growing number of reformist evangelicals speak of ecclesiology in terms reminiscent of the *Scofield Reference Bible*. John Sanders, for instance, argues against charges of open theist heterodoxy on the contingency of divine prophecy by aligning himself with the classical dispensationalist understanding of the church as "a previously non-prophesied mystery/parenthesis."[108] This is not a minor detail in Sanders's proposal. Instead, Sanders adopts a *bona fide* Kingdom-offer theology that would have outraged even Scofield. Indeed, for Sanders, even the cross is contingent and comes about "only through God's interaction with humans in history."[109] Clark Pinnock likewise praises classical dispensationalism for recognizing the "flexibility of God: God offered Israel the kingdom in Jesus and his plan was thwarted, which led to a fresh initiative."[110] And yet, this "fresh initiative" is the Body of Christ, the church. Does Pinnock really wish to retread the diminished ecclesiology of classical dispensationalism?[111]

This deemphasis on the church in the plan of God by reformist evangelicalism springs from the exact same root the early evangelical theologians identified in classical dispensational fundamentalism: a failure to see the Christocentric character of Scripture. Bernard Ramm, for instance, faulted classical dispensationalism with speculation about prophecy charts and theories about postponed kingdoms and resumed animal sacrifices because dispensationalism failed to see how the whole scope of the divine purposes was related to the identity and mission of Jesus.[112] Classical dispensationalism abstracted both Israel and the church from the overarching purposes of God putting all things under the feet of Jesus as the focal point of all the creational intent and covenantal promise of God. Reformist evangelicalism, in several of its current forms, is returning to this exact same error. What does it do to the Christocentric center of Scripture when open theists contend that God intended to establish the kingly line of Saul of the tribe of Benjamin for perpetual rule over Israel, "but in light of Saul's disobedience God turns to another"?[113] Not only does such a suggestion do violence to prophetic passages such as Genesis 49:8-12, 27 that grant the preeminence and kingship to Judah, even more importantly it marginalizes the centrality of the incarnate Christ to the unveiling of God's purposes in history. Open theists are not alone among postconservatives in calling for a move away from a Christocentric Kingdom ecclesiology. Stanley Grenz critiques the Stone-Campbell churches for "limiting" their discussion of the church to "Christological images" such as the Body of Christ because such limitation "risks losing sight of the wealth of biblical metaphors that connect the church to the other Trinitarian persons, as well as overlooking the connection between the church and its Old Testament foundation."[114] Grenz contrasts Temple of the Spirit and royal priesthood imagery to "Christological images." And yet, this New Testament imagery is explicitly defined in terms of the identity of the triumphant Jesus as the Temple, the Spirit-anointed Messiah, and the true Israelite (Eph. 1:20–2:22; 1 Pet. 4:14; Rev. 1:5-6).

Without a clearly developed doctrine of the church, the benefits of inaugurated eschatology are virtually nullified, as it is almost impossible to differentiate between the "already" and the "not yet" aspects of the Kingdom. The move toward a Kingdom ecclesiology maintains rightly that the definition of the "already" reign of Christ is the church. This means that the righteousness and justice of the messianic order cannot be found, in the present age, in the arenas of the political, social, economic, or academic orders. Instead, the reign of Christ is focused in this age solely on His reign as Messiah over the people called into the Kingdom, namely, those who make up the church. The resurrection and ascension of Jesus are presented in the New Testament Scriptures as indeed granting to Jesus the cosmic ruling authority promised to the Son of David (Eph. 1:20-21), but this ruling authority is only visible, indeed in one sense only "already" fulfilled, in the context of the regenerate community of those in voluntary submission to the Kingdom of God in Christ (Eph. 1:22). Thus, in the Pauline writings, the mystery of the age, culminating in the universal reign of Christ, is seen in this present age only "through the church," wherein "the manifold wisdom of God might now be made known to the rulers and authorities in the heavenly places" (Eph. 3:9-10, ESV). This is likewise why Paul can write of Christ's headship over "the body, the church" in the same context as he writes of the exhaustively cosmic (and therefore, by definition, political) reign of Christ. The cosmic reign finds its expression, for now, within the church. And so the doctrine of the church brings together the prevalent biblical themes of the preeminence of Christ, the warfare against the demonic powers, and the restoration of the cosmos.

Seeing the church in this way, in terms of an already developed view of the Kingdom, the emerging consensus rightly maintains the New Testament interrelationship between Christology, pneumatology, and ecclesiology. A doctrine of the Holy Spirit unloosed from the doctrines of the Kingdom of God and the person and work of Christ can be a dangerous doctrinal path for Christian theology. In terms similar to those of Richard Gaffin and Sinclair Ferguson, moral philosopher Oliver O'Donovan persuasively makes the point, for example, that Christians can understand the Holy Spirit only by understanding Him to be the Spirit *of Christ*. This carries important ramifications for ecclesiology. "If we forget this, our talk of the Holy Spirit floats free of its Christological reference, and the dangers of Montanism are not far away," O'Donovan warns. "Too often the church's life has been discussed in isolation from the historical existence of Christ, a distortion which can lead not only to the charismatic waywardness traditionally associated with Montanism but to the institutional stiffness of the self-posited church order."[115] O'Donovan's prescription for maintaining a Christological and eschatological doctrine of the Holy Spirit is in perfect concert with that of the emerging evangelical consensus, namely, to link ascension and Pentecost by understanding "the special gifts and manifestations of the Spirit as the consequence of Christ's coronation."[116]

This is supported exegetically by texts such as Ephesians 4:8, in which the church's gifts are seen as directly related to the inaugurated reign of the resurrected and ascended Christ. In so doing, the development toward a Kingdom-oriented ecclesiology takes seriously the manner in which the New Testament uses "Kingdom-like" language in reference to the community of the church. In the classical debates among evangelicals over church/Kingdom relationships, both sides rarely have focused the argument where the varying sides now seem to have found consensus, namely, the way in which the New Testament focuses both the Kingdom and the church on a common Christological referent. Thus, Douglas Farrow rightly gives attention to this theme when he argues,

> Ephesians, for example, makes it quite plain that the church is founded in and with the ascension of Christ, who by virtue of his heavenly session is given to it as "head over everything." The ecclesial communion as such is the prophetic sign to the world that God has organized all things around the one whom he has enthroned at his right hand. The church has cosmic significance, precisely in its anticipation of the appearance of that order.[117]

The church, then, does not exhaustively define everything that the canon means by "Kingdom," a point that Jesus seems to accentuate when He refuses to disclose to the apostolic community the "times or epochs" of the coming Israelite restoration (Acts 1:6-7). Nonetheless, the church is a vehicle or sign of the Kingdom inasmuch as it now reflects the rule of the very same Jesus who one day will exercise global monarchy.

At the same time, the developing Kingdom ecclesiology better maintains the New Testament understanding of the relationship between ecclesiology and soteriology, a connection that, again, covenant theology guarded more carefully than traditional dispensationalism, although both streams had their problematic areas at this point. The emerging consensus recognizes the centrality of the church in the purpose of salvation, a centrality too often overlooked in evangelical revivalism. While the conversionist zeal of American evangelicalism rightly rebelled against sacramental notions of grace mediated through ecclesiastical bodies, the disjunction between salvation and the church has failed far too often to come to grips with New Testament warnings that present those who are out of fellowship with the church as unbelievers on the brink of the wrath of God (Heb. 10:19-39; 1 John 2:19). Thus, the New Testament does not present the sacrificial, substitutionary atonement as directed toward isolated individuals.[118] Instead, the atonement is directed in the New Testament toward the gathering of a church (Acts 20:28; Eph. 5:22-33). Thus, the Pauline transfer from the "domain of darkness" into the Kingdom of Christ (Col. 1:13) is directed corporately and not merely individualistically.[119] Hence, even the most individual-oriented of New Testament texts present the goal of salvation as salvation into the community of the church. The Pauline teaching on election in the first chapter of Ephesians, for example, deals with individual election and not with some notion of "corporate election."[120] Nonetheless, the purpose of Paul's teaching here is not simply to expound on the way of individual redemption, but also to demonstrate how sinful, wrath-deserving *individuals* find themselves in a new community, "the church, which is his body, the fullness of him who fills all in all" (Eph. 1:22-23, ESV).[121] Thus, as Tom J. Nettles points out, even the New Testament doctrine of individual election has to do with corporate relationships within the covenant community of the church.[122]

The recognition of the Kingdom orientation of the church likewise serves to make sense of the specific way in which the church is the arena in which the holistic and relational aspects of the Kingdom salvation manifest themselves. Theologian Gerry Breshears rightly notes that the manifestation of the Kingdom in the present age is not theocratic rule over the nations, but is instead "the presence, gifts, and fruit of the Spirit, forgiveness, regeneration, justification, and authority to proclaim redemption from spiritual bondage."[123] Nonetheless, evangelical theology too often has failed to note that these Kingdom blessings are described in the New Testament as being experienced within the locus of the church, and not simply in the isolation of the believer's personal experience. Thus, the apostle Paul does not simply conclude that reconciliation between Jew and Gentile is a future-oriented Kingdom reality, although he writes of it in eschatological terms.[124] Instead, he argues that this Kingdom reconciliation finds expression in the current social relationships within the church (Eph. 2:11-22). Paul calls for the Corinthian church to create a countercultural system for dealing with internal political and economic conflicts, based on the fact that the church will "judge the world" in the eschaton (1 Cor. 6:1-11). Immediately after describing the dual outcomes of the ways of the flesh and the Spirit in terms of eternal Kingdom existence, Paul commands the Galatian congregation to maintain ministry to outsiders, but especially to those "of the household of faith" (Gal. 6:10, ESV). Likewise, James directs the churches to order their internal socioeconomic relationships based on their eschatology. Because the poor, though marginalized in the larger society, will one day share in the eschatological rule over the nations with Christ, they should have equal standing in the social and political relationships within the church (James 2:1-7).

With such being the case, these developments successfully retrieve the emphasis of both the Old and New Testaments on the communal nature of the Kingdom of God, in both the "already" of the present age and the "not yet" of the age to come. This is a theme that encompasses both the Mosaic and Johannine language of the redemption of the people of God, a redemption that transforms the people into "a kingdom of priests" (Ex. 19:6; Rev. 1:6). In this respect, Stanley Grenz and his followers in the call for "reformist evangelicalism" are correct to challenge the inordinate individualism inherent in evangelical theology in light of the biblical emphasis on community, a concern that is unique neither to Grenz's contemporaries nor to the reformist project.[125] Indeed, the call to rein in evangelical individualism with a more biblical model of community, focused on the church, was offered by no less a parachurch activist than Francis Schaeffer.[126] In seeking to revision a "communitarian" understanding of Christian theology, Grenz rightly argues that the New Testament focus on the church is often confused in contemporary evangelicalism with the individual believer as the primary starting point for theological reflection, an emphasis reflected in the piety and hymnody of evangelicalism as well as in the folk mores influenced by evangelicalism and fundamentalism.[127]

Grenz is on shakier footing, however, when he argues that this downgraded ecclesiology is a result of a Kingdom focus rather than a "community" focus as the integrative motif of evangelical theology.[128] This is to be attributed, Grenz argues, to the lack of content inherent in the term "Kingdom," a very real concern in light of the multifarious uses of the "Kingdom" concept in the twentieth century.[129] Grenz proceeds to argue further that biblical ecclesiology demonstrates that the centrality of the Kingdom is superseded in Scripture by a more fundamental interpretive motif, that of community, so that "the concept of community forms the content of the kingdom of God." This contention is problematic in light of the fact that, as noted in this study, the nature of the "Kingdom" in contemporary evangelical theology is rather sharply defined. Grenz's preferred alternative of "community," however, suffers from competing and contradictory definitions even from those who share Grenz's postmodern communitarian commitments.[130]

Grenz's further contention that the Kingdom motif is subservient to the community motif in Scripture is even more dubious. While Grenz is correct that the goal of the eschatological Kingdom is, as noted above, not merely a Kingdom but a Kingdom community, he is less persuasive when he defines the biblical priorities. "When God's reign is present—that is, when God's will is done—community emerges," Grenz writes. "Or, stated in the opposite manner, the emergence of community marks the presence of God's rule and the accomplishing of God's will."[131] And yet, Scripture does not argue that the emergence of just *any* community signals the reign of God, only a community formed by the Spirit under the sovereign lordship of the exalted Christ.[132]

Thus, the New Testament presents the Kingdom community in terms of its relationship to a Head and King, the sovereign covenant Messiah who is establishing His reign in the midst of the Body (Matt. 18:20; John 14:18; 18:37; 1 Cor. 12:12-31; 2 Cor. 6:14-18; Eph. 2:20-21; 3:21; 5:23; Phil. 3:20; Col. 1:18; 2:6-15; 1 Pet. 2:4-10; 1 John 5:19-20; Rev. 1:19-3:22). The developments toward an evangelical Kingdom ecclesiology, especially within the modified covenant and dispensational traditions, maintain Grenz's helpful call for a community focus while at the same time understanding that it is the Kingdom that defines the community, and not the other way around.[133] In so doing, the emerging consensus maintains the New Testament emphasis on the church as community without sacrificing its Christocentric and eschatological orientation.[134]

These developments toward a Kingdom ecclesiology likewise do justice to the New Testament description of the church's witness to the reality of the coming Kingdom. This is illustrated in the Petrine description of the church as "living stones," which proclaim by their very existence as a corporate body "the excellencies of Him who has called you out of darkness into His marvelous light" (1 Pet. 2:4-10). This internal ordering of the church, according to Peter, has an external focus as the countercultural Kingdom community witnesses to the Gentile nations (1 Pet. 2:12) and particularly to the governing authorities (1 Pet. 2:13-17) and to the economic authorities (1 Pet. 2:18-24) of the righteousness of the Kingdom manifested in their midst, a Kingdom described in the decidedly messianic and Davidic language of submission to the "Shepherd" (1 Pet. 2:25). Thus, the "salt and light" (Matt. 5:13-14) aspect of Christian relationship to the world structures is not biblically limited to Christians as individuals, but to them corporately as the church, a point that is bolstered by Jesus' reference to believers in this context as a community—a "city on a hill"—before the watching world (Matt. 5:14-16), placing the new covenant people of God in continuity with Israel's charge to be a "light to the peoples" (Isa. 51:4, ESV) in terms of their relationship to the Davidic monarch and in terms of their internal justice and righteousness.

Thus, the newer developments toward a Kingdom ecclesiology, especially in terms of sociopolitical engagement, resolve many of the tensions among evangelicals on the relationship between Israel and the church. Whatever differences may exist among evangelicals on the relationship between the Old Testament theocracy and the New Testament assembly, it is indisputable that the New Testament texts do offer the (usually poor) example of Old Testament Israel in the ordering of the internal life of the *ekklesia*. In 1 Corinthians 5:9-13, for example, the apostle Paul cites the political structuring of Old

Testament Israel from Deuteronomy in his admonition for the church to maintain internal purity. While the apostle uses decidedly political language to command church discipline, he simultaneously negates the church's coercive power over the social and political structures: "For what have I to do with judging outsiders?" (1 Cor. 5:12). This is consistent with the teaching of Jesus, who used the standard of justice from the law code of Old Testament Israel (Deut. 19:15) when speaking of principles of congregational disciplinary practices (Matt. 18:16), an application repeated by the apostle Paul in a virtually identical context (1 Tim. 5:19).

If covenant theologians were more theologically sound in maintaining the essential continuity between church and Kingdom, it must also be noted that the older dispensationalist tradition was at least partially right in its fear of an over-developed ecclesiology. Evangelical theologian Donald Bloesch rightly warns, "In forging a new eschatological vision, we should not minimize the role of the church."[135] This is a call largely heeded by the emerging evangelical consensus on ecclesiology. Still, Bloesch also calls evangelicals to repudiate the ecclesiastical skepticism of the apocalyptic tradition: "Evangelicals of the dispensationalist variety often refer to the 'twilight of the church' and issue a call to separation from the institutional church, which they regard as apostate."[136] Bloesch's critique here is partly right, since the dispensational Bible conference movement did seem to have an inherently anti-ecclesiological focus, and often this was closely tied to a particular view of the eschatological apostasy of the visible church.[137] Even so, it must be conceded that dispensationalists noticed, perhaps long before others in conservative American Protestantism, that many of the mainline Protestant churches were, in fact, apostate.[138] Thus, dispensationalism engendered a healthy skepticism. The church is indeed to point to the Kingdom, but the New Testament makes clear that it can do otherwise. Just as the church is to be wary of a totalitarian anti-Christ government, the older dispensationalist tradition rightly maintained, Christians must beware a spiritually totalitarian anti-Christ church government.[139] While this skepticism might have been fueled, and perhaps often perverted, by an inordinate apocalypticism, it is in continuity with the Reformation tradition itself. After all, several Reformed confessional documents speak of the papal office as "antichrist," not out of a populist apocalypticism, but out of a concern that the Roman church structure had co-opted the kingly prerogatives belonging only to Christ.[140] This skepticism could serve as an antidote to a Reformed tradition that has too often found itself in recent years unable to articulate theologically a reaction to doctrinal deviations within its own ecclesiastical structures.[141]

This skepticism, however, along with the previously examined problem of evangelical individualism, leads directly into what may be the most obvious area of theological significance in this project toward an integration of Kingdom theology and ecclesiology; namely, the consideration of ecclesiology itself. Fundamentalists and evangelicals can hardly be blamed for seeking parachurch avenues for ministry, after orthodox Protestants increasingly were disenfranchised by liberals and moderates within the mainline denominations.[142] At a time when the mainline denominations were redefining the mission of Christianity in terms of social action, evangelicals can be appreciated for seeking to salvage their soteriology from their ecclesiology. Perhaps unwittingly, however, evangelicals saw themselves as protecting the gospel from the church. The first casualties of the parachurch nature of evangelicalism were what evangelical leaders considered "denominational distinctives" not conducive to parachurch cooperation and a united front against modernism. E. J. Carnell, therefore, in frustration dismissed denominational confessional attention to distinctives as a hindrance to world evangelization.[143] At the same time, the opening convocation of the National Association of Evangelicals featured a similar assault on "denominational distinctives" by Harold J. Ockenga:

> If the cross of Christ Himself cannot unite true Christians there is no other possibility for their unification. Baptism should not be a reason for separation of Christ-believing Christians today. Why cannot we have tolerance enough to understand both sides? Different church governments and many other differences are insignificant and almost foolish if Christ is put in the highest place where He belongs. Moreover, denominations are no longer the boundary line between the world and the church but rather help to increase the confusion; denominations are only monuments of old arguments of our forefathers; the reasons for most of these have long since passed out of existence and only the separation caused by the arguments continues to live on. Yes, between many of us in our denominations there is less fellowship than there would be in a good Rotary club, for the simple reason that we do not have any sense of unity.[144]

Henry meanwhile almost triumphantly announced the arrival of a genuinely evangelical parachurch movement that could unite conservative Christians "without overstressing denominational distinctions."[145]

Such statements by Henry, Ockenga, and Carnell are instructive when examined alongside those of Social Gospel pioneer Walter Rauschenbusch, who said,

> The Kingdom of God is not confined within the limits of the Church and its activities. It embraces the whole of Christian life. It is the Christian transfigu-

ration of the social order. The Church is one social institution alongside of the family, the industrial organization of society, and the State. The Kingdom of God is in all these, and realizes itself through them all.[146]

While evangelicals would never have equated the church with the "industrial organization" and so forth, they committed a very similar error by subsuming the emphasis on the church and its biblical prerogatives and distinctives to an amorphous "movement," which was clearly of first importance to them. Despite all their best efforts to oppose the Social Gospel liberals, at the point of ecclesiology Henry and the postwar evangelical movement fell into precisely the same error as Rauschenbusch—namely, the tendency to replace the church with "Kingdom priorities."

Henry's call for an evangelical ecclesiology, therefore, could hardly have amounted to much when he responded to critics of the parachurch orientation of his movement in the following manner:

How does a group of devoted church members, actively engaged in the Church's primary task, become "isolated from the Church"? In such a context, what does "isolation from the Church" mean? Is it anything more than isolation from the ecclesiastical bureaucracy? Is it time someone asked the ecumenical critics of evangelicals, "What is this 'Church' from which some evangelical missionaries are isolated?"[147]

This sarcasm-laced response reveals perhaps more than Henry consciously intended. If the sum and substance of biblical ecclesiology is the devotional instruction of individuals and cooperation for world evangelization (hence, Henry's contention that parachurch evangelicals were "engaged in the Church's primary task"), then "the church" could indeed be seen as groups ranging from Campus Crusade for Christ to Young Life to the National Association of Evangelicals. Thus, evangelical theologians such as Henry were able to divorce the "large" questions of epistemology and the content of the gospel from the "insignificant" matters of the church.[148] It is difficult to refute Reformed historian John Muether's contention that "Henry's commitment 'for Christ and his Kingdom' (to use the motto of his alma mater) does not seem to work itself out through the church."[149]

And yet, as many even among Henry's most ardent supporters admit, the plastic nature of the parachurch coalition he envisioned spelled the doom of the evangelical "movement" itself.[150] This is seen in the fact that Henry's theological and apologetic legacy is maintained, not within the broad mainstream of parachurch evangelicalism, but instead within the conservative wing of the

Southern Baptist Convention, whose commitment to "denominational distinctives" would no doubt have been labeled "sectarian" by the early evangelical theologians, Henry included. "It would not be going too far to say that
Henry has been a mentor for nearly the whole SBC conservative movement,"
observes one historian, citing Henry's influence on Baptist conservatives such
as R. Albert Mohler, Jr., Richard Land, and Mark T. Coppenger.[151] When
Henry's *God, Revelation, and Authority* volumes were republished near the
end of the twentieth century, it was the result of cooperative efforts between
an evangelical publisher and a think tank led by confessional Southern
Baptists.[152]

Indeed, a confessional evangelicalism, informed at crucial points by
Henry's theological contributions, must confront an evangelical left that is now
even more "parachurch" than Henry and his postwar colleagues. This is true,
in spite of the "community of faith" emphasis of Stanley Grenz and his fellow
reformists. By refusing to see the church as the unique locus of the work of the
Spirit, through the proclamation of divine revelation, Grenz unwittingly
expands "parachurch" to include popular culture as a vehicle for divine revelation. This has profound—and profoundly negative—consequences for evangelical ecclesiology. Grenz argues that evangelical theology "must move
beyond the widely-held assumption that the church is the *sole* repository of *all*
truth, and the *only* location in which the Holy Spirit is operative."[153] Instead,
Grenz proposes that evangelical theology must realize that "God's Spirit—who
is the Creator Spirit—is present everywhere in the world, and consequently the
Holy Spirit can speak through many media."[154] One would be hard-pressed to
find an evangelical who has ever held that the church is the source of "all
truth." Nonetheless, Grenz seriously errs when he obscures here the church as
the unique manifestation of the Kingdom of God in the midst of the kingdoms
of this world, a uniqueness that is maintained specifically by the manner in
which Messiah governs His community through biblical revelation.

With this "uneasy conscience" of evangelical ecclesiology, the renewed
attention to the doctrine of the church offered by the various expressions of
Kingdom theology should be welcomed. It is this problem realization that
prompts theologians such as Richard Lints to suggest that the movement needs
fewer "evangelical theologians" and more "Baptist theologians, Presbyterian
theologians, and so on."[155] It is, however, the "so on" at the end of this statement that reveals the lingering problem of evangelical ecclesiology. This is perhaps the most flawed aspect of the emerging moves toward an evangelical
Kingdom ecclesiology. After all, the developments, especially within dispensationalism and Reformed theology, have thus far been an almost exclusively

parachurch matter, as scholars from both sides have discussed the issues within the context of professional theological society meetings and scholarly monographs. Mark Noll, therefore, is correct when he notes that, whatever progressive dispensationalist theologians such as Craig Blaising may argue about Hal Lindsey and the popular apocalyptic writers as "an eccentric deviation from dispensationalism," the "magnitude of sales, however, seems to show that the kind of dispensationalism represented by *The Late Great Planet Earth* reflects a much wider swath of evangelical thinking than the carefully qualified theological conclusions of the progressive dispensationalists."[156] Noll's point is bolstered when the church's appropriation of dispensationalism at the congregational level is more clearly seen in the *Left Behind* novels than in any theological proposal.[157]

Still, the efforts to construct a Kingdom theology do indeed offer a first step to a reconsideration of the doctrine of the church. The New Testament doctrine of the church, however, is never treated in isolation from the *definition* of the church, a definition that must be articulated not only in terms of relationships with Old Testament Israel and the eschatological Kingdom but in terms of the *membership* and *ordinances* of the church as well.[158] A consideration of evangelical ecclesiology will also necessitate a reconsideration of the lingering parachurch mentality of the evangelical coalition itself.[159] The early fundamentalists and evangelicals were correct that issues such as baptism, the Lord's Supper, church polity, and the biblical basis for church membership are not "first-order" issues requiring separation in terms of cooperative interdenominational endeavors, unlike the "fundamentals" of biblical authority at stake in the denominational skirmishes. It is a mistake, however, to assume that these "distinctives" are *not* matters of biblical authority, or that they have nothing to do with the church's "primary task" of evangelism and missions.

Evangelical theologian Wayne Grudem, for instance, vigorously contends that "baptism in the New Testament was carried out in one way: the person being baptized was *immersed* or put completely under the water and then brought back up again."[160] He asserts that the meaning of the word *baptizo* is "'to plunge, dip, immerse' something in water."[161] Nonetheless, he (remarkably) concludes this robust definition of baptism by asserting that "baptism is not a major doctrine of the faith," meaning that Baptists and paedobaptists should not make the meaning and mode of baptism a matter of congregational membership, but should leave such questions to individual conscience.[162] Can there be such an option if the meaning of the word *baptizo* is clearly, as Grudem suggests, the immersion of a believer? Nor is Grudem alone at this point. Millard Erickson, for instance, points to biblical evidence, marshaling the arguments of George Beasley-Murray and Karl Barth, to argue for the New Testament equation of *baptizo* with immersion. He concludes his treatment of the issue, however, by noting that immersion "may not be the only valid form of baptism," but that it "fully preserves and accomplishes the meaning of baptism."[163] Erickson then counsels, "Whatever mode be adopted, baptism is not a matter to be taken lightly."[164] One must wonder about the logical consistency here: if baptism is defined in the New Testament as the immersion of believers, then how can evangelicals take seriously a baptism that is not, in fact, baptism? Moreover, how are evangelicals to recognize the reign of Christ over His church through the Scriptures when the central command given by Christ to the church is described in terms of "whatever mode" the congregation deems best to use? If the word uttered as a command by the resurrected Christ to "baptize" the converts of all nations (Matt. 28:19) did indeed mean specifically the immersion of a believer, how can evangelical theology, much less local congregations and mission boards, consider it a "minor matter" best left to individual decision?[165]

These matters are not unrelated to the Kingdom orientation of biblical ecclesiology. Evangelical ecclesiology is, after all, ultimately related to evangelical epistemology, meaning that ecclesiology cannot be separated from the larger issue of the authority of Christ. When backed against the wall by the *Sword of the Lord* on the right and the World Council of Churches on the left, some of the movement's leaders seemed to equate frank confessional dialogue on the nature of the church with the earlier fundamentalist factionalism, even seeming to equate ecclesiological discussion with the fundamentalist tendency to make secondary issues of primary importance.[166] And yet this is a misdiagnosis, at least at one level, of the conservative attitude toward ecclesiological issues, during the controversies early in the century. The fundamentalists were, after all, quite trans-denominational, as the varying confessional commitments of the contributors to *The Fundamentals*[167] will demonstrate. The most heated ecclesiological battles were between the same parties who were sparring over matters of biblical authority. This is precisely because, quite often, these two issues were being fought on the same battlefield.[168] If evangelicals are to recover fully a doctrine of the church, this kind of ecclesiological gravity must be recovered, including within its discussion the uncomfortable tensions among evangelicals on the questions of the membership, ordinances, and structure of the church.

It might be asked, then, whether the "parenthesis" theory of the church really has been rejected in conservative American Protestantism, or whether it has found a new incarnation. It is not, after all, as though these questions can somehow be segregated from the larger question of the relationship between the church and the Kingdom. The ecclesiological fuzziness of dispensationalist theologian Lewis Sperry Chafer is not difficult to explain, given his understanding of the place of the church as an interruption in the Kingdom program. He could write, therefore, that "all should be saved before they join a church; and, if saved, it is normal for the individual to choose the fellowship of the people of God in one form or another."[169] This is perfectly consistent since, for Chafer, the corporate aspects of salvation are to be received in the Kingdom, a wholly future event. It is not as easy to fit theologically the anemic ecclesiological proposals offered by contemporary evangelical theologians, who hold to no such "parenthesis."

The priority of the church ordinances and structure in the systems of some broad evangelical theologians would almost seem to be an unconscious and ironic appropriation, by the most "non-dispensational" of parachurch evangelical theologians, of an ultra-dispensationalist hermeneutic that views the ordinances and other particular directives of ecclesial life as "parenthetical" appendages of a "church age" in which believers bide time until the eschaton. Such a treatment, however, is inconsistent with a New Testament ecclesiology that (as these very theologians correctly recognize) sees the church as a manifestation of the Kingdom itself. The ordinances, therefore, are presented in the New Testament as clearly eschatological in nature. Baptism is a matter of inaugurated eschatology, considered by Paul as a sign, not only of union with Christ in the present, but also of resurrection in Him in the eschaton (Rom. 6:1-11).[170] The Petrine teaching likewise presents baptism in light of the eschatological enthronement of Christ after His resurrection, ascension, and triumph over the powers (1 Pet. 3:20-21). Likewise, Jesus treats the question of the Lord's Supper eschatologically in its institution, not only by relating it to the new covenant but also by tying it to the messianic table in the Kingdom of God (Luke 22:16-17, 20).[171]

Evangelical theology must contend with what paedobaptist evangelical theologian Donald Bloesch calls "the scandal of infant baptism."[172] As Bloesch recognizes, this "scandal" is about more than the administration of the ordinances, but rather touches on the undisciplined ethos of contemporary evangelical congregational life. Any development of a Kingdom-oriented ecclesiology must address the root of the baptism controversies, namely, the debate over a regenerate church membership. If the church is a sign of the eschaton, evangelicals must ask how this approximation can include not only those "upon whom the ends of the ages have come" (1 Cor. 10:11), but their unregenerate children as well.[173] If inaugurated Kingdom blessings are received by those who "see the Kingdom of God" through the new birth (John 3:3), then it would seem that the church, as an initial manifestation of the Kingdom, must reflect in its membership those who have experienced this new birth and are participants in the Kingdom blessings of the new covenant. This means, in short, that evangelical theology must begin to see congregational discipline as a matter of eschatological significance. Such would not be a new phenomenon, but would point back, in some ways, to the best aspects of the debates of an earlier era over church polity. As one nineteenth-century Baptist theologian recognized, for instance, a biblical ecclesiology seeks, however fallibly, "to draw the line of distinction between the church and the world, exactly where God will place it at the last day."[174]

Ecclesiology as a Political Problem

As with the postwar generation of evangelical theologians, the question of the church's relationship to the social and political powers of the present order is still a matter of controversy, though perhaps in different manifestations than in the context of mid-century Protestant cultural hegemony.[175] The developments within evangelical theology toward a Kingdom-oriented ecclesiology, however, offer a starting point for a new paradigm for evangelical sociopolitical engagement, one anticipated by evangelical pioneers such as Henry and Schaeffer. The view of the church as an initial manifestation of the Kingdom in the contemporary evangelical consensus avoids the most problematic ecclesiological features of Social Gospel liberalism, ecumenical activism, and revolutionary liberation theology by maintaining a sharp distinction between the church and the world and by locating the primary locus of Kingdom sociopolitical reconciliation within the church. Instead conservative American Protestantism was correct in the warning that the Social Gospel sought to replace, in many ways, the church with the Kingdom. Walter Rauschenbusch and his followers, therefore, did not simply wish to address the activity of the church as a Kingdom institution. They wished to redefine both the term *church* and the term *Kingdom*.[176] The disastrous results of early-twentieth-century Social Gospel activism can be linked directly to the attempt to replace the church with a "Kingdom of God" defined in societal terms, an agenda that is, on its face, as much political as theological.[177]

This problem is replicated in the theonomic movement, which seeks to apply the political elements of the Old Testament theocracy and the eschatological Kingdom, not to the church, but to the outside society.[178] The emerging consensus of the church as a Kingdom community must therefore articulate, contra attempts on both the left and the right, that the Kingdom of

God in this era is manifested in the regenerate church, not in any secular government. This is a more difficult task than it first appears since an entire generation of evangelicals has grown accustomed to seeing texts on the Old Testament theocracy or the Kingdom applied to the United States. Although such interpretations often come from evangelical pulpits and press releases (including some which are doggedly dispensationalist), they also emanate from the bully pulpits of the national civil religion, from Ronald Reagan's "shining city on a hill" metaphor to Bill Clinton's naming his 1992 platform "the New Covenant."[179]

A vigorous reconsideration of ecclesiology therefore can serve to remind evangelicals of what the Social Gospel failed to learn; namely, that, as Hauerwas notes, the primary audience of the Christian social imperative "is not America, but the church."[180] This would transform the content of some of the objectives of evangelical social and political action. For instance, First Amendment scholar Charles Haynes notes that the "culture wars" over educational reform have often been focused on what he considers to be two "failed models," that of the "sacred public school" and the "civil public school."[181] Haynes is correct to note that much of the activism within the Christian political right has assumed a model in which the system favors a "generalized Protestant Christianity," a prospect that faded with "a vanishing Protestant hegemony."[182] However, Haynes rightly observes that the model has found support in the last half of the twentieth century to return to public school "Bible classes that looked more like Sunday school instruction."[183] The conflicting impulses on such issues would be relieved by a congregationally focused engagement, one that expected a culture of explicit Christianity to flourish under the reign of Christ *in the church,* rather than expecting a "generic" Christian culture in the outside social structures.[184]

As noted above, the inordinately parachurch focus of the evangelical movement's activity bled over into the movement's *theology.* In a similar vein, the parachurch nature of the movement likewise informed evangelical sociopolitical engagement. In the 1970s and 80s, therefore, evangelical political action was not focused on the church, but on "parachurch" political entities. Carl Henry, therefore, should not have been surprised when Moral Majority and other activist groups engaged the political arena through constituency lists and direct-mail campaigns.[185] The evangelical movement *as a whole* operated through constituency lists and direct-mail campaigns in areas ranging from global missions to evangelistic crusades to hunger relief. And such had been the case from the very beginnings of the movement through the efforts of Henry, Billy Graham, and others.

This has had unforeseen, and unfortunate, implications for evangelical engagement. When the primary outlet of evangelical engagement with social and political matters is a political action committee rather than the community of the church, the shaping authority on matters of social and political outlook all too often becomes polling data or party platforms, rather than an authoritative text. Political solutions are then grounded in the social contract of a "moral majority" rather than by the righteousness of the coming Kingdom of God in Christ. In such a situation, when the "silent majority" is culturally marginalized, so is the witness of evangelical Christianity. Moreover, as Stephen Carter notes, the lack of attention to the church as the instrument to mold a truly Christian counterculture, resulted in a "process of domestication of politically active white evangelicals."[186] Carter's thesis is hard to deny given the cultural realities of the contemporary political scene. The conservative wing of evangelical social and cultural thought is arguably more countercultural than at any other time since before World War II on issues such as gender roles, human sexuality, and relations with world religions. Nonetheless, sociologists record that the grassroots evangelical constituency is more and more in tandem with the prevailing ethos on these issues and others.[187]

Also, the parachurch nature of evangelical Christianity, with its lack of sustained confessional identities at the grassroots level, it can be argued, is at least one factor that doomed the postwar evangelical movement's hopes for a cohesive presence in the public square. "The organizational ontology that comes most naturally to most evangelicals is a decentralized, voluntary association situated on a fragmented field of church groups and parachurch organizations," observes sociologist Christian Smith. "A unified, widespread conservative Christian campaign to 'reclaim the nation for Christ,' therefore, is simply not in evangelicalism's organizational 'cards' or its cultural 'DNA.'"[188] As Henry conceded in later life, "the Jesus movement, the Chicago Declaration of young evangelicals, independent fundamentalist churches and even the so-called evangelical establishment, no less than the ecumenical movement which promoted structural church unity, all suffer a basic lack, namely, a public identity as a 'people,' a conspicuously unified body of regenerate believers."[189] It now appears that this lack of cohesion was the result of expecting from a *movement* that which ultimately can come only from a *church*.

As noted above, however, this parachurch nature of evangelicalism is not a historical anomaly. It is representative of an implicit acceptance of an individualistic model of Christian existence. With such being the case, the emerging evangelical ecclesiological consensus can serve as a corrective to this model. It is certainly the case that, as one observer has opined, the renewed discussion of ecclesiology in, for example, dispensationalist circles, signals "the grudging concession among pietistic individualists that the believer, *sola*, is not the starting point for Christian thought and practice."[190] This redirection is important not only theologically, but in terms of social and political action as well because, as Edmund Clowney rightly notes, the hotly contested issues of abortion rights and homosexuality, which have most often roused contemporary evangelicals to action, have been made possible "because of the individualism that marks evangelical life."[191] Given the history of the last half of the twentieth century, it is hard to refute Clowney's contention that until evangelicals fortify "a deep biblical sense of the corporate identity of the new people of God, we will not be able to present the gospel of peace on the front lines of our 'culture wars.'"[192] The renewed attention to ecclesiology is a needed step in this direction.

At the same time, these developments avoid the similar temptation of previous applications of the "spirituality of the church," a position used by nineteenth-century Southern Presbyterian and Baptist theologians to argue against the church involving itself in the debate over human slavery.[193] Thus, Presbyterian theologian Robert Lewis Dabney spent considerable time contrasting the role of the church, which is "to teach men the way to heaven, and to help them thither," with the role of the political process, which is "to protect each citizen in the enjoyment of temporal rights."[194] He thus opposed the church taking an abolitionist or racial reconciliatory stance because "the soul is above the body, eternity is more than time, man's spiritual liberties are more indefeasible than any social relation, and God is above Caesar."[195] Therefore, he argued, the church as "Christ's kingdom" does not "wait on the politicians and conquerors of the world" to instruct it "on how she must administer her sacred charge," since addressing "political" matters such as race relations would be "a sophistical perversion of our spiritual charter."[196] As historian Paul Harvey notes, this claim was far less "apolitical" than it appeared, since a refusal to address such "political" issues was itself a political act, by propping up the status quo of a slaveholding society.[197]

As a growing number of evangelicals point both to the southern and Princeton traditions to argue for a politically disengaged church, the emerging evangelical consensus on the relationship between the church and the Kingdom may offer a more balanced alternative.[198] This is because it addresses this problem by noting that the church cannot address only personal "spiritual" matters, but instead witnesses to the whole counsel of God and to the justice of the Kingdom, through the internal discipline of the Body and through the external witness to the state and the societal structures. In doing so, it can maintain a tempered engagement in sociopolitical concerns as indeed matters of "spiritual," and thus churchly, import.

Some evangelicals refuse to speak of "political" righteousness within the church out of a well-founded fear that such would equate the church with the Kingdom of God. Such concerns are valid, especially if the word "political" is taken to mean the coercive power of the nation-state, as in the case of the Israelite theocracy and the coming global Christocracy. This, however, does not have to be the case. All evangelicals believe in some form of church *polity;* the church is governed either by the congregation or through appointed or elected leaders carrying out what they consider to be the biblical imperatives for the ordering of church life. Accordingly, the church does indeed engage in "political" relationships by virtue of its existence as a community. This is perhaps most strikingly seen in the context of church discipline, wherein the New Testament congregation is given authority to address not only "individual" vices, but matters with profound social and relational implications such as marriage relationships and economic matters (Acts 5:1-11; 1 Cor. 5:1–6:20). Thus, the first "political" charge to Christian community is self-consciously internal.

During the 1998 controversy over President Bill Clinton's cover-up of a sexual affair with a White House intern, ethicist Stanley Hauerwas offered a unique perspective on the Christian response to the issue: "The question before Christians is not whether Bill Clinton should be impeached, but why he is not excommunicated."[199] Hauerwas's question can and should be addressed by evangelical Kingdom theology. The church does not claim from the Old Testament theocracy the right to stone child molesters to death.[200] The Body does claim a mandate as the "workshop of Kingdom righteousness" to reflect justice and peace in the midst of the congregation. Therefore, the congregation is exercising a concern for social (and even political) righteousness when they expel the unrepentant child molester from the membership of the church. This is hardly a novel concept. Just as the theocratic code was essential in distinguishing Israel from the idolatrous nations of the world, church discipline has been seen in centuries past (at least by those in the Free Church tradition) as essential in maintaining the distinction between the church and the world. Baptist historian Gregory Wills makes this point when he notes that nineteenth-century Baptist congregational discipline did not mean the use of coercive force. "Baptists championed the rights of conscience and private judgment in the interpretation of Scripture, but people had these rights, they believed, as citizens of the state, not as members of the churches," he argues.[201]

As the church deals internally with matters of justice, it witnesses to the political powers-that-be of the kind of Kingdom righteousness the gospel demands, not only of individuals but also of communities. The church with a slumlord as chairman of deacons has little right to engage the city council regarding economic justice for the poor (James 5:4). Or, to use Hauerwas's example, the congregation that refuses to deal decisively with an adulterous husband among its own members can hardly protest the lack of "family values" in the White House.[202] In this, the church does not identify itself as the consummation of the Kingdom of God, but it does identify itself as a witness to the eschatological Kingdom and to its submission to the present rule of the messianic King. The development of a Kingdom theology therefore can inform evangelical public theology not only by reminding evangelicals that the call for sociopolitical righteousness is biblical, but also by reminding the church that such righteousness begins in the internal structures and relationships of the people of God (1 Pet. 4:17).

It is not only the discipline of the congregation that has the force of public sociopolitical witness, however; it is also the internal ministries and activities of the congregation. As the outside governmental and cultural structures observe Kingdom righteousness at work in alleviating poverty or resolving conflict within communities of believers, they not only find workable model solutions to social problems, but they also receive a call to come under the authority of the messianic King who brought the church together by His Spirit. This is especially true in terms of believer-to-believer ministry, an important emphasis in the New Testament writings (Acts 2:44-46; 11:29-30; 2 Cor. 9:1-14; Gal. 6:10; Phil. 4:14-17).[203] At the same time, the church models the way in which a multinational messianic Kingdom must reflect reconciliation between diverse ethnic, economic, racial, and social groups, thus testifying to the regenerative power of the Spirit and to the global scope of the coming reign of Christ. Evangelical activists seem to have recognized the need for this type of a model of racial reconciliation, but, again, contemporary efforts, such as that of the "Promise Keepers" men's movement, are focused on massive, trans-congregational efforts that fit the model of the parachurch "crusade" rather than the local congregation.[204]

Reflection at this point is especially important given the recent discussions within public policy and political theory about the role of "civil society" in the social and political fabric of the society, against the tide of what is perceived as an increasingly disconnected and individualistic American society.[205] These discussions have focused particularly on the role of "mediating institutions," such as churches and community groups, between the individual and the state.[206] Civil society proponent and evangelical commentator Marvin Olasky, for instance, has pointed to the multiracial adoption program of Minneapolis's Bethlehem Baptist Church as a model for communities to address the abortion crisis. The ministry of Bethlehem, however, proclaims that the program makes sense ultimately only in the context of the gospel of Christ.[207] It may be that ecclesiology is the *only* answer to the kind of "community" for which the civil society theorists call, since this "community" demands a cohesion and internal authority lacking in such voluntary associations as parent-teacher groups or bowling leagues.[208]

As George Marsden rightly argues, the authoritative base of the "mediating institutions" is even more crucial in light of the eclipse of authority in the current pluralistic cultural atmosphere:

> So if there is no authoritative core moral tradition to appeal to, where is the society to find its moral values? How are the universities to cultivate any positive values? The answer, it seems to me, is that the moral fiber for producing constructive citizens is going to have to come from the subtraditions of the culture. Families, of course, are crucial, but constructive families themselves have to be shaped by subtraditions. We also need mediating institutions that support these subtraditions. Taking such subtraditions seriously seems to me to be close to the essence of cultivating a healthy pluralistic society.[209]

The point Marsden makes is a healthy corrective, even to an orthodox evangelical populism that too often unwittingly seeks to maintain "family values" without an emphasis on the church. The appeal to the "family" is an important one, but it cannot be separated from the regenerate community. "Family values" is an easier point to rally a coalition around, thus avoiding the theological sticking-points of defining the church. After all, evangelical, Eastern Orthodox, Roman Catholic, and Mormon cobelligerents can define, at least for now, what a "family" is. They cannot say the same for the church.[210]

But the only structure which can cultivate the revelational atmosphere in which biblically-ordered families can thrive is the church. It is this aspect of a claim to authority that likewise protects evangelical ecclesiology from the self-conscious sectarianism of communitarians such as Stanley Hauerwas. Carl Henry is correct in maintaining that the difference between an engaged evangelical ecclesiology and the post-liberal communitarian vision of the church is the nature of the truth.[211] The church's internal counterculture is not enough, Henry rightly asserts, if "truth—universally valid truth" is "a concern as vital to the Church's public involvement as are forgiveness, hope and peace."[212] Such a view resonates with a Protestant commitment to a New Testament teaching basing the community of the church on a prior commitment to prophetic/apostolic authority.[213]

Politically, this will mean that evangelical churches often will find themselves in a clash with the culture, over the very nature of a "mediating structure." Pragmatist philosopher Richard Rorty, for example, adds a significant caveat to his endorsement of "civil society"—namely, that the "subtraditions" should be "constructive." Rorty (who is himself a biological descendant of Walter Rauschenbusch) defines these "constructive" communities in the following terms:

> My litmus tests would be the following: If a religious community has gay clergy and solemnizes gay marriages, it belongs to the constructive minority. If it preaches the social gospel, if the preachers remind the congregation that the richest country in the world at the richest point in its economic history still doesn't feed its poor, then it also qualifies. I don't think there are very many religious communities of this sort. The vast majority of them do not meet either of these litmus tests.[214]

It is for this reason that Rorty finds so "upbeat" the "gradual replacement of the churches by the universities as the conscience of the nation."[215] Of course, evangelical churches cannot biblically meet the criteria of a "constructive minority" here. They must view themselves, not simply as voluntary associations that help to prop up the American experiment, but as manifestations of a yet-future Kingdom, governed now by an authoritative, external revelation. This may increasingly bring struggles with the culture, and thereby with the state, but such struggles will not be the first for the community of the Messiah.

A commitment to establishing the "parallel structures" of the church in terms of civil society may prove to be a special imperative to politically conservative evangelicals wary of the power of government. By emphasizing simply the governmental and political mechanisms of social change, these conservatives have unwittingly given aid to the idea of a robust central government. As conservative legal theorist Robert Bork argues, the power of government grows when the smaller, more representative forms of community, such as the family and the church, are eroded. "Chaos, which only government can control, results when other sources of authority are denigrated and diminished," he argues.[216] Similarly, political philosopher Stuart Hampshire has rightly noted that the essence of socialism is "the commitment to political agency far beyond the domain recognized in earlier centuries and in other political philosophies."[217] Hampshire rightly notes that Marxist philosophy, by def-

inition, seeks to make political institutions "the first resource for counteract-
ing the great evils, in the place of religious institutions and their charities."[218]
Evangelicals who neglect the church in favor of the picket line or Capitol Hill
inadvertently concede the very intrusive nature of government against which
they protest.

At the same time, this does not mean that evangelicals should abandon the
public square for the sake of the church. There is a call to retrenchment issuing
from a resurgent isolationism within remnants of the "new Christian right."
Religio-political activist Paul Weyrich, who actually coined the phrase "Moral
Majority," is one such example. Calling for an evangelical "separation" into
parallel structures, Weyrich points to the homeschooling movement's successful endeavor to "secede" from a secularized public school system, arguing that
evangelicals should do the same across the entire spectrum of public life.[219] This
is precisely the isolationist stance described and denounced in Henry's *Uneasy
Conscience*. Contrary to this position, the orientation of the church as a manifestation of the Kingdom means that evangelicals cannot be concerned only
about the "counterculture" of the churches, because the scope of the Kingdom
informs the scope of evangelical concern. Thus, the concerns of the community
itself at times require attention to matters of political concern, including electoral politics.[220] Culture informs politics, and is therefore the more important
of the two. Nonetheless, history bears out that treacherous cultural movements
are given teeth through political processes.[221]

At the same time, the developments toward a Kingdom ecclesiology
remind evangelicals of the limits of political activity. Political solutions are first
implemented within the community of the local church. When political solutions are offered to the outside world, they must always be couched in language
that recognizes the futility of cultural reform without personal regeneration
and baptism into the Body of Christ. The church, as a multinational Spirit-
body, has been forbidden the power of the sword by the Son of David Himself
(John 18:11). The church, understanding its place in the Kingdom program,
cannot then proclaim itself or any national government to be a "new Israel"
with the authority to enforce belief in Christ or any conformity to revealed religion.[222] As such, it recognizes the inherent distinction between the church and
the state. Realizing that the church is not the full consummation of the
Kingdom prevents the church from seizing the Constantinian sword, as did the
application of Augustinian Kingdom theology early in the history of the
church.[223] The reality of a church disconnected from its identity as a Kingdom
outpost among the kingdoms of the world is seen in the capitulation of established churches to the totalitarian regimes of both Nazi Germany and the

Soviet Union during the twentieth century. Maurice Hindus, a mid-century observer of Russian culture, noted the following of the relationship between the Soviet state and the Russian Orthodox Church:

> Though the Church of course repudiates materialism, it has become reconciled to the economics of communism and teaches that the accumulation of riches and property is sin. It points to Christ as the first real communist, who denounced exploiters and drove the moneychangers from the temple. In its favor in this period of fervent nationalism is the fact that historically it is as Russian as the Kremlin walls, and its unswerving patriotism, past and present, has won it not only respectability but prestige. Orthodoxy may be attacked and reviled in the press, but the Church has no more quarrels with the Kremlin over domestic and foreign policies than it had with the Czars. Whoever occupies the seat of power in the Kremlin has its blessing, now as in the past.[224]

The dangers of such civil religion therefore can be avoided only by a concentrated effort to maintain a biblical and theological understanding of the nature and mission of the church in relation to the Kingdom of God.[225] As evangelicals move toward a coherent Kingdom ecclesiology, it becomes clearer that the church is inherently eschatological and soteriological. In an inaugurationist Kingdom theology, the church is reminded that, as Henry argues, the people of God live "with renewable visas" on earth, even as they live out their heavenly citizenship in the counterculture of the church.[226] At the same time, every church building represents by its very existence a latent political challenge to the powers that be. Because the evangelical consensus at this point recognizes the church as an initial form of a coming global monarchy, they proclaim by their very presence on the landscape that the status quo will one day be shaken apart in one decisive act of sovereign authority. Therefore, the evangelical conscience remains always a bit "uneasy" even as it engages vigorously the social and political structures. This is because the doctrine of the church is, after all, the concrete display of the "already/not yet" of the Kingdom. As such, it reminds evangelicals that, although they are to submit to the governing authorities, they are claimed by no transient political entity, but by a coming messianic Kingdom, which they see even now breaking in around them through Spirit-propelled reconciliation, peace, and unity.

5

CONCLUSION

"We vote as many, but we pray as one," remarked 1952 Democratic presidential nominee Adlai Stevenson.[1] American evangelicalism now faces the situation in which the movement prays as many, but votes as one. The evangelical consensus on the Kingdom of God provides a first step to establishing a coherent theological foundation for social and political engagement in the public square. It does so by, among other things, ensuring that evangelicals do not engage the issues on an issue-by-issue basis as they have often done in the past. By following such a course, previous attempts at evangelical sociopolitical engagement have proven especially vulnerable to the whims of demagoguery and party platform electioneering. As this study has indicated, evangelical theology has achieved a remarkable commonality on the question of the relationship of the Kingdom of God to the present task of the community of Christ. This does not mean, however, that evangelicalism has achieved the kind of theological cohesion needed to serve as a vital force in the arenas of culture and politics. Instead, even as evangelicals have drawn closer together on the previously divisive issues of the Kingdom, they seem to be splintering apart at other points. These matters of dispute, moreover, involve questions on which they enjoyed a near unanimous consensus at the founding of the movement after World War II. Thus, the gains of a Kingdom consensus are jeopardized by an evangelical coalition that is increasingly fracturing over the more basic questions of theological identity, questions that threaten the very possibility of united evangelical action.

EVANGELICAL ENGAGEMENT AND THE PROMISE
OF EVANGELICAL THEOLOGY

On the one hand, the developments within evangelicalism toward a consensus Kingdom theology demonstrate the best aspects of the postwar evangelical movement. This is because the move toward a theology of the Kingdom recognizes precisely what the evangelical theological leadership so rightly asserted after World War II—namely, that the differences between the new evangelical-ism and the older fundamentalism were *theological,* not simply methodologi-cal. Accordingly, Henry correctly zeroed in on the root of the "uneasy conscience"—a problem of reconciling biblical texts on the nature of the Kingdom of God, especially in relation to the present age. In so doing, Henry identified an issue of colossal importance for the entire spectrum of theological and biblical inquiry in the twentieth century. Henry did not simply seek to "tri-angulate" methodologically between the isolationist fundamentalists and the politicized modernists. Instead, he sought to turn evangelicals to the real issue behind their political irrelevance—competing and faulty views of the Kingdom.

The move toward an evangelical consensus on the Kingdom, however, has not simply repackaged the conclusions of the larger world of exegetical and theological scholarship on the Kingdom.[2] Wolfhart Pannenberg rightly notes that the centrality of the Kingdom motif from Puritan Calvinism through Albrecht Ritschl through the Social Gospel and beyond had not been enough, even though these movements have accurately communicated, at least in name, the central thrust of the preaching of Jesus.[3] Instead, as Pannenberg con-tends, this deficiency is due to two factors. The Kingdom idea had "been deprived of its exegetical foundations" in liberal Protestantism.[4] Moreover, the attempts at Kingdom theology were hampered by "problematic questions" of how the biblical text can be "inextricably woven" with the idea of the Kingdom as both future and present.[5] The evangelical consensus, however, has come about less as an attempt to achieve a consensus than through sustained biblical reflection. It thereby reflects the *sola Scriptura* principle illustrated in John Calvin's 1543 retort that when his interlocutor Pighius "flings at us the consensus of the church, let him have this single sentence as his reply: the only consensus of the church is that which is throughout suitably and fittingly in agreement with the word of God."[6]

This is precisely the genius of the emerging evangelical consensus. They have not simply avoided the divisive issues of eschatology, soteriology, and ecclesiology. Instead, they have recognized that the emphases of the disparate traditions are based on partial truths from the biblical revelation itself. Dispensationalist evangelicals have rightly interpreted Scripture to indicate that the mission of the church is to proclaim a coming apocalyptic judgment on the entire world system. They have furthermore accurately interpreted the New Testament teaching that the church is not the triumphant, visible Kingdom of God, but is instead a suffering pilgrim band of followers in an age of darkness. Dispensationalists have recovered something of the ethos of the New

Testament itself by stirring evangelical Christianity to long for the imminent unveiling of the Messiah. They have also correctly maintained that the priority of the church in the present age is to proclaim rescue from the wrath to come through the atonement of Christ.

Covenant theologians have rightly emphasized the biblical teaching that the "Kingdom" cannot be abstracted from the "Christ," thereby maintaining that the Kingdom has come with Christ. They have recovered the New Testament teaching that the Kingdom is not just an eschatological governmental order, but it is a spiritual reign of peace and righteousness. Covenant theologians have moreover correctly argued that God's Kingdom purposes are not disjointed but are unified and are being revealed through redemptive history to the glory of Christ. The Kuyperian and postmillennial strands of Reformed theology have also added the biblical truth that the Kingdom is not just about personal salvation, or "spirituality," but is also about the vocation of the believing community, the worldview of the church, and the salvation of the cosmos. With the various traditions reexamining their theological presuppositions, a remarkable coalescence has occurred, as evangelical theology has arrived at a Kingdom model that synthesizes these biblical truths, seeing them in harmony with one another. The consensus was not the result of a public relations "manifesto" in which the participants agreed upon ambiguously worded definitions of the Kingdom. Instead, the consensus emerged from the long process of exegetical exploration and theological reflection. Thus, evangelical theology has an opportunity to move toward a "Reformed dispensationalism" or an "apocalyptic Kuyperianism," a viewpoint that holds in tension the Kingdom realities of a church truly militant but not yet visibly triumphant. This has clear implications for a theology of evangelical engagement—a theology that has both reachable goals and defined limitations.

"What are we to make of a rabbi who claims for the Mishnah and the Talmud that they guarantee the right to strike—thereby providing the Holy Writ with the satisfaction of having paved the way for the National Labor Relations Act?" asked neo-conservative thinker Irving Kristol in 1948. "What is this but an oblique way of saying that one of the merits of Judaism is that it permits its believers to read the *New Republic* with an untroubled soul?"[7] Similarly, evangelicals should indeed examine whether their Kingdom theology exists in order that they might read the *New Republic* (or, more likely, the *National Review*) with an untroubled soul. Having said this, unlike Walter Rauschenbusch and the Social Gospel, evangelical theology did not start with a social or political agenda, and then seek to find a theology to fit it.[8] This is crucial to the evangelical nature of evangelical theology. As evangelical theology rejects the isolation of the older fundamentalism, it should not reject the reasons behind this isolation, even if they were often misapplied. J. Gresham Machen, after all, was right when he warned American Protestantism, even of a "Kingdom theology" gone awry:

> Christianity will indeed accomplish many useful things in this world, but if it is accepted in order to accomplish those useful things it is not Christianity. Christianity will combat Bolshevism; but if it is accepted in order to combat Bolshevism, it is not Christianity: Christianity will produce a unified nation, in a slow but satisfactory way; but if it is accepted in order to produce a unified nation, it is not Christianity: Christianity will produce a healthy community; but if it is accepted in order to produce a healthy community, it is not Christianity: Christianity will promote international peace; but if it is accepted in order to promote international peace, it is not Christianity. Our Lord said: "Seek ye first the Kingdom of God and His righteousness and all these things shall be added unto you." But if you seek first the Kingdom of God and His righteousness *in order that* all those other things may be added unto you, you will miss both those other things and the Kingdom of God as well.[9]

By contrast, the implications for evangelical sociopolitical engagement have emerged almost as a byproduct of a theological product toward a coherent theological system in much the same way that Velcro strips were a byproduct of the United States aerospace program. For the most part, both the participants and the observers have largely ignored the sociopolitical implications of the project. And yet, the move toward a Kingdom theology has answered the problems addressed in Carl Henry's *Uneasy Conscience of Modern Fundamentalism* by removing the Kingdom barriers between the various subtraditions of American conservative Protestantism. The discussion thereby clears the way for a renewed conversation about the Kingdom and the public square on the basis of a coherent theological foundation for such engagement. As such, it offers an antidote to the twentieth century's failed attempts at a theologically vacuous political activism.

It does so by holding forth the hope of a theologically cohesive evangelical movement, exactly that for which Henry pleaded as necessary for an evangelical penetration of the public square. The flight from theological reflection lent itself to a politically activated populism that was able to mobilize evangelicals on issues such as abortion, homosexual rights, and a host of other high-profile issues. Unfortunately, this populism, divorced from doctrinal cohesion, is not only theologically problematic, but politically unsustainable as well. A populism based on direct-mail activism can grapple with clearer issues such as partial birth abortion or the rights of home-schooling families. It is not so certain that it can handle the more complicated issues such as stem-cell research, therapeutic cloning, or governmental funding of faith-based charities. Even a secularist conservative observer laments the way in which a doctrinally ambiguous evangelicalism flounders in the public arena:

> Perhaps because the theological liberals scooped up the best divinity schools and the richest congregations in the great schism of the early twentieth century, or perhaps because contemporary evangelicalism puts so much emphasis on emotion rather than doctrine, the evangelical church is a decapitated institution. It fulfills the spiritual yearnings of millions, but it has trouble justifying itself to scoffers and doubters. Henry Ward Beecher, the great mid-nineteenth-century evangelist, commanded the respect even of his antagonists. Pat Robertson doesn't.[10]

This approach can only lead evangelicals back, as indeed it has done, to the impulse toward fundamentalist withdrawal. As one conservative commentator has rightly observed,

> Instead of a serious politics, conservatives turn to primal-scream therapy and escapist fantasies (think Alan Keyes). Or they drop out of politics altogether, telling themselves that strengthening civil society is more important—as though politics and culture occupied separate, hermetically sealed boxes. When the Promise Keepers held a big rally in Washington a few years back, their spokesmen were at pains to disavow any political intent. But then, why not rally in New York—or Butte?[11]

Moreover, an evangelical coalition not held together by theological conviction must be held together by *something*. For many in the various attempts at evangelical political activism, this something was *someone*—a unifying personality around whom the movement could unite. Henry rightly showed some uneasiness with this approach when many evangelicals (including conservatives such as Pat Robertson) rallied around President Jimmy Carter. Henry conceded Carter's evangelical piety, but warned that "that devotion is not without a theological ambiguity that reflects the doctrinal imprecision found in many professedly evangelical churches where the end results are problematical."[12] This would be even more evident in the 1980s when evangelical activists sought to unite around a president who, unlike Carter, shared the convictions of most conservative evangelicals on social and cultural issues—Ronald Reagan. "Heaven was a long way away, and we needed something to help us make it through the political night," reflected a couple of disillusioned moral majoritarians. "In Reagan we trusted."[13]

The Kingdom consensus, by returning to the root concerns of the original call to evangelical engagement, addresses these key concerns. It furthermore provides a starting point for theologically driven, rather than public policy driven, conversation on issues of cultural, social, and political concern. This is necessary to prevent the evangelical witness in the public arena from becoming an *ad hoc,* issue-by-issue defensive posture. United States Supreme Court associate justice Antonin Scalia has argued that a coherent and comprehensive foundation of legal theory not only serves to inform individual decisions, but it also serves as a restraint on later temptations to judicial activism, either from the left or right wings of the political spectrum. "For when, in writing for the majority of the Court, I adopt a general rule, and say, 'This is the basis of our decision,' I not only constrain lower courts, I constrain myself as well," Scalia points out. "If the next case should have such different facts that my political or policy preferences regarding the outcome are quite the opposite, I will be unable to indulge those preferences; I have committed myself to the governing principle."[14] The same can be said of a common vision of the Kingdom of God that informs the limits and possibilities of social and political action in the present era. It can serve not only as the motive for political action when it is biblically and theologically warranted, it can restrain a zeal for believing that a Balanced Budget Amendment is the initial fulfillment of the eschaton, or that an intrusive education bill is the first seal of the Apocalypse.

A coherent Kingdom consensus also protects evangelicalism from the temptation to ground authority on social and political matters in the Republican or Democratic Party platforms, rather than in the biblical witness to the Kingdom of God. This is increasingly important as the conservative coalition, under which religious conservatives have found a home with Jewish neo-conservatives, free market libertarians, and anti-communist cold warriors, gives evidence of fragmenting apart at several points in the post-Reagan era.[15] As conservative political values such as the free market and the preservation of the traditional family collide, evangelicals must rely on something more than polling data and political coalitions to decide between such priorities. Only a comprehensive theological agenda can provide a starting point for such a discussion. A common vision of the Kingdom of God, as Henry argued a half-century ago, can offer just such a theoretical foundation. As evangelical theology informs the evangelical coalition about the theological basis for sociopolitical engagement, it does not do so by ignoring the central "political theory" of the Old and New Testament canon—namely, that "The scepter shall not depart from Judah, nor the ruler's staff from between his feet, until he comes to whom it belongs and the obedience of the nations is his" (Gen. 49:10, NIV).

EVANGELICAL ENGAGEMENT AND THE FAILURE
OF EVANGELICAL THEOLOGY

The Kingdom consensus does indeed address the matter of theological fragmentation of the evangelical coalition first lamented by Henry mid-century.
Nonetheless, the theological context here was not simply a matter of Kingdom
disunity. After all, as noted above, the problems were not preeminently those
of political strategy but of theology, a theology that was not a negation but an
expansion of the orthodoxy of the earlier fundamentalists. After all, the neo-
evangelical objections to both the Social Gospel and fundamentalism were theological, but they were fundamentally different. The opposition of Henry to
the Social Gospel, for example, was not different in any significant way from
the opposition offered by other Protestant "fundamentalists."[16] Thus, the evangelical debate over the present reality of the Kingdom of God cannot be understood apart from the undercurrents of the earlier Fundamentalist-Modernist
controversy. After all, the arguments earlier in the century over the Social
Gospel's view of the Kingdom were not primarily about the best method of
Christian social action. These vehement disagreements were not primarily
political matters, or even primarily eschatological matters. Rather, they were
struggles over the most basic matters of the doctrines of God and revelatory
authority, thereby addressing derivative theological concerns that ran the
gamut from anthropology to Christology.

Ironically, contemporary American evangelical theology has indeed
achieved virtual unanimity on the question of the Kingdom of God, thereby
overcoming the impasse preventing united action in the public square, even as
the movement splinters apart over issues of first-order importance for the survival of evangelicalism as a theological movement. While the postwar neo-
evangelicals were divided on issues such as the nature of the Kingdom, they
were united initially with each other (and with the fundamentalists from
whence they came) on issues such as biblical authority and the attributes of
God. The "reformist" element within the evangelical theological coalition does
not challenge this early unanimity on these matters, but instead laments it as
an example of an unduly narrow Reformed hegemony that must be overcome.[17] Accordingly, the current debates threatening to split the evangelical
theological consensus have to do with the locus of biblical authority and the
nature of truth (in the debate over postmodern and communitarian evangelicalism); the question of whether God has exhaustive foreknowledge (in the
debate over "open theism"); and other issues.[18] The controversies over God
and Scripture are not unrelated, but are a continuation, as one "reformist"
evangelical puts it, of an ongoing controversy since the 1970s between theo-

logical innovators and "neo-fundamentalist evangelicals who reject innovative, constructive theological reflection."[19] In some ways, these debates have had a positive effect on evangelical theology, by forcing orthodox theologians to respond to the new proposals with a vigorous exploration of the meaning and implications of the doctrines of God and Scripture.[20] Nonetheless, the long-term ramifications of this debate cast uncertainty on the prospects of ever developing an evangelical theological consensus.[21] This is because, among other reasons, behind these debates looms a much larger question—what does it mean *theologically* to be called an "evangelical"?[22] It is not just the break-down of theological consensus here, however, that threatens the prospect of a Kingdom theology of evangelical engagement. The issues at stake are funda-mental both to a theology of the Kingdom of God and to the task of evangel-ical sociopolitical engagement.

The question of revelatory authority, after all, was at the heart of conser-vative Protestantism's rejection of the mainline denominations' political forays. A new generation of evangelical theologians should perhaps ask whether a scriptural revelation that is inerrant in "spiritual" matters but not on "worldly" matters such as history and philosophy has anything at all to say to political thought and social action. Moreover, the current conflicts over the nature of biblical authority and propositional revelation should press evan-gelical theology to seek to define itself more clearly at this point, which the postwar generation failed to do. This was, once again, the result of an evan-gelical movement that sought to define itself more in terms of a common coali-tion than in terms of a common confession. Thus, in order to keep otherwise conservative, non-inerrantist scholars such as F. F. Bruce within the boundaries of evangelicalism, Henry and others proposed that biblical inerrancy was a matter of evangelical "consistency," not evangelical "authenticity."[23] The land-scape changes, however, when "inconsistent evangelicals" are in the main-stream, if not the majority of evangelical institutions and publications. Moreover, it is doubtful that Henry and his colleagues could ever have imag-ined a "united evangelical action" for social and political righteousness in an era when it is easier to find a creationist at the University of California at Berkeley than it is to find a biblical inerrantist at Fuller Theological Seminary.

This is especially true when matters of political and social agenda are, as one analyst rightly observes, "inseparable from the question of truth in moral matters."[24] This is relevant as evangelicals and other Christian traditionalists grapple with the question of how to achieve epistemological common ground with a secularized culture.[25] The prior issue, however, is how evangelical the-ology can maintain a common epistemological grounding even within its own movement. Moreover, the fracturing evangelical consensus on revelatory authority already has a precedent in terms of sociopolitical engagement in the constituencies of the mainline Protestant left—which share less and less of an epistemological common ground, resulting in a kind of theological "identity politics" among various "interest groups" rather than a coherent, sustained public theology. As Scott Hafemann has warned prophetically,

> Finally, evangelicals are increasingly unwilling to study the Bible because for many the Bible is no longer the primary locus of nor criterion for evaluating divine revelation *per se*. Instead the experience of God's people in the present is the most reliable guide for what God is like and how he acts in the world. The paradigm of revelation is thus no longer the Bible as a fixed canon but the experiences of the poor and oppressed, or the feminist critique of society, or in the same way the experiences of gold-standard, supply-side economists and upper middle class whites.[26]

The debate over the doctrine of God took evangelicalism perhaps more by surprise than did the "Battle for the Bible." This is despite the fact that some postwar evangelical theologians, notably Roger Nicole, warned as far back as 1959 that the doctrine of God's foreknowledge might soon be compromised even within the evangelical coalition.[27] This controversy carries with it the same implications for a united evangelical witness in the public square. After all, the problem that fundamentalists and evangelicals had with the Social Gospel also centered on disparate views of theology proper. Thus, Henry directly correlated the limited and impersonal Hegelian God of Protestant liberalism with the politicized moralism of the Social Gospel. God was not seen as a monarchial Creator reigning providentially sovereign over the cosmos, so God eventually became simply the metaphysical grounding for human activism:

> For God was viewed as man's moral equal, endowed only with larger perfections. In the realm of morals, the voice of God was equated with the voice of conscience. Deity never demanded more than the higher self, except in terms of other higher human selves. God's thoughts and ways are our highest thoughts and ways, except on a grander scale. Thus theological students were told that "God is at least as good as the Red Cross, or as the Y.W.C.A." and not infrequently the deity concept was impersonally merged with "the sum total of the forces at work for righteousness in our environment." The moral "otherness" or holiness of God was obscured.[28]

Of course, the open theist proposal within evangelical theology does not challenge the holiness, personality, or "otherness" of God. Nonetheless, open theism is following Social Gospel Protestantism in seeking to maintain the centrality of the Kingdom of God while redefining the sovereignty of God. For all his talk of the "Kingdom" concept being rescued by the Social Gospel, Walter Rauschenbusch disliked the concept of God as a King. Thus, Rauschenbusch argued that Jesus, by calling God "Father" instead of "King," had "democratized the conception of God" as He disconnected the idea of God "from the coercive and predatory State, and transferred it to the realm of family life, the chief social embodiment of solidarity and love."[29] Rauschenbusch's language here, shifting a "governing" imagery (perhaps the governance of a "Kingdom"?) to a "family" imagery, is remarkably similar to the "family room" imagery sought by Clark Pinnock and others to preserve God's "relationality."[30]

Moreover, Rauschenbusch was able to articulate his utopian vision of upward human progress only because he posited that the universe "is not a despotic monarchy, with God above the starry canopy and ourselves down here; it is a spiritual commonwealth with God in the midst of us."[31] A growing number of open theists are articulating a very similar model, even as they embrace the construct of an inaugurated eschatology. Gregory Boyd, for instance, in language starkly similar to Rauschenbusch, proposes that evangelicals think of the cosmos as "by divine choice, more of a democracy than it is a monarchy."[32] John Sanders likewise laments the "domineering ways" in which the metaphor of God as King has influenced evangelical theology.[33] Perhaps even more remarkable is the way in which Sanders attempts to have a Christocentric and canonical Kingdom theology after having thus redefined "monarchial" ideas about God. "Indeed the reading of the Old Testament legitimately provides for a world-ruling messiah, but God simply chose differently in Jesus," Sanders concludes.[34] It is quite difficult to see how evangelical theology can maintain, under such circumstances, a consensus view of a "world-ruling Messiah" who has initiated His all-encompassing Kingdom—a Kingdom granted to Him by the sovereignty of His Father—over the pilgrim community of the regenerate church. Henry's warning that evangelical engagement cannot "go on eschatology alone," but must be centered on the doctrine of God, which grounds creation, redemption, and consummation, is precisely on target at this point.[35]

Even starker are the ways in which feminist theological proposals are moving some sectors of reformist evangelicalism away from Kingdom-centered theology. John Sanders commends open theism for replacing the "operative root metaphor" of classical theism of "God as creator, judge, and king" with that of "God as savior, lover, and friend."[36] Sanders elucidates this root metaphor revision by noting that open theism has benefited from feminist theology's critiques of traditional models of divine providence, which Sanders characterizes as portraying God as "a real Marlboro man."[37] In the same vein, Sanders gives a qualified endorsement of some feminist theologians' rejection of meticulous sovereignty as "divine rape."[38]

Similarly, open theist Clark Pinnock insists that evangelical theology should abandon the Kingdom of God as a root metaphor, since a "Kingdom theology" drives one toward a traditional understanding of God's relationship to the cosmos.[39] Pinnock directly ties an open theist understanding of sovereignty to an evangelical feminist view of gender roles, particularly in contradistinction to the confessional commitments of the Southern Baptist Convention (SBC) in favor of both classical theism and a complementarian view of gender distinctions. "I get suspicious when the same people who want to protect God's sovereignty also want to keep women in their subordinate place," Pinnock argues. "Why do they not see that the Father whom they claim to exalt is not the 'father' of patriarchal power but the God of Jesus Christ who woos us through his self-giving love?"[40]

At the same time, evangelical feminism is likewise revising the Kingdom concept. Mainline feminist theology long ago dispensed with language of God as "King" or "Father" as too distinctively "male" in its cast.[41] Such a move is about much more than language, however, as the language shift reveals an underlying revision also in the God/cosmos relationship itself—away from sovereignty and toward "cooperation" between the Creator and the creation.[42] As the move toward "inclusive God-language" (including "Mother God" liturgy and Sophia Christology) gains ground among evangelical feminists, the example of such moves in mainline Protestantism should give evangelicals pause. Far from expressing the "relationality" of the immanent God, such proposals have resulted in the marginalizing of personal language in Scripture to the category of metaphor, resulting in a God concept that is ambiguous at best and impersonal at worst.[43]

The developing evangelical consensus on Kingdom theology cannot afford to jettison its fundamentalist past on questions such as biblical authority and classical theism. As Henry has rightly noted, any attempt at Christian political engagement apart from the moral restraints of an objective propositional revelation cannot consistently escape being "pharaoh-like" in seeking political activism for the sake of political activism.[44] Though such concerns are derided as a "slippery slope" argument from evangelical progressives, conservative evangelical inerrantists have a history of doctrinal deviation on their side as they warn against the equivocation on the issues of revelation and authority.[45] Moreover, the Kingdom idea, as Richard Niebuhr has argued, protects classical theism from the Aristotelian/Thomistic synthesis of a detached, apathetic God concept so opposed by relational theists.[46] It does so by reflecting the biblical emphasis that the sovereignty of God is not revealed as an atemporal, self-directed attribute, but is instead revealed in the context of the dynamic relation between God and His creation as He sovereignly directs it toward its appointed end—the summing up of all things in Christ (Eph. 1:10).

At stake here are both the Kingdom theological synthesis and the cohesiveness of evangelicalism as a movement. This has far-reaching implications for any theologically grounded agenda of evangelical engagement. As one commentator has noted about the entire spectrum of American religion, "Those who look to the churches for the salvation of civic life or for the renovation of politics should realize that organized religion will have its hands full coping with purely internal issues in the coming generation."[47] This is true of a mainline Protestant structure that is now splintered apart over issues as basic as homosexual marriage. But it is also true of an evangelical movement splintered apart on what Henry correctly has identified as the two most basic foundations of orthodox Christianity—the ontological axiom of the living God and the epistemological axiom of divine revelation. Henry rightly notes, "On these basic axioms depend all the core beliefs of biblical theism, including divine creation, sin and the Fall, the promise and provision of redemption, the Incarnation of God in Jesus of Nazareth, the regenerate church as a new society, and a comprehensive eschatology."[48]

Now, however, evangelical theology resembles less the "united action" of theological allies envisioned by the movement's founders and more the theologically fractured coalition of the fundamentalists from whence they came. At least, however, the fundamentalist coalition could unite around a minimal set of doctrinal affirmations, however sketchy and reactionary they might have been. Reformist evangelical theology has been unable thus far to articulate what unites the movement beyond a vague commitment to an undefined "high view of Scripture" and an even more undefined "family resemblance" of shared evangelical identity.[49]

This crisis of theological identity can be seen in a recent monograph by reformist evangelicals Gregory Boyd and Paul Eddy, which seeks to explain the "spectrum" of evangelical theology on a range of issues.[50] The authors note in the introduction that they will only discuss evangelical options, and thus do not include debates over issues such as transubstantiation, earth worship, or universalism. The authors then, however, offer discussions of supposedly "intramural" disputes over issues on which evangelical theology has been united until the very recent past—issues such as the inspiration of Scripture, the foreknowl-

edge of God, and the substitutionary atonement of Christ. The prewar fundamentalists may have had an *ad hoc* creedalism, united around the doctrines
under attack from modernists, but at least there was an underlying logic to their
coalition. The post-conservative *ad hoc* creedalism simply cannot sustain evangelical theological reflection—largely because it is no longer possible to distinguish between primary, secondary, and tertiary doctrinal matters.

Henry's proposal for a politically engaged evangelicalism has been
achieved, as the fragmented streams of the evangelical coalition have now
reached a virtual consensus on the broad themes of the relationship between
the Kingdom and political activity. At the same time, however, evangelical theology is divided, perhaps now more than ever, over issues of God, revelation,
and authority. As evangelical theology faces the future, it must supplement a
biblical and theological synthesis on the Kingdom of God with a renewed
attempt at a theological basis for evangelical identity and cooperation. Without
such a consensus, the disparate voices of the evangelical Kingdom activity in
the public square may only prove that, sometimes, an easy conscience is not
enough.

NOTES

INTRODUCTION
[1] Carl F. H. Henry, *The Uneasy Conscience of Modern Fundamentalism* (Grand Rapids, Mich.: Eerdmans, 1947).

CHAPTER ONE
[1] Russell Baker, "Mr. Right," *New York Review of Books,* May 17, 2001, 8.

[2] Charles Colson's conversion was the subject of his popular autobiography, *Born Again* (Old Tappan, N.J.: Chosen, 1976). Carter unabashedly recounted his own evangelical experience on the campaign trail and in his campaign autobiography, *Why Not the Best?* (Nashville: Broadman, 1975), published by the publishing arm of Carter's denomination, the Southern Baptist Convention (SBC). While Colson, also a Southern Baptist, would remain a fixture in the evangelical subculture, Carter's rift with conservative evangelicals would eventually manifest itself in a growing embrace of the mainline Protestant left, including the Cooperative Baptist Fellowship, a moderate dissident group within the Southern Baptist Convention. Carter links his disaffection with the denomination to the SBC's increasing support of a conservative social agenda, which the former President describes as "a threat to human rights, and to democracy and freedom" (cited in Peter G. Bourne, *Jimmy Carter: A Comprehensive Biography from Plains to Postpresidency* [New York: Scribner, 1997], 497-498).

[3] Carter expressed his frustrations with the evangelical activists on these issues in his presidential memoir, *Keeping Faith: Memoirs of a President* (New York: Bantam, 1982), 561-562. These frustrations include being accused of "secular humanism" by the conservative leadership of Carter's denomination.

[4] See, for instance, Sara Diamond, *Not by Politics Alone: The Enduring Influence of the Christian Right* (New York: Guilford, 1998), 216-235.

[5] Carl F. H. Henry, *The Uneasy Conscience of Modern Fundamentalism* (Grand Rapids, Mich.: Eerdmans, 1947).

[6] The "Evangelicals for McGovern" campaign was spearheaded in part by Anabaptist theologian Ronald J. Sider. It would provide the basis for the 1973 politically liberal "Chicago Declaration" and, later, the formation of Sider's Evangelicals for Social Action. See Tim Stafford, "Ron Sider's Unsettling Crusade," *Christianity Today,* April 27, 1992, 18-22; and Ronald J. Sider, ed., *The Chicago Declaration* (Carol Stream, Ill.: Creation House, 1974). The Chicago Declaration included some political and theological liberals whose "evangelical" credentials were dubious even at the time, such as Southern Baptist ethicists Foy Valentine and James Dunn. It also included some who would be the mainstay in the call for a new evangelical left, such as Sider, Richard Pierard, John Howard Yoder, Jim Wallis, and Richard Mouw. Surprisingly, the declaration's signers also included Bernard Ramm and Carl F. H. Henry. Henry later wrote

that he was shocked and disappointed by the leftist tone of the final draft of the document, which "called for a bold attack on 'maldistribution of the nation's wealth and services' but remained silent about Marxism's inability to produce wealth" (Carl F. H. Henry, *Confessions of a Theologian* [Waco, Tex.: Word, 1986], 348).

[7] This would include magazines such as *Sojourners* and *The Other Side,* which increasingly came to rely on Roman Catholic liberation theologies and mainline ecumenical political theologies in articulating their concerns. *The Other Side* grew closer and closer to the sexual libertarianism rejected by most of the Chicago Declaration evangelicals until it finally embraced the cultural left's acceptance of homosexual relationships as a matter of social justice. The leftist evangelicals often sought to transcend the Reformed/dispensationalist alliance of the previous generation by pointing evangelicals back to the nineteenth-century traditions of Arminian postmillennial revivalist abolitionists such as Charles G. Finney. See, for example, Ronald J. Sider, "An Historic Moment for Biblical Social Concern," in *Chicago Declaration,* 12-13; and *One-Sided Christianity? Uniting the Church to Heal a Lost and Broken World* (Grand Rapids, Mich.: Zondervan, 1993), 17-19. See also Jim Wallis, *Who Speaks for God? An Alternative to the Religious Right— A New Politics of Compassion, Community, and Civility* (New York: Delacorte, 1996), 16-22. Wallis sees a "hijacking" of this earlier progressive evangelical tradition by the conservatives emerging from the Fundamentalist-Modernist controversy. Ironically, Wallis was reared in the dispensationalist tradition of J. N. Darby's Plymouth Brethren churches and began his radical social activism at Trinity Evangelical Divinity School. See Garry Wills's foreword to Wallis's *The Soul of Politics: A Practical and Prophetic Vision for Change* (Maryknoll, N.Y.: Orbis, 1994), ix-x. Wallis takes on the political assumptions of Reformed evangelicals, even those of a moderately liberal stripe, by charging that "the problem is not that we are not political, but that we are not political in the same way that our Reformed critics are—and the way they think Christians ought to be." In the place of a Reformed paradigm, Wallis posits an Anabaptist one. Jim Wallis, "What Does Washington Have to Say to Grand Rapids?" *Sojourners,* July 1977, 3-4.

[8] Jules Witcover, *Marathon: The Pursuit of the Presidency* (New York: Viking, 1977), 270-272.

[9] William Martin offers a glimpse of the dynamics involved in such meetings, contrasting the language used by 1980 Republican presidential candidates John Connally and Ronald Reagan during two separate meetings with evangelicals. Using the terminology of his "Evangelism Explosion" training course, Presbyterian pastor D. James Kennedy asked Connally what reason he would give should he die and God were to ask him why he should be admitted into heaven. Martin quotes a participant at the meeting: "Connally said, 'Well, my mother was a Methodist, my pappy was a Methodist, my grandmother was a Methodist, and I'd just tell him I ain't any worse than any of the other people that want to get to heaven.' Well, that fell like a stone on all these Christian leaders." When Kennedy asked Reagan the same question later, "Reagan dropped his eyes, looked at his feet, and said, 'I wouldn't give God any reason for letting me in. I'd just ask for mercy, because of what Jesus Christ did for me at Calvary.'" Reagan, of course, won the support of most of the evangelical leaders present despite the fact that, as Martin notes, "he was not a regular churchgoer and would surely have been soundly defeated by Jimmy Carter in the 'Sword Drills,' contests Southern Baptist youngsters use to sharpen and show off their knowledge of Scripture" (William Martin, *With God on Our Side: The Rise of the Religious Right in America* [New York: Broadway, 1996], 208-209).

[10] George W. Bush, *A Charge to Keep* (New York: William Morrow, 1999), 135-139. Bush did face controversy regarding his religious beliefs. It was because of his appearance at the racially segregated Bob Jones University during the South Carolina primary and because he cited Jesus as his favorite political philosopher in a primary debate.

Unlike Jimmy Carter, however, Bush ignited no political firestorm when he declared himself to be a "born again" Christian. Indeed, Bush relied on evangelicals to give him the margin of victory in his primary campaign against the reformist (and relatively secularist) John McCain.

11 "Yes, let us pray for the salvation of all those who live in that totalitarian darkness—pray they will discover the joy of knowing God. But until they do, let us be aware that while they preach the supremacy of the state, declare its omnipotence over individual man, and predict its eventual domination over all peoples on the earth, they are the focus of evil in the modern world" (Ronald Wilson Reagan, "Remarks at the Annual Convention of the National Association of Evangelicals, Orlando, Florida, March 8, 1983," in Ronald Reagan, *Speaking My Mind: Selected Speeches* [New York: Simon & Schuster, 1989], 178). The term "evil empire" almost immediately replaced "focus of evil in the modern world" in the parlance of public opinion and media commentators.

12 Robert Nisbet, *Conservatism: Dream and Reality* (Minneapolis: University of Minnesota Press, 1986), 104.

13 James Nuechterlein, "Conservative Confusions," *First Things,* May 2000, 7.

14 Christian Coalition leader Ralph Reed, for example, appealed to the mainstream nature of the Christian right in the 1990s by arguing, "The movement is best understood as an essentially defensive struggle by people seeking to sustain their faith and values. They want good schools, safe neighborhoods, faith-knit communities, and lower government debt to protect the financial future of their children. They are far less interested in legislating against the sins of others, and far more interested in protecting their own right to practice their religion and raise their children in a manner consistent with their values" (Ralph Reed, *After the Revolution: How the Christian Coalition Is Impacting America* [Dallas: Word, 1996], 18).

15 Thus, one Jewish neo-conservative writes, "Evangelical and fundamentalist Christians were once content to render unto Caesar what was Caesar's and to concentrate on saving their own souls. What drew them into politics, first behind Jerry Falwell's Moral Majority and then to Pat Robertson's Christian Coalition, was not any wish to impose their own views and mores on the rest of us. To the contrary: Far from being an aggressive move, it was a defensive one. They were trying to protect their own communities from the aggressions the liberal culture was committing against *them,* with the aid of the courts, the federal bureaucracies, and the ubiquitous media" (Norman Podhoretz, "The Christian Right and Its Demonizers," *National Review,* April 3, 2000, 31-32).

16 Stephen L. Carter, *God's Name in Vain: The Wrongs and Rights of Religion in Politics* (New York: Basic, 2000), 2.

17 One Protestant liberal ethicist, for example, argues that behind many of the positions of the populist Christian right leaders "is the work of such conservative theologians of a previous generation as Francis Schaeffer, Cornelius Van Til, and Carl F. H. Henry" (J. Philip Wogaman, *Christian Perspectives on Politics,* rev. and expanded ed. [Louisville: Westminster/John Knox, 2000], 129).

18 "Most nonevangelicals wouldn't know an errantist from an inerrantist, a pre- from a post- from an a-millennialist, and think being 'born again' is a warm tingle in the toes," observed Lutheran historian Martin E. Marty in the mainline Protestant magazine *Christian Century.* "But they do know that the evangelical-moralist sector has made most of the news in the past 12 years, and that it includes much more than the evangelism of Billy Graham" (Martin E. Marty, "The Years of the Evangelicals," *Christian Century,* February 15, 1989, 171). The fact that Marty's analysis of evangelicalism was written in the aftermath of the well-publicized string of sexual and financial scandals within the media empires of television evangelists such as Jim Bakker and Jimmy Swaggart only serves to strengthen Marty's point.

[19] As one observer notes, "Evangelical conservatives often confused the issue by claiming that their concern was to defend the private family and Christian norms against the larger, public, secular world. This view tended to obscure the fact that the issues were inevitably public with great public consequences" (Robert Booth Fowler, *A New Engagement: Evangelical Political Thought, 1966–1976* [Grand Rapids, Mich.: Eerdmans, 1982], 191).

[20] Jerry Falwell, "An Agenda for the 1980s," in *Piety and Politics: Evangelicals and Fundamentalists Confront the World,* ed. Richard John Neuhaus and Michael Cromartie (Washington, D.C.: Ethics and Public Policy Center, 1987), 113.

[21] Reed, *After the Revolution,* 11.

[22] Thus, evangelical theologians such as Carl Henry were horrified to find some in the Christian right "attaching Christian identity to specific legislative proposals such as a balanced-budget amendment or line item veto" (Carl F. H. Henry, *Has Democracy Had Its Day?* [Nashville: ERLC Publications, 1996], 53).

[23] For instance, two early leaders of Moral Majority later wondered whether evangelicals had forgotten that societal ills can be remedied only "by his Spirit, not through the Republican or Democratic party; and only through individual human hearts, not through human institutions, and most especially not through those representing the kingdoms of this world" (Cal Thomas and Ed Dobson, *Blinded by Might: Can the Religious Right Save America?* [Grand Rapids, Mich.: Zondervan, 1999], 178).

[24] Robert H. Bork, *Slouching Towards Gomorrah: Modern Liberalism and American Decline* (New York: HarperCollins, 1996). Compare Bork's outlook with that of Jerry Falwell, who proclaimed in his 1980 manifesto that "Americans want to see this country come back to basics, back to values, back to biblical morality, back to sensibility, back to patriotism" (Jerry Falwell, *Listen, America!* [Garden City, N.Y.: Doubleday, 1980], 19). This optimism was not limited to the religious conservative activists. Patrick J. Buchanan, then a syndicated columnist and former Nixon White House aide, had expressed the same sentiments in traditionalist conservative terms in the post-Watergate era, arguing that the basically conservative will of the people was subverted consistently by a center-left coalition in the government and party structures (Patrick J. Buchanan, *Conservative Votes, Liberal Victories: Why the Right Has Failed* [New York: Quadrangle, 1975]). As late as the 1990s, the Christian Coalition's Pat Robertson likewise expressed his belief that most Americans were ideologically in sync with the religious right (Pat Robertson, *The Turning Tide: The Fall of Liberalism and the Rise of Common Sense* [Waco, Tex.: Word, 1993]).

[25] Richard John Neuhaus sparked this discussion with a symposium on the "judicial usurpation of politics" in his *First Things* magazine. "What is happening now is the displacement of a constitutional order by a regime that does not have, will not obtain, and cannot command the consent of the people. If enough people do not care or do not know, that can be construed as a kind of negative consent, but it is not what the American people were taught to call government by the consent of the governed" (Richard John Neuhaus, "The End of Democracy? The Judicial Usurpation of Politics," *First Things,* November 1996, 18). The resulting controversy is recorded in Mitchell S. Muncy, *The End of Democracy?* (Dallas: Spence, 1997); and *The End of Democracy? II: A Crisis of Legitimacy* (Dallas: Spence, 1999).

[26] As the editor of the Billy Graham Evangelistic Association's *Decision* magazine would note, "The book dropped like a bomb into the peaceful summer Bible conference atmosphere of the postwar evangelical community" (Sherwood Eliot Wirt, *The Social Conscience of the Evangelical* [New York: Harper & Row, 1968], 47).

[27] This was not only in the social and political arenas. Henry sought to form an evangelical movement that would engage robustly the current streams of philosophy, soci-

ology, scientific thought, and political theory. See, for instance, Carl F. H. Henry, *Remaking the Modern Mind* (Grand Rapids, Mich.: Eerdmans, 1946).

[28] Evangelicalism was not a repudiation of fundamentalism but a reform movement within it. Henry, even in his most insistent criticisms of fundamentalism, asserted that he wished to "perform surgery" on fundamentalism, not to kill it (Henry, *Uneasy Conscience of Modern Fundamentalism*, 9). Indeed, Henry even maintained that his sharpest attack on contemporary fundamentalism was part of "self-examination currently going on in alert fundamentalist circles," rather than "a direct assault on basic convictions" such as those being lodged by continental theologians such as Emil Brunner (Carl F. H. Henry, *The Protestant Dilemma: An Analysis of the Current Impasse in Theology* [Grand Rapids, Mich.: Eerdmans, 1948], 58 n. 43). Indeed one observer reflected on the emergence of the postwar evangelical movement, not as a counterinsurgency against fundamentalism, but simply as "the fundamentalist reconsideration of itself" (Ronald H. Nash, *The New Evangelicalism* [Grand Rapids, Mich.: Zondervan, 1963], 29).

[29] Harold J. Ockenga, "Introduction," in Henry, *Uneasy Conscience of Modern Fundamentalism*, 14.

[30] Jon R. Stone, *On the Boundaries of American Evangelicalism: The Postwar Evangelical Coalition* (New York: St. Martin's Press, 1997), 138. Others have noted an even broader sense in which Henry and the early evangelical theologians sought to find a middle way theologically. Carl Trueman sees this mediating position especially in Henry's *God, Revelation, and Authority:* "Henry's entire work—of which *GRA* is the greatest single example—must be understood as an attempt to restate conservative Protestant theology in a manner which takes seriously the epistemological concerns of the Enlightenment without surrendering the content and truth-claims of orthodox Christianity. In doing so, Henry defined himself over against theological traditions on both the left and right of the spectrum: on the left, the reduction of theology to reflection upon the religious self-consciousness found in Schleiermacher and his progeny, and the anti-metaphysical trajectory of Kantian theology evident in Ritschl, Herrmann, and, latterly, Barth and the neo-orthodox; on the right, the 'fundamentalist' obscurantism of those who denied the relevance of education, learning, or cultural/social/political engagement to the life of the Christian church—a position which had characterized much, though by no means all, of American conservative Protestantism in the twenties and thirties in the wake of the disastrous Scopes' monkey trial and the equally unfortunate era of Prohibition" (Carl R. Trueman, "Admiring the Sistine Chapel: Reflections on Carl F. H. Henry's *God, Revelation, and Authority,*" *Themelios* 25 [2000]: 49).

[31] Carl F. H. Henry, *Aspects of Christian Social Ethics* (Grand Rapids, Mich.: Eerdmans, 1964), 116.

[32] By segregating political concerns from the gospel, Henry asserted, the fundamentalist evacuation from the public square had conceded it to liberals such as Walter Rauschenbusch, Harry Emerson Fosdick, and their more radical successors. He lamented the fact that the inadequacies of the Social Gospel were not devastated by conservative orthodoxy, but instead by the Christian realism of Reinhold Niebuhr, which was "as destructive of certain essential elements of the biblical view as it was reconstructive of others" (Carl F. H. Henry, *A Plea for Evangelical Engagement* [Grand Rapids, Mich.: Baker, 1971], 34-35).

[33] Henry, *Aspects of Christian Social Ethics*, 21. The language used by the Social Gospel pioneers themselves only bolsters Henry's critique. "We have a social gospel," Walter Rauschenbusch proclaimed. "We need a systematic theology large enough to match it and vital enough to back it" (Walter Rauschenbusch, *A Theology of the Social Gospel* [New York: Macmillan, 1917; reprint, Louisville: Westminster/John Knox, 1997], 1).

34 Carl F. H. Henry, "Dare We Renew the Controversy? Part II: The Fundamentalist Reduction," *Christianity Today*, June 24, 1957, 23.

35 Henry, *Remaking the Modern Mind*, 12. Henry's argument here would continue as he later argued that "only three formidable movements insist that man can know ultimate reality" in the context of modern Western thought. He identified these as communist materialism, Catholic Thomism, and evangelical Protestantism (Carl F. H. Henry, *Evangelicals at the Brink of Crisis* [Waco, Tex.: Word, 1967], 7).

36 The "kaleidoscope" imagery was articulated by Timothy L. Smith, "The Evangelical Kaleidoscope and the Call to Unity," *CSR* 15 (1986): 125-140. The "kaleidoscope" metaphor, which replaces Smith's earlier imagery of an evangelical "mosaic," is challenged by traditionalist conservatives such as R. Albert Mohler, Jr., "Reformist Evangelicalism: A Center Without a Circumference," in *A Confessing Theology for Postmodern Times*, ed. Michael S. Horton (Wheaton, Ill.: Crossway, 2000), 135-136.

37 Sydney Ahlstrom, *A Religious History of the American People* (New Haven, Conn.: Yale University Press, 1972), 812-813, 816. Ahlstrom's thesis finds agreement in Ernest R. Sandeen, who argues that this Reformed-dispensationalist coalition was not surprising since both groups were united in "general mood and in the elaboration of their central theme of biblical authority," particularly in the doctrine of the inerrancy of the scriptural autographs. As such, Sandeen notes, conservative American Protestantism "was comprised of an alliance between two newly-formulated nineteenth century theologies, dispensationalism and the Princeton theology, which, though not wholly compatible, managed to maintain a united front against modernism until about 1918" (Ernest R. Sandeen, "Toward a Historical Interpretation of the Origins of Fundamentalism," *Church History* 36 [1967]: 67, 74). See also Sandeen's *The Roots of Fundamentalism: British and American Millennialism, 1800–1930* (Grand Rapids, Mich.: Baker, 1970). This basic alliance between dispensationalists and covenantalists united against modernism is likewise seen in, for example, Richard D. Land, "Southern Baptists and the Fundamentalist Interpretation in Biblical Interpretation, 1845–1945," *Baptist History and Heritage* 19 (1984): 29. Land compellingly points to this alliance in the dispensationalist and Reformed contributors to the manifesto of early American conservative Protestantism, *The Fundamentals: A Testimony to the Truth*, 4 vols. (Los Angeles: Bible Institute of Los Angeles, 1917).

38 This acknowledges that the Sandeen thesis does have problems. George Marsden, for example, argues persuasively that Sandeen seems to subsume fundamentalism under the larger category of millennialism (George Marsden, "Defining Fundamentalism," *CSR* 1 [1971]: 141-151). Also, Sandeen errs by categorizing biblical inerrancy as a historical innovation fueled by the Princeton-dispensationalist alliance, a point that is challenged and corrected in John D. Woodbridge and Randall H. Balmer, "The Princetonians and Biblical Authority: An Assessment of the Ernest Sandeen Proposal," in *Scripture and Truth*, ed. D. A. Carson and John D. Woodbridge (Grand Rapids, Mich.: Baker, 1992), 244-279. D. G. Hart claims that Sandeen overemphasizes the hegemony between dispensational premillennialists and confessional Calvinists, largely because Hart equates "fundamentalism" with apocalypticism and young-earth creationism rather than with more "fundamental" issues such as biblical inerrancy and the historical nature of the Christian faith (D. G. Hart, "Machen, Confessional Presbyterianism, and Twentieth-Century Protestantism," in *Reforming the Center: American Protestantism, 1900 to the Present*, ed. Douglas Jacobsen and William Vance Trollinger, Jr. [Grand Rapids, Mich.: Eerdmans, 1998], 132). Nonetheless, few scholars would challenge Sandeen's basic identification of confessional Calvinism and dispensationalism as, for better or for worse, formative influences on American fundamentalism, and, ultimately, American evangelicalism. This is true even of those who also would emphasize other theological streams, such as the holiness tradition. See, for instance, Phillip E. Hammond, *The*

Protestant Presence in Twentieth-Century America: Religion and Political Culture (Albany: State University of New York Press, 1992), 46; and Richard Quebedeaux, *The Young Evangelicals: The Story of the Emergence of a New Generation of Evangelicals* (New York: Harper & Row, 1974), 7-14.

[39] For a discussion of the "fusionist" agenda of Buckley and Frank S. Meyer in the formation of the American conservative movement, see George H. Nash, *The Conservative Intellectual Movement in America Since 1945* (Wilmington, Del.: Intercollegiate Studies Institute, 1996). See also Godfrey Hodgson, *The World Turned Right Side Up: A History of the Conservative Ascendancy in America* (New York: Houghton-Mifflin, 1996).

[40] Henry wrote, "What concerns me more is that we have needlessly invited criticism and even ridicule, by a tendency in some quarters to parade secondary and sometimes even obscure aspects of our position as necessary frontal phases of our view. To this extent we have failed to oppose the full genius of the Hebrew-Christian outlook to its modern competitors. With the collapse of Renaissance ideals, it is needful that we come to a clear distinction, as evangelicals, between those basic doctrines on which we unite in a supernaturalistic world and life view and the area of differences on which we are not in agreement while yet standing true to the essence of biblical Christianity" (Henry, *Uneasy Conscience of Modern Fundamentalism*, 10).

[41] See, for example, Harold J. Ockenga, "The Unvoiced Multitudes," in *Evangelical Action! A Report of the Organization of the National Association of Evangelicals for United Action* (Boston: United Action Press, 1942), 27; and Edward John Carnell, *The Case for Orthodox Theology* (Philadelphia: Westminster, 1959), 114-119.

[42] Carl F. H. Henry, *Evangelicals in Search of Identity* (Waco, Tex.: Word, 1976), 29.

[43] This is seen in the contentious battles within the Presbyterian communion over the 1941 General Assembly of the Presbyterian Church in the United States controversy as to whether dispensationalism was within the bounds of the Westminster Confession of Faith. This move was denounced by Dallas Seminary president Lewis Sperry Chafer in "Dispensational Distinctions Challenged," *BibSac* 100 (1943): 337-343.

[44] As Sydney Ahlstrom observes, "[Dispensationalism] aroused strong resistance among American Protestants by denying what most evangelicals and all liberals firmly believed—that the Kingdom of God would come as part of the historical process. They could not accept the dispensationalist claim that all Christian history was a kind of meaningless 'parenthesis' between the setting aside of the Jews and the restoration of the Davidic Kingdom. This claim aroused violent reactions because it provided a rationale for destructive attitudes and encouraged secession from existing denominations. Especially objectionable was the tendency of dispensationalists to look for the Antichrist among the 'apostate churches' of this 'present age'" (Ahlstrom, *Religious History of the American People*, 811).

[45] The primary task of the theological vision of *Uneasy Conscience* was, as chapter 3 notes, the attempt to find a mediating position between the "Kingdom then" concept of fundamentalist dispensationalism and the "Kingdom now" concept of the liberal Social Gospel. In so doing, Henry would challenge the Kingdom concepts of both groups, as in, for instance, his treatment of the law in his *Christian Personal Ethics* (Grand Rapids, Mich.: Eerdmans, 1957), 278-326. Here Henry sides with the Reformed evangelicals against the dispensationalists in his insistence that the Sermon on the Mount is a particularization of the requirements of God for new covenant Christians. Henry also maintains here that the moral law, as summarized in the Mosaic Decalogue, is binding on new covenant believers.

[46] For Ladd's work on the Kingdom, see George Eldon Ladd, *Crucial Questions About the Kingdom of God* (Grand Rapids, Mich.: Eerdmans, 1952); *The Gospel and the*

Kingdom: Scriptural Studies in the Kingdom of God (Grand Rapids, Mich.: Eerdmans, 1959); *The Presence of the Future: The Eschatology of Biblical Realism* (Grand Rapids, Mich.: Eerdmans, 1974); and Ladd's magnum opus, *A Theology of the New Testament* (Grand Rapids, Mich.: Eerdmans, 1974). For examples of dispensationalist and Reformed covenantalist responses to Ladd, see Ladd's interchanges with dispensationalist Herman Hoyt, amillennialist Anthony Hoekema, and postmillennialist Loraine Boettner in *The Meaning of the Millennium,* ed. Robert G. Clouse (Downers Grove, Ill.: InterVarsity Press, 1977).

[47] Henry, *Uneasy Conscience of Modern Fundamentalism,* 51.

[48] Ibid.

[49] So Henry contended that *Uneasy Conscience* was written in order "to urge upon evangelicals the necessity for a deliberate restudy of the whole kingdom question, that the great evangelical agreements may be set effectively over against the modern mind, with the least dissipation of energy on secondary issues" (ibid.).

[50] Ibid., 57.

[51] For a discussion of the varying conceptions of the Kingdom in American Protestant theology and biblical scholarship, see Gösta Lundström, *The Kingdom of God in the Teaching of Jesus: A History of Interpretation from the Last Decades of the Nineteenth Century to the Present Day,* trans. J. Bulman (Edinburgh: Oliver & Boyd, 1963); Norman Perrin, *The Kingdom of God in the Teaching of Jesus* (Philadelphia: Westminster, 1963); Ladd, *Presence of the Future,* 3-42; Ladd, *Theology of the New Testament,* 54-67; and Mark Saucy, *The Kingdom of God in the Teaching of Jesus in Twentieth-Century Theology* (Dallas: Word, 1997).

[52] Dispensationalist fundamentalist William B. Riley, for instance, began his 1912 work on the Kingdom by repudiating liberal Protestant John Watson's sentence, "Two claims have been made within recent years: the Divine Fatherhood of God and the Kingdom of God." Riley countered that the Kingdom had never been lost by orthodox Christianity, but instead had been infused with new meaning by liberalism (William B. Riley, *The Evolution of the Kingdom* [New York: Charles C. Cook, 1912], 7-21). Similarly, covenant theologian Geerhardus Vos expressed mistrust toward "modern attempts to make the kingdom of God the organizing center of a theological system," precisely because Protestant liberals were restricting the idea of the Kingdom to ethical norms derivative from the concept of the universal fatherhood of God (Geerhardus Vos, *The Teaching of Jesus Concerning the Kingdom of God and the Church* [New York: American Tract Society, 1903], 5-8).

[53] Geerhardus Vos, *Biblical Theology: Old and New Testaments* (Grand Rapids, Mich.: Eerdmans, 1948), 412.

[54] Ibid.

[55] The key monographs articulating this viewpoint are Craig A. Blaising and Darrell L. Bock, eds., *Dispensationalism, Israel, and the Church: The Search for Definition* (Grand Rapids, Mich.: Zondervan, 1992); Craig A. Blaising and Darrell L. Bock, *Progressive Dispensationalism* (Wheaton, Ill.: Victor, 1993); and Robert L. Saucy, *The Case for Progressive Dispensationalism: The Interface Between Dispensational and Non-dispensational Theology* (Grand Rapids, Mich.: Zondervan, 1993). Widely recognized as a precursor to the concepts within progressive dispensationalism is Robert L. Saucy, *The Church in God's Program* (Chicago: Moody, 1972).

[56] Thus while numerous scholarly monographs and articles have debated the shifts in dispensational thought, covenantalists have been forced at times to make the case that significant changes within their sectors of Reformed theology even exist. See, for example, Richard Gaffin, "A Cessationist View," in *Are Miraculous Gifts for Today? Four Views,* ed. Wayne A. Grudem (Grand Rapids, Mich.: Zondervan, 1996), 29.

57 John M. Frame, "In Defense of Something Close to Biblicism: Reflections on *Sola Scriptura* and History in Theological Method," *WTJ* 59 (1997): 278. Willem VanGemeren likewise attributes to Vos a pivotal role in the formation of a new synthesis in American Reformed thought, particularly through Vos's impact on Westminster faculty such as John Murray. VanGemeren links the influence of Vos with the influence of Dutch Reformed theology via theologians such as Abraham Kuyper as formative for the development of contemporary American Reformed theology (Willem VanGemeren, "Systems of Continuity," in *Continuity and Discontinuity: Perspectives on the Relationship Between the Old and New Testaments,* ed. John S. Feinberg [Westchester, Ill.: Crossway, 1988], 47-50). Richard Gaffin points to Vos's contributions to biblical theology, along with those of Herman Ridderbos, as the root from which modified covenantalism has grown (Richard B. Gaffin, Jr., ed., "A New Paradigm in Theology?" *WTJ* 56 [1994]: 380). Similarly, Richard Lints cites an essential continuity between Vos and "the decidedly Vosian" theologies of Ridderbos, Ladd, and Westminster covenantalists such as Poythress, Gaffin, and Clowney (Richard Lints, "Two Theologies or One? Warfield and Vos on the Nature of Theology," *WTJ* 54 [1992]: 236 n. 6).

58 David L. Turner, "'Dubious Evangelicalism'?—A Response," *GTJ* 12 (1992): 267. Turner contrasts the growing move toward consensus between dispensationalists and covenantalists involved in this dialogue with the ongoing debates between the groups that represent "a throwback to earlier days where there was frequently more heat than light produced in this type of discussion." Here Turner specifically points to John Gerstner's *Wrongly Dividing the Word of Truth: A Critique of Dispensationalism* (Waco, Tex.: Word, 1991).

59 Craig Blaising laments the fact that dispensationalism since C. I. Scofield has had no Kingdom theology, "but competing interpretations which have had varying levels of influence" (Craig A. Blaising, "Contemporary Dispensationalism," *SWJT* 36 [1994]: 9). He outlines at least four representative Kingdom theologies proposed by more traditionalist dispensationalists, none of which focus on the Kingdom as the unifying center of theology (Blaising and Bock, *Progressive Dispensationalism,* 39-45). Robert Saucy argues that the Kingdom concept is not merely an integrative motif for theology but is instead "the unifying principle of biblical history" (Saucy, *Case for Progressive Dispensationalism,* 27-28).

60 Blaising and Bock, *Progressive Dispensationalism,* 48. This Kingdom theology is contested by the more traditionalist dispensationalists who find in it echoes of George Eldon Ladd. See, for instance, Stephen J. Nichols, "The Dispensational View of the Davidic Kingdom: A Response to Progressive Dispensationalism" (paper presented at the annual meeting of the Evangelical Theological Society, Philadelphia, November 18, 1995), 3.

61 Vern Poythress, *Understanding Dispensationalists,* 2nd ed. (Phillipsburg, N.J.: Presbyterian & Reformed, 1994), 41-43. Likewise, Anthony Hoekema, an early pioneer in the modified covenantalist project, starts his analysis with the centrality of the Kingdom as an integrative motif for the whole of theology, defining the Kingdom as "the reign of God dynamically active in human history through Jesus Christ, the purpose of which is the redemption of God's people from sin and from demonic powers, and the final establishment of the new heavens and the new earth" (Anthony Hoekema, *The Bible and the Future* [Grand Rapids, Mich.: Eerdmans, 1979], 45).

62 Note Kuyper's insistence on the centrality of the Kingdom of God as the integrative motif of Reformed theology in his 1898 Stone Lectures at Princeton: "The dominating principle was not, soteriologically, justification by faith, but in the widest sense cosmologically, the sovereignty of the Triune God over the whole cosmos, in all its spheres and kingdoms, visible and invisible" (Abraham Kuyper, *Lectures on Calvinism* [Grand Rapids, Mich.: Eerdmans, 1931], 79). Theologian John Bolt likewise maintains that the Kuyperian tradition safeguarded an important part of the Reformed theological heritage:

"The theme of the kingdom of God underscores the role of the Calvinist/Puritan tradition in shaping American Christianity," he writes. "It is the common (Calvinist!) conviction of the sovereignty of God through the reign of Christ that must be lived *on earth as it is in heaven* that also links the public theology and practice of Jonathan Edwards and Abraham Kuyper" (John Bolt, *A Free Church, A Holy Nation: Abraham Kuyper's American Public Theology* [Grand Rapids, Mich.: Eerdmans, 2001], 193).

63 Mark Noll, *The Scandal of the Evangelical Mind* (Grand Rapids, Mich.: Eerdmans, 1994), 169.

64 Covenant theologian D. G. Hart warns that the call for a Kingdom-oriented theology by Henry and others leads to a perilous "politicizing" of the church. Hart traces the "worldview Calvinism" of Henry, Francis Schaeffer, and others back to the culture-transformative theology of Kuyper, a "neo-Calvinist" tradition that, for Hart, diverges from the heritage of J. Gresham Machen (D. G. Hart, "Christianity, Modern Liberalism, and J. Gresham Machen," *Modern Age* 39 [1997]: 234-245). Hart dismisses what he calls "the so-called 'kingdom perspective'" of "those who trumpet a Reformed world and life view" as inconsistent with authentic Reformed identity (D. G. Hart, *"Christianity and Liberalism* in a Postliberal Age," *WTJ* 56 [1994]: 342). Among dispensationalist traditionalists, Robert Lightner warned early on that Henry's call to engagement might prove to be a Trojan horse for evangelical appropriation of Walter Rauschenbusch's Social Gospel, precisely because of Henry's rejection of the classical dispensationalist view of the Kingdom (Robert Lightner, *Neoevangelicalism Today* [Schaumburg, Ill.: Regular Baptist Press, 1978], 43-53). In the same vein, Charles Ryrie counters the Kingdom emphasis of progressive dispensationalism by arguing that the Scriptures "call us to obey church ethics, not kingdom ethics" (Charles C. Ryrie, *Dispensationalism* [Chicago: Moody, 1995], 176).

CHAPTER TWO

1 Ockenga argued, "That there is little agreement concerning the Kingdom is shown from the contrast between the writings of Stanley Jones and A. C. Gaebelein. It has always been easiest for me to think of the Kingdom as one, but with several forms—theocratic, church, millennial, but *all* the Kingdom of God. Unless the continuity and the breaks, along with the coterminous principles and ends, of the forms of the Kingdom are recognized this question becomes a hopeless puzzle to men" (Harold John Ockenga, "Introduction," in Carl F. H. Henry, *The Uneasy Conscience of Modern Fundamentalism* [Grand Rapids, Mich.: Eerdmans, 1947], 13-14).

2 It must also be said that Henry did so without intentionally alienating the strong dispensationalist element within conservative Protestantism. Even as Henry criticized elements of dispensational theology, he never reached for the kind of anti-dispensational polemic used by Carnell. See, for instance, the attack on dispensationalism as a feature of "cultic" fundamentalism in E. J. Carnell, *The Case for Orthodox Theology* (Philadelphia: Westminster, 1959), 117-119. Henry was not only more irenic toward the dispensationalists, but stood with them on at least some key points. Historian George Marsden, for example, quotes Harold Lindsell as listing Henry, along with himself, Wilbur Smith, Gleason Archer, and Charles Woodbridge as the "Pre-Trib Men" on the Fuller Theological Seminary faculty circa 1955 (George Marsden, *Reforming Fundamentalism: Fuller Seminary and the New Evangelicalism* [Grand Rapids, Mich.: Eerdmans, 1987], 151).

3 This is not the only time that Henry would make clear that he did not equate the errors of fundamentalism with the errors of liberalism. Henry corresponded with Billy Graham in June of 1950 expressing his reservations about whether Henry would be the best choice for the editorship of *Christianity Today* because of his firm convictions on this very matter. "I was convinced that liberalism and evangelicalism do not have equal right

and dignity in the true church" (Carl F. H. Henry, *Confessions of a Theologian* [Waco, Tex.: Word, 1986], 142). "It is quite popular at the moment to crucify the fundamentalist," he wrote earlier. "That is not the object of this series of articles; there is no sympathy here for the distorted attack on fundamentalism so often pressed by liberals and humanists. . . . The fundamentalist is placed on the cross, while the liberal goes scot-free in a forest of weasel words" (Henry, *Uneasy Conscience of Modern Fundamentalism*, 60-61).

[4] Henry, *Uneasy Conscience of Modern Fundamentalism*, 60.

[5] Rauschenbusch wrote, "Why should they erect a barbwire fence between the field of Socialism and Christianity which makes it hard to pass from one to the other? Organized Christianity represents the largest fund of sobriety, moral health, good will, moral aspiration, teaching ability, and capacity to sacrifice for higher ends, which can be found in America. If Socialists will count up the writers, lecturers, and organizers who acquired their power of agitation and moral appeal through the training they got in church life, they will realize what an equipment for propaganda lies stored in the Christian churches" (Walter Rauschenbusch, *Christianizing the Social Order* [New York: Macmillan, 1912], 398-399).

[6] See, for example, the discussion of Rauschenbusch's debate with premillennialist critic James Willmarth, an influential Northern Baptist pastor, in Philadelphia (Paul M. Minus, *Walter Rauschenbusch: American Reformer* [New York: Macmillan, 1988], 90-91).

[7] Rauschenbusch argued, therefore, "Our chief interest in any millennium is the desire for a social order in which the worth and freedom of every least human being will be honored and protected; in which the brotherhood of man will be expressed in the common possession of economic resources of society; and in which the spiritual good of humanity will be set high above the private profit interests of all materialistic groups. We hope for such an order for humanity as we hope for heaven for ourselves" (Walter Rauschenbusch, *A Theology for the Social Gospel* [New York: Macmillan, 1917; reprint, Louisville: Westminster/John Knox, 1997], 224).

[8] Forty years after the publication of *Uneasy Conscience,* Henry explained, "I had no inclination whatever to commend the modernist agenda, for its soft and sentimental theology could not sustain its 'millennial fanaticism.' Discarding historic doctrinal convictions and moving in the direction of liberalism would not revitalize fundamentalism." Carl F. H. Henry, *Twilight of a Great Civilization: The Drift Toward Neo-Paganism* (Westchester, Ill.: Crossway, 1988), 165.

[9] For example, Henry tied the Social Gospel's optimistic view of human progress to the nineteenth-century paeans by Herbert Spencer to the inevitability of evolutionary improvement (Henry, *Uneasy Conscience of Modern Fundamentalism*, 48; he cites Spencer, *Social Statistics* [New York: D. Appleton, 1883], 78).

[10] Henry, *Uneasy Conscience of Modern Fundamentalism*, 48.

[11] Ibid.

[12] Carl F. H. Henry, *The Protestant Dilemma: An Analysis of the Current Impasse in Theology* (Grand Rapids, Mich.: Eerdmans, 1949), 134.

[13] Henry, *Uneasy Conscience of Modern Fundamentalism*, 49.

[14] Ibid., 26.

[15] Ibid., 32.

[16] Ibid.

[17] Thus, Henry explained, "Dispensational theology resisted the dismissal of biblical eschatology and its import for ethics. But in its extreme forms it also evaporates the present-day relevance of much of the ethics of Jesus. Eschatology is invoked to postpone the significance of the Sermon and other segments of New Testament moral teaching to

a later Kingdom age. Dispensationalism erects a cleavage in biblical ethics in the interest of debatable eschatological theory. Dispensationalism holds that Christ's Kingdom has been postponed until the end of the Church age, and that Kingdom-ethics will become dramatically relevant again only in the future eschatological era. Liberalism destroyed biblical eschatology and secularized Christian ethics; and the interim ethic school abandoned the literal relevance of Jesus' eschatology and ethics alike; and extreme dispensationalism holds literally to both eschatology and ethics, but moves both into the future. New Testament theology will not sustain this radical repudiation of any present form of the Kingdom of heaven" (Carl F. H. Henry, *Christian Personal Ethics* [Grand Rapids, Mich.: Eerdmans, 1957], 550-551).

[18] And so he argued, "In the aftermath of the second World War, evangelical postmillennialism almost wholly abandoned the field of kingdom preaching to premillennialism and amillennialism, united in the common conviction that the return of Christ is a prerequisite for the future golden age, but divided over whether it will involve an earthly millennium. Assured of the ultimate triumph of right, contemporary evangelicalism also avoids a minimizing of earthly hostility to the gospel, as well as rejects the naturalistic optimism centering in evolutionary automatic progress. The bright hope of the imminent return of Christ is not minimized, and the kingdom hope is clearly distinguishable from the liberal confidence in a new social order of human making only" (Henry, *Uneasy Conscience of Modern Fundamentalism*, 134).

[19] Ibid., 50.

[20] Carl F. H. Henry, "The Vigor of the New Evangelicalism," *Christian Life*, January 1948, 32, emphasis his.

[21] Henry, *Uneasy Conscience of Modern Fundamentalism*, 51.

[22] Ibid.

[23] This is confirmed by Henry's defense of a premillennial eschatology nearly thirty years after the publication of *Uneasy Conscience* in his most systematic treatment of evangelical theology. Here Henry repeats his avoidance of a dispensational concentration on "prophetic minutiae" such as the events of the tribulation period or the revival of the Roman Empire. He sets forth, however, a positive defense of premillennialism. "The case for a millennial kingdom rests on three arguments: (1) The Old Testament prophets speak so emphatically of a coming universal age of earthly peace and justice that to transfer this vision wholly to a transcendent superterrestrial kingdom is unjustifiable; (2) because the historical fall of Adam involves all human history in its consequences it requires an historical redemption that extends 'far as the curse is found' to complete Christ's victory over sin; (3) the most natural interpretation of Revelation 20 seems to suggest an earthly millennial reign of Christ prior to the inauguration of God's eternal kingdom" (Carl F. H. Henry, *God, Revelation, and Authority*, 6 vols. [Waco, Tex.: Word, 1983; reprint, Wheaton, Ill.: Crossway, 1999], 6:504).

[24] Carl F. H. Henry, *A Plea for Evangelical Demonstration* (Grand Rapids, Mich.: Baker, 1971), 42.

[25] Henry contended, "The fact that the Bible holds before man the assured prospect of a coming age of universal peace and justice provides no basis for any forcible Christian imposition of social ideals. Social activists seeking to supply a Christian basis for the theology of revolution emphasize that catastrophic judgment is integral to biblical messianism and eschatology, and on that ground argue that revolutionary social action is basic to the dynamic nature of all God's action in history. But to transpose the end-time messianic prerogatives in this way to the church in history is sheer presumption. That the Son of God will descend at last upon the nations in cataclysmic final judgment and in power and great glory is beyond doubt. But vengeance belongs to God alone, and not to the twentieth century avant-garde" (ibid., 104).

26 With such in the background, Henry, in the pages of dispensationalist Donald Grey Barnhouse's *Eternity* magazine, rallied evangelicals to oppose communism, not on the basis of nationalism alone, but to confront Marxism with a resurgent orthodox counter-eschatology: "That the whole social order needs to be destroyed, and a new order set in its place, is a theme with an almost New Testament radicalness. Christianity had declared that the whole socio-historical movement is sinful and headed for divine wrath, that only supernatural redemption and regeneration can retard its decline, and that the ideal historical order waits the return of Jesus Christ in power and glory. This biblical verdict on history seemed too pessimistic for western man, with his philosophies of exaggerated divine immanence and evolutionary ascent. But today almost half the population of the world is controlled by a philosophy which calls, in a naturalistic spirit, for the complete inversion of the social order" (Carl F. H. Henry, "Christianity and the Economic Crisis," *Eternity*, June 1955, 15). This article was taken from an address given by Henry to the thirteenth annual convention of the National Association of Evangelicals, meeting in Chicago in April 1955.

27 Ibid.

28 Henry charged, therefore, "The fact that the West surrendered the radical biblical judgment on history and took Hegel and Darwin rather than Jesus and Paul as its guides, and substituted the optimistic 'social gospel' for the redemptive good news, opened this door for a radical critique of the social order from the Marxist rather than Christian sources. There was plenty to criticize in the sphere of economics a century ago, even as there is today, even if the Marxists overstate and distort the situation. Christianity holds out no hope for the achievement of absolute economic and social righteousness in present history" (Henry, *Uneasy Conscience of Modern Fundamentalism*, 52).

29 Ibid., 53.

30 Henry argued, "He proclaimed kingdom truth with a constant, exuberant joy. It appears as the central theme of His preaching. To delete His kingdom references, parabolic and non-parabolic, would be to excise most of His words. The concept 'kingdom of God' or 'kingdom of heaven' is heard repeatedly from His lips, and it colors all of His works" (ibid., 52).

31 For evidence of this reality in the New Testament, Henry surveyed the preaching of the apostles in Acts, the references both to a present manifestation of the Kingdom and to a future consummation in the epistles of Paul and the writer of Hebrews, and the Apocalypse of John.

32 Henry, *Uneasy Conscience of Modern Fundamentalism*, 53.

33 Ibid., 54.

34 Henry, "Vigor of the New Evangelicalism," 32.

35 Henry included dispensationalists such as W. A. Criswell, Charles Feinberg, Wilbur Smith, and John Walvoord, and covenant theologians such as Edmund Clowney and Herman Ridderbos. Papers were presented on topics such as a debate between Feinberg and Clowney on whether a physical temple would be rebuilt in Jerusalem in fulfillment of biblical prophecy, or whether the final temple had reached its fulfillment in the person of Christ. These papers are collected in Carl F. H. Henry, ed., *Prophecy in the Making: Messages Prepared for the Jerusalem Conference on Biblical Prophecy* (Carol Stream, Ill.: Creation House, 1971).

36 Henry set forth this view in the following terms: "Professor Oscar Cullmann has depicted the present shifting eschatological situation in the graphic imagery of a cosmic conflict. While the crucial battle has already been fought and won, the cease-fire is yet future, and warfare will continue for an indeterminate and uncertain time span. The decisive battle has occurred and has already been won by the incarnation and resurrection of the crucified One; warring continues, however, until that future victory day when

at the Redeemer's return all weapons will be laid silent in consequence and crowning of all previous salvation history" (Carl F. H. Henry, "Jesus Christ and the Last Days," in *Prophecy in the Making,* 180).

[37] Ladd's eschatological scholarship included monographs such as *Crucial Questions About the Kingdom of God* (Grand Rapids, Mich.: Eerdmans, 1952); *The Gospel of the Kingdom: Scriptural Studies in the Kingdom of God* (Grand Rapids, Mich.: Eerdmans, 1959); *The Blessed Hope* (Grand Rapids, Mich.: Eerdmans, 1956); *A Commentary on the Revelation of John* (Grand Rapids, Mich.: Eerdmans, 1972); *The Presence of the Future: The Eschatology of Biblical Realism* (Grand Rapids, Mich.: Eerdmans, 1974); and *A Theology of the New Testament* (Grand Rapids, Mich.: Eerdmans, 1974), along with articles such as "Eschatology and the Unity of New Testament Theology," *Expository Times* 68 (1957): 268-273; "The Revelation of Christ's Glory," *Christianity Today,* September 1, 1958, 13-14; "Revelation 20 and the Millennium," *RevExp* 57 (1960): 167-175; and "The Kingdom of God—Reign or Realm?" *JBL* 81 (1962): 230-238.

[38] Henry, for instance, cites his dependence upon Ladd's critique of the dispensationalist distinction between the "Kingdom of God" and the "Kingdom of heaven" (Henry, *Christian Personal Ethics,* 550-551).

[39] George Eldon Ladd, *Jesus and the Kingdom: The Eschatology of Biblical Realism* (New York: Harper & Row, 1964), 3-40. This work was later revised, updated, and republished in 1974 as *The Presence of the Future.*

[40] Ladd, *Jesus and the Kingdom,* 35. "For Kümmel, the Kingdom of God by definition is the future eschatological age, the eschaton which Jesus expected to appear in the near future," Ladd explained. "However, Kümmel takes a decisive step beyond most writers who hold this view by recognizing that the eschaton was already present in Jesus' person" (ibid., 28). In his treatment of Kümmel, Ladd interacts with Werner Georg Kümmel, *Verheissung und Erfüllung* (Zurich: Zwingli, 1953).

[41] Ladd, for instance, expressed agreement with Kümmel's exegesis of Matthew 12:28 to assert that the Kingdom was somehow present in the person of Jesus. Ladd disagreed with Kümmel's assertion, however, that what was present was a "sign" of the imminent eschatological Kingdom. "Such expedients do not satisfy the demands of the text if a better solution can be found," Ladd argued. "The verse does not say that the signs of the kingdom, or powers of the kingdom, or the preaching of the kingdom, are present; the kingdom itself is present" (Ladd, "Kingdom of God—Reign or Realm?" 237).

[42] Eldon Jay Epp, "Mediating Approaches to the Kingdom: Werner George Kümmel and George Eldon Ladd," in *The Kingdom of God in Twentieth-Century Interpretation,* ed. Wendell Willis (Peabody, Mass.: Hendrickson, 1987), 46.

[43] See, for instance, Ladd's statement of indebtedness to both Cullmann and Vos in *Gospel of the Kingdom,* 25, 34, 115; and in Ladd's *A Theology of the New Testament,* rev. ed. (Grand Rapids, Mich.: Eerdmans, 1993), 44-45, 66-67.

[44] For a survey of this debate, especially focusing on the divergence between the consistent eschatology of Johannes Weiss and Albert Schweitzer, the realized eschatology of C. H. Dodd, and the existentialist eschatology of Rudolf Bultmann, see Wendell Wills, "The Discovery of the Eschatological Kingdom: Johannes Weiss and Albert Schweitzer"; and Richard Hiers, Jr., "Pivotal Reactions to the Eschatological Interpretations: Rudolf Bultmann and C. H. Dodd," in *Kingdom of God in Twentieth-Century Interpretation,* 1-33. See also the survey by Mark Saucy, *The Kingdom of God in the Teaching of Jesus in Twentieth-Century Theology* (Dallas: Word, 1997), 3-21. Ladd appraises the debate in this field from Ritschl to Kümmel and beyond in *Crucial Questions About the Kingdom of God,* 21-39.

[45] George Eldon Ladd, "Why Not Prophetic-Apocalyptic?" *JBL* 76 (1957): 192-200.

[46] Epp, "Mediating Approaches to the Kingdom," 46.

[47] Ladd elaborated on his concern at this point by noting, "Amillennialists deny the future earthly reign of Christ; premillennialists, at least of the dispensational persuasion, tend to minimize if not to deny a present spiritual kingdom inaugurated by Christ. . . . There has not been written a comprehensive study of the kingdom of God in the New Testament from a conservative, premillennial position which takes into account the critical literature; in fact, there does not exist an up-to-date conservative critical treatment of the kingdom of God from any point of view" (Ladd, *Crucial Questions About the Kingdom of God,* 59).

[48] Ladd, *Theology of the New Testament,* 54-132.

[49] Ladd, *Crucial Questions About the Kingdom of God,* 97, emphasis his.

[50] This emphasis he explained in the following terms: "Jesus was continually concerned with two emphases in his portrayal of the eschatological drama: its ultimate accomplishment, and its immediate application. The ultimate consummation will involve the perfect realization of God's reign in all creation; and the immediate application involves the personal realization of God's reign within the lives of men by which they are prepared to enter the future kingdom" (ibid.).

[51] "Evangelical Christians have been so exercised with the eschatological or future aspects of the Kingdom of God that it has often ceased to have immediate relevance to contemporary Christian life, except as a hope. Thus the very term, the 'Kingdom of God,' to many Christians means first of all the millennial reign of Christ on earth. This, however, misplaces the emphasis of the Gospels. The distinctive characteristic about Jesus' teaching is that in some real sense, the Kingdom of God has come in his person and mission (Matt. 12:28)" (Ladd, *Presence of the Future,* xi).

[52] This is the thrust of the argument in, among numerous works, Alva J. McClain, *The Greatness of the Kingdom* (Grand Rapids, Mich.: Zondervan, 1959).

[53] George Eldon Ladd, "Dispensational Theology," *Christianity Today,* October 12, 1959, 39.

[54] John F. Walvoord, review of *Jesus and the Kingdom,* by George Eldon Ladd, *BibSac* 122 (1965): 74.

[55] Ibid.

[56] Ibid., 74-75.

[57] John F. Walvoord, review of *The Presence of the Future: The Eschatology of Biblical Realism,* by George Eldon Ladd, *BibSac* 131 (1974): 273.

[58] Walvoord, review of *Jesus and the Kingdom,* 75.

[59] J. Dwight Pentecost, *Things to Come: A Study in Biblical Eschatology* (Grand Rapids, Mich.: Zondervan, 1958), 142. Here Pentecost distinguishes between seven different ways the term "kingdom" is used in the Hebrew and Greek Scriptures. The "spiritual" Kingdom is thus to be distinguished both from the political, millennial Kingdom and from the "mystery form" of the Kingdom of God.

[60] Pentecost argued therefore, "The mystery was the fact that when the One in whom this program was to be realized was publicly presented He would be rejected and an age would fall between His rejection and the fulfillment of God's purpose of sovereignty at His second advent. The mystery form of the kingdom, then, has reference to the age between the two advents of Christ. The mysteries of the kingdom of heaven describe the conditions that prevail on the earth in that interim while the king is absent. These mysteries thus relate this present age to the eternal purposes of God in regard to His kingdom" (ibid., 143).

[61] Ladd, *Crucial Questions About the Kingdom of God,* 117.

62 George Eldon Ladd, "Historic Premillennialism," in *The Meaning of the Millennium: Four Views*, ed. Robert G. Clouse (Downers Grove, Ill.: InterVarsity Press, 1977), 31.

63 Ladd, *Theology of the New Testament*, 372-373.

64 Ibid.

65 Ibid., 373.

66 Ladd, "Historic Premillennialism," 32.

67 Ladd, *Theology of the New Testament*, 373.

68 Ladd, "Historic Premillennialism," 29-30.

69 Charles L. Feinberg, *Millennialism: The Two Major Views* (Chicago: Moody, 1980), 145. This monograph is the third edition of Feinberg's work, first published in 1936, with updates in 1954, 1961, and 1980. This fact alone demonstrates the pace at which the eschatological debates within evangelicalism have proceeded.

70 Arthur W. Kuschke, Jr., review of *Crucial Questions About the Kingdom of God,* by George Eldon Ladd, *WTJ* 15 (1953): 156.

71 Ibid., 157. "Of course the underlying issue is the interpretation of Old Testament prophecy. If the Old Testament itself shows that its prophecies were intended to have a spiritual sense and the New Testament shows that these spiritual prophecies are intended to describe the present kingdom, then the kingdom which our Lord announced is truly that which was promised" (ibid.).

72 Ladd, "Revelation 20 and the Millennium," 170. Ladd here cites Louis Berkhof, *The Kingdom of God* (Grand Rapids, Mich.: Eerdmans, 1951), 166.

73 Ladd, *Crucial Questions About the Kingdom of God*, 56.

74 "The kingdom, the rule of God, is indeed to have a glorious manifestation when Christ, as the glorious King, rules over the earth in fulfillment of the Old Testament prophecies. But before that manifestation of God's rule there must intervene another revelation of God's regal power in a spiritual realm as the King comes among men in humility to inaugurate a new reign of God in the hearts of men. This is not to deny the future millennial rule; to do so is to do injustice to other passages of Scripture. To insist that the spiritual reign of Christ, the present inner aspect of God's kingdom, is the entirety of the kingdom and thereby to deny a future glorious manifestation, is to make as one-sided an emphasis as to insist that the kingdom is nothing but a future earthly reign of Christ and has no present spiritual reality. Both the present and the future are included in the fullness of the revelation of God's kingly power" (ibid., 116-117).

75 Stanley J. Grenz, "The Deeper Significance of the Millennium Debate," *SWJT* 36 (1994): 20.

76 Craig L. Blomberg, "A Response to G. R. Beasley-Murray on the Kingdom," *JETS* 35 (1992): 31. Of this trend, Blomberg remarks, "As a slightly tongue-in-cheek aside, one might observe that if a theological perspective is held jointly by such a diverse but impressive array of scholars such as Trilling, Kümmel, Jeremias, Ladd, Marshall, Beasley-Murray, Saucy, and Blaising, it must almost certainly be true. In view of the tenacity at the grassroots level of older dispensationalism on the one hand and the resurgence of idiosyncratic studies like Clayton Sullivan's wholesale rejection of realized eschatology on the other hand, a vigorous promotion of inaugurated eschatology is surely not out of place" (ibid., 32). Blomberg here cites Clayton Sullivan, *Rethinking Realized Eschatology* (Macon, Ga.: Mercer University Press, 1988).

77 This is a matter of similar method and not a matter of similar doctrinal exposition. Grudem is a historic premillennialist in the tradition of George Eldon Ladd, and thus, a very definite departure from Hodge. Nonetheless, Grudem does not utilize to any measurable extent Ladd's eschatological focus, much less his focused treatment of the "already" and "not yet" aspects of the Kingdom. To the contrary, the Kingdom of God

is treated in only two pages in Grudem's entire systematic project, and that under the doctrine of the church. Eschatology is largely limited to the end, in a section entitled "The Doctrine of the Future" (Wayne A. Grudem, *Systematic Theology* [Grand Rapids, Mich.: Zondervan, 1994]).

78 Millard J. Erickson, *A Basic Guide to Eschatology: Making Sense of the Millennium* (Grand Rapids, Mich.: Baker, 1998).

79 Millard J. Erickson, *Christian Theology*, 2nd ed. (Grand Rapids, Mich.: Baker, 1998), 1158-1159. To be fair, Erickson identifies Jürgen Moltmann as his foil for making eschatology "the whole of theology." Nonetheless, he seems to move on from there to the general notion that in some circles Christianity "is seen as so thoroughly eschatological that 'eschatological' is attached as an adjective to virtually every theological concept" (ibid.).

80 Ibid., 1159. Having observed this, however, it is important to note that Erickson himself affirms the "already/not yet" Kingdom consensus, even if he does not emphasize it. In his conclusions on eschatology, Erickson writes, "We need to recognize that eschatology does not pertain exclusively to the future. Jesus did introduce a new age, and the victory over the powers of evil has already been won, even though the struggle is still to be enacted in history" (ibid., 1170).

81 Gordon R. Lewis and Bruce A. Demarest, *Integrative Theology*, 3 vols. (Grand Rapids, Mich.: Zondervan, 1994), 3:307-499.

82 Henry's later writings are in essential doctrinal continuity with those of his earlier years in the formative stages of the evangelical movement. This is contra Roger Olson, who holds that Henry's later writings "retreated more and more toward a narrow, almost fundamentalistic mentality" (Roger Olson, *The Story of Christian Theology: Twenty Centuries of Tradition and Reform* [Downers Grove, Ill.: InterVarsity Press, 1999], 595). While Henry's later writings do show an increased alarm about the prospects of evangelicalism and the cultural situation in Western civilization, Olson has not demonstrated any substantive doctrinal shift in Henry's thought.

83 Henry, *God, Revelation, and Authority*, 4:575.

84 For the fullest development of Henry's inaugurated eschatology, see Carl F. H. Henry, "Reflections on the Kingdom of God," *JETS* 35 (1992): 39-49.

85 Henry, *God, Revelation, and Authority*, 4:612.

86 For Henry's use of inaugurated eschatology in discussion of theodicy, see, for example, *God, Revelation, and Authority*, 6:303-304, 457. For his treatment of inaugurated eschatology in terms of contemporary Jewish Christological questions about the non-appearance of the messianic Kingdom, see ibid., 3:118-146.

87 For a sketch of Boyd's "warfare worldview" in opposition to what he calls the traditional Reformed "meticulous blueprint" view of divine providence, see Gregory A. Boyd, *God at War: The Bible and Spiritual Conflict* (Downers Grove, Ill.: InterVarsity Press, 1997), 9-27. For a classical theist rebuttal of the open theism of Boyd and his like-minded colleagues, see Bruce A. Ware, *God's Lesser Glory: The Diminished God of Open Theism* (Wheaton, Ill.: Crossway, 2000).

88 Boyd, *God at War*, 171-268. Boyd, however, radically alters the traditional perspective of evangelical Kingdom theology on the relationship between the eschatological Kingdom and the general sovereignty of God, with his view that the cosmos is ultimately "more of a democracy than it is a monarchy."

89 It is interesting to note here that Boyd's *God at War* received a commendation from C. Peter Wagner, the Fuller Theological Seminary church growth scholar who has drawn heavily from the "power evangelism" thought of John Wimber.

90 This is especially clear in Grenz's treatment of Christology and pneumatology (Stanley

J. Grenz, *Theology for the Community of God* [Grand Rapids, Mich.: Eerdmans, 2000], 327-334, 361-371).

[91] Ibid., 609.

[92] Ibid.

[93] Bruce A. Ware, "New Dimensions in Eschatology," in *New Dimensions in Evangelical Thought: Essays in Honor of Millard J. Erickson,* ed. David S. Dockery (Downers Grove, Ill.: InterVarsity Press, 1998), 358.

[94] Ibid., 355.

[95] Of course, the word "relatively" is of importance here since, as Craig Blaising has noted, there has always been some degree of diversity within dispensational theological circles, even on some aspects of this issue (Craig A. Blaising, "Dispensationalism: The Search for Definition," in *Dispensationalism, Israel, and the Church: The Search for Definition,* ed. Craig A. Blaising and Darrell L. Bock [Grand Rapids, Mich.: Zondervan, 1992], 13-36).

[96] Ibid., 52. In addition to Chafer, Ladd also cited as influential on the dispensational theology of his day such works as W. E. Blackstone, *Jesus Is Coming* (New York: Revell, 1908); A. C. Gaebelein, *The Harmony of the Prophetic Word* (New York: Our Hope, 1907); and W. B. Riley, *The Evolution of the Kingdom* (New York: Charles C. Cook, 1913).

[97] Theologian Walter Elwell, for example, notes such in a review of Robert Saucy's *Case for Progressive Dispensationalism.* "In 96 exhaustive footnotes, dispensational heavyweights Lewis Sperry Chafer and John Walvoord do not appear once, whereas Ridderbos, Ladd, Perrin, Cranfield, Barrett, and even O. T. Allis are extensively—and favorably—quoted," he observes. "Saucy's is as good a summary on the kingdom as one will find and is in the 'already/not yet' mold of Werner Kümmel" (Walter A. Elwell, "Dispensationalisms of the Third Kind," *Christianity Today,* September 12, 1994, 28). Meanwhile, Craig Blomberg marvels that inaugurated eschatology, with a robust present role for the Kingdom of God, "has been increasingly approximated by some in the dispensationalist study group of the Evangelical Theological Society, most notably Robert Saucy and Craig Blaising" (Blomberg, "Response to G. R. Beasley-Murray on the Kingdom," 32).

[98] "Bock's views on the kingdom and the present session of Christ are a return to the theology of George Eldon Ladd. Consequently, progressive dispensationalism, insofar as Bock's influence, is rooted in concepts foreign to dispensationalism" (Stephen J. Nichols, "Already Ladd—Not Yet Dispensationalism: D. Bock and Progressive Dispensationalism" [paper presented at the eastern regional meeting of the Evangelical Theological Society, Philadelphia, April 2, 1993], 2-3; see also Stephen J. Nichols, "The Dispensational View of the Davidic Kingdom: A Response to Progressive Dispensationalism," *The Master's Seminary Journal* 7 [1996]: 232).

[99] See, for example, Darrell L. Bock, "The Reign of the Lord Christ," in *Dispensationalism, Israel, and the Church,* 37-67; "Current Messianic Activity and OT Davidic Promise: Dispensationalism, Hermeneutics, and NT Fulfillment," *TrinJ* 15 (1994): 85-102; and "The Son of David and the Saints' Task: The Hermeneutics of Initial Fulfillment," *BibSac* 150 (1993): 440-457.

[100] Bock, "Reign of the Lord Christ," 38.

[101] Robert Saucy is more reluctant than other progressives to argue that the healing and exorcism ministries are "signs" of the Kingdom rather than an "already" manifestation of the Kingdom itself. He ties these signals of the coming Kingdom specifically to the power of the Spirit upon Jesus as the "anointed one" of Old Testament prophecy. Saucy says this view of inaugurated eschatology is close to those of Ladd and Herman Ridderbos (Robert L. Saucy, *The Case for Progressive Dispensationalism: The Interface*

Between Dispensational and Non-dispensational Theology [Grand Rapids, Mich.: Zondervan, 1993], 98-100). Saucy cites Ladd, *Presence of the Future,* 211; and Herman Ridderbos, *The Coming of the Kingdom* (Philadelphia: Presbyterian & Reformed, 1962), 115.

[102] Bock, "Reign of the Lord Christ," 42.

[103] Ibid., 44.

[104] Ibid., 49.

[105] Craig A. Blaising and Darrell L. Bock, *Progressive Dispensationalism* (Wheaton, Ill.: Victor, 1993), 84.

[106] Bock argues, "The kingdom is earthly. Jesus will rule as a Davidite on the earth and bring a total deliverance to it as he exercises his sovereignty over all. Such hope is most strongly expressed in Luke 1:32,33, 46-55, 69-75. The eschatological discourses and the remarks of Acts 1:11 and 3:18-21 show that the future hope has not been consumed in the present inauguration, but remains alive, connected to its OT roots. God is faithful and brings all of his promises to fruition, even those made to Israel. Spiritual deliverance, however, is also his. Jesus is the rising sun who shines on those in darkness and leads them into the path of peace (Luke 1:78-79). The promise of the Spirit (Luke 3:15-18; 24:49; Acts 1:8) and the hope of forgiveness of sins (Luke 24:47) are central here. Jesus' miracles over demons and other forces show that he is able to bring such promises to realization" (Darrell L. Bock, *Luke 1:1–9:50,* Baker Exegetical Commentary on the New Testament [Grand Rapids, Mich.: Baker, 1994], 3a:32).

[107] Saucy, *Case for Progressive Dispensationalism,* 70-76.

[108] Ibid., 80.

[109] Robert L. Saucy, "The Presence of the Kingdom in the Life of the Church," *BibSac* 145 (1988): 44.

[110] Mark Saucy, "Exaltation Christology in Hebrews: What Kind of Reign?" *TrinJ* 14 (1993): 41-62. Darrell Bock convincingly refutes Saucy's contention that the early church regarded Jesus as "Lord," without reference to Him as "King." The debate extends even to the catacomb drawings of the early Roman church. Against the assertion that these drawings picture Jesus in the roles of a philosopher, miracle worker, or good shepherd, though never as a monarch, Bock responds correctly that shepherd imagery is explicitly monarchial, coming from Old Testament passages such as Ezekiel 34:22-24, which speak of the Davidic Son ruling over a flock as a shepherd (Bock, "Current Messianic Activity and OT Davidic Promise," 65).

[111] Saucy, "Exaltation Christology in Hebrews," 61.

[112] For a discussion of the present activity of the ascended Messiah from a traditionalist dispensationalist perspective, see John F. Walvoord, "The Present Work of Christ on Earth," *BibSac* 122 (1965): 291-301.

[113] Bock, "Son of David and the Saints' Task," 448.

[114] Ibid., 451.

[115] Blaising and Bock, *Progressive Dispensationalism,* 176.

[116] Darrell L. Bock, "Why I Am a dispensationalist with a Small 'd'," *JETS* 41 (1998): 391.

[117] For a discussion of popular dispensational apocalypticism, see Paul Boyer, *When Time Shall Be No More: Prophecy Belief in Modern American Culture* (Cambridge, Mass.: Harvard University Press, 1992); and Richard Kyle, *The Last Days Are Here Again: A History of the End Times* (Grand Rapids, Mich.: Baker, 1998), 99-138.

[118] These would include, for example, former Dallas Seminary president John Walvoord's popular monograph explaining the events coinciding with the Persian Gulf War in terms of biblical prophecy (John Walvoord, *Armageddon, Oil and the Middle*

East Crisis: What the Bible Says About the Future of the Middle East and the End of Western Civilization [Grand Rapids, Mich.: Zondervan, 1990]).

[119] Darrell L. Bock, "Charting Dispensationalism," *Christianity Today,* September 12, 1994, 28.

[120] Ibid., 29.

[121] Blaising and Bock, *Progressive Dispensationalism,* 19-20.

[122] Craig A. Blaising, "Premillennialism," in *Three Views on the Millennium and Beyond,* ed. Darrell L. Bock (Grand Rapids, Mich.: Zondervan, 1999), 189-190.

[123] Blaising and Bock, *Progressive Dispensationalism,* 101.

[124] Ibid., 116-123.

[125] Charles C. Ryrie, *Dispensationalism* (Chicago: Moody, 1995), 167.

[126] "Although progressive dispensationalism has certain affinities with covenant premillennialism (especially as in the work of G. Ladd), progressive dispensationalism's concept of the millennium is far more 'Israelitish' than that of the latter," concedes one traditionalist dispensationalist (Stephen J. Nichols, review of *Progressive Dispensationalism,* by Craig A. Blaising and Darrell L. Bock, *TrinJ* 15 [1994]: 255).

[127] Gerry Breshears, "Dispensational Study Group Discussion," *GTJ* 10 (1989): 162. Breshears here quotes Craig Blaising from the Study Group minutes of the 1989 meeting.

[128] Ware recognizes that this is because of the nature of covenant theology itself: "If there is one covenant of grace spanning the history of fallen and redeemed humankind, it stands to reason that God's kingdom or rule, while always and only one unified kingdom, may be manifest in various partial expressions leading up to its ultimate eschatological realization" (Ware, "New Dimensions in Eschatology," 355).

[129] Robert L. Saucy, "Response to *Understanding Dispensationalists,* by Vern S. Poythress," *GTJ* 10 (1989): 144.

[130] As the Westminster Confession of Faith (1646) states, "Man, by his fall, having made himself incapable of life by that covenant, the Lord was pleased to make a second, commonly called the covenant of grace, whereby he freely offereth unto sinners life and salvation by Jesus Christ; requiring of them faith in him that they may be saved, and promising to give unto all those that are ordained to eternal life his Holy Spirit, to make them willing and able to believe" (see "The Westminster Confession of Faith," in *Creeds of the Churches: A Reader in Christian Doctrine from the Bible to the Present,* 3rd edition, ed. John H. Leith [Louisville: John Knox, 1982], 202).

[131] John R. Murray, *The Covenant of Grace: A Biblico-Theological Study* (Phillipsburg, N.J.: Presbyterian & Reformed, 1953), 23.

[132] Berkhof, *Kingdom of God,* 167.

[133] Louis Berkhof, *Systematic Theology* (Grand Rapids, Mich.: Eerdmans, 1941; reprint, Edinburgh: Banner of Truth, 1958), 410-411.

[134] Anthony Hoekema, *The Bible and the Future* (Grand Rapids, Mich.: Eerdmans, 1979), 45. Hoekema cites Ladd, *Presence of the Future,* 331. This is one of numerous citations of both Ladd and Ridderbos in Hoekema's work. To further elaborate his viewpoint here, Hoekema explains, "The kingdom of God, therefore, is to be understood as the reign of God dynamically active in human history through Jesus Christ, the purpose of which is the redemption of God's people from sin and from demonic powers, and the final establishment of the new heavens and the new earth. It means that the great drama of the history of salvation has been inaugurated, and that the new age has been ushered in. The kingdom must not be understood as merely the salvation of certain individuals or even as the reign of God in the hearts of his people; it means nothing less than the reign of God over his entire created universe" (Hoekema, *Bible and the Future,* 45).

135 The importance of Gaffin for understanding the role of inaugurated eschatology within Reformed evangelicalism would be difficult to overestimate. Sinclair Ferguson credits Gaffin with synthesizing the theological advances of Geerhardus Vos and John Murray, providing a biblical-theological starting point for Reformed theology that appropriates the insights both of Princeton and of Amsterdam (Sinclair Ferguson, "The Whole Counsel of God: Fifty Years of Theological Studies," *WTJ* 50 [1988]: 261). Traditionalist covenant theologian Mark Karlberg meanwhile argues that Gaffin is largely responsible for a "recasting of Reformed theology" that has impacted the Westminster tradition, notably Ferguson (Mark W. Karlberg, review of *The Holy Spirit,* by Sinclair B. Ferguson, *JETS* 42 [1999]: 529).

136 Richard B. Gaffin, Jr., "The Usefulness of the Cross," *WTJ* 41 (1979): 229.

137 Ibid., 230.

138 Ibid.

139 Ibid.

140 Richard B. Gaffin, Jr., "A New Paradigm in Theology?" *WTJ* 56 (1994): 381.

141 Vern S. Poythress, "Currents Within Amillennialism," *Presbyterion* 26 (2000): 24.

142 This is especially true in, for instance, Vos's essay, "Our Lord's Doctrine of the Resurrection," in *Redemptive History and Biblical Interpretation: The Shorter Writings of Geerhardus Vos,* ed. Richard B. Gaffin, Jr. (Phillipsburg, N.J.: Presbyterian & Reformed, 1980), 317-323.

143 Richard B. Gaffin, Jr., *Resurrection and Redemption: A Study in Paul's Soteriology* (Phillipsburg, N.J.: Presbyterian & Reformed, 1987), 59. As Gaffin argues, "The resurrection of Christ is the beginning of a new and final world-order, an order described as spiritual and heavenly. It is the dawn of the new creation, the start of the eschatological age. In terms of the conceptual framework with which Paul views the whole of history, it is the commencement of the 'age to come'" (ibid., 89-90).

144 Ibid., 33-58.

145 Ibid., 62-66.

146 So Gaffin argues, "The resurrection of Christ is simply that—the resurrection of 'the Christ,' who in his experience is one with those on whose behalf he has been anointed. Or to express his solidaric, messianic factor in a broader, more distinctly Pauline category, it is the resurrection of the second Adam (1 Cor 15:22, 45). The resurrection of Jesus is just as thoroughly messianic and adamic as are his sufferings and death. His resurrection is as equally representative and vicarious as his death. Believers no longer live to themselves but to the Christ, 'who for their sake died and was raised' (2 Cor 5:15)" (ibid., 65-66).

147 Sinclair Ferguson, *The Holy Spirit* (Downers Grove, Ill.: InterVarsity Press, 1996), 105. For this view Ferguson claims dependence upon Vos's work in Pauline pneumatology and eschatology.

148 Gaffin argues, "What must also be recalled here—by now, after nearly a century, a virtual consensus across the broad front of NT scholarship—is the eschatological dimension or context of this Christocentric focus. Paul (and the other NT writers), faithful to the kingdom proclamation of Jesus, have a broadened, already/not yet understanding of eschatology. For them eschatology is defined in terms of his first as well as his second coming. Specifically Christ's resurrection is an innately eschatological event—in fact, the key inaugurating event of eschatology. His resurrection is not an isolated event in the past but, in having occurred in the past, belongs to the future consummation and from that future has entered history" (Richard B. Gaffin, Jr., "'Life-Giving Spirit': Probing the Center of Paul's Pneumatology," *JETS* 41 [1998]: 575).

149 Hoekema, *Bible and the Future,* 55-67.

[150] Ibid., 55.

[151] Ibid.

[152] Ferguson, "The Whole Counsel of God," 279.

[153] Ferguson, *Holy Spirit,* 87.

[154] Even as he contrasts their views, Gaffin notes that Vos was Warfield's Princeton Seminary colleague and his walking partner for twenty years (Richard B. Gaffin, Jr., "A Cessationist View," in *Are Miraculous Gifts for Today? Four Views,* ed. Wayne A. Grudem [Grand Rapids, Mich.: Zondervan, 1996], 29 n. 11).

[155] "That is primarily because [Warfield] did not have an adequate conception of the *eschatological* nature of the work of the Holy Spirit. (By *eschatological* I mean 'characteristic of the "age to come"'; see Matt. 12:32; Eph. 1:21; Heb. 6:5.) Briefly, one of the most important developments in biblical studies in this century has been the rediscovery of the already/not yet structure of New Testament eschatology. This broadened understanding of eschatology, which has now virtually reached the status of consensus, has brought a growing recognition that for the New Testament writers (most clearly Paul), the present work of the Spirit in the church and within believers is inherently eschatological. The Holy Spirit and eschatology, rarely related together in traditional Christian doctrine and piety, are now seen as inseparable" (ibid., 29).

[156] Poythress, "Currents Within Amillennialism," 22.

[157] Ibid. Poythress cites Meredith G. Kline, "The First Resurrection," *WTJ* 37 (1974): 366-375; Kline, "The First Resurrection: A Reaffirmation," *WTJ* 39 (1976): 110-119; and Gregory K. Beale, *The Book of Revelation: A Commentary on the Greek Text* (Grand Rapids, Mich.: Eerdmans, 1999), 972-1031.

[158] Poythress, "Currents Within Amillennialism," 21.

[159] Michael Williams, "A Restorational Alternative to Augustinian Verticalist Eschatology," *Pro Rege* 20 (1992): 11.

[160] Ibid.

[161] Ibid., 11-12.

[162] Poythress, "Currents Within Amillennialism," 21-22.

[163] Cited in Hoekema, *Bible and the Future,* 275. Hoekema cites John F. Walvoord, *The Millennial Kingdom* (Findlay, Ohio: Dunham, 1958), 298.

[164] Hoekema, *Bible and the Future,* 275-276.

[165] For manifestations of this impulse in Dutch Reformed eschatology, see, for instance, the eschatological themes in Kuyper's Princeton Stone Lectures, in Abraham Kuyper, *Lectures on Calvinism* (Grand Rapids, Mich.: Eerdmans, 1931). For a contemporary use of this eschatological impulse, see Henry R. Van Til, *The Calvinistic Concept of Culture* (Grand Rapids, Mich.: Baker, 1959).

[166] William D. Dennison, "Dutch Neo-Calvinism and the Roots for Transformation: An Introductory Essay," *JETS* 42 (1999): 278.

[167] Vern S. Poythress, *Understanding Dispensationalists,* 2nd ed. (Phillipsburg, N.J.: Presbyterian & Reformed, 1994), 47.

[168] Vern S. Poythress, "Response to Paul S. Karleen's Paper 'Understanding Covenant Theologians,'" *GTJ* 10 (1989): 148.

[169] Ibid.

[170] Poythress, "Currents Within Amillennialism," 23.

[171] C. S. Lewis, *The Problem of Pain* (New York: Macmillan, 1962; reprint, New York: Simon & Schuster, 1996), 129-130.

[172] David Stricklin, *A Genealogy of Dissent: Southern Baptist Protest in the Twentieth Century* (Lexington: University Press of Kentucky, 1999), 93-94.

173 In further confirmation of the diverse streams within early-twentieth-century funda-
mentalism, fundamentalists commissioned both the principal of the Toronto Bible
Training School and a professor at Princeton Theological Seminary to defend the doc-
trine in *The Fundamentals* (See John C. McNicol, "The Hope of the Church," and
Charles R. Erdman, "The Coming of Christ," in *The Fundamentals: A Testimony to the
Truth,* 4 vols. [Los Angeles: Bible Institute of Los Angeles, 1917], 4:287-313).

174 For the reasons for a fundamentalist emphasis on the virginal conception, see J.
Gresham Machen, *The Virgin Birth of Christ* (New York: Harper & Brothers, 1930).

175 Harry Emerson Fosdick, "Shall the Fundamentalists Win? A Sermon Preached at the
First Presbyterian Church, New York, May 21, 1922," 10. This sermon tract is reprinted
in Joel A. Carpenter, ed., *The Fundamentalist-Modernist Conflict: Opposing Views on
Three Major Issues* (New York: Garland, 1988), 287-313.

176 Such eschatological expectations, Fosdick said, "always had a new resurrection when
desperate circumstances came and man's only hope seemed to lie in divine intervention"
(ibid.).

177 Shailer Mathews, *Will Christ Come Again?* (Chicago: University of Chicago, 1917),
2, emphasis mine. This tract is reprinted in Carpenter, ed., *The Fundamentalist-
Modernist Conflict.*

178 For Mathews's constructive work on the Social Gospel, see Shailer Mathews, *The
Individual and the Social Gospel* (New York: Missionary Education Movement of the
United States and Canada, 1914). For an examination of the role of eschatological con-
siderations in early-twentieth-century Protestant liberalism, see James H. Moorhead,
"Engineering the Millennium: Kingdom Building in American Protestantism,
1880–1920," *Princeton Seminary Bulletin* 3 (1994): 104-128.

179 Fosdick, "Shall the Fundamentalists Win?" 11.

180 Contrast the evangelical view with, for example, the "theology of hope" of Jürgen
Moltmann. For an analysis of Moltmann's use of eschatology in his theological method,
see Randall E. Otto, *The God of Hope: The Trinitarian Vision of Jürgen Moltmann*
(Lanham, Md.: University Press of America, 1991).

181 For example, John Shelby Spong, who argues in language strikingly similar to that
of Fosdick and other twentieth-century modernists, asserts that the idea of a second
coming of Jesus is predicated upon a three-story universe that cannot be acceptable to
a post-Enlightenment populace (John Shelby Spong, *Here I Stand: My Struggle for a
Christianity of Integrity, Love, and Equality* [San Francisco: HarperCollins, 2000], 453-
454). See also Marcus Borg, who expresses the view that the apocalyptic eschatology of
the New Testament, which focused on a visible, bodily Second Coming, was the product of the post-Easter Christian community in order to express their experience that
Jesus was Lord (Marcus Borg, "The Second Coming Then and Now," in Marcus J. Borg
and N. T. Wright, *The Meaning of Jesus: Two Visions* [San Francisco: HarperCollins,
1999], 189-196). Borg's "Jesus Seminar" colleague Robert W. Funk likewise calls for
the new "quest for the historical Jesus" to "exorcize" apocalyptic elements, which he
deems "world-denying and vindictive," from the faith (Robert W. Funk, *Honest to
Jesus: Jesus for a New Millennium* [San Francisco: HarperCollins, 1996], 314).

182 G. B. Caird, *New Testament Theology,* ed. L. D. Hurst (New York: Oxford
University Press, 1994), 73.

183 N. T. Wright is in harmony with the apostolic witness of Paul in 1 Corinthians 15
when Wright asserts of Paul, "For him it was not a matter of the opening up of a new
religious experience. Nor was it proof of survival, of life after death. It meant that the
kingdom of God had arrived, that the new age had broken into the midst of the present
age, had dawned upon a surprised and unready world. It all happened 'according to the
Scriptures'; which, as I have argued elsewhere, does not mean that Paul could find a few

biblical proof-texts for it if he hunted hard enough, but that the entire biblical narrative had at last reached its climax, had come true in these astonishing events" (N. T. Wright, *The Challenge of Jesus: Rediscovering Who Jesus Was and Is* [Downers Grove, Ill.: InterVarsity Press, 1999], 142).

[184] Benjamin R. Barber, *The Truth of Power: Intellectual Affairs in the Clinton White House* (New York: Norton, 2001), 139.

[185] This Christocentric redemptive focus of the biblical Kingdom message is considered in more detail in chapter 4.

[186] See, for instance, Jesus' use of Psalm 61 to declare His messianic mission, as well as Peter's Pentecost definition (in Acts 2) of what it means for Jesus to be exalted as "Christ."

[187] This is especially true in Luke/Acts, though certainly not limited to this material. For a critical interaction with the Davidic covenant theme in Luke/Acts, see Mark L. Strauss, *The Davidic Messiah in Luke–Acts: The Promise and Its Fulfillment in Lukan Christology* (Sheffield, England: Sheffield Academic, 1995).

[188] Adrio König, *The Eclipse of Christ in Eschatology: Toward a Christ-Centered Approach* (Grand Rapids, Mich.: Eerdmans, 1989).

[189] Contra Old Testament theologian Walter Brueggemann, who argues that the Old Testament Scriptures affirm the Messiah only as a human agent, with "Son of God" referring only to a royal, liturgical title and not to an ontological, metaphysical claim, which he sees as a lamentable accretion by the early Christian ecumenical councils' creedal formulations (Walter Brueggemann, *Theology of the Old Testament* [Minneapolis: Fortress, 1997], 620-621). The view advocated here more closely accords with that of Old Testament theologian Paul R. House, who argues that the Old Testament prophetic writings themselves attribute to the Davidic ruler the title of "Mighty God" (Isa. 9:6) and repeatedly describe the King in terms of the actual attributes of deity in an ontological, and not merely adoptive sense (Paul R. House, *Old Testament Theology* [Downers Grove, Ill.: InterVarsity Press, 1998], 279).

[190] As Vern Poythress notes, "Sometimes we who are orthodox may not reckon directly enough with passages such as Luke 3:22 and Romans 1:3-4, which are favorites for an Adoptionist. In the midst of a controversy with Adoptionists, we should be asking how we can use their 'strong point' (i.e., such texts) in a positive manner. The answer, I believe, lies in appreciating the truth that, in the course of redemptive history, there are transformations in Jesus' role and even in his very mode of existence *with respect to his human nature*. Those points of transition also represent important transitions in God's salvific relation to the world, since through Christ as mediator we are reconciled to God" (Vern S. Poythress, *Symphonic Theology: The Validity of Multiple Perspectives in Theology* [Phillipsburg, N.J.: Presbyterian & Reformed, 1987], 97).

[191] For a discussion of the critical and theological issues involved in the interpretation of Romans 1:3-4, see Thomas R. Schreiner, *Romans,* Baker Exegetical Commentary on the New Testament (Grand Rapids, Mich.: Baker, 2000), 6:39-45.

[192] As Blaising and Bock argue, this emphasis on the present session of Christ as that of *Davidic* King means that evangelicals here avoid another ancient Christological heresy, that of Nestorianism: "Following the traditional belief in the unity of Christ's person and the integrity of divine and human natures (because we believe this interpretation to be confirmed by the church's repetitive reading of Scripture), we nevertheless seek to understand the revelation of His deity and the meaning of His humanity in a historical manner. He must be understood in the light of a history of redemption revealed in the Old Testament and carried forward in the New. Our study of the covenants and the kingdom confirms this. In other words, He is that Messiah, that anointed King of the eschaton, who will fulfill the covenant promises" (Blaising and Bock, *Progressive Dispensationalism,* 298).

193 This does not mean that the Reformed and dispensationalist traditions will jettison cessationist arguments, as some in the traditionalist wings of both camps fear. Instead, modified covenantalists such as Gaffin and Ferguson, for example, argue that a Kingdom-oriented eschatology actually bolsters the cessationist argument since the sign gifts of the Spirit are a manifestation of the onset of the eschaton. As Ferguson argues, "Pentecost, like the visible manifestations of every coronation, is by its very nature *sui generis*. It is no more repeatable *as an event* than is the crucifixion or the resurrection or the ascension of our Lord. It is an event in redemptive history (*historia salutis*), and should not be squeezed into the grid of the application of redemption (*ordo salutis*)" (Ferguson, *Holy Spirit*, 87).

194 For the indebtedness of Wimber and Wagner to Ladd, see Robert H. Krapohl and Charles H. Lippy, *The Evangelicals: A Historical, Thematic, and Biographical Guide* (Westport, Conn.: Greenwood, 1999), 263. For an explanation of "power evangelism" and the "signs and wonders" movement, see John Wimber with Kevin Springer, *Power Evangelism* (San Francisco: Harper & Row, 1986).

195 Ryrie, *Dispensationalism*, 169.

196 The assertion of these prophecies is that the coming Davidic ruler will have and use the Spirit precisely in His role as kingly "shepherd" over the people of God. For a discussion of the fulfillment of these Ezekiel passages in Christ, see Bock, "Son of David and the Saints' Task," 454.

197 Thus, as Edmund Clowney correctly points out, the "coming of the kingdom is one with the coming of the king" (Edmund P. Clowney, "The Politics of the Kingdom," *WTJ* 41 [1972]: 293).

198 The prophet Zechariah here proclaims, "And in that day living waters will flow out of Jerusalem, half of them toward the eastern sea and the other half toward the western sea; it will be in summer as well as in winter. And the LORD will be king over all the earth; in that day the LORD will be the only one, and His name the only one" (Zech. 14:8-9).

199 Ryrie, *Dispensationalism*, 167.

200 Gerry Breshears, for example, wrote early in the discussion, "The idea of Jesus inaugurating Davidic kingship in heaven is at the edge of dispensational thinking and has not won many adherents. On the other hand, the church as the place where many aspects of the kingdom of God are manifested is much more widely accepted" (Gerry Breshears, "New Directions in Dispensationalism" [paper presented at the annual meeting of the Evangelical Theological Society, Kansas City, Mo., November 23, 1991], 16).

201 "Perhaps no truth of the divine revelation has suffered more at the hands of interpreters than that concerning the kingdom. Following the Roman Catholic interpretation, Protestant theology has very generally taught that all the kingdom promises, and even the great Davidic covenant itself, are to be fulfilled in and through the church. The confusion thus created has been still further darkened by the failure to distinguish the different phases of kingdom truth indicated by the expressions 'kingdom of heaven' and 'kingdom of God'" (Lewis Sperry Chafer, *The Kingdom in History and Prophecy* [Philadelphia: Sunday School Times, 1922], 5).

202 Lewis Sperry Chafer, *Systematic Theology*, 8 vols. (Dallas: Dallas Seminary Press, 1948), 5:321. For a similar viewpoint in the succeeding generation, see J. Dwight Pentecost, *Thy Kingdom Come* (Wheaton, Ill.: Victor, 1990), 156.

203 Chafer, *Kingdom in History and Prophecy*, 87.

204 This is not to say that dispensationalists and covenantalists do not differ on the roles of Israel and the church, as discussed in the next chapter. It does mean that neither holds to ultimate dual destinies for Israel and the church.

205 This indeed is what links the Kingdom realities of the present epoch with the one

overarching Kingdom goal. "By linking Spirit and kingdom, Davidic regal hope is tied to the promise of the Spirit in the new covenant as well as to the hope of Abraham," Blaising and Bock argue (Blaising and Bock, *Progressive Dispensationalism*, 101). As Bock explains, "Progressive dispensationalists get their name because they argue that each dispensation, or each administrative period, in the plan of God builds on the previous one and advances the plan of God. There is a unity to the plan tied to God's people in terms of salvation benefits. There are no parentheses for the Kingdom in progressive dispensationalism. So the Abrahamic Covenant, the Davidic Covenant, and the New Covenant all have an initial realization that is focused in Jesus Christ and that has been inaugurated as a result of this initial coming and resurrection. Those benefits belong to the church. Fuller benefits await God's people in the Millennium to come" (Darrell L. Bock, "Does the New Testament Reshape Our Understanding of the Old Testament?" *Modern Reformation*, July/August 2000, 49).

[206] This case is bolstered by papers presented by Blaising, covenant theologian Richard Gaffin, and traditionalist dispensationalist John Master at the 1994 meeting of the Dispensational Study Group. Ironically, both Blaising and Gaffin seem more willing to assert a qualitatively unique post-Pentecost work of the Spirit than does Master. See Craig A. Blaising, "The Baptism with the Holy Spirit in the History of Redemption"; Richard B. Gaffin, Jr., "Pentecost: Before and After"; and John R. Master, "A Perspective of the Ministry of the Holy Spirit in the Old and New Testaments" (papers presented to the Dispensational Study Group at the annual meeting of the Evangelical Theological Society, Philadelphia, November 17, 1994). The uniqueness of the new covenant work of the Spirit is explained by the advance of the inbreaking Kingdom of the Davidic Messiah. As one progressive dispensationalist New Testament scholar notes, "Since Paul makes such a close association between the kingdom of God and righteousness, peace, and joy in the Holy Spirit (Rom. 14:17), the presence of the Spirit among God's people must be related to the advance of the kingdom" (Carl B. Hoch, Jr., *All Things New: The Significance of Newness for Biblical Theology* [Grand Rapids, Mich.: Baker, 1995], 35; see also Larry D. Pettegrew, *The New Covenant Ministry of the Holy Spirit* [Grand Rapids, Mich.: Kregel, 2001]).

[207] "We should anticipate, then, given the overall coherence of his teaching, that Paul's understanding of the Spirit will prove to be 'eschatological in nature and Christocentric in quality.' Without denying the presence of other determining factors, Christology and eschatology especially shape the matrix of his pneumatology. The death and resurrection of Christ in their eschatological significance control Paul's teaching on the work of the Spirit" (Gaffin, "'Life-Giving Spirit'," 575).

[208] Mark Karlberg, for instance, charges Ferguson with embodying "distinctive elements found in dispensational theology," particularly because of Ferguson's suggestion that the *"permanent* indwelling of the Spirit is understood here as strictly a new covenant experience" (Mark W. Karlberg, review of *The Holy Spirit,* by Sinclair Ferguson, 529).

[209] Compare, for instance, the teachings of modified covenantalist Sinclair Ferguson and progressive dispensationalist Bruce Ware on the role of the Spirit in the old and new covenants. Ferguson argues, "The Spirit had been active among God's people; but his activity was enigmatic, sporadic, theocratic, selective, and in some respects external. The prophets had longed for better days. Moses desired, but did not see, a fuller and universally widespread coming of the Spirit on God's people (Num. 11:29). By contrast, in the anticipated new covenant, the Spirit would be poured out in a universal manner, dwelling in them personally and permanently" (Ferguson, *Holy Spirit,* 30). In almost total agreement, Ware sees the work of the Spirit in the old covenant as being selective, temporary, and task-oriented. He argues that the new covenant work of the Spirit is, by contrast, a permanent and universal giving of the Spirit to the people of God in Christ

(Bruce A. Ware, "The New Covenant and the People[s] of God," in *Dispensationalism, Israel, and the Church,* 75-82).

[210] Richard B. Gaffin, Jr., *Perspectives on Pentecost: New Testament Teaching on the Gifts of the Holy Spirit* (Phillipsburg, N.J.: Presbyterian & Reformed, 1979), 25.

[211] It also opens up an inconsistency within covenant theology as it relates to baptism. If the Spirit permanently and individually indwells the members of the new covenant community, in distinction from the temporary and task-oriented nature of the Spirit's work in the old covenant community, then modified covenantalists such as Ferguson must ask how some members of the new covenant community (namely the infants of believing parents) can be members without sharing in the blessing of the Spirit.

[212] See, for instance, J. Gresham Machen's valiant defense of the historical nature of Jesus' resurrection, along with the other miraculous elements of His life, in Machen's *Christianity and Liberalism* (Grand Rapids, Mich.: Eerdmans, 1923), 80-116.

[213] See, for example, Charles Hodge's rather uneven treatment of the crucifixion and the resurrection in his *A Commentary on Romans* (Philadelphia: William S. & Alfred Martien, 1864; reprint, Edinburgh: Banner of Truth, 1986), 129. "His resurrection was no less necessary [than the cross], first, as a proof that his death had been accepted as an expiation for our sins. Had he not risen, it would have been evident that he was not what he claimed to be. . . . And secondly, in order to secure the continued application of the merits of his sacrifice, he rose from the dead." Hodge presents a similar perspective on the resurrection in his *Systematic Theology,* 3 vols. (New York: Scribner, 1873; reprint, Grand Rapids, Mich.: Eerdmans, 1995), 2:626-630. It is noteworthy that Hodge here takes up a relatively minute four pages of text to relate the resurrection of Jesus to His exaltation as the Christ.

[214] Gaffin, *Resurrection and Redemption,* 13.

[215] B. B. Warfield is here representative of the older Reformed tradition in American fundamentalism in asserting of the resurrection "that we have in it a decisive proof of the divine origin of Christianity; a revolutionary revelation of the reality of immortality, a demonstration of the truth of all Christ's claims and trustworthiness of all his promises, an assurance of the perfection of his saving work, and a pledge of our own resurrection" (Benjamin B. Warfield, "Resurrection—A Fundamental Doctrine," in *Selected Shorter Writings of Benjamin B. Warfield,* ed. John E. Meeter, 2 vols. [Phillipsburg, N.J.: Presbyterian & Reformed, 1970], 1:201). Warfield's article was originally published in *The Homiletic Review* 32 (1896): 291-298. The comparison between Warfield and Vos on the eschatological nature of the resurrection of Jesus is a major point of discussion in Gaffin, *Resurrection and Redemption,* 100-106; and Richard Lints, *The Fabric of Theology: A Prolegomenon to Evangelical Theology* (Grand Rapids, Mich.: Eerdmans, 1993), 186.

[216] Reformed theologian Richard Mouw hails this dispensational eschatological expectancy in his *The Smell of Sawdust: What Evangelicals Can Learn from Their Fundamentalist Heritage* (Grand Rapids, Mich.: Zondervan, 2000), 95-104.

[217] Craig Blaising is right when he observes that the "heavenly" passages of the New Testament refer most often to the believer's present experience in union with Christ rather than to the hope of future consummation (Blaising, "Premillennialism," 196).

[218] Craig Blaising explains this eschatological model as follows: "In the spiritual vision model of eternity, heaven is the highest level of ontological reality. It is the realm of spirit as opposed to base matter. This is the destiny of the saved, who will exist in that non-earthly, spiritual place as spiritual beings engaged eternally in spiritual activity" (Blaising, "Premillennialism," 161). For a discussion of the doctrinal development of the beatific vision and the heavenly hope, see Colleen McDannell and Bernhard Lang, *Heaven: A History* (New Haven, Conn.: Yale University Press, 1988). Blaising contrasts

this model with the "new creation" model of eternity, in which the redeemed participate in an eternal Kingdom within a regenerated cosmos. "The key point is that whereas
the spiritual vision model abstracts spirit from matter, hierarchalizes it ontologically,
and sees perfection in a changeless, atemporal state, the new creation model affirms a
future holistic creation blessed with the perfection of righteousness and everlasting life"
(Blaising, "Premillennialism," 163-164). This idea of cosmic regeneration is considered
in more detail in the next chapter of this study.

[219] Hodge, *Systematic Theology*, 3:862-863. Hodge's criticism of the carnal nature of
the millennial Kingdom hope is similar to that of the Lutheran Augsburg Confession of
1530, which states, "Rejected, too, are certain Jewish opinions which are even now making an appearance and which teach that, before the resurrection of the dead, saints and
godly men will possess a worldly kingdom and annihilate all the godless" (see
"Augsburg Confession," in *Creeds of the Churches*, 73).

[220] As Chafer asserted, "Because the supreme divine purpose in this age is the outcall-
ing of the Church, there is but one message to be preached to all men, namely salvation
into heavenly glory through faith in Christ" (Chafer, *Systematic Theology*, 4:417,
emphasis mine).

[221] As Blaising and others have noted, dispensationalists such as Ryrie and Walvoord
did away with the dual eternal destinies of Israel and the church. Dispensationalism still,
however, tended to speak of the eternal hope as heaven, rather than a Kingdom in the
new heavens and new earth (Blaising, "Premillennialism," 184-186). See, for example,
Erich Sauer, *The Triumph of the Crucified: A Survey of Historical Revelation in the New
Testament*, trans. G. H. Lang (London: Paternoster, 1951; reprint, Grand Rapids,
Mich.: Eerdmans, 1994), 167. "But where is the church during the Millennial kingdom?" Sauer asked. "As it would appear, with Christ in heaven, not regularly on the
earth."

[222] From the early teachings of J. N. Darby through Scofield and Chafer to Ryrie and
Walvoord, it would seem that the progressive dispensationalists are right to note that
the ultimate hope of the dominant forms of dispensationalism has been what Blaising
calls the "spiritual vision" model of eschatology, consistent with the Augustinian and
medieval traditions. Dispensationalist theologian Gary Nebeker is right to tie the
emphasis on the pretribulational rapture doctrine with this vision of hope. Nebeker is
also correct to wonder whether this Augustinian verticalist eschatology has been challenged, if not superseded, by the developments in contemporary dispensationalism (Gary
L. Nebeker, "The Theme of Hope in Dispensationalism," *BibSac* 158 [2002]: 3-20).

[223] Vern Poythress picks up this charge against premillennialism, a charge previously
made by Anthony Hoekema and others (Poythress, "Response to Paul Karleen's
Paper," 149).

[224] Blaising and Bock, *Progressive Dispensationalism*, 121.

[225] Ladd, *Theology of the New Testament*, 680.

[226] Covenant theologians were likewise correct to repudiate the dispensational premillennialist interpretation of a resumption of animal sacrifices as "memorials" in the millennial temple, a position in conflict with Hebrews 9–10 on the finality of the sacrifice
of the Messiah. With the developments in dispensationalism, however, this "memorial
sacrifice" view is less and less common. Craig Blaising rebuts this as a straw man in his
"A Premillennial Response to Robert B. Strimple," in *Three Views of the Millennium
and Beyond*, ed. Darrell L. Bock (Grand Rapids, Mich.: Zondervan, 1999), 143.
Blaising is correct at least inasmuch as virtually no historic premillennialists and few progressive dispensationalists would hold such a view. It is not, therefore, essential to a premillennial interpretation of biblical theology.

[227] Poythress, *Understanding Dispensationalists*, 132-133.

[228] Craig A. Blaising, "A Premillennial Response to Kenneth L. Gentry Jr.," in *Three Views on the Millennium and Beyond*, 79.

[229] The same is true for Zechariah 14, in which the wicked in the restored earth are said to be punished. Poythress therefore conceded, "Zechariah 14, if read in a straightforward manner, is particularly difficult for an amillennialist. In fact, if I were to defend premillennialism in a debate, I would probably choose Zechariah 14 as a main text" (Vern S. Poythress, "Response to Robert L. Saucy's Paper," *GTJ* 10 [1989]: 158).

[230] The "Zionic" dispensation is described in Blaising and Bock, *Progressive Dispensationalism*, 121.

[231] Ladd, "Revelation of Christ's Glory," 14; Ladd, *Theology of the New Testament*, 680-681.

[232] The issue of the glory of God in the reign of Christ will be examined more carefully in the next chapter's discussion of soteriology and the Kingdom of God.

[233] C. Marvin Pate is thus correct to note that an amillennial interpretation of Revelation 20 falls apart in light of the following two exegetical factors: "(a) A spiritual resurrection can hardly explain the compensation provided for the martyrs mentioned in verse 4. From John's perspective they are physically dead but spiritually alive. What they need is a bodily resurrection. (b) The best understanding of the verb *ezesan* ('they lived') in verse 4 is that it refers to a bodily resurrection" (C. Marvin Pate, "A Progressive Dispensationalist View of Revelation," in *Four Views on the Book of Revelation*, ed. C. Marvin Pate [Grand Rapids, Mich.: Zondervan, 1998], 171).

[234] G. B. Caird is thus correct in his interpretation of the nature of resurrection hope when he argues that "the gift of immortality is not in itself an adequate answer to the cry of the martyrs. They have died for God's word, and no theodicy can justify their death except the triumph of the cause for which they gave their lives. It is for the vindication of God's justice within earthly history that they are 'told to wait patiently a little while longer'" (Caird, *New Testament Theology*, 244).

[235] Bock, *Luke 1:1–9:50*, 116-117.

[236] Walter Eichrodt, *Theology of the Old Testament*, trans. J. A. Baker, 2 vols. (Philadelphia: Westminster, 1961), 1:447.

[237] Ibid., 1:448.

[238] Contra Old Testament theologian Walter Brueggemann, who argues against the "exclusive" appropriation of Davidic kingship to the person of Jesus of Nazareth. "Old Testament theology, it seems to me, may acknowledge the linkage made to Jesus but may at the same time wonder about the exclusiveness of the claim, since it is in the nature of the Old Testament witness to allow for other historically designated agents to do Yahweh's work of justice and righteousness in the earth" (Brueggemann, *Theology of the Old Testament*, 620). Brueggemann assaults therefore the arrogance of Christian theology in "appropriating for Christology the highest claims of kingship (witness the use of Pss 2, 110) and assigning to Judaism the demands of Torah" (ibid., 610). For an evangelical view that sees the Old Testament theology of the Davidic covenant as compatible with the New Testament identification of Jesus as the messianic King, see House, *Old Testament Theology*, 241-279.

[239] George M. Marsden, *Fundamentalism and American Culture: The Shaping of Twentieth-Century Evangelicalism, 1870–1925* (New York: Oxford University Press, 1980), 210-211.

[240] Rick Perlstein, *Before the Storm: Barry Goldwater and the Unmaking of the American Consensus* (New York: Hill and Wang, 2001), 465.

[241] For an analysis of this application, see Donald W. Dayton, *Discovering an Evangelical Heritage* (Peabody, Mass.: Hendrickson, 1976), 121-135.

242 Marsden notes, "During the half-century before World War I, premillennialists developed very little in the way of political theory. After the war when communist and other conspiracy theories arose as explanations of what was going wrong, they had little basis for evaluating these theories on their own merits. The conspiracy theories did, however, appeal to their general disposition of thought. Like their premillennialism, the political threats could be placed in the framework of the conflict between the forces of God and of Satan. The two types of conspiracy theory, the political and the religious, might well have appealed to a single mind-set in such a way as to override the difficulty of reconciling specific details" (Marsden, *Fundamentalism and American Culture*, 211).

243 Mark Noll, *The Scandal of the Evangelical Mind* (Grand Rapids, Mich.: Eerdmans, 1994), 168. Noll points to the example of anti-Semitic Gerald Winrod and dispensationalist Canadian radio preacher/elected official William Aberhart.

244 Ibid., 169. Noll, in fact, can cite only one "rudimentary effort" at prewar fundamentalist political reflection, Judson E. Conant, *The Growing Menace of the "Social Gospel"* (Chicago: Bible Institute Colportage, 1937).

245 Henry did not, however, end the debate. In the 1970s, Richard Quebedeaux, for instance, took Henry's argument to the next level by insisting that dispensationalism must repudiate dispensationalism before it could ever find a workable theology for social and political engagement since, in dispensational theology, "getting ready for the rapture becomes the all-embracing concern of the church." While Henry implied that dispensational eschatological commitments were unwittingly impeding biblical social and political mandates, Quebedeaux suggested that the eschatological commitments were "convenient" excuses to jettison the ethical demands of Christianity and to support the biblical status quo. He commented that he found it "interesting to note the tendency among many dispensationalists to identify as the Antichrist-Beast (Revelation 13, 17) prominent national or world political leaders who take the side of the oppressed and downtrodden or who work avidly for peace" (Richard Quebedeaux, *The Young Evangelicals: The Story of the Emergence of a New Generation of Evangelicals* [New York: Harper & Row, 1974], 79-80).

246 As Timothy Weber observes, the premillennial pessimism of the early twentieth century may have discouraged social and political action, but it was wielded in the arena of personal ethics as fundamentalists "discovered in their own particular doctrine a way of reinforcing slipping evangelical mores," on issues ranging from skirt lengths to theater attendance. Weber cites, for instance, dispensationalist Reuben A. Torrey's use of the pretribulational rapture as an incentive for Christian avoidance of "worldliness," a situation that Weber suggests Torrey used in every possible life situation. "Do not do anything that you would not be glad to have your Lord find you doing if He should come," Torrey preached. "[I]t is simply wonderful how that clears things up" (Timothy Weber, *Living in the Shadow of the Second Coming: American Premillennialism, 1875–1925* [New York: Oxford University Press, 1979], 61).

247 Boyer, *When Time Shall Be No More*, 108.

248 Ibid.

249 Jon R. Stone, *On the Boundaries of American Evangelicalism: The Postwar Evangelical Coalition* (New York: St. Martin's, 1997), 61.

250 Carl F. H. Henry, "Martyn Lloyd-Jones: From Buckingham to Westminster," *Christianity Today*, February 8, 1980, 33.

251 Ibid.

252 Lloyd-Jones saw the rising democracies as even more indication of this. He held that the future held "either dictatorship or complete chaos" since "666 is the number of man, and this is democracy—man worshipping himself, his own likeness" (ibid., 34).

253 Henry said, in what reads more like a series of assertions for debate than a line of

questioning, "Would you agree that even if we might have only 24 or 48 hours, to with-hold a witness in the political or any other arena is to withdraw prematurely from the social responsibility of the Christian and to distrust the providence of God? Might He not do something even in the last few hours that He had not done before? The closer we get to the end time, isn't it that much more important to address the public con-science? Must we not press claims of Christ in all the arenas of society and remind peo-ple, whether they receive Christ or not, of the criteria by which the returning King will judge men and nations?" (ibid., 33).

254 Ibid.

255 Cal Thomas and Jay Sekulow, "What Role for Religious Conservatives?" *The American Enterprise,* April/May 2000, 15. This article was a revised transcript of a debate between Thomas and Sekulow on Christian political engagement at the February 2000 national convention of the National Religious Broadcasters.

256 Gary North, *Rapture Fever: Why Dispensationalism Is Paralyzed* (Tyler, Tex.: Institute for Christian Economics, 1993), 186.

257 Ibid., 193.

258 Gary North, *Westminster's Confession: The Abandonment of Van Til's Legacy* (Tyler, Tex.: Institute for Christian Economics, 1991), 162.

259 Ibid.

260 See, for example, Jürgen Moltmann, *God for a Secular Society: The Public Relevance of Theology,* trans. Margaret Kohl (Minneapolis: Fortress, 1999), 219-220; and Gary North, *Millennialism and Social Theory* (Tyler, Tex.: Institute for Christian Economics, 1990), 71-95.

261 This does not mean that evangelicals will be able to solve all human rights abuses, but it does mean that the coming "justice" of the King is to be a priority for the com-munity now. Progressive dispensationalist Robert Pyne, for example, calls upon evan-gelicals to pursue justice in American society and in seemingly intractable social situations such as India since such justice is "part of the King's agenda" according to passages such as Psalm 72:12-14 (Robert Pyne, "New Man and Immoral Society" [paper presented at the annual meeting of the Evangelical Theological Society, Santa Clara, Calif., November 20, 1997], 15).

262 John Paul II (pope), *The Gospel of Life [Evangelium Vitae]* (New York: Random House, 1995).

263 Sara Diamond, *Not by Politics Alone: The Enduring Influence of the Christian Right* (New York: Guilford, 1998), 197.

264 Ibid., 202.

265 Ibid., 9-10.

266 Friedrich Nietzsche, *Unpublished Writings from the Period of Unfashionable Observations,* trans. Richard T. Gray (Stanford, Calif.: Stanford University Press, 1999), 168.

267 For a discussion of the issues involved in working this out, see Michael Cromartie, ed., *Caesar's Coin Revisited: Christians and the Limits of Government* (Grand Rapids, Mich.: Eerdmans, 1996).

268 This is the controversy over judicial usurpation and the future of democracy in America. Two monographs were published containing the debates over this subject: Mitchell S. Muncy, ed., *The End of Democracy? The Celebrated First Things Debate with Arguments Pro and Con* (Dallas: Spence, 1997); and Mitchell S. Muncy, ed., *The End of Democracy? II: A Crisis of Legitimacy* (Dallas: Spence, 1999). Questioning the legitimacy of the regime is therefore appropriate, even if the growing "anti-American temptation" of some sectors of the Christian right is unwarranted, as it would seem. For

a compelling critique of the "end of democracy" rhetoric, see David Brooks, "The Right's Anti-American Temptation," *Weekly Standard*, November 11, 1996, 23-26; and Gertrude Himmelfarb, "On the Future of Conservatism: A Symposium," *Commentary*, February 1997, 29-32.

269 Henry thus rightly notes that "Christianity stipulates no one permanent form of government in the name of divine revelation." He underscores this point through the lens of eschatology and history: "Just government can in theory prevail quite apart from majority rule. Monarchy need not be unjust; many Christians anticipate a Christocratic millennium" (Carl F. H. Henry, *Has Democracy Had Its Day?* [Nashville: ERLC Publications, 1996], 3). Nonetheless, Henry correctly commends democracy because it "is a political process that champions religious liberty and that sustains an atmosphere in which voluntary religion can thrive" (ibid., 59).

270 For a helpful, though short, discussion of just war theory, history, and eschatology, see John S. Feinberg and Paul D. Feinberg, *Ethics for a Brave New World* (Wheaton, Ill.: Crossway, 1993), 364.

271 Robert P. Kraynak, *Christian Faith and Modern Democracy: God and Politics in the Fallen World* (Notre Dame, Ind.: University of Notre Dame Press, 2000).

272 As seen in, for instance, the competing papers at the 1971 Jerusalem Conference on Biblical Prophecy.

273 For a historical analysis of the roots of American evangelical support for a Jewish state, especially as it has been informed by dispensationalism, see David A. Rausch, *Zionism Within Early American Fundamentalism, 1879–1918* (New York: Edwin Mellen, 1979); John C. Green et al., eds., *Religion and the Culture Wars: Dispatches from the Front* (Lanham, Md.: Rowman & Littlefield, 1996), 330-355; and Timothy Weber, "How Evangelicals Became Israel's Best Friend," *Christianity Today*, October 5, 1998, 39-49.

274 One commentator gives the rather extreme example of conservative Christian support for renegade Israeli groups bent on destroying the Dome of the Rock in Jerusalem in order that their prophetic expectations regarding a rebuilt Jewish temple might be expedited (Daniel Wojcik, *The End of the World as We Know It: Faith, Fatalism, and Apocalypse in America* [New York: New York University Press, 1997], 146).

275 Thus, as historian Martin Marty notes, Protestant liberals during and after World War II (such as the editorial board of *The Christian Century*) received talk of Zionism with ambivalence, if not outright hostility, while "Protestant fundamentalists, who backed Zionism, gave a theological interpretation of events that was friendly to Israel but that no Jew could accept" (Martin Marty, *Under God, Indivisible*, vol. 3 of *Modern American Religion* [Chicago: University of Chicago Press, 1996], 63-64). Jewish political "support" for such evangelical eschatological interpretations is seen in the Jewish signatories of the *Dabru Emet* statement on Jewish-Christian relations, which hails evangelicals for recognizing that the Palestinian land is part of an eternal covenant between God and the Jewish people. "Many Christians support the State of Israel for reasons far more profound than mere politics," they note. "As Jews, we applaud this support" ("Dabru Emet: A Jewish Statement on Christians and Christianity" [paid advertisement], *New York Times*, September 10, 2000, 23).

276 This is not to say that there are not a multitude of other geopolitical and human rights reasons for supporting the current Israeli state. For a compelling defense of support for Israel by the international community, see Benjamin Netanyahu, *A Durable Peace: Israel and Its Place Among the Nations* (New York: Warner, 2000).

277 At Henry's 1971 prophecy conference in Israel, for example, Herman Ridderbos expressed "embarrassment" that the evangelicals gathered there were focused on the place of the secular state in biblical prophecy, rather than on an evangelistic endeavor

to convert its Jewish citizens to faith in Christ (Herman Ridderbos, "The Future of Israel [View I]," in *Prophecy in the Making*, 321-322).

278 O. Palmer Robertson, *The Israel of God: Yesterday, Today, and Tomorrow* (Phillipsburg, N.J.: Presbyterian & Reformed, 2000), 194.

279 Blaising and Bock, *Progressive Dispensationalism*, 296-297.

280 The soteriological ramifications of the future for political Israel will be examined in the next chapter's discussion of the Kingdom and salvation.

281 Timothy George, writing for the Baptist Peace Fellowship of North America, denounced the 1982 attempt by some conservatives to pass a resolution "On Support of Israel" at the Southern Baptist Convention. George rightly opposed the eschatological positions underlying much of this support and rightly pointed to church/state separation as a reason for refusing to give "unqualified support to any political figure or entity." Nonetheless, George and the Baptist pacifists did not deal with the very real threat to Israel's very existence, not only by hostile Arab neighbors but by an often-hostile United Nations constituency as well (Timothy George, "Peacemaker Preface," *Baptist Peacemaker,* April 1983, 2).

282 The most sensational of all was the wildly popular end-times speculator Hal Lindsey, who applied Jesus' teaching in Matthew 24:34 that "this generation will not pass away until all these things take place" to refer to current events, especially the "budding of the fig tree" in the establishment of Israel in 1948, thus starting a "countdown to Armageddon." Lindsey argued, "A generation in the Bible is something like forty years. If this is a correct deduction, then within forty years or so of 1948, all these things could take place. Many scholars who have studied prophecy all their lives believe that this is so" (Hal Lindsey, *The Late Great Planet Earth* [Grand Rapids, Mich.: Zondervan, 1971], 53-54).

283 Jürgen Moltmann, for instance, laments the fact that American evangelicals in the 1980s were "politicized through 'the moral majority' of Jerry Falwell and others, who since the time of Ronald Reagan have linked this apocalyptic fundamentalism with the political right in the USA, and with the preparation for a nuclear Armageddon" (Jürgen Moltmann, *The Coming of God: Christian Eschatology,* trans. Margaret Kohl [Minneapolis: Fortress, 1996], 159).

284 Richard Kyle, *Last Days Are Here Again*, 17. Kyle cites this quotation from Robert Jewett, "Coming to Terms with the Doom Boom," *Quarterly Review* 4 (1984): 9.

285 Other fearful theological analyses of Reagan's supposed dependence on popular evangelical apocalypticism include Larry Jones and Gerald T. Sheppard, "The Politics of Biblical Eschatology: Ronald Reagan and the Impending Nuclear Armageddon," *TSF Bulletin,* September/October 1984, 16-18. "In 1980, a public confession of being 'born again' was almost required of serious presidential contenders," the authors warn. "We hope that the presidential election in 1984 does not become a mandate to experimentally test the dispensationalist hypothesis with a war of our own making" (ibid., 18).

286 Not to mention the irony of the fact that Reagan, supposedly influenced by the Doomsday scenarios of pessimistic premillennialism, was derided for his "Morning in America" optimism by his more liberal critics, not least of which was his 1984 Democratic opponent Walter Mondale, who was the heir of a rich tradition of Social Gospel Methodism.

287 The reference is from Ezekiel 38. Many prophecy teachers in the 1970s and 80s identified this northern enemy of Israel with the Soviet Union, thus prompting them to predict a coming invasion of Israel by the USSR. For a discussion of the place of Russia and the USSR in popular evangelical apocalypticism, see Boyer, *When Time Shall Be No More,* 154-180.

288 This includes the dispensationalist tradition within evangelicalism. As Timothy

Weber argues, the newer generation of progressive dispensationalists employs a "toned down" rhetoric, which minimizes the "excesses and sensationalism of its predecessors" since the progressives are "less inclined to engage in map drawing and categorical predictions" (Weber, "How Evangelicals Became Israel's Best Friend," 49). It is doubtful, however, that this doctrinal development will end the kind of politicized apocalypticism the progressives reject since, as Richard Kyle notes, the popular message of novelists and speculators has reached the grassroots of American evangelicalism in a way that these theological developments have not (Kyle, *Last Days Are Here Again,* 117).

[289] Social Gospel proponent Shailer Mathews, for instance, applied his Kingdom theology to a struggle for more progressive views of women throughout the world, noting that it was a combination of British colonialism and William Carey's missionary endeavors that ended the ancient Indian practice of widows burning themselves on the funeral pyres of their deceased husbands. Likewise, he interpreted the improving status of women in Japan as due to "the influence of Christianity; in part to the social traditions of the Japanese; but most of all to the extraordinary spirit of progress which marks the new Japan" (Shailer Mathews, *The Individual and the Social Gospel,* 26-27). It is noteworthy that Mathews's praise for the "Christianity" and "progress" of Japan came not too many years before the Japanese empire's 1941 attack on the United States. It is also noteworthy to see the cultural context of this Social Gospel eschatology. After all, such sentiments expressed later in the twentieth century would be denounced by many within Protestant liberal academia as hopelessly imperialistic. For a neo-feminist attempt to "rescue" the Social Gospel, see Christopher H. Evans, "Gender and the Kingdom of God: The Family Values of Walter Rauschenbusch," and Rosemary Skinner Keller, "Women Creating Communities—and Community—in the Name of the Social Gospel," in *The Social Gospel Today,* ed. Christopher H. Evans (Louisville: Westminster/John Knox, 2001), 38-66.

[290] It should be remembered that although premillennialists have had more often to combat the "pessimism" charge in relation to political activity, theonomic postmillennialists charge both groups with a similarly hopeless prospect for social and political victory in the present era. See, for instance, North, *Millennialism and Social Theory,* 71-95.

[291] Thus, as one Arminian critic of conservative evangelicalism puts it, premillennialism "expresses the same pessimistic view about human ability and action that is found in the high Calvinism of Princeton—and perhaps thus provides another explanation for the coalescing of traditions in the late nineteenth century to produce modern fundamentalism" (Donald W. Dayton, "The Social and Political Conservatism of Modern American Evangelicalism: A Preliminary Search for the Reasons," *Union Seminary Quarterly Review* 32 [1977]: 78).

[292] See, for instance, Moorhead, "Engineering the Millennium."

[293] This is therefore quite distinct from what Shailer Mathews called "the true premillenarianism," which he defined as an age of "conflict with sinful men and sinful social institutions, but the victory will be with the Holy Spirit who will take the things of Christ and lead men to truth and holiness and love like that of God" (Mathews, *Will Christ Come Again?* 21). It is for this reason that Mathews could affirm the "second coming of Christ": "Will Christ come again? We answer in all reverence, not in the sense in which the early Christians in their perpetuation of Jewish beliefs expected. Never in the sense that the premillenarians of today assert. The prophecies of the Old Testament are not highly ingenious puzzles to be worked out—always mistakenly, in charts, diagrams, and 'fulfillments.' They are the discovery of his laws in social evolution. The pictures of the 'last things' in the New Testament are not scientific statements but figures of speech expressing everlasting spiritual realities" (ibid.).

[294] This will be explored in more depth in the examination of the Kingdom and soteriology in chapter 4.

[295] Henry, *Protestant Dilemma,* 128-129.

[296] Carl F. H. Henry, "The Undoing of the Modern Mind," in *Evangelical Roots: A Tribute to Wilbur Smith,* ed. Kenneth S. Kantzer (Nashville: Thomas Nelson, 1978), 114.

[297] Niebuhr identifies Rauschenbusch's Social Gospel eschatology not simply with utopianism but with Pelagianism, seeing in it not only a problematic view of history but also a problematic view of human sin (Reinhold Niebuhr, *The Nature and Destiny of Man,* vol. 1, *Human Nature* [New York: Charles Scribner's Sons, 1941], 245-248). As Eugene McCarraher notes, "Neoorthodoxy was the grim face of liberal Protestantism and the Niebuhrian moment marked the immersion of the social gospel in the muddied waters of liberal religious idealism" (Eugene McCarraher, *Christian Critics: Religion and the Impasse in Modern American Social Thought* [Ithaca, N.Y.: Cornell University Press, 2000], 65).

[298] Stanley J. Grenz, "The Deeper Significance of the Millennium Debate," 20. Grenz also highlights helpful aspects of evangelical postmillennial optimism and amillennial realism. While Grenz's epistemological view that the Spirit speaks through contradictory eschatological views is problematic, he nonetheless makes the point that the pessimism of premillennialists (and Reformed amillennialists) in the early part of the century served to provide a biblical counterbalance to the triumphalism of earlier generations of postmillennialism.

[299] Saucy, *Kingdom of God in the Teaching of Jesus in Twentieth-Century Theology,* 300.

[300] Revolutionary liberation theology would seem to be languishing due to the decline of global Marxism and the rise of Pentecostal evangelicalism in the Third World. Nonetheless, its message of an immanent Kingdom associated with politically left ideology would seem to be resurgent in some sectors of evangelical political theology. See, for instance, the resemblance between the Kingdom theology of Gustavo Gutierrez's *A Theology of Liberation: History, Politics, and Salvation* (Maryknoll, N.Y.: Orbis, 1973) and that of James Wallis's evangelical political manifesto *The Soul of Politics: A Practical and Prophetic Vision for Change* (Maryknoll, N.Y.: Orbis, 1994), an affinity that does not end with the fact that both were published by the same liberationist Roman Catholic publisher.

[301] Edmund P. Clowney, *Another Foundation: The Presbyterian Confessional Crisis* (Philadelphia: Presbyterian & Reformed, 1965), 20.

[302] Ibid.

[303] Gaffin, "Usefulness of the Cross," 246.

[304] Carl F. H. Henry, *The God Who Shows Himself* (Waco, Tex.: Word, 1966), 7.

[305] Mark A. Noll, *Adding Cross to Crown: The Political Significance of Christ's Passion* (Grand Rapids, Mich.: Baker, 1996), 15.

[306] Ibid., 42-44.

[307] Perhaps no one has more biblically balanced Kingdom with cross than Richard Gaffin, who appeals to an inaugurated eschatology view of the Kingdom in his polemic against theonomy and other forms of dominion theology: "Looking in one direction, we must agree that New Testament eschatology is most assuredly an eschatology of victory, and of victory presently being realized. But, any outlook that fails to see that for the church, between the resurrection and return of Christ and *until* that return, the eschatology of victory is an eschatology of suffering, any outlook that otherwise tends to remove the dimension of suffering from the present *triumph* of the church, distorts the gospel and confuses the (apostolic) mission of the church in the world. The church does indeed carry the eschatological victory of Jesus into the world, but only as it takes up the cross after him. Its glory, always veiled, is revealed in its suffering with him" (Gaffin, "Usefulness of the Cross," 245).

[308] This eschatological dualism is emphasized by the various manifestations of Kingdom

eschatology within the evangelical coalition. It is not, however, new to them. The early Baptist arguments for religious liberty and church/state separation carried similar arguments, though without a clearly worked out inaugurated eschatology. See, for instance, Stanley Grenz's analysis of the relevance of eschatology in the religious liberty arguments of early American Baptist leader Isaac Backus in *Isaac Backus—Puritan and Baptist: His Place in History, His Thought, and Their Implications for Modern Baptist Theology* (Macon, Ga.: Mercer University Press, 1983), 317-324.

[309] Ladd, *Gospel of the Kingdom,* 56.

[310] For an example of the more recent attempts to synthesize secular apocalypticism and leftist utopianism, see Michael Hardt and Antonio Negri, *Empire* (Cambridge, Mass.: Harvard University Press, 2001), which combines Marxist social theory with contemporary environmentalist theory.

[311] For an example of contemporary secular apocalypticism, see the arguments of Albert Gore, Jr., then a United States senator and later Vice-President of the United States, in his *Earth in the Balance: Ecology and the Human Spirit* (New York: Penguin, 1992). Gore, for example, warns darkly of global extinction based on the ozone and global warming dangers stemming from human inattention and technology such as the internal combustion engine.

[312] As does, for instance, Jürgen Moltmann in *Coming of God,* 202-217.

[313] Ladd, *Blessed Hope,* 5-6.

[314] Philosopher Isaiah Berlin contends that the Western concepts of utopia "tend to contain the same elements: a society lives in a state of pure harmony, in which all its members live in peace, love one another, are free from physical danger, from want of any kind, from insecurity, from degrading work, from envy, from frustration, experience no injustice or violence, live in perpetual, even light, in a temperate climate, in the midst of infinitely fruitful, generous nature." He notes that the assumption on which utopianism is based "is that men have a certain fixed, unfaltering nature, certain universal, common, immutable goals" (Isaiah Berlin, *The Crooked Timber of Humanity: Chapters in the History of Ideas,* ed. Henry Hardy [Princeton, N.J.: Princeton University Press, 1959; reprint, Princeton, N.J.: Princeton University Press, 1990], 20). As Jean Elshtain notes, it is because Berlin is right about the commonality of utopian visions that they are so inherently anti-democratic. "Democracy is precisely an institutional, cultural, habitual way of acknowledging the pervasiveness of conflict and the fact that our loyalties are not one; our wills are not single; our opinions are not uniform; our ideals are not cut from the same cloth" (Jean Bethke Elshtain, *Democracy on Trial* [New York: Basic, 1995], 113). The dangerous tendencies and historical consequences of utopianism are analyzed further in Thomas Molnar, *Utopia: The Perennial Heresy* (New York: Sheed & Ward, 1967).

[315] Eric Voegelin, *The New Science of Politics* (Chicago: University of Chicago Press, 1952), 107-132.

[316] Eric Voegelin, *Science, Politics and Gnosticism: Two Essays* (Washington, D.C.: Regnery, 1968), 62-63. For a helpful analysis of the role of utopianism in both Nazi and Marxist totalitarianism, see A. James Gregor, *The Faces of Janus: Marxism and Fascism in the Twentieth Century* (New Haven, Conn.: Yale University Press, 2000).

[317] Daniel Bell, *The End of Ideology: On the Exhaustion of Political Ideas in the Fifties* (Cambridge, Mass.: Harvard University Press, 1988), 431.

[318] Richard J. Ellis, *The Dark Side of the Left: Illiberal Egalitarianism in America* (Lawrence: University Press of Kansas, 1998).

[319] Ibid., 53.

[320] For a contemporary restatement of the conservative evangelical stance during the Fundamentalist-Modernist controversy, see Peter P. J. Beyerhaus, *God's Kingdom and*

the Utopian Error: Discerning the Biblical Kingdom of God from Its Political Counterfeits (Wheaton, Ill.: Crossway, 1992).

321 Russell Jacoby, *The End of Utopia: Politics and Culture in an Age of Apathy* (New York: Basic, 1999), 181.

322 Ladd, *Presence of the Future,* 303.

323 Carl F. H. Henry, *Gods of This Age or God of the Ages?* (Nashville: Broadman & Holman, 1994), 81.

324 Barth and his colleagues struggled against the Nazi regime precisely because the "German Christian" movement attempted to recast German identity and historical progress with the Kingdom of God. Against this, the confessing church maintained the sole and unrivaled place of Christ as the Head of His Kingdom. For an analysis, see Rolf Ahlers, *The Barmen Theological Declaration of 1934: The Archaeology of a Confessional Text* (Lewiston, N.Y.: Edwin Mellen, 1986).

CHAPTER THREE

1 Carl F. H. Henry, *Faith at the Frontiers* (Chicago: Moody, 1969), 47.

2 For a discussion of the centrifugal role of Graham, see Mark Silk, "The Rise of the 'New Evangelicalism': Shock and Adjustment," in *Between the Times: The Travail of the Protestant Establishment in America, 1900–1960,* ed. William R. Hutchison (New York: Cambridge University Press, 1989), 282-291.

3 Carl F. H. Henry, "Evangelicals in the Social Struggle," in *Salt and Light: Evangelical Political Thought in Modern America,* ed. Augustus Cerillo, Jr., and Murray W. Dempster (Grand Rapids, Mich.: Baker, 1989), 31.

4 The official history of the National Association of Evangelicals, after all, referred to Social Gospel soteriology as "the Great Apostasy," noting that against this background "all evangelical thought and action may be seen in its true perspective and significance" (James Deforest Murch, *Cooperation Without Compromise: A History of the National Association of Evangelicals* [Grand Rapids, Mich.: Eerdmans, 1956], 19).

5 Northern Baptist premillennialist fundamentalist William Bell Riley began his 1912 study on the Kingdom by repudiating the soteriological implications of the contention of one Social Gospel proponent that "Two finds have been made within recent years: the Divine Fatherhood of God and the Kingdom of God." Riley countered that the Kingdom had never been "lost" by orthodox Protestantism, but had been infused with a new, and decidedly political meaning by a liberalism wishing to abandon orthodox soteriology (William B. Riley, *The Evolution of the Kingdom* [New York: Charles C. Cook, 1912], 7). Similarly, Reformed theologian Geerhardus Vos argued that the "Kingdom" salvation of Protestant liberalism abandoned soteriology, replacing it with ethics (Geerhardus Vos, *The Teaching of Jesus Concerning the Kingdom of God and the Church* [New York: American Tract Society, 1903], 5-8; *Biblical Theology: Old and New Testaments* [Grand Rapids, Mich.: Eerdmans, 1948], 412).

6 So Stanley Hauerwas argues against the essentially soteriological revisionist project of the Social Gospel: "For example, Protestant theologians, no longer sure of the metaphysical status of Christian claims, sought to secure the ongoing meaningfulness of Christian convictions by anchoring them in anthropological generalizations and/or turning them into ethics. No longer convinced that Jesus is the resurrected Messiah, his significance is now said to be found in the proclamation of the Kingdom of God. The Kingdom is the outworking in human history of the fatherhood of God and the brotherhood of man. Theology, at least Protestant liberal theology, became ethics, but the ethics it became was distinctively Kant's ethics dressed in religious language" (Stanley Hauerwas, "How 'Christian Ethics' Came to Be," in *The Hauerwas Reader,* ed. John Berkman and Michael Cartwright [Durham, N.C.: Duke University Press, 2001], 45).

[7] As New Testament scholar Norman Perrin observes, Rauschenbusch's understanding of the Kingdom attempted to domesticate the Kingdom by preserving eschatology without a soteriology, an unworkable construct from the point of view of the New Testament writers (Norman Perrin, *The Kingdom of God in the Teaching of Jesus* [Philadelphia: Westminster, 1963], 46-49).

[8] H. Richard Niebuhr, no "fundamentalist" by almost any definition, noted the soteriological vacuity of the modernist "Kingdom of God." For Niebuhr, the "Kingdom" as articulated by Protestant liberals such as Ritschl and his heirs represented "the complete reconciliation of Christianity and culture," a goal long sought by the ecumenical left. Like the fundamentalists, Niebuhr noted that, for liberal Protestants "the word 'God' seems to be an intrusion" in the phrase "Kingdom of God," a problem solved, he commented, when liberalism eventually "substituted the phrase 'brotherhood of man' for 'kingdom of God.'" With such being the case, Niebuhr charged, modernism had no doctrine of salvation, or even a theological concept of the Kingdom, but instead coalesced under a vaguely defined theological gloss on Immanuel Kant's "kingdom of ends" or Thomas Jefferson's universal human family (H. Richard Niebuhr, *Christ and Culture* [New York: Harper & Row, 1951], 98-99).

[9] Carl F. H. Henry, *A Plea for Evangelical Demonstration* (Grand Rapids, Mich.: Baker, 1971), 39.

[10] Murch, *Cooperation Without Compromise,* 166.

[11] Carl F. H. Henry, "A Troubled Conscience Fifty Years Later" (paper presented at the inaugural Carl F. H. Henry Lectures, The Southern Baptist Theological Seminary, Louisville, January 28, 1998), 4.

[12] Ibid.

[13] Elements within the older fundamentalism, such as *Sword of the Lord* editor John R. Rice, reacted to Henry's proposal for a socially and politically engaged evangelical movement by charging the neo-evangelicals with abandoning the emphasis on personal regeneration found in *The Fundamentals* (Los Angeles: Bible Institute of Los Angeles, 1917), thus providing a "bridgehead" between modernists and fundamentalists (John R. Rice, "Don't Be Fooled," *AGC Reporter,* September 1958, 2; cited in Louis Gasper, *The Fundamentalist Movement, 1930–1956* [Grand Rapids, Mich.: Baker, 1981], 120). Others simply equated the new evangelical call to engagement with the evangelization of social structures rather than the evangelization of individuals, namely the denominational liberalism they had fled in the controversies of the last generation and against which they now contended in the form of the highly politicized gospel of the World Council of Churches. "It is closer to the 'social gospel' of liberal theology than it is to the 'ye must be born again' of biblical evangelism," charged fundamentalist Raymond Pratt as late as the 1970s (Raymond Pratt, "The Social Emphasis of New Evangelicalism," *Central Bible Quarterly* 21 [1978]: 24). At times, this fear of a tie to the societal view of soteriology espoused by the Social Gospel liberals may have been fanned by the intellectual training of new evangelical theologians such as Henry. Historian Joel Carpenter seems to grant credence to at least some of the fundamentalists' fears: "Carl Henry, for example, was studying under Edgar Brightman and the other 'personalist' theologians at Boston University who were deeply devoted to the Social Gospel. Two years after they approved Henry's dissertation, they would be imparting some of their vision to another extraordinary student, Martin Luther King, Jr. Henry has claimed that his encounter with Brightman and the others had little to do with his developing a critique of fundamentalism's lack of social concern. But it is hard to believe that it was only a coincidence that Henry was putting the finishing touches on *The Uneasy Conscience of Modern Fundamentalism* (1947) in the summer of 1946 while he was studying in Boston" (Joel A. Carpenter, *Revive Us Again: The Reawakening of American Fundamentalism* [New York: Oxford University Press, 1997], 193).

[14] This does not mean that Henry's call to emphasize both personal responsibility and social reform was successful in transforming the evangelical movement, or even, for that matter, the ministry of Graham. Some historians have tied Henry's *Uneasy Conscience* to Graham's later involvement in issues such as nuclear non-proliferation (Robert K. Johnston, *Evangelicals at an Impasse: Biblical Authority in Practice* [Atlanta: John Knox, 1979], 78-79). Graham biographer William Martin, however, presents a more ambiguous relationship, writing that Graham was "particularly impressed by Carl Henry's book, but his passion for winning souls outweighed his social concerns, and his solutions to major social problems were typically those of evangelical individualism— get individuals to attend church, read their Bible, and pray, and social problems will vanish—and he showed only limited appreciation for corporate efforts to effect social change" (William Martin, *A Prophet With Honor: The Billy Graham Story* [New York: William Morrow, 1991], 164).

[15] Carl F. H. Henry, *The God Who Shows Himself* (Waco, Tex.: Word, 1966), 50.

[16] In the preface to *Uneasy Conscience,* he argued that, apart from a rebirth of sociopolitical engagement on the part of conservative evangelicals, American fundamentalism would "be reduced either to a tolerated cult status, or in the event of Roman Catholic domination in the United States, become once again a despised and oppressed sect" (Carl F. H. Henry, *The Uneasy Conscience of Modern Fundamentalism* [Grand Rapids, Mich.: Eerdmans, 1947], 9). Henry's argument built on those of others such as Harold J. Ockenga, who warned in his keynote address at the initial meeting of the National Association of Evangelicals that a politically and socially disengaged evangelicalism was on the verge of being overcome by a growing Roman Catholic presence and "that terrible octopus of liberalism, which spreads itself throughout our Protestant church, dominating innumerable organizations, pulpits, and publications, as well as seminaries and other schools" (Harold John Ockenga, "The Unvoiced Multitudes," in *Evangelical Action! A Report on the Organization of the National Association of Evangelicals for United Action* [Boston: United Action Press, 1942], 26-27).

[17] By segregating social and political concerns from the gospel, Henry charged, the fundamentalists had conceded the public square to modernists such as Walter Rauschenbusch, Harry Emerson Fosdick, and their even more radical successors. Fundamentalist isolation had ensured, Henry chided, that the theological inadequacies of the Social Gospel would be answered and, in many instances, replaced, not by Christian orthodoxy, but instead by alternatives such as Reinhold Niebuhr's "Christian realism," a system that was "as destructive of certain essential elements of the biblical view as it was reconstructive of others" (Henry, *Plea for Evangelical Demonstration,* 34-35).

[18] Henry, *Uneasy Conscience of Modern Fundamentalism,* 44-45.

[19] Ibid., 27-28.

[20] "Infected with Hegelian speculation, Protestant liberalism not only surrendered the Biblical redemptive-regenerative view of man and the world to optimistic evolutionary expectations about the future, but also lost all transcendent and eschatological elements of the Kingdom of God," Henry asserted. "It promulgated, rather, a wholly immanent and essentially politico-economic conception of the Kingdom" (Henry, *Plea for Evangelical Demonstration,* 117).

[21] Henry complained that, for those who "shared the glow of Dean Shailer Mathews' prospect for a better world," the fundamentalists "who stood with the Hebrew-Christian tradition in a more pessimistic view of contemporary culture were accused of not having any social program." In fact, Henry countered, many of these fundamentalists did indeed have no social program, "though modernism was unjustified in assuming they could have none since they were not optimistic about man" (Carl F. H. Henry, *Remaking the Modern Mind* [Grand Rapids, Mich.: Eerdmans, 1946], 41).

22 Henry, *Plea for Evangelical Demonstration*, 92.

23 Carl F. H. Henry, *Evangelicals at the Brink of Crisis: The Significance of the World Congress on Evangelism* (Waco, Tex.: Word, 1967), 68.

24 "The evangelical vision of the new society, or the Kingdom on earth, is therefore messianic, and is tied to the expectation of the return of Christ in glory," Henry concluded. "It is distrustful of world power, of attempts to derive a just society from unregenerate human nature. And this verdict on human affairs is fully supportive of the biblical verdict on fallen history" (ibid.).

25 Carl F. H. Henry, *Christian Personal Ethics* (Grand Rapids, Mich.: Eerdmans, 1957), 234.

26 Henry, *God Who Shows Himself*, 39.

27 Henry, *Christian Personal Ethics*, 303.

28 Ibid., 420. Unlike E. J. Carnell, however, Henry did not condemn fundamentalist personal morality on issues such as alcohol and tobacco as "cultic" legalism. Henry instead warned that an emphasis only on personal evils might represent a degradation of the moral law in terms of an incipient Pelagianism. "Smoking can be a subject of legislation; pride cannot," he noted (ibid., 421).

29 Ibid., 152.

30 Henry, *God Who Shows Himself*, 62.

31 Henry, *Christian Personal Ethics*, 572.

32 Ibid., 230.

33 So Henry asserted, "Surely evangelical Christianity has more to offer mankind than its unique message of salvation, even if that is its highest and holiest mission. While it rightly chides the liberal for regarding the world as a unity (rather than divided into unregenerate and regenerate), it also has a message for all men as members of one society. The Christian is not, by his church identification, isolated from humanity, or from involvement in the political and economic orders. Not only is he called to identify with society: he *is* identified, by the very fact of his humanity, and as a Christian he bears a double responsibility in relation to the social needs and goals of mankind. Social justice is a need of the individual, whose dignity as a person is at stake, and of society and culture, which soon collapse without it" (Henry, *God Who Shows Himself*, 61).

34 George Eldon Ladd, *Crucial Questions About the Kingdom of God* (Grand Rapids, Mich.: Eerdmans, 1952), 84.

35 Ladd contended, "We have seen that the present activity of the Kingdom of God in Jesus' person and mission included both a positive and a negative aspect. It meant salvation for those who received his message and judgment for those who rejected it. This salvation and judgment were interpreted primarily in individual terms, but not exclusively so" (George Eldon Ladd, *The Presence of the Future: The Eschatology of Biblical Realism* [Grand Rapids, Mich.: Eerdmans, 1974], 321).

36 Noting that biblical terms such as "eternal life" and "the Kingdom of God" are future realities, Ladd contended that nonetheless "every Sunday School child knows that Jesus came to give men eternal life here and now; for he who believes on the Son *has* eternal life" (George Eldon Ladd, "The Revelation of Christ's Glory," *Christianity Today*, September 1, 1958, 14).

37 "Long ago, Professor Geerhardus Vos pointed out in his *Pauline Eschatology* that the great themes of redemption—justification, the Holy Spirit, as well as eternal life and the kingdom of God—are 'semi-eschatological' realities," Ladd wrote. "That is, although they belong to the age to come, they have entered into human history, through the incarnation and redemptive work of Christ" (ibid.).

38 Ladd, *Crucial Questions About the Kingdom of God*, 83.

³⁹ Ladd, *Presence of the Future,* 331.

⁴⁰ "The theological confusion stems from a basic failure to understand the nature of Christ's mediatorial ministry; and this in turn derives from an unwillingness to accept the New Testament definition of the kingdom of God and to reinterpret the Old Testament in light of the New Testament definition," Ladd wrote of the Kingdom theology of dispensationalist Alva McClain (George Eldon Ladd, "Dispensational Theology," *Christianity Today,* October 12, 1959, 39).

⁴¹ Ladd, *Crucial Questions About the Kingdom of God,* 56-57.

⁴² George Eldon Ladd, *A Theology of the New Testament* (Grand Rapids, Mich.: Eerdmans, 1974), 602.

⁴³ Ibid., 339.

⁴⁴ George Eldon Ladd, *The Gospel of the Kingdom: Scriptural Studies in the Kingdom of God* (Grand Rapids, Mich.: Eerdmans, 1959), 69.

⁴⁵ Ladd, *Theology of the New Testament,* 74. See also George Eldon Ladd, "The Kingdom of God and the Church," *Foundations* 4 (1961): 169-171.

⁴⁶ Ladd, *Theology of the New Testament,* 74.

⁴⁷ See Demarest's survey of historical models of regeneration in Bruce Demarest, *The Cross and Salvation* (Wheaton, Ill.: Crossway, 1997), 278-291.

⁴⁸ Ibid., 297-300.

⁴⁹ Millard J. Erickson, *Christian Theology,* 2nd ed. (Grand Rapids, Mich.: Baker, 1998), 657-674. Erickson summarizes his treatment in this way: "Social sin is prevalent in our society and exists alongside individual sin. Persons who oppose sin on a personal level may be drawn into the corporate nature of sin through the evil acts of government, economic structures, or other forms of group identification. The Bible identifies the evil that comes through the world, the powers, and corporate personality which draws both believers and non-believers into the evil of society. Our hope lies in Christ, who has overcome the world. But we also need to be proactive in opposing social sin by finding strategies that will respond to social sin" (ibid., 657).

⁵⁰ Erickson lists the options for confronting structural and social sin as strategies of regeneration, reform, and revolution (ibid., 658).

⁵¹ So Henry writes, "The messianic vision comprehends a restoration of the unity of man and nature," because of the cosmic implications of the fall of humanity (Carl F. H. Henry, *God, Revelation, and Authority,* 6 vols. [Waco, Tex.: Word, 1976; reprint, Wheaton, Ill.: Crossway, 1999], 2:101).

⁵² Ibid., 2:99.

⁵³ Ibid., 6:111-112.

⁵⁴ Thus, Henry writes, "Jesus in his own person is the embodied sovereignty of God. He lives out that sovereignty in the flesh. He manifests the kingdom of God by enthroning the creation-will of God and demonstrating his lordship over Satan. Jesus conducts himself as Lord and true King, ruling over demons, ruling over nature at its fiercest, ruling over sickness, conquering death itself. With the coming of Jesus the kingdom is not merely immanent; it gains the larger scope of incursion and invasion. Jesus points to his release of the victims of Satan, and to his own devastation of demons and the demonic, as attesting that 'the kingdom of God has come upon you' (Matt. 12:28). He reveals God's royal power in its salvific activity" (Carl F. H. Henry, "Reflections on the Kingdom of God," *JETS* 35 [1992]: 42).

⁵⁵ Stanley J. Grenz, *Theology for the Community of God* (Grand Rapids, Mich.: Eerdmans, 2000), 348.

⁵⁶ Ibid.

⁵⁷ Boyd sketches this "warfare worldview" in two volumes, Gregory A. Boyd, *God at*

War: The Bible and Spiritual Conflict (Downers Grove, Ill.: InterVarsity Press, 1996); and *Satan and the Problem of Evil: Constructing a Trinitarian Warfare Theodicy* (Downers Grove, Ill.: InterVarsity Press, 2001). Boyd couches this "warfare worldview" in terms of his "open theism," in which God does not meticulously govern the affairs of the cosmos. Thus, God sometimes suffers defeat at the hands of cosmic agents, both angelic and human.

[58] Ironically, Boyd traces part of his understanding of the cosmic implications of salvation to the work of a prominent European dispensationalist, Erich Sauer. See, for instance, Boyd, *God at War*, 106-110; and *Satan and the Problem of Evil*, 315-316.

[59] To the contrary, Finney mixed his conversionist revivalism with a type of nineteenth-century postmillennial fervor and a passion for social justice causes such as revivalism. He is not unique in this respect, but he is perhaps the most influential of the Second Great Awakening's revivalist evangelist/theologians. As Donald Dayton notes, "Charles Grandison Finney, however, was greater than either the secular caricature of a ranting, hell-fire evangelist or the evangelical images of a deeply spiritual preacher given totally to the 'saving of souls.' In the words of American historian Richard Hofstadter of Columbia University, he 'must be reckoned among our great men.' Though first and foremost an evangelist, Finney's work and the way he understood the gospel 'released a mighty impulse toward social reform' that shook the nation and helped destroy slavery" (Donald W. Dayton, *Discovering an Evangelical Heritage* [Peabody, Mass.: Hendrickson, 1976], 15). Dayton cites Richard Hofstadter, *Anti-Intellectualism in American Life* (New York: Alfred A. Knopf, 1964), 92; and Gilbert Hobbs Barnes, *The Anti-Slavery Impulse, 1830–1844* (New York: Harcourt, Brace & World, 1964), 11.

[60] Thus, as one historian notes, dispensationalists generally did not oppose the cooperative crusade efforts of cooperative evangelism of the evangelical movement (John Fea, "Fundamentalism, Neo-Evangelicalism, and the American Dispensationalist Establishment in the 1950s," *Michigan Theological Journal* 4 [1993]: 131). As an example of this phenomenon, Fea points to the glowing reception Graham received from the dispensationalist magazine *Moody Monthly* in the 1950s in contrast to the articles in separatist fundamentalist periodicals such as *Sword of the Lord*.

[61] Robert Pyne, "New Man and Immoral Society" (paper presented at the annual meeting of the Evangelical Theological Society, Santa Clara, Calif., November 20, 1997), 2.

[62] Richard K. Curtis, *They Called Him Mister Moody* (Garden City, N.Y.: Doubleday, 1962), 266-267. Stanley Grenz is one of many who cite Moody's famous comparison of the world to a wrecked sea vessel as a metaphor for worsening conditions in world history (Stanley J. Grenz, *Theology for the Community of God*, 506). Timothy Weber points to C. I. Scofield's use of the metaphor strikingly as he preached a 1912 memorial service in Belfast for the drowned passengers of the world's most infamous "sinking ship," the *Titanic* (Timothy Weber, *Living in the Shadow of the Second Coming: American Premillennialism, 1875–1925* [New York: Oxford University Press, 1979], 71).

[63] Darrell L. Bock, "Why I Am a dispensationalist with a Small 'd'," *JETS* 41 (1998): 393. Bock's contention bears much weight when the dispensationalist influence on parachurch evangelistic movements, such as Campus Crusade for Christ, is examined.

[64] Such as that of Vern Poythress: "One cannot contemplate a millennium in which salvation is in union with one man, the last Adam, Jesus Christ, but in which that union is undermined by the distinctiveness of two peoples of God with two inheritances and two destinies, on earth and in heaven" (Vern S. Poythress, *Understanding Dispensationalists*, 2nd ed. [Phillipsburg, N.J.: Presbyterian & Reformed, 1994], 129).

[65] Craig A. Blaising, "Lewis Sperry Chafer," in *Handbook of Evangelical Theologians*, ed. Walter A. Elwell (Grand Rapids, Mich.: Baker, 1993), 93-94. The dual salvific des-

tinies of the "heavenly" church and the "earthly" Israel are not limited to Scofield and Chafer, but are widespread throughout the early dispensationalist theological writings. Even continental dispensationalist Erich Sauer, who was in many ways a forerunner of some of the revisions of the progressive dispensationalists, could write, "Thus the church stands far above Israel. The Jews are the subjects of Christ, the members of the church are His co-regents (2 Tim. 2:12; Matt. 19:28); the Jews belong to the kingdom, the church is His wife; the Jews are God's earthly people (Isa. 60:21), the church His heavenly people (Eph. 1:3), and as the heaven is higher than the earth so are the spiritual blessings of the church higher than the earthly blessings of the at last converted people of Israel" (Erich Sauer, *The Triumph of the Crucified: A Survey of the History of Salvation in the New Testament*, trans. G. H. Lang [Grand Rapids, Mich.: Eerdmans, 1951], 167). At times, these dual goals of salvation were also related to other theological concepts, such as the "gap" theory of the creation days, in which Lucifer's pre-Fall reign over the earth from the heavens is compared to the reign of the church in the millennial Kingdom (G. H. Pember, *Earth's Earliest Ages* [London: Hodder & Stoughton, 1876; reprint, Grand Rapids, Mich.: Kregel, 1975], 55).

66 Lewis Sperry Chafer, *The Kingdom in History and Prophecy* (Philadelphia: Sunday School Times, 1922), 9.

67 This does not mean, however, that progressives do away with the differentiation between Israel and the new covenant church. This distinction will be noted later in this study.

68 Craig A. Blaising, "Dispensationalism: The Search for Definition," in *Dispensationalism, Israel, and the Church: The Search for Definition*, ed. Craig A. Blaising and Darrell L. Bock (Grand Rapids, Mich.: Zondervan, 1992), 33.

69 Bruce A. Ware, "The New Covenant and the People(s) of God," in *Dispensationalism, Israel, and the Church*, 68-97.

70 Charles C. Ryrie, *Dispensationalism* (Chicago: Moody, 1995), 165.

71 Dispensationalists have found a soteriological distinctive in the effect that the system, with its imminent parousia, has on the personal sanctification of the individual believer. See, for instance, Charles L. Feinberg, *Millennialism: The Two Major Views* (Chicago: Moody, 1980), 29-30.

72 So, for instance, Elliott E. Johnson, "Prophetic Fulfillment: The Already and Not Yet," in *Issues in Dispensationalism*, ed. Wesley R. Willis and John R. Master (Chicago: Moody, 1994), 198.

73 Walvoord warns, "Such an approach builds upon the assumption that the Davidic kingdom is basically soteriological and points to Christ. This eliminates any real physical, political kingdom of David if his kingdom is viewed as exclusively soteric. By downplaying the idea of a physical, political Davidic kingdom, the argument for a future millennial kingdom following Christ's second advent is weakened. It may be concluded that the amillennial understanding of the kingdom has been influenced, in large measure, by failing to distinguish the various ways that the word *kingdom* is used in the Scriptures, specifically not recognizing the difference between the Davidic kingdom and the kingdom of God" (John F. Walvoord, "Biblical Kingdoms Compared and Contrasted," in *Issues in Dispensationalism*, 85).

74 Craig A. Blaising and Darrell L. Bock, *Progressive Dispensationalism* (Wheaton, Ill.: Victor, 1993), 297.

75 Blaising and Bock write, "In Jesus Christ, divine and human rule come together in one Person. This is the revelation of ultimate reconciliation. The tension between the Davidic and divine rulership is eliminated in the unity of the person and action of Christ. Thus the Incarnation is crucial to guaranteeing the salvation of human beings, for at least this human being has an everlasting, eternal human life. His atonement is crucial for

bringing forgiveness and justification to all. His resurrection from the dead reveals human immortality as well as divine power" (ibid., 298).

[76] For a survey of these revisions in various dispensationalist models, see Blaising, "Dispensationalism: The Search for Definition," 23-29.

[77] Chafer, *Kingdom in History and Prophecy*, 87.

[78] Blaising writes, "Beginning in the late 1950s, some dispensationalists began to abandon classical dispensationalism's dualism of heavenly and earthly eternal states. This meant that a choice had to be made in favor of either a spiritual vision model or a more earthly model of eternity. Some (such as Charles Ryrie and John Walvoord) chose the former, believing that all the redeemed would share an eternal destiny that was spiritual in nature (even though the redeemed would be segregated between Israel and the church). Others (such as Alva J. McClain and J. Dwight Pentecost) believed that eternity for all the redeemed of all dispensations would be on the new earth in a new creation experience of final salvation (still segregated, however, as Israel and the church)" (Craig A. Blaising, "Premillennialism," in *Three Views on the Millennium and Beyond*, ed. Darrell L. Bock [Grand Rapids, Mich.: Zondervan, 1999], 185-186).

[79] As one progressive dispensationalist remarks, in answering the question of the object of Christian hope, "Is Christian hope, then, a hope for heaven—specifically, to be raptured into heaven—to there abide for a period of three and a half years, and then to return to the earth with Christ as glorified saints? Or is Christian hope *ultimately* a millennial and earthly hope that finds its terminus on the restored earth (Rom 8:18-23)? Or is Christian hope a *combination* of both of these ideas?" (Gary L. Nebeker, "The Theme of Hope in Dispensationalism," *BibSac* 158 [2001]: 4-5).

[80] Blaising, "Dispensationalism," 26.

[81] Blaising, "Premillennialism," 189.

[82] Robert L. Saucy, "The Crucial Issue Between Dispensational and Non-dispensational Systems," *Criswell Theological Review* 1 (1986): 156-158.

[83] Ibid., 157.

[84] Ibid.

[85] One progressive dispensationalist traces out this view of salvation in the following way: "Such a renovation involves both continuity and discontinuity as the old Adamic order is transformed into the new messianic order. There is continuity in that the new heaven and new earth will be substantially one with the present heaven and earth. There is also discontinuity in that the new heaven and earth will be radically transformed from the bondage of the disobedience of the first Adam to the freedom of the obedience of the second Adam, Jesus Christ. The new universe in Christ is none other than the old Adamic universe gloriously liberated from its cacophonous groan to a harmonious song of praise to the One who sits on the throne" (David L. Turner, "The New Jerusalem in Revelation 21:1–22:5: Consummation of a Biblical Continuum," in *Dispensationalism, Israel, and the Church*, 265).

[86] Craig A. Blaising, "Law, Gospel, and the Unity of Scripture in Progressive Dispensationalism" (paper presented to the Biblical Theology Study Group at the Evangelical Theological Society national meeting, Colorado Springs, November 15, 2001), 1.

[87] "The kingdom which Jesus proclaimed was as much a spiritual as a physical kingdom. This is not a contradiction because the adjective *spiritual* does not imply a change in metaphysical status of God's subjects. It refers to the presence of God with His creation in which He renews and blesses it" (Blaising and Bock, *Progressive Dispensationalism*, 242).

[88] Ibid., 248.

[89] Ryrie, *Dispensationalism*, 176.

[90] Ibid., 180 n. 40.

[91] Lewis Sperry Chafer, *Systematic Theology,* 8 vols. (Dallas: Dallas Seminary Press, 1948), 3:105-108.

[92] Ibid., 108.

[93] As Robert Saucy argues contra Vern Poythress and the covenant theologians, "We would argue that the redemptive work of the Messiah involves not only a personal inner spiritual salvation, but a socio-political salvation as well" (Robert L. Saucy, "Response to *Understanding Dispensationalists* by Vern S. Poythress," *GTJ* 10 [1989]: 145).

[94] For Saucy, the eternal state cannot be the focal point of these national aspects of salvation, contra Hoekema, because in the regeneration, all persons know God, and thus do not need the mediatorial function of national Israel (Robert L. Saucy, "A Rationale for the Future of Israel," *JETS* 28 [1985]: 439).

[95] Ibid., 440-441.

[96] As Saucy notes, "God's kingly rule is brought to the earth through the mediation of the kingdom of the Messiah. According to biblical prophecy, the coming of the kingdom involves the redemption of creation from all the effects of sin through the personal salvation of individuals, the socio-political salvation of the nations, and finally the salvation of the earth and heavens through re-creation. This pervasive mediatorial kingdom program, ultimately fulfilled through the reign of Christ, is the theme of Scripture and the unifying principle of all aspects of God's work in history" (Robert L. Saucy, *The Case for Progressive Dispensationalism: The Interface Between Dispensational and Non-dispensational Theology* [Grand Rapids, Mich.: Zondervan, 1993], 28).

[97] Thus, neo-Arminian theologian Clark Pinnock points to this tradition in his critique of Millard Erickson's soteriology: "Having blamed Erickson for being too Calvinistic in theology proper, I now object to his not being Calvinistic enough when it comes to the holistic scope of salvation. He narrows down the atonement to penal substitution (p. 815) and discusses the nature of salvation in very nearly exclusively individualistic terms (part 10). He even says, 'Jesus made it clear that the eternal spiritual welfare of the individual is infinitely more important than the supplying of temporal needs' (p. 905). Is this perhaps the reason why the kingdom of God as a topic is not treated either under Christology or under salvation? Is it any wonder that forty million American evangelicals have been unable to impart to the public square a tangy Christian flavor? How could they if they have no hope for culture except to be taken out of it by our returning Lord Jesus?" (Clark H. Pinnock, "Erickson's Three-Volume *Magnum Opus,*" *TSF Bulletin,* January-February 1986, 30).

[98] Abraham Kuyper, *Lectures on Calvinism* (Grand Rapids, Mich.: Eerdmans, 1931). This published monograph is taken from Kuyper's six Stone Lectures delivered at Princeton University in 1898.

[99] Thus Kuyper proclaimed at Princeton, "He placed the spiritual center of this cosmos on our planet, and caused all the divisions of the kingdoms of nature, on this earth, to culminate in man, upon whom, as the bearer of His image He called to consecrate the cosmos to His glory. In God's creation, therefore, man stands as the prophet, priest and king, and although sin has disturbed these high designs, yet God pushes them onward. He so loves His world that He has given Himself to it, in the person of His Son, and thus He has again brought our race, and through our race, His whole cosmos, into a renewed contact with eternal life. To be sure, many branches and leaves fell off the tree of the human race, yet the tree itself shall be saved; on its new root in Christ, it shall once more blossom gloriously. For regeneration does not save a few isolated individuals, finally to be joined together mechanically as an aggregate heap" (ibid., 59). For more detailed Kuyperian attempts at relating salvation to an overarching Kingdom theology, see, for example, Henry R. Van Til, *The Calvinistic Concept of Culture* (Grand Rapids, Mich.:

Baker, 1959; reprint, Grand Rapids, Mich.: Baker, 2001); Albert M. Wolters, *Creation Regained: Biblical Basics for a Reformational Worldview* (Grand Rapids, Mich.: Eerdmans, 1985); and Gordon J. Spykman, *Reformational Theology: A New Paradigm for Doing Dogmatics* (Grand Rapids, Mich.: Eerdmans, 1992).

[100] Thus Warfield argued, "The redemption of Christ, if it is to be worthily viewed, must be looked at not merely individualistically, but also in its social, or better in its cosmical relations. Men are not discrete particles standing off from one another as mutually isolated units. They are members of an organism, the human race; and this race itself is an element in a greater organism which is significantly termed a universe. Of course the plan of salvation as it lies in the divine mind cannot be supposed to be concerned, therefore, alone with individuals as such: it of necessity has its relations with the greater unities into which these individuals enter as elements. We have only partially understood the redemption in Christ, therefore, when we have thought of it only in its modes of operation and effects on the individual" (Benjamin B. Warfield, *The Plan of Salvation* [Grand Rapids, Mich.: Eerdmans, 1935; reprint, Eugene, Ore.: Wipf & Stock, 2000], 102).

[101] Ladd, *Crucial Questions About the Kingdom of God*, 54-57.

[102] See, for instance, Oswald T. Allis's definition of the Kingdom of God as spiritual, universal, and redemptive in his *Prophecy and the Church* (Philadelphia: Presbyterian & Reformed, 1945), 56. It is against this view of the Kingdom that Ladd took special issue in his treatment of covenant theology (Ladd, *Crucial Questions About the Kingdom of God*, 56).

[103] Louis Berkhof, *Systematic Theology* (Grand Rapids, Mich.: Eerdmans, 1941; reprint, Edinburgh: Banner of Truth, 1958), 406-407.

[104] Ibid., 408.

[105] Edmund P. Clowney, "The Politics of the Kingdom," *WTJ* 41 (1979): 292.

[106] Saucy, *Case for Progressive Dispensationalism*, 20. Some may even say more so, given the profound emphasis on God's self-glorification in the Westminster Confession of Faith and in the theological writings of Reformed theologians ranging from John Calvin to Jonathan Edwards. For a more recent appropriation of Edwards's theology of the glory of God as the goal of redemptive history, see John Piper, *The Pleasures of God: Meditations on God's Delight in Being God*, rev. and expanded ed. (Sisters, Ore.: Multnomah, 2000).

[107] Poythress, *Understanding Dispensationalists*, 129.

[108] Vern S. Poythress, *Symphonic Theology: The Validity of Multiple Perspectives in Theology* (Phillipsburg, N.J.: Presbyterian & Reformed, 1987), 96-99.

[109] Richard B. Gaffin, Jr., *Resurrection and Redemption: A Study in Paul's Soteriology* (Phillipsburg, N.J.: Presbyterian & Reformed, 1987), 116-134.

[110] Sinclair B. Ferguson, *The Holy Spirit* (Downers Grove, Ill.: InterVarsity Press, 1996), 34-56.

[111] Ibid., 33. Similarly, Gaffin argues, "A basic factor emerging from our discussion, one that controls both the Christology and the pneumatology of the New Testament, is the thorough *integration*, the complete *correspondence*, the total *congruence*, there is in the church and the experience of believers between the work of the exalted Christ and the work of the Holy Spirit. We may say not only that at Pentecost Christ pours out on the church the gift of the Spirit, but also that Pentecost is the coming to the church of Christ Himself as the life-giving Spirit. The Spirit of Pentecost is the resurrection life of Jesus, the life of the exalted Christ effective in the church" (Richard B. Gaffin, Jr., "The Holy Spirit," *WTJ* 43 [1980]: 58).

[112] See, for instance, Richard B. Gaffin, Jr., "'Life-Giving Spirit': Probing the Center of Paul's Pneumatology," *JETS* 41 (1998): 573-589.

[113] Anthony Hoekema, *Created in God's Image* (Grand Rapids, Mich.: Eerdmans, 1986), 74.

[114] Dan G. McCartney, "*Ecce Homo:* The Coming of the Kingdom as the Restoration of Human Vicegerency," *WTJ* 56 (1994): 2.

[115] This is not to say that salvation is simply a return to Adamic innocence, he argues, but instead this creation order brought to its eschatological fulfillment. "It is thus an advance over the Adamic state" (ibid.).

[116] Ibid.

[117] Ibid., 16.

[118] Vern S. Poythress, "Currents Within Amillennialism," *Presbyterion* 26 (2000): 24.

[119] Ibid.

[120] Therefore Poythress argues, "Redemption and recreation therefore also take place by way of a representative head, a new human head, namely the incarnate Christ (1 Cor 15:45-49). As there is one humanity united under Adam through the flesh, so there is one new humanity united under Christ through the Spirit. Just as the subhuman creation was affected by Adam's fall (Rom 8:20), so it is to be transformed by Christ's resurrection (v. 21). Christ himself, as head and representative of all the redeemed, is the unifying center of God's acts in redemption and recreation" (ibid., 42).

[121] Poythress, for instance, points not only to the corporeality of Jesus' resurrection body, but to His claim to exhaustive lordship over the created order: "Christ is Lord of our *bodies,* Lord of the *community* of God's people, not simply Lord of the individual soul" (ibid., 44).

[122] Michael D. Williams, "Regeneration in Cosmic Context," *Evangelical Journal* 7 (1989): 68.

[123] Hoekema thus asserts, "The renewal of the image of God, therefore, involves a broad comprehensive vision of the Christian view of man. The process of sanctification affects every aspect of life: man's relationship to God, to others, and to the entire creation. The restoration of the image does not concern only religious piety in the narrow sense, or witnessing to people about Christ, or 'soul saving' activities; in its fullest sense it involves the redirection of all of life" (Hoekema, *Created in God's Image,* 88).

[124] Gaffin, for instance, answers objections to his cosmic understanding of salvation in the following way: "To this we reply with Abraham Kuyper that we will not yield one square inch of the crown rights of our King Jesus over the whole creation, and we will insist that the gospel offers the present reality of eschatological life in Christ, and present renewal and transformation of the believer in his entirety, according to the inner man, with the redirection and reintegration of human life in all its aspects. And we will have much more to say as to the cosmic scope of redemption and the awesome breadth of the gospel of the Kingdom. But, at the same time we must also insist with Paul in Romans 8 (vv. 18ff.) on this cosmic truth: that the whole creation groans, that there is not one square inch of creation which is not now groaning in anxious longing for the revelation of the sons of God. And in the meantime, until that revelation at Jesus' coming, these adopted sons, under the power of the Spirit (vs. 23), also groan, not in isolation from creation or by withdrawing from everyday life and responsibilities, but they groan *with* creation; they groan out of their deep, concentrated solidarity with the rest of creation. They groan by entering fully and with hope for the entire creation (vv. 20, 24f.)" (Richard B. Gaffin, Jr., "The Usefulness of the Cross," *WTJ* 41 [1979]: 245-246).

[125] Williams, "Regeneration in Cosmic Context," 73.

[126] Gaffin, "'Life-Giving Spirit'," 577. For Gaffin, this means the "eschatological body is the believer's hope of total (psycho-) physical transformation, and in that sense our bodies too, enlivened and renovated by the Spirit."

[127] "Man, then, exists in a state of psychosomatic unity. So we were created, so we are now, and so we shall be after the resurrection of the body. For full redemption must include the redemption of the body (Rom. 8:23; 1 Cor. 15:12-57), since man is not complete without the body. The glorious future of human beings in Christ includes both the resurrection of the body and a purified, perfected new earth" (Hoekema, *Created in God's Image*, 218).

[128] Michael Williams, "Of Heaven and History: The Verticalist Eschatology of Geerhardus Vos," *Pro Rege* 20 (1992): 18.

[129] George Marsden, for instance, argues that "the widest influence of Kuyperianism spread in a mild form through the neoevangelical movement after World War II" (George Marsden, "Introduction: Reformed and American," in *Reformed Theology in America: A History of Its Modern Development*, ed. David F. Wells [Grand Rapids, Mich.: Baker, 1997], 10). Brian Walsh likewise writes, "When Carl Henry spoke of the need to challenge the controlling presuppositions of the secular mind and clearly to articulate a Christian 'world and life view' in his 1947 work, *The Uneasy Conscience of Modern Fundamentalism,* he was directly indebted to the tradition of Kuyper" (Brian J. Walsh, "Worldviews, Modernity, and the Task of Christian College Education," *Faculty Dialogue: Journal of the Institute for Christian Leadership* 18 [1992]: 14). This is not to say that Henry was a full-fledged Kuyperian in his understanding of the extent of the cultural mandate and human salvation. In fact, Henry rejected much of what the Dutch Reformed tradition had to offer in terms of a political theology, especially as American Kuyperianism took a decidedly left turn. See, for instance, Henry's response to Reformed critics of his model of evangelical engagement such as Lewis Smedes and *Reformed Journal* (Henry, *Faith at the Frontiers,* 104-118). Henry offers a qualified theological endorsement of many of the theoretical arguments of his Christian Reformed interlocutors, while dismissing their propensity for democratic socialism and a confessional state.

[130] D. G. Hart, "Christianity, Modern Liberalism, and J. Gresham Machen," *Modern Age* 39 (1997): 234-245.

[131] D. G. Hart, "What Can Presbyterians Learn from Lutherans?" *Logia* 8 (1999): 3-8. Hart also applies his critique of a Kingdom worldview perspective to Christian higher education, particularly as related to the arguments of neo-evangelicals such as Henry and Ockenga and Kuyperian historians such as Mark Noll and George Marsden. "Here the Lutheran notion of the paradoxical relation between the affairs of man and the ways of God may prove to offer a better approach for evangelical scholars than the Reformed notion of taking every thought captive for Christ" (D. G. Hart, "Christian Scholars, Secular Universities, and the Problem with the Antithesis," *CSR* 30 [2001]: 385).

[132] At the onset of the evangelical movement, even Henry's colleague E. J. Carnell feared that dispensationalism's soteriology could only destabilize evangelicalism because it "honors the distinctives of Judaism" rather than those of the historic Christian gospel (Edward John Carnell, *The Case for Orthodox Theology* [Philadelphia: Westminster, 1959], 118). Similarly, see the heated soteriological polemic in, for instance, John Gerstner, *Wrongly Dividing the Word of Truth: A Critique of Dispensationalism,* 2nd ed., ed. Don Kistler (Moran, Pa.: Soli Deo Gloria, 2000), 115-304; and Zane Hodges, "Calvinism Ex Cathedra: A Review of John H. Gerstner's *Wrongly Dividing the Word of Truth: A Critique of Dispensationalism,*" *Journal of the Grace Evangelical Society* 4 (1991): 69-70.

[133] As Vern Poythress writes of the new consensus, "Covenant theologians within this framework still believe in the unity of a single covenant of grace. But what does this unity amount to? The single 'covenant of grace' is the proclamation, in various forms, of the single way of salvation. Dispensationalists do not really disagree with this unity!" (Poythress, *Understanding Dispensationalists,* 40).

134 In this Craig Blaising speaks for progressive dispensationalists and modified covenantalists when he describes salvation in the following Kingdom terms: "In the history of salvation, law reveals sin, instructs believers, orders Israel nationally in relationship to God, and prior to the appearing of Christ, points to Christ's coming. Gospel refers to the promise of blessing in Christ for individual Jews and Gentiles and for Jews and Gentiles nationally, points to the constancy of grace through faith in God's promise of redemption through the history of salvation while also testifying to the progression in the bestowal of grace, looking ultimately to the shalom of the eschaton where grace renders the redeemed informed by God's law to the complete exclusion of sin" (Blaising, "Law, Gospel, and the Unity of Scripture in Progressive Dispensationalism," 4).

135 Perrin, *Kingdom of God in the Teaching of Jesus,* 47.

136 This is an emphasis that continues among more traditionalist dispensationalists. Charles Ryrie, for example, writes, "To the normative dispensationalist, the soteriological, or saving, program of God is not the only program but one of the means God is using in the total program of glorifying Himself. Scripture is not man-centered as though salvation were the main theme, but it is God-centered because His glory is at the center" (Ryrie, *Dispensationalism,* 40).

137 As has been conceded by, among others, Saucy, *Case for Progressive Dispensationalism,* 20-21.

138 The glory of God in Christ as the central theme of Pauline theology is ably defended by Thomas R. Schreiner in his *Paul, Apostle of God's Glory in Christ: A Pauline Theology* (Downers Grove, Ill.: InterVarsity Press, 2001), 16-19. This Christocentric and Kingdom-oriented definition of God's self-glorification is not entirely alien even to the theocentric and doxological theology of American Puritan Jonathan Edwards, whose theology of the centrality of God's glory has been highly influential on contemporary evangelicals such as Daniel Fuller and John Piper. Edwards, for instance, defines the doxological purpose of history thusly: "The end of God's creating the world, was to prepare a kingdom for His Son (for He is appointed heir of the world), which should remain to all eternity" (Jonathan Edwards, "A History of the Work of Redemption [1773]," in *The Works of Jonathan Edwards,* ed. Edward Hickman, 2 vols. [London: William Ball, 1834; reprint Edinburgh: Banner of Truth, 1974], 1:584).

139 David J. MacLeod rightly identifies this theme in the Pauline epistle to the Philippians as in continuity with "the OT pattern of messianic kingship." As MacLeod argues, "Paul did not think of the exalted Christ as displacing or rivaling God the Father. As the apostle's hymn makes clear, the authority of the exalted Jesus is 'a derived authority—God [the Father] exalted Him. . . . God conferred on Him the superlative [name]; God purposed that created beings worship and obey Him. Hence, only God the Father has ultimate authority and sovereignty . . . (cf. 1 Cor 15:28; Rev 3:21; John 13:31).' So when the universe confesses that 'Jesus Christ is Lord,' God the Father will be pleased for His purposes will be fulfilled and His plans realized. The lordship of Christ glorifies the Father for in His earthly ministry Christ accomplished the Father's will and work (Rom 15:7-9; 2 Cor 1:20)" (David J. MacLeod, "The Exaltation of Christ: An Exposition of Philippians 2:9-11," *BibSac* 158 [2001]: 449).

140 This is in agreement with James D. G. Dunn's contention that in Romans 8:29, "The Adam Christology is clear: Christ is the image of God which Adam was intended to be, the Son as the pattern of God's finished product." Furthermore, Dunn also rightly argues that the end result of salvation envisioned here by Paul is "not simply a return to pristine purity, but the fuller glory which Adam never attained, including life *from* death" (James D. G. Dunn, *Romans 1–8,* Word Biblical Commentary, vol. 38a [Dallas: Word, 1988], 483-484).

141 Charles Hodge, *A Commentary on Romans* (Philadelphia: William S. & Alfred Martien, 1864; reprint, Edinburgh: Banner of Truth, 1986), 285-286.

[142] Supralapsarianism finds its most enthusiastic contemporary evangelical proponent in Reformed theologian Robert Reymond, who argues that no doctrine "signalizes the *soli Deo gloria* more and no doctrine humbles proud people more than the supralapsarian vision of predestination" (Robert L. Reymond, *A New Systematic Theology of the Christian Faith* [Nashville: Thomas Nelson, 1998], 501). Reymond continues a supralapsarian Calvinist tradition carried in the beginnings of the postwar evangelical movement by Gordon H. Clark. See Clark's defense of this view in Gordon H. Clark, "Reply to Roger Nicole," in *The Philosophy of Gordon H. Clark: A Festschrift,* ed. Ronald H. Nash (Philadelphia: Presbyterian & Reformed, 1968), 468-484. As one Reformed critic rightly notes, Reymond's "restricted view of creation flows from Reymond's commitment to supralapsarianism (chapter 13), for if God's first thought was his choice of elect and non-elect before he considered creating anything, it follows that creation is ancillary and subservient to his predestinating purpose." This is perhaps why, as Letham later laments, Reymond "focuses almost entirely on the cross" in his section on the work of Christ with "only one short paragraph each on Christ's intercession, kingship, or his prophetic role in declaring the will of the Father" (Robert Letham, review of *A New Systematic Theology of the Christian Faith* by Robert L. Reymond, *WTJ* 62 [2000]: 316).

[143] Erich Sauer, *King of the Earth: The Nobility of Man According to the Bible and Science* (Grand Rapids, Mich.: Eerdmans, 1962).

[144] John Sailhamer rightly identifies Genesis 49 as an explicit reference both to the coming Davidic covenant and to the eschatological and cosmic reign of Jesus. This is because, Sailhamer points out, the "most startling aspect" of this narrative is that "the obedience of the nations" belongs to the tribe of Judah. "The use of the plural word *nations* rather than the singular suggests that Jacob had in view a kingship that extended beyond the boundaries of the Israelites to include other nations as well" (John H. Sailhamer, *The Pentateuch as Narrative: A Biblical-Theological Commentary* [Grand Rapids, Mich.: Zondervan, 1992], 235).

[145] Ladd, *Theology of the New Testament,* 143.

[146] For an evaluation of the contemporary "spiritual warfare" movements, see Charles E. Lawless, Jr., "The Relationship Between Evangelism and Spiritual Warfare in the North American Spiritual Warfare Movement, 1986–1997" (Ph.D. diss., The Southern Baptist Theological Seminary, 1997).

[147] Norman Perrin, for example, cites Johannes Weiss's criticism of Albrecht Ritschl for ignoring the apocalyptic antithesis between the Kingdom of God and the kingdom of Satan in the biblical materials, such as Matthew 12:25-29, a reluctance that Perrin ties directly with liberal Protestantism's insistence that the Kingdom is built by human progress rather than by the cataclysmic action of God (Perrin, *Kingdom of God in the Teaching of Jesus,* 17). Perrin's critique certainly rings true in an analysis of Walter Rauschenbusch's dismissal of the idea of a satanic "kingdom of evil" as an unworkable construct for modern persons since belief in demonic activity is "confined to narrow circles, mostly of premillennialists" (Walter Rauschenbusch, *A Theology for the Social Gospel* [New York: Macmillan, 1917; reprint, Louisville: Westminster/John Knox, 1997], 87).

[148] Boyd fails to ground adequately his charge that a "meticulous blueprint worldview," which holds to the exhaustive sovereignty of God in providence and salvation, is fundamentally incompatible with a "warfare worldview" which sees the history of redemption in terms of a conflict between the Triune God and the satanic powers. Boyd is correct that his view of dark forces that are able to thwart the decretive will of God is indeed incompatible with the classical theist view of sovereignty most often held within evangelical theology. For a convincing critique of Boyd's faulty theological method and

presuppositions, see D. A. Carson, "God, the Bible and Spiritual Warfare: A Review Article," *JETS* 42 (1999): 251-270.

[149] So Donald Bloesch included this "warfare" interpretation of Kingdom theology as a distinctive element of neo-evangelical theology: "While Barth and Bonhoeffer spoke as if the whole world were now the kingdom of Christ, the evangelicals see the two kingdoms at war with one another—the kingdom of God and the kingdom of Satan. The devil and his hosts have been overthrown by the cross of Christ, but they are not reconciled servants of Christ (as Cullmann, for example, maintains) but rather rebels against the rule of Christ. God accomplishes His will in a secret way through the devil and in spite of the devil, but this is not to suppose that the devil is now an agent of the kingdom of God" (Donald G. Bloesch, *The Evangelical Renaissance* [Grand Rapids, Mich.: Eerdmans, 1973], 39).

[150] Boyd is hardly the only contemporary evangelical scholar to emphasize the divine warrior theme. See Tremper Longman III and Daniel G. Reid, *God Is a Warrior* (Grand Rapids, Mich.: Zondervan, 1995).

[151] John Eldredge, *Wild at Heart: Discovering the Secret of a Man's Soul* (Nashville: Thomas Nelson, 2001).

[152] Leon Podles, *The Church Impotent: The Feminization of Christianity* (Dallas: Spence, 1999), 201-209.

[153] For a contemporary evangelical defense of effectual calling, see Bruce A. Ware, "Effectual Calling and Grace," in *Still Sovereign: Contemporary Perspectives on Election, Foreknowledge and Grace,* ed. Thomas R. Schreiner and Bruce A. Ware (Grand Rapids, Mich.: Baker, 2000); and Tom J. Nettles, *By His Grace and For His Glory: A Historical, Theological, and Practical Study of the Doctrines of Grace in Baptist Life* (Grand Rapids, Mich.: Baker, 1986), 285-296.

[154] Stanley J. Grenz, "'Fideistic Revelationalism': Donald Bloesch's Antirationalist Theological Method," in *Evangelical Theology in Transition: Theologians in Dialogue with Donald Bloesch,* ed. Elmer M. Colyer (Downers Grove, Ill.: InterVarsity Press, 1999), 56.

[155] For an excellent discussion of this issue, see H. Wayne House, "Creation and Redemption: A Study of Kingdom Interplay," *JETS* 35 (1992): 3-17.

[156] Francis A. Schaeffer, *The God Who Is There* (London: Hodder & Stoughton, 1968; reprint, Downers Grove, Ill.: InterVarsity Press, 1998), 201.

[157] So Henry writes, "The writer of Genesis emphasizes [Adam's] superiority to the animal world in this regard. To unfallen Adam the Creator gave the privilege of naming the lower creatures in Eden. This task involved the ability to discriminate their essential nature, and clearly implied the ability to discriminate his own nature from theirs. Among them he could not find a help meet. When Eve was brought to him, he saw their relatedness in character. The total impression of the creation narrative is that Adam, while not gifted with omniscience and universal knowledge nor with a direct insight into obscure mysteries, clearly *was* gifted with the rational and moral qualities necessary for ethical judgment and behavior in conformity with eternal principles of right and wrong" (Henry, *Christian Personal Ethics,* 152).

[158] Henry, *God, Revelation, and Authority,* 2:142.

[159] For an examination of the downgrade of rationality in the contemporary zeitgeist, see Douglas Groothuis, *Truth Decay: Defending Christianity Against the Challenges of Postmodernism* (Downers Grove, Ill.: InterVarsity Press, 2000), a book that Groothuis appropriately dedicates to Henry and Schaeffer, postwar evangelical theology's foremost defenders of what Schaeffer called "true truth."

[160] See Mark Seifrid's incisive critique of Bultmann on this point in Mark A. Seifrid, "The 'New Perspective on Paul' and Its Problems," *Themelios* 25 (2000): 7.

[161] For an examination of the therapeutic soteriology so prevalent at the grassroots of evangelical thought and practice, see David F. Wells, *No Place for Truth, or, Whatever Happened to Evangelical Theology?* (Grand Rapids, Mich.: Eerdmans, 1993), 137-186.

[162] David F. Wells, *God in the Wasteland: The Reality of Truth in a World of Fading Dreams* (Grand Rapids, Mich.: Eerdmans, 1994), 176.

[163] See, for instance, Carl Henry's charge that Protestant liberalism failed, at least in part, because it failed to relate justification and sanctification with the new creation of the believer in Christ (Carl F. H. Henry, *The Protestant Dilemma: An Analysis of the Current Impasse in Theology* [Grand Rapids, Mich.: Eerdmans, 1949], 158).

[164] Ladd, *Presence of the Future,* 321.

[165] As G. B. Caird points out, "To see the Kingdom of God, to enter it, to be born of the Spirit, and to have eternal life are interchangeable descriptions of the one experience of salvation which is to become available to enquirers like Nicodemus only when Jesus has been 'lifted up' (3:15 [*sic*]). Jesus is indeed already King of Israel (1:50 [*sic*]; 12:13, 15; cf. 20:31), but not in the only sense his enemies could understand" (G. B. Caird, *New Testament Theology,* ed. L. D. Hurst [New York: Oxford University Press, 1994], 131).

[166] Henry, *God, Revelation, and Authority,* 2:67. Henry here cites the underpinnings of the cosmic and personal nature of redemption from Isaiah 9:1-6; 11:1-9; and chapters 40–55.

[167] At least, that is, of personal sins, defined as transgressions against the law of God. The Social Gospel, and its successors in the liberation theology movements, emphasized sin, but usually did so in the corporate and structural sense of the term.

[168] Andrew T. Lincoln, *Paradise Now and Not Yet: Studies in the Role of the Heavenly Dimension in Paul's Thought with Special Reference to His Eschatology* (Cambridge: Cambridge University Press, 1981), 192.

[169] "Having 'the first place in everything' corresponds to being 'the highest of all the kings of the earth' in Psalm 89:27," Blaising and Bock rightly observe, referencing Colossians 1:18. "Revelation 1:5 is even more explicit in applying Psalm 89:27 to Jesus' present position by describing Him as 'the firstborn of the dead, and the ruler of the kings of the earth'" (Blaising and Bock, *Progressive Dispensationalism,* 179).

[170] As noted above, this authority to rule over the earth is presented in Scripture as belonging to those resurrected from the dead, not to disembodied spirits in heaven awaiting resurrection. It would appear, therefore, that the reign referred to in Revelation 20:4-6 speaks in consonance with the rest of the biblical witness to a bodily resurrection of believers in Christ, contra the historic arguments of amillennialism.

[171] Thomas Schreiner and Ardel Caneday are right, therefore, to argue that those who "attempt to distinguish the kingdom of God from eternal life, so that the former refers only to blessings in the present life, are seriously mistaken. The same criticism applies to those who try to keep salvation distinct from the kingdom of God" (Thomas R. Schreiner and Ardel B. Caneday, *The Race Set before Us: A Biblical Theology of Perseverance and Assurance* [Downers Grove, Ill.: InterVarsity Press, 2001], 81). Here Schreiner and Caneday ably apply a Kingdom-focused understanding of salvation, informed by inaugurated eschatology, to the evangelical debates over "lordship salvation."

[172] For a sketch of the inclusivist view of soteriology in relation to the Kingdom of God, see Clark H. Pinnock, "Toward a More Inclusive Eschatology," in *Looking into the Future: Evangelical Essays in Eschatology,* ed. David W. Baker (Grand Rapids, Mich.: Baker, 2001), 249-262. For a helpful critique of "evangelical" inclusivism, see Ronald H. Nash, *Is Jesus the Only Savior?* (Grand Rapids, Mich.: Zondervan, 1994).

[173] Erickson, *Christian Theology,* 197. For a more developed outworking of Erickson's viewpoint here, see Millard J. Erickson, *How Shall They Be Saved? The Destiny of Those Who Do Not Hear of Jesus* (Grand Rapids, Mich.: Baker, 1996).

[174] Erickson, *Christian Theology,* 197.

[175] Clark H. Pinnock, *Flame of Love: A Theology of the Holy Spirit* (Downers Grove, Ill.: InterVarsity Press, 1996), 194.

[176] Ibid.

[177] Ibid., 196.

[178] Ibid.

[179] Amos Yong, "Discerning the Spirit(s) in the World of Religions," in *No Other Gods Before Me? Evangelicals and the Challenge of World Religions,* ed. John G. Stackhouse, Jr. (Grand Rapids, Mich.: Baker, 2001), 38. The eclipse of Christology in the soteriological proposals of Pinnock and Yong is continued in Grenz, who suggests that "the finality of Christ" means "Jesus is the vehicle through whom we come to the fullest understanding of what God is like" so that through "the Spirit who was poured out into the world at the exaltation of Jesus, therefore, we enter into a fuller community with God than is enjoyed in any other religious tradition" (Stanley J. Grenz, "Toward an Evangelical Theology of the Religions," *Journal of Ecumenical Studies* 31 [1994]: 64).

[180] See especially Pinnock, "Toward a More Inclusive Eschatology," 254-261.

[181] Boyd, *God at War,* 238-268. Pinnock combines a "Christus Victor" model with a reconstruction of Irenaeus' "recapitulation" theory of the atonement (Pinnock, *Flame of Love,* 102-111). These challenges to the penal substitutionary model of the atonement are derivative of Gustaf Aulén, *Christus Victor: An Historical Study of the Three Main Types of the Idea of the Atonement,* trans. A. G. Hebert (New York: Macmillan, 1969).

[182] Boyd, *God at War,* 267-268.

[183] Joel B. Green and Mark D. Baker, *Recovering the Scandal of the Cross: Atonement in New Testament and Contemporary Contexts* (Downers Grove, Ill.: InterVarsity Press, 2000), 149.

[184] For a defense of the essentially penal and substitutionary nature of the atonement, see Leon Morris, *The Apostolic Preaching of the Cross,* 3rd ed. (Grand Rapids, Mich.: Eerdmans, 1965); Demarest, *The Cross and Salvation,* 166-199; and Reymond, *A New Systematic Theology for the Christian Faith,* 631-642.

[185] As one Reformed theologian rightly contends, "By sin, the serpent makes all the woman's seed into children of the devil; but by the grace of redemptive judgment, God determines to make a division among the woman's fallen seed, promising to convert a remnant into children of God" (R. Fowler White, "Agony, Irony, and Victory in Inaugurated Eschatology: Reflections on the Current Amillennial-Postmillennial Debate," *WTJ* 62 [2000]: 170).

[186] See also the "holistic" definition of the "deeds of the flesh" in Galatians 5:19-21, a definition that includes "internal" acts such as "jealousy" and "envying" as well as "bodily" acts such as "drunkenness" and "carousing."

[187] Green and Baker, *Recovering the Scandal of the Cross,* 150.

[188] These are the proposals for a "theological megashift" in evangelical theology as articulated by many on the reformist wing of evangelical theology. See, for instance, Clark H. Pinnock and Robert C. Brow, *Unbounded Love: A Good News Theology for the Twenty-first Century* (Downers Grove, Ill.: InterVarsity Press, 1994); and Robert C. Brow, "The Evangelical Megashift," *Christianity Today,* February 19, 1990, 12-14. For a critique of these proposals, see R. Albert Mohler, Jr., "'Evangelical': What's in a Name?" in *The Coming Evangelical Crisis: Current Challenges to the Authority of Scripture and the Gospel* (Chicago: Moody, 1996), 33-36. Other challenges to forensic justification and other aspects of Reformation soteriology increasingly come from within the evangelical coalition's Pentecostal tradition. In 2000, for instance, the pres-

ident of the Society for Pentecostal Studies argued, "When I first read the Catholic response to the Reformation in the Councils and Decrees of Trent, my heart was 'strangely moved.' I found there much that had been missing from the shallow well of the forensic model. Here was an attempt to view justification as something that God not only declares but does. God makes us right with the divine life by a justice that redeems and heals. The Italian Pentecostal church of my youth which leveled so many anathemas against the Catholic Church would have been surprised to discover that in some ways their understanding of the New Testament texts that speak of justification was actually closer to Trent than to certain Reformers" (Frank D. Macchia, "Justification and the Spirit: A Pentecostal Reflection on the Doctrine by Which the Church Stands or Falls," *Pneuma* 22 [2000]: 5). See also Frank D. Macchia, "Justification Through New Creation: The Holy Spirit and the Doctrine by Which the Church Stands or Falls," *Theology Today* 58 (2000): 202-217.

[189] This is a point that Jesus further makes when He speaks of the justification of guilty tax collectors and prostitutes in terms of their entrance into the Kingdom of God (Matt. 21:31-32). Thus, Peter Stuhlmacher is at least partially correct in his assessment that justification is an eschatological matter for Paul: "The Pauline doctrine of justification is the doctrine about the implementation of God's righteousness through Christ for the entire creation. Its goal is the establishment of the kingdom of God" (cited in Ted Dorman, "The Joint Declaration on the Doctrine of Justification: Retrospect and Prospects," *JETS* 44 [2001]: 434).

[190] This is magnified in the way in which J. Gresham Machen addressed the atonement question during the controversy itself against liberal Protestant interlocutors. He did not see disagreement over the substitutionary nature of the work of Christ as an intramural debate among Christians. Instead, he proposed that an alternative to penal substitutionary atonement was itself a different religion from Christianity: "According to Christian belief, Jesus is our Savior, not by virtue of what He said, or even by virtue of what He was, but by what He did. He is our Savior, not because He inspired us to live the kind of life He lived, but because He took upon Himself the dreadful guilt of our sins and bore it instead of us on the cross. Such is the Christian conception of the cross of Christ. It is ridiculed as being a 'subtle theory of the atonement.' In reality, it is the plain teaching of the word of God; we know absolutely nothing about an atonement that is not a vicarious atonement, for that is the only atonement of which the New Testament speaks" (J. Gresham Machen, *Christianity and Liberalism* [New York: Macmillan, 1923; reprint, Grand Rapids, Mich.: Eerdmans, 2001], 117).

[191] This is in agreement with Mark Seifrid's cosmic and Kingdom-oriented view of justification, in which "the event which took place in Christ is final and incapable of revision, a prolepsis of the day of judgment. This forensic setting means that Paul's thought excludes any idea of an infused, imparted or inherent righteousness, which treats the human being as one in need of healing or repair. Justification is a matter of death and life, wrath and vindication" (Mark A. Seifrid, *Christ, Our Righteousness: Paul's Theology of Justification* [Downers Grove, Ill.: InterVarsity Press, 2000], 184).

[192] This represents the argument of John Sanders, *The God Who Risks: A Theology of Providence* (Downers Grove, Ill.: InterVarsity Press, 1998), 98-106.

[193] It should be noted that this, not "the future of ethnic Israel," is at the heart of the debate. The issue at dispute is not, however, whether a restored ethnic Israel will participate in the salvific blessings of Christ. Even an unreconstructed covenant theologian such as Charles Hodge could affirm a future conversion of ethnic Israel on the basis of New Testament passages such as Romans 11 (Charles Hodge, *Systematic Theology*, 3 vols. [New York: Scribner, 1873; reprint, Grand Rapids, Mich.: Eerdmans, 1995], 3:805-812). The question instead is whether, as Robert Saucy notes, Israel will bless the world by fulfilling "this mission as a distinct national entity among the nations of the

world in accordance with the prophetic picture" (Saucy, *Case for Progressive Dispensationalism,* 306).

[194] Thus, one Reformed theologian argues, "The future messianic kingdom will embrace equally the whole of the newly created cosmos, and will not experience a special manifestation of any sort in the region of the 'promised land.'" O. Palmer Robertson, *The Israel of God: Yesterday, Today and Tomorrow* (Phillipsburg, N.J.: Presbyterian & Reformed, 2000), 95. Vern Poythress meanwhile claims that the growing soteriological and eschatological consensus between covenantalist and dispensationalist evangelicals has rendered the dispute largely moot since the newer covenantalists join with dispensationalists in seeing the goal of salvation as an earthly, this-worldly Kingdom in which redeemed Israel (and the redeemed of all ages) will rule with Christ (Poythress, *Understanding Dispensationalists,* 40-51). In this, Poythress is in agreement with Anthony Hoekema (Anthony Hoekema, *The Bible and the Future* [Grand Rapids, Mich.: Eerdmans, 1979], 274-287).

[195] Blaising and Bock, *Progressive Dispensationalism,* 181.

[196] Henry, *God, Revelation, and Authority,* 3:120.

[197] Poythress, *Understanding Dispensationalists,* 42-43.

[198] Compare the progressive dispensational view with, for example, Ladd's treatment of the Hebrews 8:8-13 "reinterpretation" of the new covenant prophecy of Jeremiah 31:31-34 (George Eldon Ladd, "Historic Premillennialism," in *The Meaning of the Millennium: Four Views,* ed. Robert G. Clouse [Downers Grove, Ill.: InterVarsity Press, 1977], 25).

[199] This is true, at least, in terms of those who hold to a "complementarian" view of differing male/female roles. For a defense of this view from a Reformed theologian, see Vern S. Poythress, "The Church as Family: Why Male Leadership in the Family Requires Male Leadership in the Church," in *Recovering Biblical Manhood and Womanhood: A Response to Evangelical Feminism,* ed. John Piper and Wayne Grudem (Wheaton, Ill.: Crossway, 1991), 233-247.

[200] Craig Blaising, for instance, argues, "In Christ, the blessings of the cross, the resurrection, and the gift of the Holy Spirit are given without distinction. But soteriological equality does not lead to androgyny" (Craig A. Blaising, "The Future of Israel as a Theological Question," *JETS* 44 [2001]: 448).

[201] For a compelling refutation of evangelical feminist appropriations of Galatians 3:28, see Peter R. Schemm, Jr., "Galatians 3:28: Prooftext or Context?" *Journal for Biblical Manhood and Womanhood* 8 (2003): 23-30.

[202] Oskar Skarsaune, *In the Shadow of the Temple: Jewish Influences on Early Christianity* (Downers Grove, Ill.: InterVarsity Press, 2002), 271.

[203] R. C. Sproul, Jr., "Coram Deo," *Tabletalk,* December 1998, 2.

[204] One dispensationalist New Testament scholar makes an important point here on the question of the shared blessings of Jews and Gentiles in the "engrafting onto the Olive Tree" teaching of Romans 11: "The question that is immediately raised is, 'A sharer with whom?' The most natural and consistent Pauline answer is that believing Gentiles become fellow sharers with believing Jews in the fatness of the tree, that is, in the blessings of the Abrahamic covenant. There is no hint of Gentiles replacing Israel en toto or the church replacing Israel. The facts are that believing Gentiles fill up the place left by unbelieving Jews, while the remnant of Jews within the church share with Gentiles what always belonged to Jews" (Carl B. Hoch, *All Things New: The Significance of Newness for Biblical Theology* [Grand Rapids, Mich.: Baker, 1995], 316). Hoch's analysis here demonstrates that the impasse between dispensationalists and covenantalists, even on this point, should not be impossible to overcome.

[205] In this Barnhouse is, to say the least, a unique figure in evangelical history. His broad

THE KINGDOM OF CHRIST

evangelical credentials came with his editorship of the highly influential *Eternity* magazine. He was a dispensational premillennialist, widely esteemed for his prophetic writings and Bible conference speaking schedule. He was also a confessional Calvinist, pastor of Philadelphia's historic Tenth Presbyterian Church.

206 Donald Grey Barnhouse, "Social Problems," *Eternity,* January 1955, 9.

207 Clowney, "Politics of the Kingdom," 292.

208 Ibid.

209 See, for instance, the analysis on the differing conceptions of "the gospel" even between a neo-conservative Roman Catholic convert and the Marxist liberation theologians (Richard John Neuhaus, "Liberation Theology and the Cultural Captivity of the Gospel," in *Liberation Theology,* ed. Ronald H. Nash [Grand Rapids, Mich.: Baker, 1988], 215-236).

210 Carl F. H. Henry, *Gods of This Age or God of the Ages?* (Nashville: Broadman & Holman, 1994), 241.

211 Reformed theologian Michael Williams rightly identifies this essentially soteriological definition of the Kingdom: "The kingdom of God is the comprehensive term for all that messianic salvation includes. This salvation, however, must not be restricted to the soul of man, but must be understood as cosmic in scope. The goal of redemption is nothing less than the restoration of the entire cosmos. Because man's fall affected not only himself but the rest of creation, redemption must involve God's entire creation. The kingdom of God, therefore, implies cosmic redemption" (Michael Williams, "A Restorational Alternative to Augustinian Verticalist Eschatology," *Pro Rege* 20 [1992]: 16).

212 See, for instance, Carl Henry's treatment of the cultural mandate, creational restoration, and work in his *Aspects of Christian Social Ethics* (Grand Rapids, Mich.: Eerdmans, 1964), 31-71. It is interesting to note that Henry credits his view of human vicegerency and the cultural mandate not only to the Kuyperian tradition, but also to a dispensationalist European theologian Erich Sauer (ibid., 47).

213 For a helpful starting point on a Christian theological perspective on the role of the welfare state in alleviating poverty, see Marvin Olasky, *The Tragedy of American Compassion* (Washington, D.C.: Regnery; Wheaton, Ill.: Crossway, 1992).

214 So argues Kuyperian theologian Albert Wolters: "Even the great crisis that will come on the world at Christ's return will not annihilate God's creation or our cultural development of it. The new heaven and the new earth the Lord has promised will be a continuation, purified by fire, of the creation we now know. There is no reason to believe that the cultural dimensions of earthly reality (except insofar as they are involved in sin) will be absent from the new, glorified earth that is promised. In fact, the biblical indications point in the opposite direction. Describing the new earth as the New Jerusalem, John writes that 'the kings of the earth will bring their splendor into it. . . . The glory and honor of the nations will be brought into it' (Rev. 21:24, 26). This very likely refers to the cultural treasures of mankind that will be purified by passing through the fires of judgment, like gold in a crucible" (Wolters, *Creation Regained,* 40). Picking up on the Kuyperian theme, evangelical philosopher/theologian Douglas Groothuis likewise posits that Isaiah 60 and Revelation 21 teach against the view that the Triune God will "obliterate every aspect of human culture or only use it as the furniture of hell"; he holds to the eternal conscious damnation of the wicked, "but some of the works of their hands may endure as blessings—although to the praise of God" (Groothuis, *Truth Decay,* 253).

215 Richard Mouw correctly notes that the view of cultural aspects of common grace surviving into the eschaton is "something that is enshrouded in mystery," and that it "posits multiple divine purposes in the world." In pointing to his agreement with Abraham Kuyper and Herman Bavinck on the "eschatological ingathering of the fruits of humankind's cultural labors," Mouw is on solid theological footing when he argues,

"Alongside God's clear concern about the eternal destiny of individuals are his designs for the larger creation" (Richard J. Mouw, *He Shines in All That's Fair: Culture and Common Grace* [Grand Rapids, Mich.: Eerdmans, 2001], 50).

[216] Hence this answers the objections of social critic Wendell Berry, who points out, "People who quote John 3:16 as an easy formula for getting to Heaven neglect to see the great difficulty implied in the statement that the advent of Christ was made possible by God's love for the world—not the world as it might be but for the world as it was and is" (Wendell Berry, *Sex, Economy, Freedom and Community* [New York: Pantheon, 1992], 97).

[217] For Kirk's defense of this view, see Russell Kirk, *The Politics of Prudence* (Wilmington, Del.: Intercollegiate Studies Institute, 1993), 15-29.

[218] As argued in the next chapter, however, politics is still necessary in order to preserve the God-ordained order in which cultural forces are both sustained and restrained.

[219] As Michael Williams notes, this is an advance over the almost singularly "spiritual" soteriology of Geerhardus Vos. It can therefore fuel a Reformed commitment to social and political action: "While Christian activism is not inherently wrong for Vos, it always runs the risk of losing sight of the heavenly object of the Christian religion. Thus he dismisses Christian social action as bordering on a humanistic terrestrialization of the faith. The kingdom of God's present theater of operation lies in the invisible, the spiritual, and the thoroughly ethico-religious. There is no room nor fitting place for the Genesis mandate to function as God's stewards and representatives within the creation" (Williams, "Of Heaven and History," 17-18). Williams here cites Vos's comments on Christian sociopolitical engagement from Geerhardus Vos, *The Pauline Eschatology* (Grand Rapids, Mich.: Eerdmans, 1952), 359, 364-365.

[220] For O'Donovan, the resurrection of Jesus is the "sign that God has stood by his created order," implying that "this order with mankind in its proper place within it, is to be totally restored at the last." As O'Donovan applies this to Christian ethics, he notes, "This invites a comment upon a debate which has occupied too much attention, the debate between the so-called 'ethics of the kingdom' and the 'ethics of creation'. This way of posing the alternatives is not acceptable, for the very act of God which ushers in his kingdom is the resurrection of Christ from the dead. A kingdom ethics which was set up in opposition to creation could not possibly be interested in the same eschatological kingdom as that which the New Testament proclaims" (Oliver O'Donovan, *Resurrection and Moral Order: An Outline for Evangelical Ethics*, 2nd ed. [Grand Rapids, Mich.: Eerdmans, 1994], 15).

[221] Francis A. Schaeffer, *A Christian Manifesto* (Westchester, Ill.: Crossway, 1982), 68-69.

[222] "Abortion Decision: A Death Blow?" *Christianity Today*, February 16, 1973, 48.

[223] Ibid.

[224] Kenneth Woodward, "Sex, Sin, and Salvation," *Newsweek*, November 2, 1998, 37.

[225] This would be true by informing a conservative evangelical response to arguments such as those of Southern Baptist ethicist Paul D. Simmons: "There can be no doubt about the personhood of the woman. Her rights to bodily integrity, conscientious belief, and family planning decisions should be unequivocally supported, though women have often been ignored in the debate. Notions of fetal personhood are, at best, problematic. Certainly where a conceptus (fertilized ovum) is concerned, it is metaphysical speculation to declare it a person" (Paul D. Simmons, "The Pastor as Prophet: How Naked the Public Square?" *RevExp* 86 [1989]: 528).

[226] See, for instance, the recent debate within the conservative-led Southern Baptist Convention regarding the SBC's revision of the article on "The Christian and the Social Order" in the denomination's statement of faith, the *Baptist Faith and Message*. While many moderates condemned adding issues such as abortion to the confession as "polit-

ical" matters, the conservative majority saw these issues as necessary for a theological definition of the common ground on which the churches were to cooperate. The SBC's left flank had had no such problems with understanding the theological nature of social problems such as racism earlier in the century. Instead, some Southern Baptist progressives boldly confronted the segregationist culture of the Jim Crow-era SBC precisely because they understood that the issues were theological, not simply social, in nature. See, for instance, Henlee H. Barnette, *Introducing Christian Ethics* (Nashville: Broadman, 1961), 128-143.

[227] See, for instance, Norma Ramos, "Pornography Is a Social Justice Issue," in *Feminism and Pornography: Oxford Readings in Feminism,* ed. Drucilla Cornell (New York: Oxford University Press, 2000), 45-47.

[228] Such conversations are ongoing. See, for example, the eschatologically- and soteriologically-informed arguments of the Interfaith Council for Environmental Stewardship's response to the environmentalist charge that the Judeo-Christian view of creation is "anthropocentric," in "A Biblical Perspective on Environmental Stewardship," in *Environmental Stewardship in the Judeo-Christian Tradition: Jewish, Catholic and Protestant Wisdom on the Environment,* ed. Michael B. Barkley (Grand Rapids, Mich.: Acton Institute for the Study of Religion and Liberty, 2000), 64-68.

[229] Contra many of the arguments of animal-rights ethicists and others such as, for example, Peter Singer, *Animal Liberation* (New York: Random House, 1975).

[230] Thus answering the complaint by evangelical Reformed theologian John Jefferson Davis that evangelical theology has had little to say to the question of environmental stewardship because of a failure to relate creation to cosmic redemption (John Jefferson Davis, "Ecological 'Blind Spots' in the Structure and Content of Recent Evangelical Systematic Theologies," *JETS* 43 [2000]: 273-286).

[231] This point is analyzed in Michael A. Bullmore, "The Four Most Important Biblical Passages for a Christian Environmentalism," *TrinJ* 19 (1998): 139-162. The insights of modified covenantal Kingdom theology are helpful here, in discussing the link between the Christocentric nature of regeneration and the cosmic regeneration, because of the covenantal commonality both have in the role of humanity in fall and redemption. Michael Williams correctly observes, "Why must God regenerate, give new life and direction to *ta panta* (all things)? Because all things have been drawn into the mutiny of the human race (Rom 8:19-24). Humanity plays the pivotal role here. Just as the fall of the first Adam was the ruin of the whole earthly realm, so the atoning death of the second Adam is the salvation of the whole world. Our present spiritual regeneration is inseparable from cosmic regeneration because our present restoration to life is the first stage in the eschatological restoration of all creation to its proper vitality and direction. We are *firstfruits*" (Michael Williams, "Regeneration in Cosmic Context," 73).

[232] Van Til, *Calvinistic Concept of Culture,* 39.

[233] So, as Brevard Childs notes, the Old Testament writers employ bodily organs such as heart, liver, or kidneys "in a metaphorical-like manner to describe realistically different aspects of total life as a human being" (Brevard S. Childs, *Old Testament Theology in a Canonical Context* [Philadelphia: Fortress, 1985], 199).

[234] Carl F. H. Henry, "Fortunes of the Christian Worldview," *TrinJ* 19 (1998): 164.

[235] See, for example, Ronald J. Sider, *One-Sided Christianity? Uniting the Church to Heal a Lost and Broken World* (Grand Rapids, Mich.: Zondervan, 1993).

[236] It must be remembered, after all, that even leaders of the Social Gospel maintained in writing the necessity of personal, individual regeneration, however ambiguously this might have been defined. Shailer Mathews, for instance, was quick to argue, "In the center of Christian teaching is the crucified Son of God, and as long as the memory of his death endures, Christianity will begin its ministry of salvation by convicting the world

of sin" (Shailer Mathews, *The Individual and the Social Gospel* [New York: Missionary Education Movement of the United States and Canada, 1914], 5).

237 Robert Saucy, "Dispensationalism and the Salvation of the Kingdom," *TSF Bulletin,* May-June 1984, 6.

238 For a critique of revivalism in American history, especially the legacy of Charles G. Finney, see Iain Murray, *Revival and Revivalism: The Making and Marring of American Evangelicalism, 1750–1858* (Edinburgh: Banner of Truth, 1994).

239 Schaeffer, *Christian Manifesto,* 65.

240 Martin, *Prophet with Honor,* 362.

241 Henry seemed to recognize this point as well, by recounting, "In Copenhagen, when evangelist Billy Graham opened his crusade, a heckler interrupted him with the cry: 'Why didn't you march in Selma?' But Graham had been integrating meetings in the South long before the marchers had become existentialized and, moreover, had done so in the context of biblical Christianity" (Henry, *God Who Shows Himself,* 67).

242 Thus, the Jerusalem Council can call for social reconciliation between Jewish and Gentile believers because both have experienced the Davidic blessings of the one Holy Spirit (Acts 15:8, 14-19). Likewise, the apostle Paul can appeal to Jews that "Gentiles are fellow heirs, members of the same body" because they are "partakers of the promise in Christ Jesus through the gospel" (Eph. 3:6, ESV).

243 Henry, *God Who Shows Himself,* 71.

244 This reflects the apostle Paul's admonition that Timothy offer up prayers for those in offices of political authority, precisely so that the church may have the tranquility in which to proclaim the purpose of God to save sinners through the gospel of Christ (1 Tim. 2:1-6).

245 Henry actually argues that a government commitment to justice unintentionally aids the church's evangelistic task by inculcating into the culture the importance of justice and righteousness, therefore preparing the way, as it were, for the conviction of sin through the proclamation of the gospel (Henry, *Aspects of Christian Social Ethics,* 94-95).

246 This thus necessitated the neo-orthodox critique of liberal Christian social and political ethics, chiefly in the person of Reinhold Niebuhr.

247 Henry, *Aspects of Christian Social Ethics,* 169.

248 This is contra the arguments of scholars who propose that the message of forensic justification through the imputation of the alien righteousness of Christ is politically destabilizing, with Martin Luther's gospel preparing the way for Adolf Hitler's Third Reich. See, for instance, James D. G. Dunn and Alan M. Suggate, *The Justice of God: A Fresh Look at the Old Doctrine of Justification by Faith* (Grand Rapids, Mich.: Eerdmans, 1993), 49-59.

249 Henry brilliantly noted this truth when he asserted in the anti-authoritarian tumult of the 1960s, "Those who know that God deals with men justly and not arbitrarily, and who also have a share in the justification that reinforces His justice in the grace of Golgotha, stand today at the crossroads of a crisis in modern civilization. If they find vision for our day, they can put the world on notice regarding God's claim in creation and redemption, by calling men everywhere to behold anew the demand for justice and the need for justification" (Henry, *Evangelicals at the Brink of Crisis,* 72).

CHAPTER FOUR

1 Stanley Hauerwas, *Sanctify Them in the Truth: Holiness Exemplified* (Nashville: Abingdon, 1998), 157.

2 Hence historian George Marsden correctly identifies an incipient anti-ecclesiological spirit at work in the movement's assembling of theological "stars" such as Henry,

Harold J. Ockenga, and E. J. Carnell for the Pasadena experiment: "These individual-ists were remarkably free from external controls. None of them had a taste for strong denominational authority, and all were thus attracted to a situation free from such restraints. An independent seminary, they were convinced, could serve the whole church. When they thought of the church, however, they did not think first of institu-tions but rather of the 'invisible' body of all evangelical believers. The church was essen-tially a collection of converted individuals. So the planners could act freely without being subject to any ecclesiastical authority. Free enterprise was at work" (George M. Marsden, *Reforming Fundamentalism: Fuller Seminary and the New Evangelicalism* [Grand Rapids, Mich.: Eerdmans, 1987], 29).

[3] This tension was evident in, among other things, Henry's loss of his American Baptist Convention retirement fund upon his appointment to the Fuller faculty (Carl F. H. Henry, *Confessions of a Theologian* [Waco, Tex.: Word, 1986], 118).

[4] Thus, the rationale for the formation of a National Association of Evangelicals as an orthodox alternative to the ecumenical Federal Council of Churches included the par-ticular complaint about the FCC: "It indicated both in pronouncements and practice that it considered man's need and not God's grace as the impelling motive to Christian action and that the amelioration of the social order is of primary concern to the Church. In this connection it attacked capitalism, condoned communism and lent its influence toward the creation of a new social order" (James Deforest Murch, *Cooperation Without Compromise: A History of the National Association of Evangelicals* [Grand Rapids, Mich.: Eerdmans, 1956], 47).

[5] "Insofar as the professing Church is unregenerate and hence a stranger to the power of true love, it should surprise no one that it conceives its mission to be the Christianizing of the world rather than the evangelizing of mankind, and that it relies on other than supernatural dynamic for its mission in the world," Henry noted. "Even ecclesiastical leaders cannot rely on a power they have never experienced" (Carl F. H. Henry, *The God Who Shows Himself* [Waco, Tex.: Word, 1966], 15).

[6] Carl F. H. Henry, *Evangelicals at the Brink of Crisis: The Significance of the World Congress on Evangelism* (Waco, Tex.: Word, 1967), 74. Henry therefore summed up the defective political ecclesiology of the Protestant left by noting, "The authentic mis-sion of the church is thus asserted to be that of changing the structures of society and not that of winning individual converts to Christ as the means of renewing society. The 'gospel' is said to be addressed not to individuals but to the community. This theory is connected with a further assumption, that individuals as such are not lost in the tradi-tional sense, and that the mission of the Church in the world is therefore no longer to be viewed as the regeneration of a doomed world, but the Church is rather to use the secular structures (political, economic, and cultural) as already on the way to fulfillment of God's will in Christ" (ibid., 74-75).

[7] Carl F. H. Henry, "Church and Political Pronouncements," *Christianity Today*, August 28, 1964, 29.

[8] Carl F. H. Henry, *Aspects of Christian Social Ethics* (Grand Rapids, Mich.: Eerdmans, 1964), 136-137.

[9] Henry, "Church and Political Pronouncements," 29.

[10] Carl F. H. Henry, "Somehow, Let's Get Together!" *Christianity Today*, June 9, 1957, 24.

[11] Ibid.

[12] "Neglect of the doctrine of the Church, except in defining separation as a special area of concern, proved to be another vulnerable feature of the fundamentalist forces. This failure to elaborate the biblical doctrine of the Church comprehensively and convinc-ingly not only contributes to the fragmenting spirit of the movement but actually hands

the initiative to the ecumenical enterprise in defining the nature and relations of the churches. Whereas the ecumenical movement has busied itself with the question of the visible and invisible Church, the fundamentalist movement has often been preoccupied with distinguishing churches as vocal or silent against modernism" (Carl F. H. Henry, *Evangelical Responsibility in Contemporary Theology* [Grand Rapids, Mich.: Eerdmans, 1957], 35).

[13] Carl F. H. Henry, *God, Revelation, and Authority,* 6 vols. (Waco, Tex.: Word, 1976; reprint, Wheaton, Ill.: Crossway, 1999), 1:133.

[14] Ironically, one of the early voices to address this problem was the editor of the Billy Graham Evangelistic Association's *Decision* magazine, Sherwood Wirt. Wirt feared that the evangelical movement's commitment to "the stance of the pristine rugged individualist" would undercut any call to evangelical public engagement. Redemption could not be merely about rescuing individuals, Wirt maintained, but instead meant the creation of a new community, the church (Sherwood Eliot Wirt, *The Social Conscience of the Evangelical* [New York: Harper & Row, 1968], 76, 149).

[15] Henry, *Evangelicals at the Brink of Crisis,* 75.

[16] "Today the wrong understanding of the Christian view of the State is compounded both by the Roman Catholic theory of union of Church and State and the Protestant liberal attempt to spawn the Kingdom of God as an earthly politico-economic development. Neither scheme has escaped the notice of totalitarian rulers who want to manipulate the Church for their own political objectives" (Henry, *Aspects of Christian Social Ethics,* 83).

[17] Carl F. H. Henry, *The Uneasy Conscience of Modern Fundamentalism* (Grand Rapids, Mich.: Eerdmans, 1947), 52.

[18] Ibid., 53.

[19] Ibid.

[20] "From his throne in the eternal order the Living Head mediated to the Body an earnest of the powers that belong to the age to come" (Henry, *Aspects of Christian Social Ethics,* 28).

[21] So Henry wrote, "Christ founded neither a party of revolutionaries, nor a movement of reformers, nor a remnant of reevaluators. He 'called out a people.' The twice-born fellowship of his redeemed Church, in vital company with its Lord, alone mirrored the realities of the new social order. This new order was no mere distant dream, waiting for the proletariat to triumph, or the evolutionary process to reach its pinnacle or truth to win its circuitous way throughout the world. In a promissory way the new order had come *already* in Jesus Christ and in the regenerate fellowship of his Church. The Lord was ascended; he reigned over all. Hence the apostolic church would not yield to other rulers or other social visions" (ibid.).

[22] Henry, *God Who Shows Himself,* 88.

[23] "In primitive Christian thought the Church was real, but it was like a temporary house put up to shelter the believers till the Lord came and the real salvation began," Walter Rauschenbusch argued. "But the Parousia did not come, and the temporary shelter grew and grew, and became the main thing." Rauschenbusch then was able to argue that the church was necessary for "the religious education of humanity" while the true realization of the Kingdom "awaits religion in the public life of humanity" (Walter Rauschenbusch, *A Theology for the Social Gospel* [New York: Macmillan, 1917; reprint, Louisville: Westminster/John Knox, 1997], 232, 145).

[24] Henry, *God Who Shows Himself,* 89.

[25] Carl F. H. Henry, *Christian Personal Ethics* (Grand Rapids, Mich.: Eerdmans, 1957), 205.

[26] Ibid.

[27] Ibid., 452.

[28] Ibid., 452-453.

[29] "It has the right and duty to call upon rulers, even pagan rulers, to maintain order and justice. It must stress the divine responsibility of government, condemn every repudiation of divine answerability, and challenge the State's neglect of its duty. The Church cannot content itself simply with denying church membership to the unjust and politically immoral. It must also criticize those who violate, misapply, or refuse to enforce the law. In Barth's words, the Church is to call the State 'into co-responsibility before God'" (Henry, *Aspects of Christian Social Ethics,* 81-82).

[30] For instance, Henry criticized Karl Barth for failing to make this distinction in the nature of the mediatorial reign of Christ by ignoring "the real difference between the divine sovereignty over the present world order and Christ's kingdom in the Age to come" since "Christ is not related to the world as Head to Body" (ibid., 151).

[31] Carl F. H. Henry, *A Plea for Evangelical Demonstration* (Grand Rapids, Mich.: Baker, 1971), 67.

[32] "The strategy stance of the church *vis-à-vis* society is not simply one of the church *for* the world, but of the church *against* the world. The church is ideally an approximate picture of what the world ought to be; the world, on the other hand, is what the church would still be were it not for the reality of grace and restoration to divine obedience. The New Testament looks ahead to Messiah's inauguration of universal social justice at his return. But it also incorporates into its preaching the divine demand for world righteousness, and in no whit relaxes God's present requirement of universal social justice" (ibid., 121-122).

[33] George Eldon Ladd, "The Kingdom of God and the Church," *Foundations* 4 (1961): 164.

[34] Ibid., 167.

[35] Ibid.

[36] "Reformed theologians continue to insist that the church is the Kingdom to the degree that it realizes the ideal order among its members," he wrote. Ladd found this view faulty since, he argued, replacing "Kingdom" with "church" in the relevant New Testament passages renders them nonsensical and because the church cannot be identified with the perfect, absolute reign of God since it is at times pictured as under the judgment of God (ibid., 165).

[37] Ibid.

[38] Ladd charged dispensational theology, as mediated through the Bible conferences and the *Scofield Bible,* with so disjointing the church and the Kingdom that it had fostered fundamentalist separatism based on the belief that the visible church is destined to apostatize as this "'mystery form' of the Kingdom is destined to become decadent, apostate and corrupt at the end of the age." For Ladd's critique of the "parenthesis" idea, see George Eldon Ladd, *Crucial Questions About the Kingdom of God* (Grand Rapids, Mich.: Eerdmans, 1952), 101-120, 166.

[39] Ladd, "Kingdom of God and the Church," 168.

[40] Ibid.

[41] Ibid., 168-169.

[42] George Eldon Ladd, *The Gospel of the Kingdom: Scriptural Studies in the Kingdom of God* (Grand Rapids, Mich.: Eerdmans, 1959), 117.

[43] George Eldon Ladd, *The Presence of the Future: The Eschatology of Biblical Realism* (Grand Rapids, Mich.: Eerdmans, 1974), 337.

[44] Ibid.

45 Ibid., 339.

46 Ladd lays out the full exegetical defense of his view in George Eldon Ladd, *A Theology of the New Testament* (Grand Rapids, Mich.: Eerdmans, 1974; reprint, Grand Rapids, Mich.: Eerdmans, 1993), 103-117.

47 Ibid., 113.

48 "Christendom's Key Issue: 25 Scholars' Views," *Christianity Today,* October 12, 1959, 29.

49 Ibid., 29-30.

50 This is ironic given the relatively scant attention given by Henry to the doctrine of the church, and the criticism he has received from more confessional evangelicals at this very point.

51 Henry, *God, Revelation, and Authority,* 4:522.

52 "Marxist exegesis is notably vague in stating what precise form the socialist utopia is to take, and where in history it has been concretely realized. Radical neo-Protestant theologians needlessly accommodate much of this Marxist obscurity over the new man and the new society. For they fail to identify Jesus Christ as the ideal man, fail to emphasize the new covenant that Scripture associates with messianic fulfillment and fail to center the content of the new society in the regenerate church's reflection of the kingdom of God" (ibid.).

53 The role of the church as covenant community, therefore, "is not to forcibly demote alien powers" but "to demonstrate what it means to live in ultimate loyalty not to worldly powers but to the risen Lord in a corporate life of truth, righteousness, and mercy" (ibid., 529).

54 Carl F. H. Henry, "Reflections on the Kingdom of God," *JETS* 35 (1992): 47.

55 Ibid., 48.

56 With such being the case, Grenz finds himself in agreement with conservative R. Albert Mohler, Jr., on the neglect of the church in the evangelical theology represented by Henry (Stanley J. Grenz, *Renewing the Center: Evangelical Theology in a Post-Theological Age* [Grand Rapids, Mich.: Baker, 2000], 288-289).

57 The central difference represented by Grenz and Henry is the relationship between the community of faith and divine revelation. Grenz holds to a communitarian understanding of truth that is categorically rejected by conservative evangelicals such as Henry, Erickson, Grudem, and Mohler, all of whom hold to a correspondence theory of truth with strong notions of divine revelation as propositional and verbal. For a contrast between these epistemological visions, contrast Stanley J. Grenz and John R. Franke, *Beyond Foundationalism: Shaping Theology in a Postmodern Context* (Louisville: Westminster/John Knox, 2001), with R. Albert Mohler, Jr., "The Integrity of the Evangelical Tradition and the Challenge of the Postmodern Paradigm," in *The Challenge of Postmodernism: An Evangelical Engagement,* 2nd edition, ed. David S. Dockery (Grand Rapids, Mich.: Baker, 2001), 53-74.

58 Grenz writes, "From this eschatological vision, the New Testament writers derive their understanding of communal life in the here and now. Although they present the anticipated fullness of community as a future reality, the early Christians were convinced that a partial, yet genuine foretaste of the eschatological fullness may be enjoyed prior to the eschaton. The New Testament writers declare that the focus of the prolepsis of the future reality is the community of Christ—the community of reconciled people in fellowship with God through Christ. In their estimation, the present experience of community with Christ, that is, the relationship of believers with their Lord and therefore with each other—is to be the harbinger of the glorious eschatological community, the society of humankind in fellowship with God. With this in view, they elevate the believing community as the focal point of bonded fellowship in the penultimate age inaugurated by the

Christ event" (Stanley J. Grenz, *The Social God and the Relational Self: A Trinitarian Theology of the Imago Dei* [Louisville: Westminster/John Knox, 2001], 281).

59 Stanley J. Grenz, *Theology for the Community of God* (Grand Rapids, Mich.: Eerdmans, 2000), 610.

60 Grenz argues, "Classical theology rightly affirms that God's program in the world is directed to individuals in the midst of human sin and need. Unfortunately, this emphasis—correct as it is—all too often settles for a truncated soteriology resulting in an inadequate ecclesiology. The program of God includes the salvation of the individual, of course, but it overflows the human person in solitary aloneness. Our salvation occurs in relationships, not in isolation. Hence, God's purpose includes human social interaction. And it moves beyond the isolated human realm to encompass all creation. God's concern does not end with the redeemed individual as an individual. Rather, he desires a reconciled humankind (Eph. 2:14-19) living in the renewed creation and enjoying his own presence (Rev. 21:1-5a)" (ibid., 481).

61 Ibid.

62 John S. Feinberg, "Systems of Discontinuity," in *Continuity and Discontinuity: Perspectives on the Relationship Between the Old and New Testaments,* ed. John S. Feinberg (Westchester, Ill.: Crossway, 1988), 83.

63 So, for instance, popular dispensationalist author F. B. Meyer at the beginning of the twentieth century emphasized the importance of understanding the reality of the church as a distinct work of the Holy Spirit in the dispensation of grace. "Just as Jesus was born on a definite day which we celebrate as Christmas day, and came into new relations with the world which will never be dissolved, so also on the day of Pentecost, the Holy Spirit came into new relations with men. Just as we date the chronology of the world from the advent of our Lord, so we should date the history of the church from the advent of the Holy Spirit. Indeed, there is a precise parallel, which you will see in a moment. Our Lord was in the world before His birth, but at His birth He took a human body. The Holy Spirit was in the world before the day of Pentecost, but at Pentecost He took on a body. He is now tenanting that body, which is composed of all believers in every age and every clime" (F. B. Meyer, *Back to Bethel* [Chicago: Moody, 1901], 89).

64 Craig A. Blaising, "Lewis Sperry Chafer," in *Handbook of Evangelical Theologians,* ed. Walter A. Elwell (Grand Rapids, Mich.: Baker, 1993), 95.

65 Darrell L. Bock, "Why I Am a dispensationalist with a Small 'd'," *JETS* 41 (1998): 393.

66 George Marsden defines this dispensationalist ecclesiology as follows: "Unlike the postponed kingdom, which has a definite material and institutional structure, the interim church age of grace is a non-institutional age of the Holy Spirit. The true church is not the institutional church, which is worldly and steadily growing in apostasy. It is rather a faithful remnant of the spiritual who are 'separate and holy' from the world" (George M. Marsden, *Fundamentalism and American Culture: The Shaping of Twentieth-Century Evangelicalism, 1870–1925* [New York: Oxford University Press, 1980], 54).

67 Michael D. Williams, "Where's the Church? The Church as the Unfinished Business of Dispensational Theology," *GTJ* 10 (1989): 166-167.

68 Ibid., 167-170.

69 Ibid., 176-177.

70 Ibid., 180.

71 Craig Blaising, for instance, traces out this view by arguing, "In contrast to classical dispensationalism, progressive dispensationalism does not see the church as a wholly separate category of grace. But neither does it see the church within the history of redemption as simply a clearer manifestation of the grace revealed in the Old Testament. Rather, progressive dispensationalism views the church as a truly new (and therefore

distinctive) phase in a progressive unfolding history of holistic redemption" (Craig A. Blaising, "The Baptism with the Holy Spirit in the History of Redemption" [paper presented to the Dispensational Study Group of the Evangelical Theological Society, Lisle, Ill., November 17, 1994], 7-8).

[72] Craig A. Blaising and Darrell L. Bock, *Progressive Dispensationalism* (Wheaton, Ill.: Victor, 1993), 285-288.

[73] Gerry Breshears, "New Directions in Dispensationalism" (paper presented at the annual meeting of the Evangelical Theological Society, Kansas City, Mo., November 23, 1991), 16.

[74] "The church's testimony to Jesus is based on the relationship which Jesus established with her from His ascended position in heaven. He had already provided the atonement which made possible a new covenant in all its blessings. His resurrection from the dead revealed and confirmed these blessings in Himself—the firstfruits from the dead. However, a few days after His ascension into heaven, on Israel's Day of Pentecost, Jesus (acting from heaven) gave His disciples a 'down payment' on the new covenant blessings of the kingdom, the gift of the Holy Spirit. This action constituted His disciples a community of the eschatological kingdom of God, under the rule and blessing of Jesus the Messiah. All who come to faith in Jesus are likewise blessed by the gift of the Spirit and join this kingdom community, which has come to be known as the church" (Blaising and Bock, *Progressive Dispensationalism,* 255).

[75] See, for instance, Darrell L. Bock, "The Reign of the Lord Christ," in *Dispensationalism, Israel, and the Church: The Search for Definition,* ed. Craig A. Blaising and Darrell L. Bock (Grand Rapids, Mich.: Zondervan, 1992), 37-67; "Current Messianic Activity and OT Davidic Promise: Dispensationalism, Hermeneutics, and NT Fulfillment," *TrinJ* 15 (1994): 85-102; and "The Son of David and the Saints' Task: The Hermeneutics of Initial Fulfillment," *BibSac* 150 (1993): 440-457.

[76] Bock writes, "In its initial phase, the kingdom as manifested in the church is a community of people who all look to the same hope in Christ. Thus, the kingdom's presence primarily is manifested in believers who all serve and are accountable to the sovereign head, Jesus Christ (Eph. 1:19-22; Col. 1:12-14). The church universal is related to the kingdom, being its present expression, but the church is not all there is to the kingdom, since there is a kingdom to come. In addition, the church is not an institution seeking to seize power on earth or exercise coercive sovereignty, but is to serve and love humankind, reflecting the love of God, his standards of righteousness, and the message of his forgiveness and love in Jesus Christ (Rom. 12:9-13:7). These elements make up the mission of the church as light in the world" (Darrell L. Bock, *Luke 9:51–24:53,* Baker Exegetical Commentary on the New Testament [Grand Rapids, Mich.: Baker, 1996], 3b:1222).

[77] These are outlined in Niebuhr's seminal work, *Christ and Culture* (New York: Harper & Row, 1951).

[78] Bock, "Son of David and the Saints' Task," 456.

[79] Bock, "Current Messianic Activity and OT Davidic Promise," 87.

[80] Blaising argues, "But one should not imply from this that the state should control local churches or that the church is a political state alongside other governmental bodies. Political authority over all nations belongs to Christ now, but how and when he will exercise his authority is a matter of his and the Father's will. Progressive dispensationalists believe that the New Testament teaches that Christ will function as both political and spiritual head among the redeemed and over the world when he comes. Prior to that time, his special activity is revealed in the formation of believing Jews and all kinds of Gentiles of faith into *a community* for the indwelling of God by the Holy Spirit. This community interpenetrates the diverse political structures of this world. Even though it

awaits the revelation of Christ's political administration at his return, it should already begin to explore within itself the social and political righteousness of Christ within its own redeemed *community* of people" (Craig A. Blaising, "Contemporary Dispensationalism," *SWJT* 36 [1994]: 13). Even progressive dispensational theologians, such as Robert Saucy, who disagree with the current reign of Christ as outlined by Blaising and Bock, agree with most of these aspects of the church/world relationship. Saucy thus places himself in agreement with the emerging consensus at this point: "Far from giving believers today the kingdom power that will someday crush all its enemies, the church today, as Ladd has said, 'is, like other men, at the mercy of the powers of this world'" (Robert L. Saucy, "The Presence of the Kingdom and the Life of the Church," *BibSac* 145 [1988]: 45). Saucy here quotes Ladd, *Presence of the Future*, 338.

[81] Charles C. Ryrie, *Dispensationalism,* rev. and expanded ed. (Chicago: Moody, 1995), 176. In the place of this church-oriented model of engagement, Ryrie has proposed a model that is much more focused on the role of the individual Christian in relation to various social and political issues. See Charles C. Ryrie, *Biblical Answers to Contemporary Issues* (Chicago: Moody, 1974).

[82] Robert Pyne, "New Man and Immoral Society" (paper presented at the annual meeting of the Evangelical Theological Society, Santa Clara, Calif., November 20, 1997), 11.

[83] Ibid., 2.

[84] Louis Berkhof, *Systematic Theology,* rev. ed. (Grand Rapids, Mich.: Eerdmans, 1941), 553-554. I am indebted to Craig Blaising for this observation.

[85] It might be argued, contra Berkhof, that the Reformed tradition perhaps has devoted more effort in establishing an ecclesiology than many other branches of the American evangelical tradition. Nonetheless, Berkhof's central point about the ambiguity at this point still stands.

[86] See, for example, Geerhardus Vos, *The Teaching of Jesus Concerning the Kingdom of God and the Church* (New York: American Tract Society, 1903), 140-168. See also Vos's treatment of the church and the Kingdom by means of the ecclesiological teachings of Jesus in Matthew 16:18-20 in *Biblical Theology: Old and New Testaments* (Grand Rapids, Mich.: Eerdmans, 1948), 426-429.

[87] See, for instance, Michael Williams's appreciative critique of Vos in "A Restorational Alternative to Augustinian Verticalist Eschatology," *Pro Rege* 20 (1992): 11-24.

[88] Edmund P. Clowney, *Another Foundation: The Presbyterian Confessional Crisis* (Philadelphia: Presbyterian & Reformed, 1965), 19.

[89] Ibid., 19-20.

[90] Clowney put this argument as follows: "The life of Christ's kingdom also has cultural manifestation among those who are his people. The church as the present form of the people of God is ordered by Christ, ruled by Christ, indwelt by Christ. The church has an eschatological form, for it awaits the coming of the kingdom. But it is also an actual fellowship in which the power of the kingdom is manifested. The whole sphere of Christian living is 'in the Lord.' In the church, life in the Lord is manifested. Other authority structures besides the church remain valid: the state continues to bear the sword by God's own ordinance; the family is closely related to the church but not identified with it. Yet only the church has been organized by Christ as the ordered form of his kingdom, the new people of God in the world. The pilgrim calling of the church subordinates some aspects of the cultural task in the present form of Christ's kingdom. The 'filling' of the earth, for example, as it is sought 'in the Lord' is brought about by the ministry of the Word of Christ by which the number of believers is multiplied and the church enriches by the gifts of the risen Lord (Eph 4:8-16)" (Edmund P. Clowney, "The Christian College and the Transformation of Culture," *CSR* 1 [1970]: 15).

[91] "The word 'church' asserts the unity of the new people of God. The Greek word

ekklesia translates the Hebrew term *qahal*. Both mean 'assembly.' The Old Testament assembly is defined by the great covenant assembly at Sinai. It is extended in the major assemblies for covenant renewal and in the festival assemblies three times a year. In assembly the people stand before their covenant Lord. They are not a tribe, defined genealogically, but a holy nation bound together by the word of God in the presence of God. At Pentecost the wind and flame of the Spirit make the feast of the first-fruits the Sinai of the New Covenant" (Edmund P. Clowney, "The Politics of the Kingdom," *WTJ* 41 [1979]: 300-301).

[92] Richard B. Gaffin, Jr., "Pentecost: Before and After" (paper presented to the Dispensational Study Group of the Evangelical Theological Society, Lisle, Ill., November 17, 1994).

[93] Vern Poythress, *Understanding Dispensationalists,* 2nd ed. (Phillipsburg, N.J.: Presbyterian & Reformed, 1987), 128-129.

[94] See, for instance, Mark Karlberg, review of *The Holy Spirit,* by Sinclair B. Ferguson, *JETS* 42 (1999): 529.

[95] Richard B. Gaffin, Jr., "'Life-Giving Spirit': Probing the Center of Paul's Pneumatology," *JETS* 41 (1998): 585.

[96] Ibid.

[97] Michael D. Williams, "Rapture or Resurrection?" *Presbyterion* 24 (1998): 23.

[98] Poythress, *Understanding Dispensationalists,* 44.

[99] Anthony A. Hoekema, *The Bible and the Future* (Grand Rapids, Mich.: Eerdmans, 1979), 216.

[100] Ibid.

[101] "Without question, the Great Commission continues fully in force, with its full cultural breadth, until Jesus returns; 'teaching them to obey everything I have commanded you' is the mandate of the exalted Last Adam to the people of his new creation. . . . That mandate, then, is bound to have a robust, leavening impact—one that will redirect every area of life and will transform not only individuals but, through them corporately (as the church), their cultures; it already has done so and will continue to do so, until Jesus comes" (Richard B. Gaffin, Jr., "Theonomy and Eschatology: Reflections on Postmillennialism," in *Theonomy: A Reformed Critique,* ed. William S. Barker and W. Robert Godfrey [Grand Rapids, Mich.: Zondervan, 1990], 220).

[102] Edmund P. Clowney, *The Church* (Downers Grove, Ill.: InterVarsity Press, 1995), 189.

[103] "Calling the state to righteousness does not mean calling it to promote the gospel with political power or to usher in the last judgment with the sword. Christians are not free to form an exclusively Christian political party that seeks to exercise power in the name of Christ. That would identify Christ's cause with one of the kingdoms of the world. Political action on the part of Christians must always be undertaken in concert with others who seek the same immediate objectives. Such objectives, promoting life, liberty and the restraint of violence, are the proper goals of civil government. They are not the goals of faith and holiness that Christ appointed for his kingdom" (ibid., 193).

[104] Clowney, "Politics of the Kingdom," 306.

[105] Ibid.

[106] Ibid., 307.

[107] For a discussion of the "harlot/bride" motif in the Old Testament, see Raymond C. Ortlund, Jr., *God's Unfaithful Wife: A Biblical Theology of Spiritual Adultery* (Downers Grove, Ill.: InterVarsity Press, 1996).

[108] This is from page 8, footnote 5, of John Sanders's paper to the Evangelical Theological Society (ETS) Executive Committee, defending himself in the fall of 2003

against charges by Roger Nicole that he should be expelled from the Society. The paper may be accessed at www.etsjets.org.

109 John Sanders, *The God Who Risks: A Theology of Providence* (Downers Grove, Ill.: InterVarsity Press, 1998), 100.

110 Clark H. Pinnock, *Most Moved Mover: A Theology of God's Openness* (Grand Rapids, Mich.: Baker, 2001), 44.

111 For an insightful critique of the older forms of dispensationalism at these points, see Michael Williams, *This World Is Not My Home: The Origins and Development of Dispensationalism* (Fearn, Ross-shire, Scotland: Mentor, 2003).

112 Bernard Ramm, *Beyond Fundamentalism: The Future of Evangelical Theology* (New York: Harper & Row, 1983), 188.

113 Sanders, *God Who Risks,* 71.

114 Stanley J. Grenz, "An Evangelical Response to Ferguson, Holloway, and Lowery: Restoring a Trinitarian Understanding of the Church in Practice," in *Evangelicalism and the Stone-Campbell Movement,* ed. William R. Baker (Downers Grove, Ill.: InterVarsity Press, 2002), 232.

115 Oliver O'Donovan, *The Desire of the Nations: Rediscovering the Roots of Political Theology* (Cambridge: Cambridge University Press, 1996), 161.

116 Ibid. Compare O'Donovan's treatment here with, for example, the way in which Gaffin makes the case for the cessation of the sign gifts of tongues and prophecy, due to their lack of an eschatological, Christological nature (Richard B. Gaffin, Jr., *Perspectives on Pentecost: New Testament Teaching on the Gifts of the Holy Spirit* [Phillipsburg, N.J.: Presbyterian & Reformed, 1979]).

117 Douglas Farrow, *Ascension and Ecclesia: On the Significance of the Doctrine of the Ascension for Ecclesiology and Christian Cosmology* (Grand Rapids, Mich.: Eerdmans, 1999), 32-33.

118 Of course, the atoning work is indeed directed toward individuals, since Christ is a covenant sacrifice bearing in His body the sins of individual sinners. Thus, the apostle Paul is able to write of "the Son of God, who loved me and gave Himself up for me" (Gal. 2:20). Nonetheless, the key word here is *isolated*. The goal of salvation is never to redeem individuals in isolation from one another. The goal of the atonement is presented in Scripture as to redeem believers in community with one another, to redeem a people. The apostle John, therefore, is able to see "myriads of myriads, and thousands of thousands, saying with a loud voice, 'Worthy is the Lamb that was slain to receive power and riches and wisdom and might and honor and glory and blessing'" (Rev. 5:11-12). These are individuals, but they are an assembly, a congregation. They are not disparate, isolated individuals redeemed for a solitary union with Christ.

119 For a convincing argument for the ecclesiological and corporate meaning of Colossians 1:12-14, contra the traditional dispensationalist or mystical individualist readings, see Gary S. Shogren, "Presently Entering the Kingdom of Christ: The Background and Purpose of Col 1:12-14," *JETS* 31 (1988): 173-180.

120 Contra William W. Klein, *The New Chosen People: A Corporate View of Election* (Grand Rapids, Mich.: Zondervan, 1990). For a compelling rebuttal of the Klein thesis, with specific reference to the election passage of Romans 9, see Thomas R. Schreiner, "Does Romans 9 Teach Individual Election unto Salvation?" in *Still Sovereign: Contemporary Perspectives on Election, Foreknowledge, and Grace* (Grand Rapids, Mich.: Baker, 2000), 89-106.

121 Peter O'Brien traces the relationship between the cosmic headship of Christ taught in Ephesians 1:22-23 and the corresponding teaching on the headship of Christ over the church: "Here Christ's headship has to do with his relation to the cosmos; then body is introduced as a description of the church to which Christ is given. . . . As head over all

things Christ exercises his sovereign rule by 'filling' the universe. But only the church is his body, and he rules it, that is, he fills it in a special way with his Spirit, grace and gifts: it is his fullness" (Peter T. O'Brien, *The Letter to the Ephesians,* The Pillar New Testament Commentary [Grand Rapids, Mich.: Eerdmans, 1999], 146, 152). Markus Barth writes of this passage, noting the relationship involving the cosmic role of Christ and his role as Head of the Body: "In Ephesians and Colossians fullness and filling denote a dynamic or unilateral relationship: the revelation of God's glory to the world through Jesus Christ; the power exerted by God in Christ and in the church for the subjection of the powers and the salvation of all mankind; the life, growth, and salvation given by Christ to his body; or, in brief, the presence of the living God and his Messiah among his chosen people for the benefit of all creation. If there is a cosmic role ascribed to the church in Ephesians then it is as a servant. She is to manifest the presence of the loving and powerful God. Not God, Christ, or the Head, but solely the body of Christ, that is, the house of God, the church is 'to grow.' Any notion of world dominion by the church is missing, but the church is equipped to do a 'work of service' and to 'stand against,' and 'resist,' the attacks of the evil powers. The idea is lacking that one day the church will fill or replace the world. Assurance is given that Christ is filling all things and that the saints will attain or will be filled with, all of God's and the Messiah's fullness" (Markus Barth, *Ephesians 1–3,* vol. 34 of *The Anchor Bible* [Garden City, N.Y.: Doubleday, 1974], 209).

[122] Nettles points specifically to the allusion in James 2:5 to unconditional election in respect to the question of partiality toward the rich and injustice to the poor within the context of the local congregation (Thomas J. Nettles, *By His Grace and for His Glory: A Historical, Theological, and Practical Study of the Doctrines of Grace in Baptist Life* [Grand Rapids, Mich.: Baker, 1986], 280).

[123] Gerry Breshears, "The Body of Christ: Prophet, Priest, or King?" *JETS* 37 (1994): 9.

[124] "When you read this, you can perceive my insight into the mystery of Christ, which was not made known to the sons of men in other generations as it has now been revealed to his holy apostles and prophets by the Spirit. The mystery is that the Gentiles are fellow heirs, members of the same body, and partakers of the promise in Christ Jesus through the gospel" (Eph. 3:4-6, ESV).

[125] See, for instance, J. Gresham Machen's critique of inordinate individualism in *Christianity and Liberalism* (New York: Macmillan, 1923; reprint, Grand Rapids, Mich.: Eerdmans, 2001), 152-156.

[126] "There must be communion and community among the people of God—not the false community that is set up as though human community were an end in itself; but in the local church, in a mission, in a school, wherever it might be, true fellowship must be evident as the outcome of original, individual salvation. This is the real church of the Lord Jesus Christ—not merely organization but a group of people individually the people of God, drawn together by the Holy Spirit for a particular task either in a local situation or over a wider area" (Francis Schaeffer, *The God Who Is There* [London: Hodder & Stoughton, 1968; reprint, Downers Grove, Ill.: InterVarsity Press, 1998], 186). While Schaeffer's definition here of this community as "whatever it might be" indicates that the parachurch nature of the movement still had a hold on him, such calls to community were a foray in the right direction.

[127] Social critics Gene Edward Veith and Thomas L. Wilmeth, for instance, find this individualistic anti-congregationalism in, of all places, the lyrics of popular country music songs of the twentieth century. Rooted in the folk music of the South, country music emphasizes both sin and piety, they argue, but references to the church are almost always related to an individual believer finding repentance in an empty or abandoned church in the countryside. Veith and Wilmeth attribute this to, among other things, suspicion of the denominational structures in light of the Fundamentalist-Modernist controversy. "In contemporary country music, the church as the place of salvation has all but dis-

appeared," they argue (Gene Edward Veith and Thomas L. Wilmeth, *Honky-Tonk Gospel: The Story of Sin and Salvation in Country Music* [Grand Rapids, Mich.: Baker, 2001], 92).

[128] Grenz, *Theology for the Community of God*, 22-24; *Renewing the Center*, 212-217.

[129] "Without a clear understanding of the nature of the kingdom, kingdom theology is inadequate to the task of indicating what the world is like when it is transformed by the divine rule" (Grenz and Franke, *Beyond Foundationalism*, 234).

[130] Robert Booth Fowler surveys the definitions of "community" offered by communitarians ranging from Robert Bellah to Stanley Hauerwas to Rosemary Radford Ruether and concludes, "No single version of community dominates present-day discussion" (Robert Booth Fowler, "Community: Reflections on a Definition," in *New Communitarian Thinking: Virtues, Institutions, and Communities*, ed. Amitai Etzioni [Charlottesville: University of Virginia Press, 1995], 88). Likewise, philosopher Raymond Plant describes "community" as having "a high level of use but a low level of meaning," making it "one of the most pervasive, yet indefinite terms" in use in public discourse (Raymond Plant, "Community," in *The Blackwell Encyclopedia of Political Thought*, ed. David Miller [Oxford: Blackwell, 1987], 88).

[131] Grenz and Franke, *Beyond Foundationalism*, 235.

[132] Grenz seems to recognize this elsewhere, as he assumes that the goal of creation and redemption is not community *qua* community, but is rather an eschatological community under the rule of the triune God. Thus, he can argue, "The central motif of biblical eschatology is the assertion that the triune God is at work in history *effecting the consummation of the divine reign by establishing community*. The biblical perspective considers the history of the world in the context of the theological question of ultimate sovereignty. Is the Creator lord over creation, or is the universe self-existing and autonomous?" (Grenz, *Theology for the Community of God*, 651, emphasis mine).

[133] After all, a "community" may exist without explicit reference to God, much less to the incarnate Christ. A "Kingdom," however, presupposes the existence of a King, defined in Scripture as a particular "community," the Triune God. As biblical scholar Marcus Borg argues, in the New Testament "the image 'Kingdom' is intrinsically corporate or communal, implying a community of people living as subjects of a king" (Marcus J. Borg, *Conflict, Holiness, and Politics in the Teachings of Jesus* [Harrisburg, Pa.: Trinity Press International, 1998], 264). It is difficult to see how the equal and opposite case could be made.

[134] In so doing, evangelical ecclesiology invariably is dependent upon a robust evangelical epistemology, especially as it distinguishes itself from a revisionist Protestant left that is often unsure how a doctrine of the church can fit within a paradigm built on dissent and mistrust of authority. See, for example, Nancy Watson, "Faithful Dissenters? Feminist Ecclesiologies and Dissent," *Scottish Journal of Theology* 51 (1998): 464-484.

[135] Donald G. Bloesch, *The Future of Evangelical Christianity: A Call for Unity amid Diversity* (Garden City, N.Y.: Doubleday, 1983), 148.

[136] Ibid.

[137] For instance, this is seen in the way nineteenth-century dispensationalist George Peters relates the "apostasy" to the church bodies of his day: "See how vast, the most powerful organizations have fallen away from the truth; how bodies counting their millions of adherents are in direct opposition to Bible doctrine and primitive belief; how hundreds of smaller sects, communities, etc., in the aggregate swelling to a great multitude, deny the most fundamental truths, dishonor Christ by their views and practices, and elevate their own human derived revelations, etc., above the Scriptures" (George N. H. Peters, *The Theocratic Kingdom of Our Lord Jesus Christ, as Covenanted in the Old Testament and Presented in the New Testament*, 3 vols. [New York: Funk &

Wagnalls, 1884; reprint, Grand Rapids, Mich.: Kregel, 1952], 3:119). It is not difficult to see how such a mistrust of the ecclesial bodies could only intensify against the backdrop of the Fundamentalist-Modernist controversy.

[138] A point made also by the preeminent twentieth-century presence among Reformed theologians, J. Gresham Machen, who recognized that the problem in the Fundamentalist-Modernist controversy was not, ultimately, varying degrees of orthodoxy. It was instead the contest between two different religions (Machen, *Christianity and Liberalism*).

[139] C. I. Scofield thus could speak in his notes on Revelation 18 of the congruity between the "ecclesiastical Babylon, which is apostate Christendom, headed up under the Papacy" and "political Babylon, which is the Beast's confederated empire, the last form of Gentile world-dominion" (C. I. Scofield, *The Scofield Study Bible* [New York: Oxford University Press, 1909; reprint, New York: Oxford University Press, 1996], 1346). Whatever the deficiencies of Scofield's prophetic historicism, he does seem to be on solid ground in noting that the New Testament does warn of the possibility of apostate pseudo-church organizations during the present era. See, for example, Paul's admonition in 2 Thessalonians 2:3-12.

[140] Similarly, the Second Helvetic Confession (1566), for example, points to the headship of Christ over the church universal as the reason Reformed Protestants "do not allow of the doctrine of the Romish prelates, who would make the Pope the general pastor and supreme head of the Church Militant here on earth, and the very vicar of Jesus Christ, who has (as they say) all fullness of power and sovereign authority in the Church" (John H. H. Leith, *Creeds of the Churches: A Reader in Christian Doctrine from the Bible to the Present,* 3rd ed. [Louisville: John Knox, 1982], 144).

[141] This problem would include, incredibly, even some of the most conservative adherents to Reformed orthodoxy. John Gerstner, for example, argues that one must remain in a denomination even when that denomination refuses to ordain men who oppose the ordination of women to the pastorate. Likewise, he argues, a person must not separate from a church that blesses homosexual unions or ordains practicing homosexuals to the ministry because it "does not cease to be a church," and therefore "could we cease to be a member of her?" (John Gerstner, "Guide Me, O Thou Great Jehovah," in *Onward, Christian Soldiers: Protestants Affirm the Church,* ed. Don Kistler [Morgan, Pa.: Soli Deo Gloria, 1999], 300-308).

[142] See, for example, the treatment of J. Gresham Machen at the hands of the Presbyterian Church, the impetus for the founding of Westminster Seminary and the Orthodox Presbyterian Church (see D. G. Hart and John Muether, *Fighting the Good Fight: A Brief History of the Orthodox Presbyterian Church* [Philadelphia: Committee on Christian Education and Committee for the Historian of the Orthodox Presbyterian Church, 1995], 11-54).

[143] "The apostles went everywhere preaching the gospel, but sectarians go everywhere preaching the Episcopal view of succession, the Lutheran view of the real presence, the Baptist view of immersion, the Methodist view of holiness, and the Pentecostal view of speaking in tongues. Church history proves that denominational distinctives trace to very ambiguous evidences. They have no right to share honors with the gospel; they are adjectives, not nouns" (Edward J. Carnell, *The Case for Orthodox Theology* [Philadelphia: Westminster, 1959], 131).

[144] Harold John Ockenga, "The Unvoiced Multitudes," in *Evangelical Action! A Report of the Organization of the National Association of Evangelicals for United Action* (Boston: United Action Press, 1942), 32-33.

[145] Carl F. H. Henry, "The Vigor of the New Evangelicalism," *Christian Life,* April 1948, 66.

146 Rauschenbusch, *Theology for the Social Gospel*, 232.

147 Carl F. H. Henry, "Isolated from the Church?" *Christianity Today*, March 29, 1968, 23.

148 Southern Baptist historian Timothy George, for instance, points to Henry as the prime culprit in the slowness of contemporary evangelical theology to "develop a distinctive understanding of the church." For George, the "3000 pages with little ink spent on the doctrine of the church" in Henry's six-volume *God, Revelation, and Authority* represents the fact that "evangelical scholars have been too preoccupied with other theological themes such as biblical revelation, religious epistemology and apologetics" to construct a workable ecclesiology (Timothy George, "What I'd Like to Tell the Pope About the Church," *Christianity Today*, June 15, 1998, 41-42). Similarly, Southern Baptist theologian R. Albert Mohler, Jr., takes Henry to task because the "most glaring omission in his theological project is the doctrine of the church," even as he counts Henry as his chief theological mentor (R. Albert Mohler, Jr., "Carl F. H. Henry," in *Baptist Theologians*, ed. Timothy George and David S. Dockery [Nashville: Broadman & Holman, 1990], 530). Such a critique is borne out, argues Presbyterian historian John Muether, in the fact that Henry is identified as an "evangelical theologian" and rarely as a "Baptist theologian," a fact that, Muether contends, is "indicative of the non-denominational character of his ministry" (John Muether, "Contemporary Evangelicalism and the Triumph of the New School," *WTJ* 50 [1988]: 340). Muether further argues that the vapid ecclesiology and lack of denominational identity represented by Henry, his fellow Fuller Seminary faculty members, and other leaders of the evangelical movement, along with the commitment of the movement to work through parachurch avenues rather than through the visible church, represents the triumph of New School Presbyterianism over the Old Princeton confessional, Reformed tradition in American conservative Protestantism.

149 Muether, "Contemporary Evangelicalism and the Triumph of the New School," 345. This does not mean, of course, that evangelicals such as Henry were personally agnostic on issues of confessional church identity. See, for instance, Henry's defense of Baptist ecclesiology, a commitment that defines baptism as the immersion of believers only, calls for a regenerate church membership, and maintains the separation of the church from the state (Carl F. H. Henry, "Fifty Years a Baptist," in *Why I Am a Baptist*, ed. Tom J. Nettles and Russell D. Moore [Nashville: Broadman & Holman, 2001], 209-217).

150 R. Albert Mohler, Jr., perhaps Henry's closest theological successor, cites Henry's goal to create "an international multi-denominational corps of scholars articulating conservative theology," and concludes that Henry emphasized the movement more than the church, thereby destabilizing the movement itself (R. Albert Mohler, Jr., "Reformist Evangelicalism: A Center Without a Circumference," in *A Confessing Theology for Postmodern Times*, ed. Michael S. Horton [Wheaton, Ill.: Crossway, 2000], 133). John Muether, for instance, rightly notes that Henry's "indifference to ecclesiology and confessionalism may explain the failures of the evangelical movement, failures he so candidly describes" (Muether, "Contemporary Evangelicalism and the Triumph of the New School," 342).

151 Barry Hankins, "The Evangelical Accommodationism of Southern Baptist Convention Conservatives," *Baptist History and Heritage* 33 (1998): 59.

152 This describes the 1999 collaboration between Crossway Books and the Carl F. H. Henry Institute for Evangelical Engagement at The Southern Baptist Theological Seminary. This is especially significant given Fuller Seminary's almost complete repudiation of the epistemological and apologetic contributions of Henry. See, for instance, the counter-proposal on issues of theological prolegomena offered by Fuller Seminary philosopher Nancey Murphey, *Beyond Liberalism and Fundamentalism: How Modern*

and Postmodern Philosophy Set the Theological Agenda (Valley Forge, Pa.: Trinity Press International, 1996).

153 Stanley J. Grenz, "What Does Hollywood Have to Do with Wheaton? The Place of (Pop) Culture in Theological Reflection," *JETS* 43 (2000): 309.

154 Ibid., 309-310.

155 Richard Lints, *The Fabric of Theology: A Prolegomenon to Evangelical Theology* (Grand Rapids, Mich.: Eerdmans, 1993), 321.

156 Mark Noll, *The Scandal of the Evangelical Mind* (Grand Rapids, Mich.: Eerdmans, 1994), 140 n. 51.

157 Tim LaHaye and his collaborator Jerry Jenkins have revived Lindsey-style apocalypticism via the series of end-times novels that skyrocketed in the late 1990s and beyond to the top of the *New York Times* bestseller list. LaHaye's popular impact is such that the Institute for the Study of American Evangelicals at Wheaton College named LaHaye the "evangelical of the century" for, among other things, "rescuing" a withering dispensational eschatology among evangelicals (Larry Eskridge, "And, the Most Influential Evangelical of the Last 25 Years Is . . . ," *Evangelical Studies Bulletin* 17 [2001]: 1-4).

158 This is true not only in terms of the Jew-Gentile membership of the churches, as discussed previously. The book of 1 Corinthians alone, for instance, discusses in detail the ordering of the church in terms of membership and church discipline (5–6), the Lord's Supper (11:23-34), the exercise of charismatic gifts (12:1–14:40), and so forth.

159 A position articulated perhaps most bluntly by Reformed theologian John Frame, who argues for an effort toward a "super-denomination" of evangelicals, undivided by "minor" matters such as baptism and church polity (John M. Frame, *Evangelical Reunion: Denominations and the Body of Christ* [Grand Rapids, Mich.: Baker, 1991]).

160 Wayne Grudem, *Systematic Theology: An Introduction to Biblical Doctrine* (Grand Rapids, Mich.: Zondervan, 1994), 967.

161 Ibid.

162 "Specifically, this would mean that Baptist churches would have to be willing to allow into membership those who had been baptized as infants and whose conviction of conscience, after careful consideration, is that their infant baptism was valid and should not be repeated. Of course, Baptist churches could be free to teach and to attempt to persuade prospective church members that they should be baptized as believers, but if some, after careful consideration, are simply not persuaded, it does not seem appropriate to make this a barrier to membership" (ibid., 982-983). Grudem follows this practice consistently, giving a suggested hymn for a believer's baptism at the end of his chapter on the subject, while suggesting that a hymn from a paedobaptist hymnal be chosen for the "baptism" of infants (ibid., 987).

163 Millard J. Erickson, *Christian Theology,* 2nd ed. (Grand Rapids, Mich.: Baker, 1998), 1114.

164 Ibid.

165 As one scholar has noted, Erickson's theological concerns seem to lie "with conservative, evangelical Christianity, seemingly without any denominational affiliation. Indeed the only locus that could be counted as evidence that Erickson was a Baptist was the brief chapter entitled, 'Initiatory Rite of the Church—Baptism.' His chapter on polity, for example, qualified its preference for congregationalism in two ways. First, it found no direct precept in the New Testament that required any polity. Rather, it derived its preference from the value of order, the priesthood of the believer, and the importance of each person to the body as a whole. Second, it admitted two exceptions: that a 'very large congregation' may require a representative or Presbyterian polity and that an ignorant or immature congregation may require that a pastor exercise greater

authority" (E. Jeffrey Mask, *At Liberty Under God: Toward a Baptist Ecclesiology* [Lanham, Md.: University Press of America, 1997], 23-24).

166 Hence the suggestions that the "denominational distinctives" were in the same category as the timing of the Rapture and other such questions of dispensational premillennial orthodoxy.

167 *The Fundamentals: A Testimony to the Truth,* 4 vols. (Los Angeles: Bible Institute of Los Angeles, 1917).

168 Note, for instance, the following reaction of fundamentalist John Roach Straton to the ecclesiology of Harry Emerson Fosdick: "Dr. Harry Emerson Fosdick, who still calls himself a Baptist, has been serving for several years as preacher at the First Presbyterian Church, in this city. In addition to rejecting other cardinal tenets of the Christian faith, Dr. Fosdick again and again has repudiated immersion as the only right and proper baptism, and in his so-called 'farewell' sermon at the First Presbyterian Church last Sunday, March 2nd, he used the following words: 'Why should things like baptism divide? If I had my way baptism would be altogether an individual affair. Any one who wanted to be immersed I would gladly immerse. Any one who wanted to be sprinkled I would gladly sprinkle. If anybody was a Quaker and had conscientious scruples against any ritual, I would gladly, without baptism, welcome him on confession of his faith. Why not?'" Straton believed Fosdick's cavalier attitude was more than denominational disloyalty, but that instead it was part of his larger rejection of the authority of Scripture (John Roach Straton, "Do True Believers Need to Keep At It?" *Religious Herald,* March 19, 1925, 3).

169 Lewis Sperry Chafer, *Major Bible Themes,* rev. John F. Walvoord (Grand Rapids, Mich.: Zondervan, 1974), 240.

170 As James D. G. Dunn argues, the baptismal teaching of Romans 6 is bound up with the Adam/Christ parallel in the preceding chapter. As such, Romans 6 deals with "epochal" issues of "a shift in the ages." Thus, "it is only possible to speak thus of the believer in the here and now because there is one who has in fact passed from one age and dominion to the other (vv 7-10) and because it is possible for the believer in the here and now to identify with that one (vv 3-5, 11)" (James D. G. Dunn, *Romans 1–8,* Word Biblical Commentary 38a [Dallas: Word, 1988], 307). Thomas Schreiner likewise sees an interweaving of inaugurated eschatology with the Pauline baptismal teaching in Romans 6. He writes that "Romans 6 teaches that believers are not free from the presence of sin, but they are free from its power, tyranny, mastery, and dominion. The already-not yet character of Paul's eschatology shows that believers have already been liberated from the mastery of sin, but that they have not yet reached the eschaton" (Thomas R. Schreiner, *Romans,* Baker Exegetical Commentary on the New Testament [Grand Rapids, Mich.: Baker, 2000], 6:317).

171 Darrell Bock distinguishes between the Passover meal, which Jesus will eat with His disciples in the Kingdom, and the Lord's Supper. He argues that the meal will commence in the Kingdom, in which "some sacrifices will be continued, but as a celebration or memorial, not as a sacrifice for sin," referencing Hebrews 8–10. Bock here seems on shaky ground, especially in light of the Hebrews passages, in resuscitating the older dispensationalist arguments for "memorial" sacrifices after the consummation. Bock does recognize, however, "that there is an element of parallelism between the Lord's Supper and this ultimate fulfillment. Just as the church is pictured in fellowship with its Lord at the Lord's table, so all believers will share that fellowship in a full physical presence at the consummation (1 Cor. 11:26)" (Darrell L. Bock, *Luke 9:51–24:53,* Baker Exegetical Commentary on the New Testament, 3b:1721-1722). Despite his problematic view of the sacrificial system, however, Bock does seem to be correct in his assertion that the Lukan narrative teaches that the regenerate community at the Lord's table is "to look backward and forward" to both the atonement and to "a greater meal yet to come" (ibid., 1729).

[172] Donald G. Bloesch, *The Reform of the Church* (Grand Rapids, Mich.: Eerdmans, 1970), 71.

[173] For a defense of believers' baptism against the charge that it reflects American individualism, see Paul K. Jewett, *Infant Baptism and the Covenant of Grace* (Grand Rapids, Mich.: Eerdmans, 1978), 221-226.

[174] R. B. C. Howell, *The Covenants* (Charleston: Southern Baptist Publication Society, 1855), 126.

[175] Commentator David Frum sums up the denominational politicization of the mainline churches in the 1970s by noting the deleterious effects of such political activism by churches which had "convinced themselves that they were losing adherents because their religion was too authoritarian, its doctrines too demanding, its moral edicts too strict, its ritual too formal, its ministers too aloof." Instead, Frum observes, "By virtue of the time he spends with the sick and the sad, even a very worldly minister acquires insight into the human soul unavailable to the comfortable and secure in his congregation. But it was an exceeding rare liberal Protestant or progressive Catholic minister who had anything to say about welfare or grapes or South Africa or nuclear weapons that his congregants had not already read in the *New York Times*. Why should they waste a Sunday morning listening to the same editorial twice?" (David Frum, *How We Got Here: The 70's—The Decade That Brought You Modern Life (For Better or Worse)* [New York: Basic, 2000], 150). This observation sums up the postwar evangelical theologians' fears about the politicization of the mainline.

[176] Thus Rauschenbusch was able to argue that the church is necessary for "the religious education of humanity" while the true realization of the Kingdom "awaits religion in the public life of humanity" (Rauschenbusch, *Theology for the Social Gospel*, 145).

[177] So argues persuasively Stephen L. Carter, *God's Name in Vain: The Wrongs and Rights of Religion in Politics* (New York: Basic, 2000), 107. This distaste for the church emerging within Protestant liberalism still exists. Note, for instance, the attempt of gadfly Episcopal Bishop John Shelby Spong to reconfigure a doctrine of the church without a commitment to theism (John Shelby Spong, *A New Christianity for a New World: Why Traditional Faith Is Dying and How a New Faith Is Being Born* [San Francisco: HarperCollins, 2001], 219-232).

[178] Thus, John Muether is right to find a "low view of the church" in movements that focus on finding "biblical blueprints" for economic policy and national defense without giving nearly so much attention to "biblical blueprints" for the church, a hermeneutical problem he correctly identifies both with theonomy and with leftist social activist Ronald Sider, since both seem to read the Old Testament simplistically as a politico-economic textbook (John R. Muether, "The Theonomic Attraction," in *Theonomy: A Reformed Critique*, ed. William S. Barker and W. Robert Godfrey [Grand Rapids, Mich.: Zondervan, 1990], 245-259).

[179] President Jimmy Carter, for instance, intended to cite 2 Chronicles 7:14 (KJV), "If my people, which are called by my name, shall humble themselves, and pray, and seek my face, and turn from their wicked ways; then will I hear from heaven, and will forgive their sin, and will heal their land," in his 1977 inaugural address. This changed when "after some second thoughts about how those who did not share my beliefs might misunderstand the words 'wicked' and 'sin,' I chose Micah 6:8" (Jimmy Carter, *Keeping Faith: Memoirs of a President* [New York: Bantam, 1982], 19).

[180] Stanley Hauerwas, "Christian Ethics in America: A Promising Obituary," in *Introduction to Christian Theology: Contemporary North American Perspectives*, ed. Roger A. Badham (Louisville: Westminster/John Knox, 1998), 106.

[181] Charles C. Haynes, "From Battleground to Common Ground: Religion in the Public Square of Twenty-first Century America," in *Religion in American Public Life: Living*

with Our Deepest Differences, ed. Azizah Y. al-Hibri, Jean Bethke Elshtain, and Charles C. Haynes (New York: W. W. Norton, 2001), 100.

[182] Ibid.

[183] Ibid.

[184] This would not end the debate over the public school system's relationship to Christianity. As recent debates have shown, the terms of the debate have shifted radically. Few evangelicals are calling for a return to state-sponsored religious instruction (though many, not only in the Christian right political movement but also in the mainstream of the evangelical subculture, called for just that in years past). The issues now are more often framed in terms of religious liberty for evangelical students who wish to exercise their rights in accordance with the free exercise clause of the United States Constitution.

[185] This is, of course, a complaint that Henry has indeed offered regarding the Christian right political movement, charging it with "the methodology of secular politics and of the secular media in the effort to lift secular politics to a new plateau" (Carl F. H. Henry, "Response," in *No Longer Exiles: The Religious New Right in American Politics,* ed. Michael Cromartie [Washington, D.C.: Ethics and Public Policy Center, 1993], 76). As noted before, it is not that Henry's critique here is baseless. The issue is, instead, whether this problem is limited to the Christian political right, or whether it extends to the evangelical movement *en masse.*

[186] Carter, *God's Name in Vain,* 57.

[187] Note, for instance, the research presented in Christian Smith, *Christian America? What Evangelicals Really Want* (Berkeley: University of California Press, 2000). Smith especially finds this true in terms of evangelical conviction on gender roles in contrast to evangelical practice. Thus, he argues, evangelicals may hold to a complementarian view of gender roles, but a "significant number of evangelicals admit that, although they believe in the headship of husbands theoretically, their daily experience reflects de facto an egalitarian model of marriage" (ibid., 181). This same thesis of "functional egalitarianism" is put forth in John P. Bartkowski, *Remaking the Godly Marriage: Gender Negotiation in Evangelical Families* (New Brunswick, N.J.: Rutgers University Press, 2001).

[188] Smith, *Christian America?* 57.

[189] Henry, *God, Revelation, and Authority,* 1:133.

[190] Ashley Woodiwiss, "Revising Our Pledges of Allegiance: From 'Christian America' to the Gospel of the Resurrection," *Touchstone,* September/October 1998, 31.

[191] Clowney, *Church,* 170.

[192] Ibid., 163-164.

[193] For a discussion of the influence of this doctrine in the Southern Presbyterian Church, see Morton Smith, "The Southern Tradition," in *Reformed Theology in America: A History of Its Modern Development,* ed. David F. Wells (Grand Rapids, Mich.: Eerdmans, 1985), 198-202.

[194] Robert Lewis Dabney, *Lectures in Systematic Theology* (St. Louis: Presbyterian Publishing Company of St. Louis, 1878; reprint, Grand Rapids, Mich.: Zondervan, 1972), 874.

[195] Robert Lewis Dabney, *Discussions: Evangelical and Theological,* 2 vols. (Richmond: Presbyterian Committee for Publication, 1891; reprint, London: Banner of Truth, 1967), 2:214.

[196] Ibid.

[197] Paul Harvey, "Race, Gender, and Southern Baptist Identity Politics" (address given to the Center for the Study of the Southern Baptist Convention, Louisville, February

27, 2001). For a fuller analysis of the racial issue among nineteenth-century Southern Baptists, see Paul Harvey, *Redeeming the South: Religious Cultures and Racial Identities Among Southern Baptists, 1845–1925* (Chapel Hill: University of North Carolina Press, 1997).

[198] For a defense of a contemporary application of the "spirituality of the church," see D. G. Hart's treatment of the issue in *"Christianity and Liberalism* in a Postliberal Age," *WTJ* 56 (1994): 329-344; "Christianity, Modern Liberalism and J. Gresham Machen," *Modern Age* 39 (1997): 234-245; and *Defending the Faith: J. Gresham Machen and the Crisis of Conservative Protestantism in Modern America* (Grand Rapids, Mich.: Baker, 1995), 133-170. The implications of the "spirituality of the church" argument still exist within evangelicalism, particularly in the Reformed communions. Note, for instance, the Presbyterian Church in America's denominational debate over whether the General Assembly could address the issue of women in combat because of the spirituality of the church (Paul R. Gilchrist, ed., *Supplement to the PCA Digest, 1994–1998: A Digest of the Minutes of the General Assembly of the Presbyterian Church in America* [Atlanta: Committee for Christian Education and Publications, 1998], 68).

[199] Stanley Hauerwas, "Why Clinton Is Incapable of Lying: A Christian Analysis," in *Judgment Day at the White House: A Critical Declaration Exploring Moral Issues and the Political Use and Abuse of Religion,* ed. Gabriel J. Fackre (Grand Rapids, Mich.: Eerdmans, 1999), 31.

[200] As one Old Testament theologian notes, it is the Mosaic code that exposes clearly in special revelation the horror with which God regards the sexual abuse of children (Paul R. House, *Old Testament Theology* [Downers Grove, Ill.: InterVarsity Press, 1998], 143).

[201] Gregory A. Wills, *Democratic Religion: Freedom, Authority, and Church Discipline in the Baptist South, 1785–1900* (New York: Oxford University Press, 1997), 87.

[202] For the relevance of church discipline in terms of the breakdown of the family in contemporary evangelical congregational life, see R. Albert Mohler, Jr., "Church Discipline: The Missing Mark," in *The Compromised Church: The Present Evangelical Crisis,* ed. John H. Armstrong (Wheaton, Ill.: Crossway, 1998), 174-175.

[203] It is at this point that the model of the church as Kingdom community differs sharply with a sociological definition of the church. Sociologist Rodney Stark, for instance, says the rapid growth of early Christian communities was the result of a "rational choice" on the part of individuals to become a part of a network of social support in troubled times (Rodney Stark, *The Rise of Christianity: A Sociologist Reconsiders History* [Princeton, N.J.: Princeton University Press, 1996]). Stark fails to note, however, that these "social networks" were not distinct from the theological nature of Christianity, but were in fact part and parcel of the early Christian doctrinal message.

[204] Darrell Bock rightly makes the case that Promise Keepers' attention to racial reconciliation represents "hints that such concerns are an element of the church's concern" and that such "impulses should be encouraged" (Darrell L. Bock, "Reconciliation: Witness to a Prepared and Redeemed People, Invitation to Real Community," in *Politics and Public Policy: A Christian Response,* ed. Timothy J. Demy and Gary P. Stewart [Grand Rapids, Mich.: Kregel, 2000], 255). Still, the failure to sustain the Promise Keepers "movement" in terms of broad influence much past the 1990s again points to the failure of parachurch activism apart from congregational confessionalism.

[205] See, for instance, Robert Nisbet, *The Quest for Community: A Study in the Ethics of Order and Freedom* (New York: Oxford University Press, 1953; reprint, San Francisco: Institute for Contemporary Studies, 1990); and Robert D. Putnam, *Bowling Alone: The Collapse and Revival of American Community* (New York: Simon & Schuster, 2000). This problem is compounded by developments in the American culture

of the late eighteenth and early nineteenth centuries. As one political theorist observes, "Americans claimed to belong to a nation composed not only of individuals but of individualists—or 'rugged individualists', in Herbert Hoover's later phrase. America was said to be not only a new nation but a new type of nation, and Americans a new type of people. America was, in short, a new kind of community—a non-communitarian community, as it were, populated by a new kind of individual" (Terence Ball, *Reappraising Political Theory* [Oxford: Clarendon, 1995], 274). Others would want to say that the move away from "rugged individualism" is actually a return to the Reformed Protestantism that represented the dominant influence on the early American experiment. See, for instance, Barry Alan Shain, *The Myth of American Individualism: The Protestant Origins of American Political Thought* (Princeton, N.J.: Princeton University Press, 1994). As another has noted, it was "mid-19th-century voices of men like Ralph Waldo Emerson and Walt Whitman, romantic American nationalists and prophets of the unconstrained self," not the founding generation, that were most responsible for an inordinate American individualism (Wilfred M. McClay, "Individualism and Its Discontents," *Virginia Quarterly Review* 77 [2001]: 396).

[206] As "civil society" theorist Don Eberly writes, "sustaining freedom requires preserving institutions that shape character (especially families and communities), real social and cultural authority, and a widespread acceptance of authority" (Don Eberly, "Introduction: The Moral and Intellectual Framework," in *Building a Healthy Culture: Strategies for an American Renaissance,* ed. Don Eberly [Grand Rapids, Mich.: Eerdmans, 2001], 11). Of the unique role of the church, evangelicals would certainly want to say more, but they surely would not want to say less.

[207] Marvin Olasky, *Compassionate Conservatism: What It Is, What It Does, and How It Can Transform America* (New York: Free Press, 2000), 157-161.

[208] "It is true that we brighten to tales of community, especially if the talk is soothing and doesn't demand very much from us," concedes one communitarian theorist. "But when discussion turns to institutions and the need to sustain authoritative institutions of all kinds—and here I include families and churches and schools as well as governing bodies—attention withers and a certain sourness sets in" (Jean Bethke Elshtain, *Augustine and the Limits of Politics* [Notre Dame, Ind.: University of Notre Dame Press, 1995], 2).

[209] George M. Marsden, "The Incoherent University," *Hedgehog Review* 2 (2000): 103-104.

[210] This is seen especially in the "unity" proposed by the Evangelicals and Catholics Together movement. The evangelicals define "unity" as another parachurch project. The Roman Catholics, however, define "unity" as a church—palpable, visible, and under the headship of Rome. For an analysis of this, see Russell D. Moore, "Of Sacraments and Sawdust: ECT, the Culture Wars, and the Quandary of Evangelical Identity," *Southern Baptist Journal of Theology* 5 (2001): 36-49.

[211] It is this lack of an ability to articulate an objective moral standard that unravels the communitarian project. See, for example, the devastating critique of theorists such as Amitai Etzioni in J. Budziszewski, "The Problem with Communitarianism," *First Things,* March 1995, 22-26.

[212] Carl F. H. Henry, "The Church in the World or the World in the Church? A Review Article," *JETS* 34 (1991): 382. Henry similarly devastates Hauerwas's claim to a distinction between the church and the world, when Hauerwas is unwilling to draw the distinction "between the faithful Church and the pseudo-church or apostate church" (ibid., 383). It would appear that Henry's critique of Hauerwas keeps in mind the similar problems with Rauschenbusch and the Social Gospel.

[213] Such that, for instance, the apostle Paul claims that "it is in the sight of God that we

have been speaking in Christ; and all for your upbuilding, beloved" (2 Cor. 12:19). The issue of apostolic biblical authority is directly correlated to the structuring of the life of the community. This is consistent with the canonical witness. It is the authority of revelation that shapes and defines the Old Testament community (Ex. 19:5-6; Deut. 27:9; 29:13). Likewise, the New Testament *ekklesia* is built on the authoritative revelation of the identity of Jesus as the Messiah (Matt. 16:13-19).

[214] Richard Rorty, "The Moral Purposes of the University: An Exchange," *Hedgehog Review* 2 (2000): 106-107.

[215] Ibid., 108.

[216] Robert H. Bork, *Slouching Towards Gomorrah: Modern Liberalism and American Decline* (New York: HarperCollins, 1996), 62.

[217] Stuart Hampshire, *Justice Is Conflict* (Princeton, N.J.: Princeton University Press, 2000), 83.

[218] Ibid.

[219] Paul Weyrich, "The Moral Minority," *Christianity Today,* September 6, 1999, 45.

[220] This means that a commitment to civil society generically, or to ecclesiology particularly, does not reduce the need for direct political engagement, a mistaken emphasis sometimes implied by civil society theorists. For a more balanced view, see Christopher Been, *The Necessity of Politics: Reclaiming American Public Life* (Chicago: University of Chicago Press, 1999).

[221] Thus William F. Buckley, Jr., rightly warns, "Our principal afflictions are the result of ideology backed by the power of government. It takes government to translate individual vices into universal afflictions. It was government that translated *Mein Kampf* into concentration camps" (William F. Buckley, Jr., *Let Us Talk of Many Things: The Collected Speeches* [New York: Random House, 2000], 107).

[222] As did some efforts at Puritan church/state alliances. For an analysis of this phenomenon, see Conrad Cherry, ed., *God's New Israel: Religious Interpretations of American Destiny,* rev. and exp. (Chapel Hill: University of North Carolina Press, 1998). For a theological interpretation of the conflict between the political theories of Puritan New England and that of dissenter Roger Williams, see A. J. Beitzinger, *A History of American Political Thought* (New York: Dodd, Mead, and Company, 1972), 51-60.

[223] Michael J. Scanlon convincingly argues that it was Augustine's recapitulation of Cyprian's understanding of the church as the Kingdom of Christ on earth that led to Charlemagne's appropriation of *The City of God* in the construction of the "Holy Roman Empire" and "the identification by medieval Christendom of the church with the kingdom of God" (Michael J. Scanlon, "Eschatology," in *Augustine Through the Ages: An Encyclopedia,* gen. ed. Allan D. Fitzgerald [Grand Rapids, Mich.: Eerdmans, 1999], 317).

[224] Maurice Hindus, *House Without a Roof: Russia After Forty-Three Years of Revolution* (Garden City, N.Y.: Doubleday, 1961), 118.

[225] Robert Kraynak then rightly condemns the "earlier mistakes when Christians forged close links between the churches and a specific political regime," of which he notes the Russian Orthodox embrace of the czar as head of the church, the Anglican view of divine right of kings, and the American Puritan attempt at a "deified America as a New Jerusalem." The church/state alliance of the Roman pontiff is conspicuously absent in the analysis offered by Kraynak, a Roman Catholic (Robert P. Kraynak, *Christian Faith and Modern Democracy: God and Politics in the Fallen World* [Notre Dame, Ind.: University of Notre Dame Press, 2001], 180).

[226] Henry, "The Church in the World or the World in the Church?" 383.

CHAPTER FIVE

1 Cited in Martin Marty, *Under God, Indivisible,* vol. 3 of *Modern American Religion* (Chicago: University of Chicago Press, 1996), 307.

2 For a discussion of these interpretations and debates, see Wendell Willis, ed., *The Kingdom of God in Twentieth-Century Interpretation* (Peabody, Mass.: Hendrickson, 1987).

3 Wolfhart Pannenberg, *Theology and the Kingdom of God,* ed. Richard John Neuhaus (Philadelphia: Westminster, 1969), 51.

4 Ibid.

5 Ibid., 52-53.

6 John Calvin, *The Bondage and Liberation of the Will: A Defense of the Orthodox Doctrine of Human Choice Against Pighius,* ed. A. N. S. Lane, trans. G. I. Davies (Grand Rapids, Mich.: Baker, 1996), 80.

7 Cited in Mark Gerson, "Reflections of a Neoconservative Disciple," in *The Neoconservative Imagination: Essays in Honor of Irving Kristol,* ed. Christopher DeMuth and William Kristol (Washington, D.C.: American Enterprise Institute, 1995), 167.

8 "We have a social gospel," Rauschenbusch proclaimed in the opening paragraph of his *magnum opus.* "We need a systematic theology large enough to match it and vital enough to back it" (Walter Rauschenbusch, *A Theology for the Social Gospel* [New York: Macmillan, 1917; reprint, Louisville: Westminster/John Knox, 1997], 1).

9 J. Gresham Machen, *Christianity and Liberalism* (New York: Macmillan, 1923; reprint, Grand Rapids, Mich.: Eerdmans, 2001), 152.

10 David Frum, *What's Right: The New Conservative Majority and the Remaking of America* (New York: Basic, 1996), 82.

11 Ramesh Ponnuru, "This We Must Do," *National Review,* January 22, 2001, 33.

12 Carl F. H. Henry, "Evangelicals: Out of the Closet but Going Nowhere?" *Christianity Today,* January 4, 1980, 18.

13 Cal Thomas and Ed Dobson, *Blinded by Might: Can the Religious Right Save America?* (Grand Rapids, Mich.: Zondervan, 1999), 22.

14 Antonin Scalia, "The Rule of Law as a Law of Rules," *University of Chicago Law Review* 56 (1989): 1179.

15 This can be seen, for instance, in the way in which libertarian conservatives and traditionalist conservatives are increasingly torn on the issue of the family. See, for instance, Jennifer Roback Morse's compelling argument that "free market" solutions to the questions of gender roles, institutionalized child care policy, and family definition are unworkable and harmful (Jennifer Roback Morse, *Love and Economics: Why the Laissez-Faire Family Doesn't Work* [Dallas: Spence, 2001]).

16 As David Weeks has observed, "Henry believes that the social gospel was based upon a truncated scriptural message. Utilizing the scientific methodologies of higher criticism, liberal social gospel theologians stripped away most of the Scripture and reduced the biblical message to the 'simple affirmation of "the fatherhood of God and the brotherhood of man" realized in the teachings of Jesus about the kingdom of God'" (David L. Weeks, "The Political Thought of Carl F. H. Henry" [Ph.D. diss., Loyola University of Chicago, 1991], 124).

17 Clark H. Pinnock, for example, compares the trajectory of contemporary evangelical theology with the trajectory of Fuller Theological Seminary. "Like the evangelical movement itself, I see Fuller beginning life with a sectarian, conservative and Reformed profile and evolving into a renewal component in the mainline denominations in a Barthian, neo-Reformed mode," Pinnock argues. He further asks, "Can there be any doubt at all what Henry's goals were? They had nothing to do with Pentecostalism or Methodism.

He wanted Fuller to be the flagship of the neo-Reformed, post-fundamentalist evangelical movement which was getting under way. I see Fuller Seminary in the light of Carl Henry, Paul Jewett, Edward Carnell, Gleason Archer, etc. These men were Reformed (often Baptist) theologians who wanted to expound a species of Calvinism which they decided to call evangelical and expound it in an intelligent manner which would give leadership to the growing post-fundamentalist movement in America" (Clark H. Pinnock, "Fuller Theological Seminary and the Nature of Evangelicalism," *CSR* 23 [1993]: 44-45).

18 Perhaps the preeminent proponent of a reconsidered evangelical epistemological model of revelation and authority is theologian Stanley Grenz. Grenz outlines his proposal most succinctly in Stanley J. Grenz, "Articulating the Christian Belief-Mosaic: Theological Method After the Demise of Foundationalism," in *Evangelical Futures: A Conversation on Theological Method*, ed. John G. Stackhouse, Jr. (Grand Rapids, Mich.: Baker, 2000), 107-138; Stanley J. Grenz, *Renewing the Center: Evangelical Theology in a Post-Theological Era* (Grand Rapids, Mich.: Baker, 2000), 184-248; and Stanley J. Grenz and John R. Franke, *Beyond Foundationalism: Shaping Theology in a Postmodern Context* (Louisville: Westminster/John Knox, 2001). The open theism proposal is articulated in, among other works, Clark H. Pinnock et al., *The Openness of God: A Biblical Challenge to the Traditional Understanding of God* (Downers Grove, Ill.: InterVarsity Press, 1994); John Sanders, *The God Who Risks: A Theology of Providence* (Downers Grove, Ill.: InterVarsity Press, 1998); and Clark H. Pinnock, *Most Moved Mover: A Theology of God's Openness* (Grand Rapids, Mich.: Baker, 2001).

19 Roger E. Olson, review of *Most Moved Mover: A Theology of God's Openness* by Clark H. Pinnock and *Searching for an Adequate God: A Dialogue Between Process and Free Will Theists* ed. by John B. Cobb, Jr., and Clark H. Pinnock, *Christian Century*, January 30–February 6, 2002, 37.

20 This is especially true in the open theism debate, in which classical theists have not simply restated the arguments of classical theism but have explored the biblical teachings on God's relationality, foreknowledge, sovereignty, and immutability. See, for instance, Millard J. Erickson, *God the Father Almighty: A Contemporary Exploration of the Divine Attributes* (Grand Rapids, Mich.: Baker, 1998); Bruce A. Ware, *God's Lesser Glory: The Diminished God of Open Theism* (Wheaton, Ill.: Crossway, 2000); and John Frame, *No Other God: A Response to Open Theism* (Phillipsburg, N.J.: Presbyterian & Reformed, 2001).

21 For instance, see Steve W. Lemke, "Evangelical Theology in the Twenty-First Century" (paper presented at the southwestern regional meeting of the Evangelical Theological Society, Fort Worth, Tex., April 7, 2000). "Like most coalitions, the evangelical coalition will break down, probably within the next ten years," Lemke predicts. "I do not know which issue or issues will drive this division—biblical inerrancy, the openness of God, the ordination of women—but I believe that a Neo-Evangelical Theological Society or a Really Neo-Evangelical Theological Society will come into existence soon."

22 For various perspectives on the debate over evangelical definitional boundaries, see R. Albert Mohler, Jr., "'Evangelical': What's in a Name?" in *The Coming Evangelical Crisis: Current Challenges to the Authority of Scripture and the Gospel*, ed. John H. Armstrong (Chicago: Moody, 1996), 29-44; Millard J. Erickson, *The Evangelical Left: Encountering Postconservative Theology* (Grand Rapids, Mich.: Baker, 1997); and Roger E. Olson, "Reforming Evangelical Theology," in *Evangelical Futures*, 201-208.

23 Henry, of course, maintained biblical inerrancy, but he dismissed the warning cries of Harold Lindsell and others, even noting that evangelical debates over inerrancies were an indulgence in "the luxury of internal conflict," thus diverting attention from the task of evangelical penetration of the larger culture (Carl F. H. Henry, *Confessions of a*

Theologian [Waco, Tex.: Word, 1986], 389). Perhaps if Henry had returned to his earlier critiques of the unworkable "penetration" of a Social Gospel bereft of biblical authority, he might have better understood the concerns of Lindsell and his cohorts.

[24] Damon Linker, "Richard Rorty: Liberal Absolutist," *Policy Review* 100 (April/May 2000): 81.

[25] This is usually of late posited in terms of some appeal to a natural law theory or the common *imago Dei*. See, for instance, J. Budziszewski, *Written on the Heart: The Case for Natural Law* (Downers Grove, Ill.: InterVarsity Press, 1997); and *The Revenge of Conscience: Politics and the Fall of Man* (Dallas: Spence, 2000); Robert P. George, *In Defense of Natural Law* (New York: Oxford University Press, 2001); and David L. Weeks, "The Uneasy Politics of Modern Evangelicalism," *CSR* 30 (2001): 403-418.

[26] Scott Hafemann, "Seminary, Subjectivity, and the Centrality of Scripture: Reflections on the Current Crisis in Evangelical Seminary Education," *JETS* 31 (1988): 140.

[27] Nicole points to E. S. Brightman's finite god hypothesis along with a denial of foreknowledge in L. D. McCabe, *Divine Nescience of Future Contingencies* (New York: Phillips & Hunt, 1882). "The emphasis upon human freedom is so strong that it more and more impairs the divine majesty," Nicole wrote. "Now, I am wholly aware that there are evangelical Arminians who do not for a moment sanction these things. But the weight of logic prevails in due time and historically those fruits have been developed" (Roger Nicole, in Carl F. H. Henry, "Feature Interview: The Debate Over Divine Election," *Christianity Today*, October 12, 1959, 6).

[28] Carl F. H. Henry, *The Protestant Dilemma: An Analysis of the Current Impasse in Theology* (Grand Rapids, Mich.: Eerdmans, 1949), 131.

[29] Thus, Rauschenbusch concludes, "He not only saved humanity; he saved God. He gave God his first chance of being loved and of escaping from the worst misunderstandings conceivable. The value of Christ's idea of the Fatherhood of God is realized only by contrast to the despotic ideas which it opposes and was meant to replace" (Rauschenbusch, *Theology for the Social Gospel*, 174-175).

[30] Clark H. Pinnock and Robert C. Brow, *Unbounded Love: A Good News Theology for the Twenty-first Century* (Downers Grove, Ill.: InterVarsity Press, 1994), 15-34.

[31] Rauschenbusch, *Theology for the Social Gospel*, 49.

[32] Gregory A. Boyd, *God at War: The Bible and Spiritual Conflict* (Downers Grove, Ill.: InterVarsity Press, 1997), 58.

[33] Sanders, *God Who Risks*, 36.

[34] Ibid., 300 n. 20.

[35] Diane Hochstedt Butler, "An Interview with Carl F. H. Henry," *TSF Bulletin*, March–April 1987, 18.

[36] Christopher A. Hall and John Sanders, *Does God Have a Future? A Debate on Divine Providence* (Grand Rapids, Mich.: Baker, 2003), 123.

[37] Ibid., 127.

[38] Ibid., 137-138.

[39] Pinnock explains, "Theologies seek root metaphors to help express their vision of God. Some make 'king' the key metaphor and generate a view of God in causal terms; others feature 'judge' and come up with a religious system of rights and duties. The open view is centered on God as a loving person and lifts up the personal relations God seeks to have with creaturely persons" (Pinnock, *Most Moved Mover*, 179).

[40] Ibid., 182.

[41] For a study of this trend within egalitarian evangelicalism, see Randy Stinson, "Our Mother Who Art in Heaven: A Brief Overview and Critique of Evangelical Feminists

and the Use of Feminine God-Language," *Journal for Biblical Manhood and Womanhood* 8 (2003): 20-33.

[42] See, for instance, Baptist theologian Molly T. Marshall, who ties a feminist-liberationist theology to a full-blown panentheism (Molly T. Marshall, *Joining the Dance: A Theology of the Spirit* [Valley Forge: Judson, 2003]).

[43] See the incisive critique of feminist revisions of the doctrine of God in Donald Bloesch, *The Battle for the Trinity: The Debate over Inclusive God-Language* (Grand Rapids, Mich.: Servant, 1985).

[44] Carl F. H. Henry, *God, Revelation, and Authority,* 6 vols. (Waco, Tex.: Word, 1976; reprint, Wheaton, Ill.: Crossway, 1999), 2:142.

[45] Thus, the early Clark Pinnock could argue, "My concern with Dr. [Daniel] Fuller's position is that the limited errancy stance can slide easily into an unlimited errancy stance. Just because the 'revelational/non-revelational' distinction is so fuzzy, he gives us a slope, not a platform. Until now he has confined his 'biblical errors' to the marginalia. May it always be so" (Clark H. Pinnock, "In Response to Dr. Daniel Fuller," *CSR* 2 [1973]: 335). This "slippery slope" is seen even in the theological project of the present-day Pinnock, who now bolsters his open theism argument by asserting that some biblical prophecies, including one made by Jesus, were simply mistaken (Pinnock, *Most Moved Mover,* 51). It is inconceivable that Pinnock could have made such a statement if he had not previously altered his view of Scripture toward a "limited inerrancy" position, along with a softening of the propositional nature of revealed truth. Just as Pinnock had warned Fuller of a "slippery slope" in the early 1970s, Pinnock's student Adrian Rogers warned him of a "slippery slope" in the mid-1980s (Adrian Rogers, "Response," in *The Proceedings of the Conference on Biblical Inerrancy* [Nashville: Broadman, 1987], 103-104).

[46] H. Richard Niebuhr, *The Kingdom of God in America* (New York: Harper & Row, 1937), 17-44.

[47] Richard N. Ostling, "America's Ever-Changing Religious Landscape," in *What's God Got to Do With the American Experiment?* ed. E. J. Dionne, Jr., and John J. DiIulio, Jr. (Washington, D.C.: Brookings Institution Press, 2000), 24.

[48] Carl F. H. Henry, *Toward a Recovery of Christian Belief* (Wheaton, Ill.: Crossway, 1990), 49.

[49] The frustration with the loss of evangelical identity can be seen in Millard Erickson's assessment of reformist evangelicalism. "It does not yet appear that these theologians have moved so far as to surrender the right to be called evangelicals," Erickson writes. "But such movement cannot be unlimited" (Erickson, *The Evangelical Left,* 147).

[50] Gregory A. Boyd and Paul R. Eddy, *Across the Spectrum: Issues in Evangelical Theology* (Grand Rapids, Mich.: Baker, 2002).

BIBLIOGRAPHY

BOOKS

Ahlers, Rolf. *The Barmen Theological Declaration of 1934: The Archaeology of a Confessional Text*. Lewiston, N.Y.: Edwin Mellen, 1986.

Ahlstrom, Sydney E. *A Religious History of the American People*. New Haven, Conn.: Yale University Press, 1972.

Allis, Oswald T. *Prophecy and the Church*. Philadelphia: Presbyterian & Reformed, 1945.

Armitage, Thomas. *A History of the Baptists Tracked by Their Vital Principles and Practices from the Time of Our Lord and Saviour Jesus Christ to the Present*. New York: Bryan, Taylor, 1893.

Aukerman, Dale. *Reckoning with Apocalypse: Terminal Politics and Christian Hope*. New York: Crossroad, 1993.

Aulén, Gustaf. *Christus Victor: An Historical Study of the Three Main Types of the Idea of the Atonement*. Translated by A. G. Hebert. New York: Macmillan, 1969.

Bahnsen, Greg L. *No Other Standard: Theonomy and Its Critics*. Tyler, Tex.: Institute for Christian Economics, 1991.

Ball, Terence. *Reappraising Political Theory*. Oxford: Clarendon, 1995.

Balmer, Randall. *Blessed Assurance: A History of Evangelicalism in America*. Boston: Beacon, 1999.

Bandow, Doug. *Beyond Good Intentions: A Biblical View of Politics*. Wheaton, Ill.: Crossway, 1988.

Barber, Benjamin R. *The Truth of Power: Intellectual Affairs in the Clinton White House*. New York: Norton, 2001.

Barker, William S., and W. Robert Godfrey, eds. *Theonomy: A Reformed Critique*. Grand Rapids, Mich.: Zondervan, 1990.

Barkley, Michael B., ed. *Environmental Stewardship in the Judeo-Christian Tradition: Jewish, Catholic, and Protestant Wisdom on the Environment*. Grand Rapids, Mich.: Acton Institute for the Study of Religion and Liberty, 2000.

Barnes, Gilbert Hobbs. *The Anti-Slavery Impulse, 1830–1844*. New York: Harcourt, Brace & World, 1964.

Barnette, Henlee H. *Introducing Christian Ethics*. Nashville: Broadman, 1961.

Barron, Bruce. *Heaven on Earth? The Social and Political Agendas of Dominion Theology*. Grand Rapids, Mich.: Zondervan, 1992.

Barth, Markus. *Ephesians 1–3*. The Anchor Bible, vol. 34. Edited by William Foxwell Albright and David Noel Freedman. Garden City, N.Y.: Doubleday, 1974.

Bartkowski, John P. *Remaking the Godly Marriage: Gender Negotiation in Evangelical Families*. New Brunswick, N.J.: Rutgers University Press, 2001.

Bateman, Herbert W. IV, ed. *Three Central Issues in Contemporary Dispensationalism: A Comparison of Traditional and Progressive Views*. Grand Rapids, Mich.: Kregel, 1989.

Bauman, Michael, and David Hall, eds. *God and Caesar: Selected Essays from the 1993 Evangelical Theological Society's Convention at Washington, D.C.* Camp Hill, Pa.: Christian Publications, 1994.

Beale, Gregory K. *The Book of Revelation: A Commentary on the Greek Text*. Grand Rapids, Mich.: Eerdmans, 1999.

Been, Christopher. *The Necessity of Politics: Reclaiming American Public Life*. Chicago: University of Chicago Press, 1999.

Beitzinger, A. J. *A History of American Political Thought*. New York: Dodd, Mead, 1972.

Bell, Daniel. *The End of Ideology: On the Exhaustion of Political Ideas in the Fifties*. Cambridge, Mass.: Harvard University Press, 1988.

Bellah, Robert N., Richard Madsen, William M. Sullivan, Ann Swindler, and Steven M. Tipton. *Habits of the Heart: Individualism and Commitment in American Life*. Berkeley: University of California Press, 1985.

Berkhof, Louis. *The Kingdom of God*. Grand Rapids, Mich.: Eerdmans, 1951.

———. *Systematic Theology*. Grand Rapids, Mich.: Eerdmans, 1941; reprint, Edinburgh: Banner of Truth, 1958.

Berlin, Isaiah. *The Crooked Timber of Humanity: Chapters in the History of Ideas*. Edited by Henry Hardy. Princeton, N.J.: Princeton University Press, 1959; reprint, Princeton, N.J.: Princeton University Press, 1990.

Berns, Walter. *Making Patriots*. Chicago: University of Chicago Press, 2001.

Berry, Wendell. *Sex, Economy, Freedom, and Community*. New York: Pantheon, 1992.

Beyerhaus, Peter P. J. *God's Kingdom and the Utopian Error: Discerning the Biblical Kingdom of God from Its Political Counterfeits*. Westchester, Ill.: Crossway, 1992.

Blackston, W. E. *Jesus Is Coming*. New York: Revell, 1908.

Blaising, Craig A., and Darrell L. Bock. *Progressive Dispensationalism*. Grand Rapids, Mich.: Baker, 1993.

Blaising, Craig A., and Darrell L. Bock, eds. *Dispensationalism, Israel, and the Church: The Search for Definition*. Grand Rapids, Mich.: Zondervan, 1992.

Bloesch, Donald. *The Battle for the Trinity: The Debate over Inclusive God-Language*. Ann Arbor, Mich.: Servant, 1985.

———. *Essentials of Evangelical Theology*. 2 vols. San Francisco: HarperCollins, 1978.

———. *The Evangelical Renaissance*. Grand Rapids, Mich.: Eerdmans, 1973.

———. *The Future of Evangelical Christianity: A Call for Unity amid Diversity*. Garden City, N.Y.: Doubleday, 1983.

———. *The Reform of the Church*. Grand Rapids, Mich.: Eerdmans, 1970.

Bock, Darrell L. *Luke*. 2 vols. Baker Exegetical Commentary on the New Testament. Grand Rapids, Mich.: Baker, 1996.

Bock, Darrell L., ed. *Three Views on the Millennium and Beyond.* Grand Rapids, Mich.: Zondervan, 1999.

Bolt, John. *A Free Church, A Holy Nation: Abraham Kuyper's American Public Theology.* Grand Rapids, Mich.: Eerdmans, 2001.

Borg, Marcus J. *Conflict, Holiness, and Politics in the Teachings of Jesus.* Harrisburg, Pa.: Trinity Press International, 1998.

Bork, Robert H. *Slouching Towards Gomorrah: Modern Liberalism and American Decline.* New York: HarperCollins, 1996.

Bourne, Peter G. *Jimmy Carter: A Comprehensive Biography from Plains to Postpresidency.* New York: Scribner, 1997.

Boxx, T. William, and Gary M. Quinlivan, eds. *Public Morality, Civic Virtue, and the Problem of Modern Liberalism.* Grand Rapids, Mich.: Eerdmans, 2000.

———. *Toward the Renewal of Civilization: Political Order and Culture.* Grand Rapids, Mich.: Eerdmans, 1998.

Boyd, Gregory A. *God at War: The Bible and Spiritual Conflict.* Downers Grove, Ill.: InterVarsity Press, 1997.

———. *Satan and the Problem of Evil: Constructing a Trinitarian Warfare Theodicy.* Downers Grove, Ill.: InterVarsity Press, 2001.

Boyd, Gregory A., and Paul R. Eddy, *Across the Spectrum: Issues in Evangelical Theology.* Grand Rapids, Mich.: Baker, 2002.

Boyer, Paul. *When Time Shall Be No More: Prophecy Belief in Modern American Culture.* Cambridge: Belknap, 1992.

Brower, Kent E., and Mark W. Elliott, eds. *Eschatology in Bible and Theology: Evangelical Essays at the Dawn of a New Millennium.* Downers Grove, Ill.: InterVarsity Press, 1997.

Bruce, F. F. *The Time Is Fulfilled: Five Aspects of the Fulfillment of the Old Testament in the New.* Reprint, Grand Rapids, Mich.: Eerdmans, 1995.

Brueggemann, Walter. *Theology of the Old Testament.* Minneapolis: Fortress, 1997.

Buchanan, Patrick J. *Conservative Votes, Liberal Victories: Why the Right Has Failed.* New York: Quadrangle, 1975.

Buckley, William F., Jr. *Let Us Talk of Many Things: The Collected Speeches.* New York: Random House, 2000.

Budde, Michael L., and Robert W. Brimlow, eds. *The Church as Counterculture.* New York: State University of New York Press, 2000.

Budziszewski, J. *The Revenge of Conscience: Politics and the Fall of Man.* Dallas: Spence, 1999.

———. *Written on the Heart: The Case for Natural Law.* Downers Grove, Ill.: InterVarsity Press, 1997.

Bush, George W. *A Charge to Keep.* New York: William Morrow, 1999.

Caird, G. B. *New Testament Theology.* Edited by L. D. Hurst. New York: Oxford University Press, 1994.

Calvin, John. *Institutes of the Christian Religion.* Vol. 2. Edited by John T. McNeill. Translated by Ford Lewis Battles. Philadelphia: Westminster, 1960.

———. *Treatises Against the Anabaptists and Against the Libertines.* Translated by Benjamin Wirt Farley. Grand Rapids, Mich.: Baker, 1982.

Carnell, Edward John. *The Case for Orthodox Theology*. Philadelphia: Westminster, 1959.

Carpenter, Joel A. *Revive Us Again: The Reawakening of American Fundamentalism*. New York: Oxford University Press, 1997.

Carpenter, Joel A., ed. *The Fundamentalist-Modernist Conflict: Opposing Views on Three Major Issues*. New York: Garland, 1988.

Carroll, James. *Constantine's Sword: The Church and the Jews*. Boston: Houghton Mifflin, 2001.

Carson, D. A. *The Gagging of God: Christianity Confronts Pluralism*. Grand Rapids, Mich.: Zondervan, 1996.

Carter, Jimmy. *Keeping Faith: Memoirs of a President*. New York: Bantam, 1982.

———. *Why Not the Best?* Nashville: Broadman, 1975.

Carter, Stephen L. *God's Name in Vain: The Wrongs and Rights of Religion in Politics*. New York: Basic, 2000.

Cerillo, Augustus, Jr., and Murray W. Dempster. *Salt and Light: Evangelical Political Thought in Modern America*. Grand Rapids, Mich.: Baker, 1989.

Chafer, Lewis Sperry. *Dispensationalism*. Dallas: Dallas Seminary Press, 1936.

———. *The Kingdom in History and Prophecy*. Philadelphia: Sunday School Times, 1922.

———. *Major Bible Themes*. Revised by John F. Walvoord. Grand Rapids, Mich.: Zondervan, 1974.

———. *Systematic Theology*. 8 vols. Dallas: Dallas Seminary Press, 1947.

———. *True Evangelism, or Winning Souls by Prayer*. New York: Gospel, 1911.

Cherry, Conrad, ed. *God's New Israel: Religious Interpretations of American Destiny*. Rev. and exp. Chapel Hill: University of North Carolina Press, 1998.

Childs, Brevard S. *Old Testament Theology in a Canonical Context*. Philadelphia: Fortress, 1985.

Chilton, David. *Paradise Restored: A Biblical Theology of Dominion*. Tyler, Tex.: Dominion Press, 1985.

Clapp, Rodney. *Border Crossings: Christian Trespasses on Popular Culture and Public Affairs*. Grand Rapids, Mich.: Baker, 2000.

———. *A Peculiar People: The Church as Culture in a Post-Christian Society*. Downers Grove, Ill.: InterVarsity Press, 1996.

Clouse, Robert G. *The Cross and the Flag*. Carol Stream, Ill.: Creation House, 1972.

Clouse, Robert G., Richard V. Pierard, and Edwin M. Yamauchi. *Two Kingdoms: The Church and Culture Through the Ages*. Chicago: Moody, 1993.

Clowney, Edmund P. *Another Foundation: The Presbyterian Confessional Crisis*. Philadelphia: Presbyterian & Reformed, 1965.

———. *The Church*. Downers Grove, Ill.: InterVarsity Press, 1995.

Colson, Charles. *Born Again*. Old Tappan, N.J.: Chosen, 1976.

Conant, Judson E. *The Growing Menace of the "Social Gospel."* Chicago: Bible Institute Colportage, 1937.

Conyers, A. J. *The Eclipse of Heaven: Rediscovering the Hope of a World Beyond*. Downers Grove, Ill.: InterVarsity Press, 1992.

Cox, William E. *An Examination of Dispensationalism.* Phillipsburg, N.J.: Presbyterian & Reformed, 1963.

Crapanzano, Vincent. *Serving the Word: Literalism in America from the Pulpit to the Bench.* New York: New Press, 2000.

Cromartie, Michael, ed. *Caesar's Coin Revisited: Christians and the Limits of Government.* Grand Rapids, Mich.: Eerdmans, 1996.

Crutchfield, Larry. *The Origins of Dispensationalism.* Lanham, Md.: University Press of America, 1992.

Cullmann, Oscar. *Christ and Time: The Primitive Christian Conception of Time and History.* Translated by Floyd V. Filson. Philadelphia: Westminster, 1950.

———. *The Christology of the New Testament.* Rev. ed. Translated by Shirley C. Guthrie and Charles A. M. Hall. Philadelphia: Westminster, 1963.

———. *Salvation in History.* Translated by S. G. Sowers. London: SCM, 1967.

Curtis, Richard K. *They Called Him Mister Moody.* Garden City, N.Y.: Doubleday, 1962.

Dabney, Robert Lewis. *Discussions: Evangelical and Theological.* Vol. 2. Richmond: Presbyterian Committee for Publication, 1891; reprint, London: Banner of Truth, 1967.

———. *Lectures in Systematic Theology.* St. Louis: Presbyterian Publishing Company of St. Louis, 1878; reprint, Grand Rapids, Mich.: Zondervan, 1972.

D'Antonio, Michael D. *Fall From Grace: The Failed Crusade of the Christian Right.* New Brunswick, N.J.: Rutgers University Press, 1992.

Davis, John Jefferson. *Evangelical Ethics: Issues Facing the Church Today.* 2nd ed. Phillipsburg, N.J.: Presbyterian & Reformed, 1993.

———. *Foundations of Evangelical Theology.* Grand Rapids, Mich.: Baker, 1984.

———. *The Victory of Christ's Kingdom: An Introduction to Postmillennialism.* Moscow, Idaho: Canon, 1996.

Dayton, Donald W. *Discovering an Evangelical Heritage.* Peabody, Mass.: Hendrickson, 1976.

Dayton, Donald W., and Robert K. Johnston, eds. *The Variety of American Evangelicalism.* Downers Grove, Ill.: InterVarsity Press, 1991.

DeMar, Gary. *Last Days Madness: Obsessions of the Modern Church.* Atlanta: American Vision, 1994.

Demarest, Bruce. *The Cross and Salvation.* Wheaton, Ill.: Crossway, 1997.

Diamond, Sara. *Not by Politics Alone: The Enduring Influence of the Christian Right.* New York: Guilford, 1998.

Dionne, E. J., Jr., and John J. DiIulio, Jr., eds. *What's God Got to Do with the American Experiment?* Washington, D.C.: Brookings Institution Press, 2000.

Dorrien, Gary J. *Reconstructing the Common Ground: Theology and the Social Order.* Maryknoll, N.Y.: Orbis, 1990.

———. *The Remaking of Evangelical Theology.* Louisville: Westminster/John Knox, 1998.

Dunn, Charles W. *American Political Theology.* New York: Praeger, 1984.

Dunn, James D. G. *Romans 1–8.* Word Biblical Commentary, vol. 38a. Dallas: Word, 1988.

Eberly, Don. *Building a Healthy Culture: Strategies for an American Renaissance*. Grand Rapids, Mich.: Eerdmans, 2001.

Edwards, David L. *Christianity: The First Two Thousand Years*. Maryknoll, N.Y.: Orbis, 1997.

Eichrodt, Walter. *Theology of the Old Testament*. Vol. 1. Translated by J. A. Baker. Philadelphia: Westminster, 1961.

Eidsmoe, John. *God and Caesar: Biblical Faith and Political Action*. Westchester, Ill.: Crossway, 1984.

Ellis, Richard J. *The Dark Side of the Left: Illiberal Egalitarianism in America*. Lawrence: University Press of Kansas, 1998.

Elshtain, Jean Bethke. *Augustine and the Limits of Politics*. Notre Dame, Ind.: University of Notre Dame Press, 1995.

———. *Democracy on Trial*. New York: Basic, 1995.

Erickson, Millard J. *A Basic Guide to Eschatology: Making Sense of the Millennium*. Grand Rapids, Mich.: Baker, 1998.

———. *Christian Theology*. 2nd ed. Grand Rapids, Mich.: Baker, 1998.

———. *The Evangelical Left: Encountering Postconservative Evangelical Theology*. Grand Rapids, Mich.: Baker, 1997.

———. *The Evangelical Mind and Heart: Perspectives on Theological and Practical Issues*. Grand Rapids, Mich.: Baker, 1993.

———. *The New Evangelical Theology*. Westwood, N.J.: Revell, 1968.

———. *Postmodernizing the Faith: Evangelical Responses to the Challenge of Postmodernism*. Grand Rapids, Mich.: Baker, 1998.

———. *Where Is Theology Going? Issues and Perspectives on the Future of Theology*. Grand Rapids, Mich.: Baker, 1994.

Evans, Christopher H., ed. *The Social Gospel Today*. Louisville: Westminster/John Knox, 2001.

Fackre, Gabriel. *The Promise of Reinhold Niebuhr*. Rev. ed. Lanham, Md.: University Press of America, 1994.

Falwell, Jerry. *Listen, America!* Garden City, N.Y.: Doubleday, 1980.

Farrow, Douglas. *Ascension and Ecclesia: On the Significance of the Doctrine of the Ascension for Ecclesiology and Christian Cosmology*. Grand Rapids, Mich.: Eerdmans, 1999.

Feinberg, Charles L. *Millennialism: The Two Major Views*. Chicago: Moody, 1980.

Feinberg, John S., ed. *Continuity and Discontinuity*. Westchester, Ill.: Crossway, 1988.

Feinberg, John S., and Paul D. Feinberg. *Ethics for a Brave New World*. Wheaton, Ill.: Crossway, 1993.

Ferguson, Sinclair B. *The Holy Spirit: Contours of Christian Theology*. Downers Grove, Ill.: InterVarsity Press, 1996.

Fowler, Robert Booth. *New Communitarian Thinking: Virtues, Institutions, and Communities*. Edited by Amitai Etzioni. Charlottesville: University of Virginia Press, 1995.

———. *A New Engagement: Evangelical Political Thought, 1966–1976*. Grand Rapids, Mich.: Eerdmans, 1982.

Frame, John M. *Evangelical Reunion: Denominations and the Body of Christ.* Grand Rapids, Mich.: Baker, 1991.

Frank, Douglas W. *Less than Conquerors: How Evangelicals Entered the Twentieth Century.* Grand Rapids, Mich.: Eerdmans, 1986.

Frum, David. *How We Got Here: The Seventies—The Decade That Brought You Modern Life (For Better or Worse).* New York: Basic, 2000.

Fuller, Daniel P. *Gospel and Law: Contrast or Continuum?* Pasadena, Calif.: Fuller Seminary Press, 1990.

The Fundamentals: A Testimony to the Truth. 4 vols. Los Angeles: Bible Institute of Los Angeles, 1917.

Funk, Robert W. *Honest to Jesus: Jesus for a New Millennium.* San Francisco: HarperCollins, 1996.

Gaebelein, A. C. *The Harmony of the Prophetic Word.* New York: Our Hope, 1907.

Gaffin, Richard B., Jr. *The Centrality of the Resurrection: A Study in Paul's Soteriology.* Grand Rapids, Mich.: Baker, 1978.

———. *Perspectives on Pentecost: New Testament Teaching on the Gifts of the Holy Spirit.* Phillipsburg, N.J.: Presbyterian & Reformed, 1979.

———. *Resurrection and Redemption: A Study in Paul's Soteriology.* Phillipsburg, N.J.: Presbyterian & Reformed, 1987.

Gasper, Louis. *The Fundamentalist Movement, 1930–1956.* Grand Rapids, Mich.: Baker, 1981.

Gauchet, Marcel, and Charles Taylor. *Disenchantment of the World: A Political History of Religion.* Translated by Oscar Burge. Princeton, N.J.: Princeton University Press, 1997.

George, Robert P. *In Defense of Natural Law.* New York: Oxford University Press, 2001.

Gerstner, John. *Wrongly Dividing the Word of Truth: A Critique of Dispensationalism.* 2nd ed. Edited by Don Kistler. Moran, Pa.: Soli Deo Gloria, 2000.

Gilchrist, Paul R., ed. *Supplement to the PCA Digest, 1994–1998: A Digest of the Minutes of the General Assembly of the Presbyterian Church in America.* Atlanta: Committee for Christian Education and Publications, 1998.

Gore, Albert, Jr. *Earth in the Balance: Ecology and the Human Spirit.* New York: Penguin, 1992.

Green, Joel B., and Mark D. Baker. *Recovering the Scandal of the Cross: Atonement in New Testament and Contemporary Contexts.* Downers Grove, Ill.: InterVarsity Press, 2000.

Green, John C., James L. Guth, Corwin E. Smidt, and Lyman A. Kellstedt, eds. *Religion and the Culture Wars: Dispatches from the Front.* Lanham, Md.: Rowman & Littlefield, 1996.

Gregor, A. James. *The Faces of Janus: Marxism and Fascism in the Twentieth Century.* New Haven, Conn.: Yale University Press, 2000.

Grenz, Stanley J. *Created for Community.* 2nd ed. Grand Rapids, Mich.: Baker, 1998.

———. *Isaac Backus—Puritan and Baptist: His Place in History, His Thought, and Their Implications for Modern Baptist Theology.* Macon, Ga.: Mercer University Press, 1983.

————. *The Millennial Maze: Sorting Out Evangelical Options.* Downers Grove, Ill.: InterVarsity Press, 1992.

————. *Renewing the Center: Evangelical Theology in a Post-Theological Era.* Grand Rapids, Mich.: Baker, 2000.

————. *Revisioning Evangelical Theology: A Fresh Agenda for the Twenty-first Century.* Downers Grove, Ill.: InterVarsity Press, 1993.

————. *The Social God and the Relational Self: A Trinitarian Theology of the Imago Dei.* Louisville: Westminster/John Knox, 2001.

————. *Theology for the Community of God.* Grand Rapids, Mich.: Eerdmans, 2000.

Grenz, Stanley J., and John R. Franke. *Beyond Foundationalism: Shaping Theology in a Postmodern Context.* Louisville: Westminster/John Knox, 2001.

Grenz, Stanley J., and Roger E. Olson. *Twentieth-Century Theology: God and the World in a Transitional Age.* Downers Grove, Ill.: InterVarsity Press, 1992.

Groothuis, Douglas. *Truth Decay: Defending Christianity Against the Challenges of Postmodernism.* Downers Grove, Ill.: InterVarsity Press, 2000.

Grounds, Vernon C. *Revolution and the Christian Faith.* Philadelphia: J. B. Lippincott, 1971.

Grudem, Wayne A., ed. *Are Miraculous Gifts for Today? Four Views.* Grand Rapids, Mich.: Zondervan, 1996.

————. *Systematic Theology.* Grand Rapids, Mich.: Zondervan, 1994.

Gundry, Robert H. *The Church and the Tribulation.* Grand Rapids, Mich.: Zondervan, 1973.

————. *First the Antichrist.* Grand Rapids, Mich.: Baker, 1997.

Gushee, David P. *Christians and Politics Beyond the Culture Wars: An Agenda for Engagement.* Grand Rapids, Mich.: Baker, 2000.

Gutierrez, Gustavo. *A Theology of Liberation: History, Politics, and Salvation.* Maryknoll, N.Y.: Orbis, 1973.

Hagopian, David G., ed. *Back to Basics: Rediscovering the Richness of the Reformed Faith.* Phillipsburg, N.J.: Presbyterian & Reformed, 1996.

Hammond, Phillip E. *The Protestant Presence in Twentieth-Century America: Religion and Political Culture.* Albany: State University of New York Press, 1992.

Hampshire, Stuart. *Justice Is Conflict.* Princeton, N.J.: Princeton University Press, 2000.

Handy, Robert T. *A Christian America: Protestant Hopes and Historical Realities.* 2nd ed., rev. and enlarged. New York: Oxford University Press, 1984.

Hardt, Michael, and Antonio Negri. *Empire.* Cambridge, Mass.: Harvard University Press, 2001.

Hart, D. G. *Defending the Faith: J. Gresham Machen and the Crisis of Conservative Protestantism in Modern America.* Grand Rapids, Mich.: Baker, 1995.

Hart, D. G., ed. *Reckoning with the Past: Historical Essays on American Evangelicalism from the Institute for the Study of American Evangelicals.* Grand Rapids, Mich.: Baker, 1995.

Harvey, Paul. *Redeeming the South: Religious Cultures and Racial Identities Among Southern Baptists, 1845–1925.* Chapel Hill: University of North Carolina Press, 1997.

Hauerwas, Stanley. *After Christendom.* Nashville: Abingdon, 1999.

———. *Against the Nations*. Minneapolis: Winston, 1985.

———. *Christian Existence Today: Essays on Church, World, and Living in Between*. Grand Rapids, Mich.: Baker, 1988.

———. *A Community of Character: Toward a Constructive Christian Social Ethic*. Notre Dame, Ind.: University of Notre Dame Press, 1981.

———. *Dispatches from the Front: Theological Engagements with the Secular*. Durham, N.C.: Duke University Press, 1994.

———. *In Good Company: The Church as Polis*. Notre Dame, Ind.: University of Notre Dame Press, 1995.

———. *Unleashing the Scripture: Freeing the Bible from Captivity to America*. Nashville: Abingdon, 1993.

Hauerwas, Stanley, and William H. Willimon. *Resident Aliens: Life in the Christian Colony*. Nashville: Abingdon, 1989.

Hegeman, David Bruce. *Plowing in Hope: Toward a Biblical Theology of Culture*. Moscow, Idaho: Canon, 1999.

Henry, Carl F. H. *Aspects of Christian Social Ethics*. Grand Rapids, Mich.: Eerdmans, 1964.

———. *Christian Countermoves in a Decadent Culture*. Portland, Ore.: Multnomah, 1986.

———. *The Christian Mindset in a Secular Society*. Portland, Ore.: Multnomah, 1984.

———. *Christian Personal Ethics*. Grand Rapids, Mich.: Eerdmans, 1957.

———. *Confessions of a Theologian*. Waco, Tex.: Word, 1986.

———. *Conversations with Carl Henry: Christianity for Today*. Lewiston, N.Y.: Edwin Mellen Press, 1986.

———. *Evangelicals at the Brink of Crisis*. Waco, Tex.: Word, 1967.

———. *Evangelicals in Search of Identity*. Waco, Tex.: Word, 1976.

———. *Faith at the Frontiers*. Chicago: Moody, 1969.

———. *God, Revelation, and Authority*. 6 vols. Waco, Tex.: Word, 1976–1983; reprint, Wheaton, Ill.: Crossway, 1999.

———. *The God Who Shows Himself*. Waco, Tex.: Word, 1966.

———. *Gods of This Age or God of the Ages?* Nashville: Broadman & Holman, 1994.

———. *Has Democracy Had Its Day?* Nashville: ERLC Publications, 1996.

———. *A Plea for Evangelical Demonstration*. Grand Rapids, Mich.: Baker, 1971.

———. *The Protestant Dilemma: An Analysis of the Current Impasse in Theology*. Grand Rapids, Mich.: Eerdmans, 1949.

———. *Remaking the Modern Mind*. Grand Rapids, Mich.: Eerdmans, 1946.

———. *Twilight of a Great Civilization: The Drift Toward Neo-Paganism*. Westchester, Ill.: Crossway, 1988.

———. *The Uneasy Conscience of Modern Fundamentalism*. Grand Rapids, Mich.: Eerdmans, 1947.

Henry, Carl F. H., ed. *Prophecy in the Making*. Carol Stream, Ill.: Creation House, 1971.

Hindus, Maurice. *House Without a Roof: Russia After Forty-Three Years of Revolution*. Garden City, N.Y.: Doubleday, 1961.

Hoch, Carl B. *All Things New: The Significance of Newness for Biblical Theology*. Grand Rapids, Mich.: Baker, 1995.

Hodge, Charles. *A Commentary on Romans*. Philadelphia: William S. & Alfred Martien, 1864; reprint, Edinburgh: Banner of Truth, 1986.

———. *Systematic Theology*. 3 vols. New York: Scribner, 1873; reprint, Grand Rapids, Mich.: Eerdmans, 1995.

Hodgson, Godfrey. *The World Turned Right Side Up: A History of the Conservative Ascendancy in America*. Boston: Houghton-Mifflin, 1996.

Hoekema, Anthony. *The Bible and the Future*. Grand Rapids, Mich.: Eerdmans, 1979.

———. *Created in God's Image*. Grand Rapids, Mich.: Eerdmans, 1986.

Hofmann, Hans. *The Theology of Reinhold Niebuhr*. Translated by Louise Pettibone Smith. New York: Charles Scribner's Sons, 1956.

Hofstadter, Richard. *Anti-Intellectualism in American Life*. New York: Alfred A. Knopf, 1964.

Hollinger, Dennis P. *Individualism and Social Ethics: An Evangelical Syncretism*. Lanham, Md.: University Press of America, 1983.

House, H. Wayne, ed. *The Christian and American Law: Christianity's Impact on America's Founding Documents and Future Direction*. Grand Rapids, Mich.: Kregel, 1998.

House, H. Wayne, and Thomas Ice. *Dominion Theology: Blessing or Curse?* Portland, Ore.: Multnomah, 1988.

House, Paul R. *Old Testament Theology*. Downers Grove, Ill.: InterVarsity Press, 1998.

Howell, R. B. C. *The Covenants*. Charleston: Southern Baptist Publication Society, 1855.

Hunt, Boyd. *Redeemed! Eschatological Redemption and the Kingdom of God*. Nashville: Broadman & Holman, 1993.

Hunter, James Davison. *American Evangelicalism: Conservative Religion and the Quandary of Modernity*. New Brunswick, N.J.: Rutgers University Press, 1983.

———. *Before the Shooting Begins: Searching for Democracy in America's Culture War*. New York: Free Press, 1994.

———. *Evangelicalism: The Coming Generation*. Chicago: University of Chicago Press, 1987.

Hutchison, William R., ed. *Between the Times: The Travail of the Protestant Establishment in America, 1900–1960*. Cambridge: Cambridge University Press, 1989.

Ice, Thomas, and Timothy Demy. *When the Trumpet Sounds*. Eugene, Ore.: Harvest, 1995.

Inch, Morris A. *The Evangelical Challenge*. Philadelphia: Westminster, 1978.

Jacobsen, Douglas, and William Vance Trollinger, Jr. *Reforming the Center: American Protestantism, 1900 to the Present*. Grand Rapids, Mich.: Eerdmans, 1998.

Jacoby, Russell. *The End of Utopia: Politics and Culture in an Age of Apathy*. New York: Basic, 1999.

Jewett, Paul K. *Infant Baptism and the Covenant of Grace*. Grand Rapids, Mich.: Eerdmans, 1978.

John Paul II (pope). *The Gospel of Life [Evangelium Vitae]*. New York: Random House, 1995.

Johnston, Robert K. *Evangelicals at an Impasse: Biblical Authority in Practice.* Atlanta: John Knox, 1979.

Kantzer, Kenneth, and Carl F. H. Henry, eds. *Evangelical Affirmations.* Grand Rapids, Mich.: Zondervan, 1990.

Keillor, Steven J. *This Rebellious House: American Christianity and the Truth of Christianity.* Downers Grove, Ill.: InterVarsity Press, 1996.

Kirk, Russell. *The Politics of Prudence.* Wilmington, Del.: Intercollegiate Studies Institute, 1993.

———. *The Roots of American Order.* Washington, D.C.: Regnery Gateway, 1991.

Klein, William W. *The New Chosen People: A Corporate View of Election.* Grand Rapids, Mich.: Zondervan, 1990.

Knight, Henry H. III. *A Future for Truth: Evangelical Theology in a Postmodern World.* Nashville: Abingdon, 1997.

König, Adrio. *The Eclipse of Christ in Eschatology: Toward a Christ-Centered Approach.* Grand Rapids, Mich.: Eerdmans, 1989.

Krapohl, Robert H., and Charles H. Lippy. *The Evangelicals: A Historical, Thematic, and Biographical Guide.* Westport, Conn.: Greenwood, 1999.

Kraynak, Robert P. *Christian Faith and Modern Democracy: God and Politics in the Fallen World.* Notre Dame, Ind.: University of Notre Dame Press, 2000.

Kromminga, D. H. *The Millennium in the Church: Studies in the History of Christian Chiliasm.* Grand Rapids, Mich.: Eerdmans, 1945.

Kuyper, Abraham. *Lectures on Calvinism.* Grand Rapids, Mich.: Eerdmans, 1931.

Kyle, Richard. *The Last Days Are Here Again: A History of the End Times.* Grand Rapids, Mich.: Baker, 1998.

Ladd, George E. *The Blessed Hope.* Grand Rapids, Mich.: Eerdmans, 1956.

———. *A Commentary on the Revelation of John.* Grand Rapids, Mich.: Eerdmans, 1972.

———. *Crucial Questions About the Kingdom of God.* Grand Rapids, Mich.: Eerdmans, 1952.

———. *The Gospel of the Kingdom: Scriptural Studies in the Kingdom of God.* Grand Rapids, Mich.: Eerdmans, 1959.

———. *Jesus and the Kingdom: The Eschatology of Biblical Realism.* New York: Harper & Row, 1964.

———. *The Meaning of the Millennium.* Edited by Robert G. Clouse. Downers Grove, Ill.: InterVarsity Press, 1977.

———. *The Presence of the Future: The Eschatology of Biblical Realism.* Grand Rapids, Mich.: Eerdmans, 1974.

———. *A Theology of the New Testament.* Grand Rapids, Mich.: Eerdmans, 1974.

Leith, John H., ed. *Creeds of the Churches: A Reader in Christian Doctrine from the Bible to the Present.* Louisville: John Knox, 1982.

Lewis, C. S. *The Problem of Pain.* New York: Macmillan, 1962; reprint, New York: Simon & Schuster, 1996.

Lewis, Gordon R., and Bruce A. Demarest. *Integrative Theology.* Vol. 3. Grand Rapids, Mich.: Zondervan, 1994.

Lienesch, Michael. *Redeeming America: Piety and Politics in the New Christian Right.* Chapel Hill: University of North Carolina Press, 1993.

Lightner, Robert. *Neoevangelicalism Today.* Schaumburg, Ill.: Regular Baptist Press, 1978.

Lincoln, Andrew T. *Paradise Now and Not Yet: Studies in the Role of the Heavenly Dimension in Paul's Thought with Special Reference to His Eschatology.* Grand Rapids, Mich.: Baker, 1981.

Lindsey, Hal. *The Late Great Planet Earth.* Grand Rapids, Mich.: Zondervan, 1971.

Lints, Richard. *The Fabric of Theology: A Prolegomenon to Evangelical Theology.* Grand Rapids, Mich.: Eerdmans, 1993.

Lundström, Gösta. *The Kingdom of God in the Teaching of Jesus: A History of Interpretation from the Last Decades of the Nineteenth Century to the Present Day.* Translated by J. Bulman. Edinburgh: Oliver & Boyd, 1963.

Machen, J. Gresham. *Christianity and Liberalism.* Grand Rapids, Mich.: Eerdmans, 1923.

———. *The Virgin Birth of Christ.* New York: Harper & Brothers, 1930.

Marsden, George M. *Fundamentalism and American Culture.* New York: Oxford University Press, 1980.

———. *Reforming Fundamentalism: Fuller Seminary and the New Evangelicalism.* Grand Rapids, Mich.: Eerdmans, 1987.

———. *Understanding Fundamentalism and Evangelicalism.* Grand Rapids, Mich.: Eerdmans, 1991.

Marsden, George M., ed. *Evangelicalism and Modern America.* Grand Rapids, Mich.: Eerdmans, 1984.

Marshall, Molly Truman. *Joining the Dance: A Theology of the Spirit.* Valley Forge, Pa.: Judson, 2003.

Martin, William. *A Prophet With Honor: The Billy Graham Story.* New York: William Morrow, 1991.

———. *With God on Our Side: The Rise of the Religious Right in America.* New York: Broadway, 1996.

Marty, Martin. *Modern American Religion.* Vol. 3, *Under God, Indivisible.* Chicago: University of Chicago Press, 1986–1991.

———. *Politics, Religion, and the Common Good: Advancing a Distinctly American Conversation About Religion's Role in Our Shared Life.* San Francisco: Jossey-Bass, 2000.

———. *The Public Church.* New York: Crossroad, 1981.

Mask, E. Jeffrey. *At Liberty Under God: Toward a Baptist Ecclesiology.* Lanham, Md.: University Press of America, 1997.

Mathews, Shailer. *The Individual and the Social Gospel.* New York: Missionary Education Movement of the United States and Canada, 1914.

McBrien, Richard P. *Caesar's Coin: Religion and Politics in America.* New York: Macmillan, 1987.

McCarraher, Eugene. *Christian Critics: Religion and the Impasse in Modern American Social Thought.* Ithaca, N.Y.: Cornell University Press, 2000.

McClain, Alva J. *The Greatness of the Kingdom*. Grand Rapids, Mich.: Zondervan, 1959.

McCown, Chester Charlton. *The Genesis of the Social Gospel: The Meaning of the Ideals of Jesus in Light of Their Antecedents*. New York and London: Alfred A. Knopf, 1929.

McDannell, Colleen, and Bernhard Lang. *Heaven: A History*. New Haven, Conn.: Yale University Press, 1988.

McGrath, Alister. *Evangelicalism and the Future of Christianity*. Downers Grove, Ill.: InterVarsity Press, 1995.

———. *A Passion for Truth: The Intellectual Coherence of Evangelicalism*. Downers Grove, Ill.: InterVarsity Press, 1996.

Melling, Philip. *Fundamentalism in America: Millennialism, Identity, and Militant Religion*. Edinburgh: Edinburgh University Press, 1999.

Menendez, Albert J. *Evangelicals at the Ballot Box*. Amherst, N.Y.: Prometheus, 1996.

Meyer, F. B. *Back to Bethel*. Chicago: Moody, 1901.

Moen, Matthew C. *The Transformation of the Christian Right*. Tuscaloosa: University of Alabama Press, 1992.

Molnar, Thomas. *Utopia: The Perennial Heresy*. New York: Sheed & Ward, 1967.

Moltmann, Jürgen. *The Coming of God: Christian Eschatology*. Translated by Margaret Kohl. Minneapolis: Fortress, 1996.

———. *God for a Secular Society: The Public Relevance of Theology*. Translated by Margaret Kohl. Minneapolis: Fortress, 1999.

Morris, Leon. *The Apostolic Preaching of the Cross*. 3rd ed. Grand Rapids, Mich.: Eerdmans, 1965.

Mouw, Richard J. *He Shines in All That's Fair: Culture and Common Grace*. Grand Rapids, Mich.: Eerdmans, 2001.

———. *The Smell of Sawdust: What Evangelicals Can Learn from Their Fundamentalist Heritage*. Grand Rapids, Mich.: Zondervan, 2000.

Muncy, Mitchell S., ed. *The End of Democracy? The Celebrated First Things Debate with Arguments Pro and Con*. Dallas: Spence, 1997.

———. *The End of Democracy? II: A Crisis of Legitimacy*. Dallas: Spence, 1999.

Murch, James Deforest. *Cooperation Without Compromise: A History of the National Association of Evangelicals*. Grand Rapids, Mich.: Eerdmans, 1956.

Murray, Iain H. *Evangelicalism Divided: A Record of Crucial Change in the Years 1950 to 2000*. Edinburgh: Banner of Truth, 2000.

———. *Revival and Revivalism: The Making and Marring of American Evangelicalism, 1750–1858*. Edinburgh: Banner of Truth, 1994.

Murray, John R. *The Covenant of Grace: A Biblico-Theological Study*. Phillipsburg, N.J.: Presbyterian & Reformed, 1953.

Nash, George H. *The Conservative Intellectual Movement in America Since 1945*. Wilmington, Del.: Intercollegiate Studies Institute, 1996.

Nash, Ronald H. *Freedom, Justice, and the State*. Lanham, Md.: University Press of America, 1980.

———. *Great Divides: Understanding the Controversies that Come Between Christians*. Colorado Springs: NavPress, 1993.

————. *Is Jesus the Only Savior?* Grand Rapids, Mich.: Zondervan, 1994.

————. *The New Evangelicalism.* Grand Rapids, Mich.: Zondervan, 1963.

————. *Why the Left Is Not Right: The Religious Left—Who They Are and What They Believe.* Grand Rapids, Mich.: Zondervan, 1996.

Nash, Ronald H., ed. *Liberation Theology.* Milford, Mich.: Mott Media, 1984.

————. *The New Evangelicalism.* Grand Rapids, Mich.: Zondervan, 1963.

————. *Process Theology.* Grand Rapids, Mich.: Baker, 1987.

Netanyahu, Benjamin. *A Durable Peace: Israel and Its Place Among the Nations.* New York: Warner, 2000.

Nettles, Tom J. *By His Grace and for His Glory: A Historical, Theological, and Practical Study of the Doctrines of Grace in Baptist Life.* Grand Rapids, Mich.: Baker, 1986.

Neuhaus, Richard John. *The End of Democracy? The Judicial Usurpation of Politics.* Dallas: Spence, 1997.

————. *The Naked Public Square.* Grand Rapids, Mich.: Eerdmans, 1984.

Neuhaus, Richard John, and Michael Cromartie, eds. *Piety and Politics: Evangelicals and Fundamentalists Confront the World.* Washington, D.C.: Ethics and Public Policy Center, 1987.

Niebuhr, H. Richard. *Christ and Culture.* New York: Harper & Row, 1951.

————. *The Kingdom of God in America.* New York: Harper & Row, 1937.

Niebuhr, Reinhold. *The Children of Light and the Children of Darkness: A Vindication of Democracy and a Critique of Its Traditional Defense.* New York: Charles Scribner's Sons, 1944.

————. *Man's Nature and His Communities.* New York: Charles Scribner's Sons, 1965.

————. *Moral Man and Immoral Society: A Study in Ethics and Politics.* New York: Charles Scribner's Sons, 1932.

————. *The Nature and Destiny of Man.* Vol. 1, *Human Nature.* New York: Charles Scribner's Sons, 1941.

Nietzsche, Friedrich. *Unpublished Writings from the Period of Unfashionable Observations.* Translated by Richard T. Gray. Stanford, Calif.: Stanford University Press, 1999.

Nisbet, Robert. *Conservatism: Dream and Reality.* Minneapolis: University of Minnesota Press, 1986.

————. *The Quest for Community: A Study in the Ethics and Order of Freedom.* New York: Oxford University Press, 1953; reprint, San Francisco: Institute for Contemporary Studies, 1990.

Noll, Mark A. *Adding Cross to Crown: The Political Significance of Christ's Passion.* Grand Rapids, Mich.: Baker, 1996.

————. *One Nation Under God? Christian Faith and Political Action in America.* San Francisco: Harper & Row, 1988.

————. *The Scandal of the Evangelical Mind.* Grand Rapids, Mich.: Eerdmans, 1994.

Noll, Mark A., Nathan O. Hatch, and George M. Marsden, eds. *The Search for Christian America.* Expanded ed. Colorado Springs: Helmers & Howard, 1989.

Noll, Mark A., and Ronald F. Thiemann, eds. *Where Shall My Wond'ring Soul Begin? The Landscape of Evangelical Piety and Thought.* Grand Rapids, Mich.: Eerdmans, 2000.

Noll, Mark A., and David F. Wells, eds. *Christian Faith and Practice in the Modern World: Theology from an Evangelical Point of View.* Grand Rapids, Mich.: Eerdmans, 1988.

Norman, R. Stanton. *More than Just a Name: Preserving Our Baptist Identity.* Nashville: Broadman & Holman, 2001.

North, Gary. *Healer of the Nations: Biblical Principles in International Relations.* Fort Worth: Dominion Press, 1987.

————. *Millennialism and Social Theory.* Tyler, Tex.: Institute for Christian Economics, 1990.

————. *Rapture Fever: Why Dispensationalism Is Paralyzed.* Tyler, Tex.: Institute for Christian Economics, 1993.

————. *Westminster's Confession: The Abandonment of Van Til's Legacy.* Tyler, Tex.: Institute for Christian Economics, 1991.

North, Gary, ed. *Theonomy: An Informed Response.* Tyler, Tex.: Institute for Christian Economics, 1991.

North, Gary, and Gary DeMar. *Christian Reconstruction: What It Is, What It Isn't.* Tyler, Tex.: Institute for Christian Economics, 1991.

O'Brien, Peter T. *The Letter to the Ephesians.* The Pillar New Testament Commentary. Edited by D. A. Carson. Grand Rapids, Mich.: Eerdmans, 1999.

O'Donovan, Oliver. *The Desire of the Nations: Rediscovering the Roots of Political Theology.* New York: Cambridge University Press, 1996.

————. *Resurrection and Moral Order: An Outline for Evangelical Ethics.* Grand Rapids, Mich.: Eerdmans, 1986.

Olasky, Marvin. *Compassionate Conservatism: What It Is, What It Does, and How It Can Transform America.* New York: Free Press, 2000.

————. *The Tragedy of American Compassion.* Washington, D.C.: Regnery, 1992.

Olson, Roger. *The Story of Christian Theology: Twenty Centuries of Tradition and Reform.* Downers Grove, Ill.: InterVarsity Press, 1999.

Ortlund, Raymond C. *God's Unfaithful Wife: A Biblical Theology of Spiritual Adultery.* Downers Grove, Ill.: InterVarsity Press, 1996.

Otto, Randall E. *The God of Hope: The Trinitarian Vision of Jürgen Moltmann.* Lanham, Md.: University Press of America, 1991.

Pate, C. Marvin, ed. *Four Views on the Book of Revelation.* Grand Rapids, Mich.: Zondervan, 1998.

Pember, G. H. *Earth's Earliest Ages.* London: Hodder & Stoughton, 1876; reprint, Grand Rapids, Mich.: Kregel, 1975.

Pentecost, J. Dwight. *Things to Come: A Study in Biblical Eschatology.* Grand Rapids, Mich.: Zondervan, 1958.

————. *Thy Kingdom Come.* Wheaton, Ill.: Victor, 1990.

Perlstein, Rick. *Before the Storm: Barry Goldwater and the Unmaking of the American Consensus.* New York: Hill & Wang, 2001.

Perrin, Norman. *The Kingdom of God in the Teaching of Jesus.* Philadelphia: Westminster, 1963.

Peters, George N. *The Theocratic Kingdom of Our Lord Jesus Christ, as Covenanted in the Old Testament and Presented in the New Testament.* 3 vols. New York: Funk & Wagnalls, 1884; reprint, Grand Rapids, Mich.: Kregel, 1952.

Pettegrew, Larry D. *The New Covenant Ministry of the Holy Spirit.* Grand Rapids, Mich.: Kregel, 2001.

Phillips, Timothy R., and Dennis L. Okholm. *Welcome to the Family: An Introduction to Evangelical Christianity.* Wheaton, Ill.: Victor, 1996.

Pinnock, Clark H. *Flame of Love: A Theology of the Holy Spirit.* Downers Grove, Ill.: InterVarsity Press, 1996.

———. *Most Moved Mover: A Theology of God's Openness.* Grand Rapids, Mich.: Baker, 2001.

Pinnock, Clark H., and Robert C. Brow. *Unbounded Love: A Good News Theology for the Twenty-first Century.* Downers Grove, Ill.: InterVarsity Press, 1994.

Pinnock, Clark H., John Sanders, William Hasker, and David Basinger. *The Openness of God.* Downers Grove, Ill.: InterVarsity Press, 1994.

Piper, John. *The Pleasures of God: Meditations on God's Delight in Being God.* Rev. and enlarged. Sisters, Ore.: Multnomah, 2000.

Poythress, Vern S. *Symphonic Theology: The Validity of Multiple Perspectives in Theology.* Phillipsburg, N.J.: Presbyterian & Reformed, 1987.

———. *Understanding Dispensationalists.* 2nd ed. Grand Rapids, Mich.: Zondervan, 1994.

Putnam, Robert D. *Bowling Alone: The Collapse and Revival of American Community.* New York: Simon & Schuster, 2000.

Quanbeck, Warren A., ed. *God and Caesar: A Christian Approach to Social Ethics.* Minneapolis: Augsburg, 1959.

Quebedeaux, Richard. *The Worldly Evangelicals.* San Francisco: Harper & Row, 1978.

———. *The Young Evangelicals: The Story of the Emergence of a New Generation of Evangelicals.* New York: Harper & Row, 1974.

Ramm, Bernard. *After Fundamentalism: The Future of Evangelical Theology.* San Francisco: Harper & Row, 1983.

———. *The Evangelical Heritage: A Study in Historical Theology.* Grand Rapids, Mich.: Baker, 1973.

Rasmusson, Arne. *The Church as Polis.* Notre Dame, Ind.: University of Notre Dame Press, 1995.

Rausch, David A. *Zionism within Early American Fundamentalism, 1879–1918.* New York: Edwin Mellen, 1979.

Rauschenbusch, Walter. *Christianity and the Social Crisis.* Louisville: Westminster/John Knox, 1991.

———. *Christianizing the Social Order.* New York: Macmillan, 1912.

———. *A Theology for the Social Gospel.* New York: Macmillan, 1917; reprint, Louisville: Westminster/John Knox, 1997.

Reagan, Ronald. *Speaking My Mind: Selected Speeches.* New York: Simon & Schuster, 1989.

Reed, Ralph. *After the Revolution: How the Christian Coalition Is Impacting America.* Dallas: Word, 1996.

Reymond, Robert L. *A New Systematic Theology of the Christian Faith*. Nashville: Thomas Nelson, 1998.

Rhodes, Arnold B., ed. *The Church Faces the Isms*. New York: Abingdon, 1958.

Ridderbos, Herman. *The Coming of the Kingdom*. Philadelphia: Presbyterian & Reformed, 1962.

Riley, W. B. *The Evolution of the Kingdom*. New York: Charles C. Cook, 1913.

Robertson, O. Palmer. *The Israel of God: Yesterday, Today, and Tomorrow*. Phillipsburg, N.J.: Presbyterian & Reformed, 2000.

Robertson, Pat. *The Turning Tide: The Fall of Liberalism and the Rise of Common Sense*. Waco, Tex.: Word, 1993.

Rogers, Jack. *Claiming the Center: Churches and Conflicting Worldviews*. Louisville: Westminster/John Knox, 1995.

Rorty, Richard. *Achieving Our Country: Leftist Thought in Twentieth-Century America*. Cambridge: Harvard University Press, 1997.

———. *Philosophy and Social Hope*. New York: Penguin, 1999.

Rushdoony, Rousas J. *Christianity and the State*. Vallecito, Calif.: Ross, 1986.

———. *God's Plan for Victory: The Meaning of Postmillennialism*. Fairfax, Va.: Thoburn, 1977.

———. *The Institutes of Biblical Law*. Nutley, N.J.: Craig, 1973.

———. *Thy Kingdom Come: Studies in Daniel and Revelation*. Phillipsburg, N.J.: Presbyterian & Reformed, 1971.

Russell, Mark J., and Clyde Wilcox, eds. *God at the Grassroots: The Christian Right in the 1994 Elections*. Lanham, Md.: Rowman & Littlefield, 1995.

Ryrie, Charles C. *Basic Theology*. Chicago: Moody, 1986.

———. *Biblical Answers to Contemporary Issues*. Chicago: Moody, 1974.

———. *Dispensationalism*. Rev. and enlarged. Chicago: Moody, 1995.

Sailhamer, John H. *The Pentateuch as Narrative: A Biblical-Theological Commentary*. Grand Rapids, Mich.: Zondervan, 1992.

Sandeen, Ernest R. *The Roots of Fundamentalism: British and American Millennialism, 1800–1930*. Grand Rapids, Mich.: Baker, 1970.

Sanders, John. *The God Who Risks: A Theology of Providence*. Downers Grove, Ill.: InterVarsity Press, 1998.

Saucy, Mark. *The Kingdom of God in the Teaching of Jesus in Twentieth Century Theology*. Dallas: Word, 1997.

Saucy, Robert L. *The Case for Progressive Dispensationalism*. Grand Rapids, Mich.: Zondervan, 1993.

———. *The Church in God's Program*. Chicago: Moody, 1972.

Sauer, Erich. *The Dawn of World Redemption*. Grand Rapids, Mich.: Eerdmans, 1955.

———. *King of the Earth: The Nobility of Man According to the Bible and Science*. Grand Rapids, Mich.: Eerdmans, 1962.

———. *The Triumph of the Crucified: A Survey of Historical Revelation in the New Testament*. Translated by G. H. Lang. London: Paternoster, 1951; reprint, Grand Rapids, Mich.: Eerdmans, 1994.

Schaeffer, Francis A. *A Christian Manifesto*. Westchester, Ill.: Crossway, 1982.

———. *The Complete Works of Francis A. Schaeffer*. 5 vols. Westchester, Ill.: Crossway, 1982.

———. *The God Who Is There*. London: Hodder & Stoughton, 1968; reprint, Downers Grove, Ill.: InterVarsity Press, 1998.

Schreiner, Thomas R. *Paul, Apostle of God's Glory in Christ: A Pauline Theology*. Downers Grove, Ill.: InterVarsity Press, 2001.

———. *Romans*. Baker Exegetical Commentary on the New Testament, vol. 6. Grand Rapids, Mich.: Baker, 1998.

———. *Still Sovereign: Contemporary Perspectives on Election, Foreknowledge, and Grace*. Grand Rapids, Mich.: Baker, 2000.

Schreiner, Thomas R., and Ardel B. Caneday. *The Race Set Before Us: A Biblical Theology of Perseverance and Assurance*. Downers Grove, Ill.: InterVarsity Press, 2001.

Seifrid, Mark A. *Christ, Our Righteousness: Paul's Theology of Justification*. Downers Grove, Ill.: InterVarsity Press, 2000.

Shepherd, Norman R. *The Call of Grace: How the Covenant Illuminates Salvation and Evangelism*. Phillipsburg, N.J.: Presbyterian & Reformed, 2000.

Shain, Barry Alan. *The Myth of American Individualism: The Protestant Origins of American Political Thought*. Princeton, N.J.: Princeton University Press, 1994.

Skarsaune, Oskar. *In the Shadow of the Temple: Jewish Influences on Early Christianity*. Downers Grove, Ill.: InterVarsity Press, 2002.

Sider, Ronald J. *Completely Pro-Life*. Downers Grove, Ill.: InterVarsity Press, 1987.

———. *Good News and Good Works: A Theology for the Whole Gospel*. Grand Rapids, Mich.: Baker, 1993.

———. *One-Sided Christianity? Uniting the Church to Heal a Lost and Broken World*. Grand Rapids, Mich.: Zondervan, 1993.

———. *Rich Christians in an Age of Hunger*. Dallas: Word, 1990.

Sider, Ronald J., ed. *The Chicago Declaration*. Carol Stream, Ill.: Creation House, 1974.

Singer, Peter. *Animal Liberation*. New York: Random House, 1975.

Smith, Christian. *Christian America? What Evangelicals Really Want*. Berkeley: University of California Press, 2000.

Snyder, Howard A. *Models of the Kingdom*. Nashville: Abingdon, 1991.

Spong, John Shelby. *Here I Stand: My Struggle for a Christianity of Integrity, Love, and Equality*. San Francisco: HarperCollins, 2000.

———. *A New Christianity for a New World: Why Traditional Faith Is Dying and How a New Faith Is Being Born*. San Francisco: HarperCollins, 2001.

Sproul, R. C. *Grace Unknown: The Heart of Reformed Theology*. Grand Rapids, Mich.: Baker, 1997.

Spykman, Gordon J. *Reformational Theology: A New Paradigm for Doing Dogmatics*. Grand Rapids, Mich.: Eerdmans, 1992.

Stackhouse, John G., Jr. *Evangelical Futures: A Conversation on Theological Method*. Grand Rapids, Mich.: Baker, 2000.

Stark, Rodney. *The Rise of Christianity: A Sociologist Reconsiders History*. Princeton, N.J.: Princeton University Press, 1996.

Stone, Jon R. *On the Boundaries of American Evangelicalism: The Postwar Evangelical Coalition.* New York: St. Martin's Press, 1997.

Strauss, Mark L. *The Davidic Messiah in Luke–Acts: The Promise and Its Fulfillment in Lukan Christology.* Sheffield, England: Sheffield Academic, 1995.

Stricklin, David. *A Genealogy of Dissent: Southern Baptist Protest in the Twentieth Century.* Lexington: University Press of Kentucky, 1999.

Sullivan, Clayton. *Rethinking Realized Eschatology.* Macon, Ga.: Mercer University Press, 1988.

Sweet, Leonard I., ed. *The Evangelical Tradition in America.* Macon, Ga.: Mercer University Press, 1984.

Thomas, Cal, and Ed Dobson. *Blinded by Might: Can the Religious Right Save America?* Grand Rapids, Mich.: Zondervan, 1999.

Tinder, Glenn E. *The Fabric of Hope: An Essay.* Atlanta: Scholars, 1999.

———. *The Political Meaning of Christianity.* Baton Rouge: Louisiana State University Press, 1989.

Tolson, Jay, ed. *The Correspondence of Shelby Foote and Walker Percy.* New York: W. W. Norton, 1997.

Unger, Merrill F. *The Baptism and Gifts of the Holy Spirit.* Chicago: Moody, 1974.

Urofsky, Melvin I., and Martha May. *The New Christian Right: Political and Social Issues.* New York: Garland, 1996.

Van Gelder, Craig. *The Essence of the Church: A Community Created by the Spirit.* Grand Rapids, Mich.: Baker, 2000.

Vangemeren, Willem. *The Progress of Redemption: The Story of Salvation from Creation to the New Jerusalem.* Grand Rapids, Mich.: Baker, 1988.

Van Til, Henry R. *The Calvinistic Concept of Culture.* With a foreword by Richard J. Mouw. Grand Rapids, Mich.: Baker, 1959; reprint, Grand Rapids, Mich.: Baker, 2001.

Veith, Gene Edward, and Thomas L. Wilmeth. *Honky-Tonk Gospel: The Story of Sin and Salvation in Country Music.* Grand Rapids, Mich.: Baker, 2001.

Voegelin, Erich. *The New Science of Politics.* Chicago: University of Chicago Press, 1952.

———. *Political Religions.* Translated by T. J. DiNapoli and E. S. Easterly III. Lewiston, N.Y.: Edwin Mellen, 1986.

———. *Science, Politics, and Gnosticism: Two Essays.* Washington, D.C.: Regnery, 1968.

Vos, Geerhardus. *Biblical Theology: Old and New Testaments.* Grand Rapids, Mich.: Eerdmans, 1948.

———. *The Pauline Eschatology.* Grand Rapids, Mich.: Eerdmans, 1961.

———. *The Teaching of Jesus Concerning the Kingdom of God and the Church.* New York: American Tract Society, 1903.

Wallis, James. *The Soul of Politics: A Practical and Prophetic Vision for Change.* Maryknoll, N.Y.: Orbis, 1994.

———. *Who Speaks for God? An Alternative to the Religious Right—A New Politics of Compassion, Community, and Civility.* New York: Delacorte, 1996.

Walsh, Brian J., and J. Richard Middleton. *Transforming Vision: Shaping a Christian Worldview.* Downers Grove, Ill.: InterVarsity Press, 1984.

Walvoord, John. *Armageddon, Oil, and the Middle East Crisis: What the Bible Says About the Future of the Middle East and the End of Western Civilization.* Grand Rapids, Mich.: Zondervan, 1990.

Ware, Bruce A. *God's Lesser Glory: The Diminished God of Open Theism.* Wheaton, Ill.: Crossway, 2000.

Warfield, Benjamin B. *The Plan of Salvation.* Grand Rapids, Mich.: Eerdmans, 1935; reprint, Eugene, Ore.: Wipf and Stock, 2000.

Webber, Robert. *Ancient-Future Faith: Rethinking Evangelicalism for a Postmodern World.* Downers Grove, Ill.: InterVarsity Press, 1999.

Weber, Max. *The Protestant Ethic and the Spirit of Capitalism.* Translated by Talcott Parsons. New York: Charles Scribner's Sons, 1958.

Weber, Robert E. *The Secular Saint: A Case for Evangelical Social Responsibility.* Grand Rapids, Mich.: Zondervan, 1979.

Weber, Timothy P. *Living in the Shadow of the Second Coming: American Premillennialism, 1875–1982.* Chicago: University of Chicago Press, 1983.

Wells, David F. *God in the Wasteland: The Reality of Truth in a World of Fading Dreams.* Grand Rapids, Mich.: Eerdmans, 1994.

———. *Losing Our Virtue: Why the Church Must Recover Its Moral Vision.* Grand Rapids, Mich.: Eerdmans, 1998.

———. *No Place for Truth: Or, Whatever Happened to Evangelical Theology?* Grand Rapids, Mich.: Eerdmans, 1993.

———. *The Search for Salvation.* Downers Grove, Ill.: InterVarsity Press, 1978.

Wells, David F., ed. *Reformed Theology in America; A History of Its Modern Development.* Grand Rapids, Mich.: Eerdmans, 1985.

Wells, David F., and John D. Woodbridge, eds. *The Evangelicals: What They Believe, Who They Are, Where They Are Changing.* Grand Rapids, Mich.: Baker, 1997.

Williams, Michael. *This World Is Not My Home: The Origins and Development of Dispensationalism.* Fearn, Ross-shire, Scotland: Mentor, 2003.

Willis, Wendell, ed. *The Kingdom of God in Twentieth-Century Interpretation.* Peabody, Mass.: Hendrickson, 1987.

Willis, Wesley R., and John R. Master, eds. *Issues in Dispensationalism.* Chicago: Moody, 1994.

Wills, Gregory A. *Democratic Religion: Freedom, Authority, and Church Discipline in the Baptist South, 1785–1900.* New York: Oxford University Press, 1997.

Wimber, John, with Kevin Springer. *Power Evangelism.* San Francisco: Harper & Row, 1986.

Wirt, Sherwood Eliot. *The Social Conscience of the Evangelical.* New York: Harper & Row, 1968.

Witcover, Jules. *Marathon: The Pursuit of the Presidency.* New York: Viking, 1977.

Wogaman, J. Philip. *Christian Perspectives on Politics.* Rev. and enlarged. Louisville: Westminster/John Knox, 2000.

Wojcik, Daniel. *The End of the World as We Know It: Faith, Fatalism, and Apocalypse in America.* New York: New York University Press, 1997.

Wolters, Albert M. *Creation Regained: Biblical Basics for a Reformational Worldview.* Grand Rapids, Mich.: Eerdmans, 1985.

Wright, N. T. *The Challenge of Jesus: Rediscovering Who Jesus Was and Is.* Downers Grove, Ill.: InterVarsity Press, 1999.

Yoder, John Howard. *Body Politics: Five Practices of the Christian Community Before the Watching World.* Nashville: Discipleship Resources, 1992.

———. *The Priestly Kingdom: Social Ethics as Gospel.* Notre Dame, Ind.: University of Notre Dame Press, 1984.

Zuck, Roy B., ed. *Vital Prophetic Issues: Examining Promises and Problems in Eschatology.* Grand Rapids, Mich.: Kregel, 1995.

ARTICLES

"Abortion Decision: A Death Blow?" *Christianity Today,* February 16, 1973, 48.

Bailey, Mark L. "Dispensational Definitions of the Kingdom." In *Integrity of Heart and Skillfulness of Hands: Biblical and Leadership Studies in Honor of Donald K. Campbell,* ed. Charles H. Dyer and Roy B. Zuck, 201-221. Grand Rapids, Mich.: Baker, 1994.

Baker, Russell. "Mr. Right." *New York Review of Books,* May 17, 2001, 4-8.

Barnhouse, Donald Grey. "Social Problems." *Eternity,* January 1955, 9.

Beale, Gregory K. "The Eschatological Conception of New Testament Theology." In *Eschatology in Bible and Theology,* ed. Kent E. Brower and Mark W. Elliott, 11-52. Downers Grove, Ill.: InterVarsity Press, 1997.

Beasley-Murray, George R. "A Century of Eschatological Discussion." *Expository Times* 64 (1952–1953): 312-316.

———. "Comments on Craig L. Blomberg's Response to 'The Kingdom of God in the Teaching of Jesus'." *Journal of the Evangelical Theological Society* 35 (1992): 37-38.

———. "The Kingdom of God in the Teaching of Jesus." *Journal of the Evangelical Theological Society* 35 (1992): 19-30.

Beckwith, Francis J. "A Critical Appraisal of Theological Arguments for Abortion Rights." *Bibliotheca Sacra* 148 (1991): 337-355.

Blaising, Craig A. "Contemporary Dispensationalism." *Southwestern Journal of Theology* 36 (1994): 5-13.

———. "Development of Dispensationalism by Contemporary Dispensationalists." *Bibliotheca Sacra* 145 (1988): 254-280.

———. "Doctrinal Developments in Orthodoxy." *Bibliotheca Sacra* 145 (1988): 133-140.

———. "The Future of Israel as a Theological Question." *Journal of the Evangelical Theological Society* 44 (2001): 435-450.

———. "Lewis Sperry Chafer." In *Handbook of Evangelical Theologians,* ed. Walter A. Elwell, 83-96. Grand Rapids, Mich.: Baker, 1993.

———. "A Premillennial Response to Kenneth L. Gentry, Jr." In *Three Views on the Millennium and Beyond,* ed. Darrell L. Bock, 72-80. Grand Rapids, Mich.: Zondervan, 1999.

———. "A Premillennial Response to Robert B. Strimple." In *Three Views of the Millennium and Beyond,* ed. Darrell L. Bock, 143-154. Grand Rapids, Mich.: Zondervan, 1999.

———. "Premillennialism." In *Three Views on the Millennium and Beyond,* ed. Darrell L. Bock, 155.-227. Grand Rapids, Mich.: Zondervan, 1999.

Blomberg, Craig L. "Eschatology and the Church: Some New Testament Perspectives." *Themelios* 23 (1998): 3-26.

———. "A Response to G. R. Beasley-Murray on the Kingdom." *Journal of the Evangelical Theological Society* 35 (1992): 31-36.

Blue, J. Ronald. "Major Flaws in Liberation Theology." *Bibliotheca Sacra* 147 (1990): 89-103.

Bock, Darrell L. "The Case for Premillennialism in Acts." In *A Case for Premillennialism,* ed. Donald K. Campbell and Jeffrey L. Townsend, 185-202. Chicago: Moody, 1992.

———. "Charting Dispensationalism." *Christianity Today,* September 12, 1994, 26-29.

———. "Current Messianic Activity and OT Davidic Promise: Dispensationalism, Hermeneutics, and NT Fulfillment." *Trinity Journal* 15 (1994): 55-87.

———. "Does the New Testament Reshape Our Understanding of the Old Testament?" *Modern Reformation,* July/August 2000, 48-50.

———. "The 'New Man' as Community in Colossians and Ephesians." In *Integrity of Heart, Skillfulness of Hands: Biblical and Leadership Studies in Honor of Donald K. Campbell,* ed. Charles H. Dyer and Roy B. Zuck, 157-168. Grand Rapids, Mich.: Baker, 1994.

———. Review of *The Gospel According to Jesus. Bibliotheca Sacra* 146 (1989): 21-40.

———. "The Son of David and the Saints' Task: The Hermeneutics of Initial Fulfillment." *Bibliotheca Sacra* 150 (October/December 1993): 440-457.

———. "Why I Am a dispensationalist with a Small 'd.'" *Journal of the Evangelical Theological Society* 41 (1998): 383-396.

Borg, Marcus J., and N. T. Wright. "The Second Coming Then and Now." In *The Meaning of Jesus: Two Visions,* 189-196. San Francisco: HarperCollins, 1999.

Breshears, Gerry. "The Body of Christ: Prophet, Priest, or King?" *Journal of the Evangelical Theological Society* 37 (1994): 3-26.

———. "Dispensational Study Group Discussion." *Grace Theological Journal* 10 (1989): 161-164.

Brock, Rita Nakashima. "And a Little Child Will Lead Us: Christology and Child Abuse." In *Christianity, Patriarchy, and Abuse: A Feminist Critique,* ed. Joanne Carlson Brown and Carole R. Bohn, 42-61. New York: Pilgrim, 1989.

Brooks, David. "God and the Neocons." *Public Interest* 126 (1997): 95-101.

———. "The Right's Anti-American Temptation." *Weekly Standard,* November 11, 1996, 23-26.

Brow, Robert C. "The Evangelical Megashift." *Christianity Today,* February 19, 1990, 12-14.

Brown, Robert McAfee. "'Eschatological Hope' and Social Responsibility." *Christianity and Crisis* 13 (1953): 146-149.

Budziszewski, J. "The Problem with Communitarianism." *First Things,* March 1995, 22-26.

Bullmore, Michael A. "The Four Most Important Biblical Passages for a Christian Environmentalism." *Trinity Journal* 19 (1998): 139-162.

Bush, L. Russ. Review of *Living in the Shadow of the Second Coming: American Premillennialism, 1875–1982,* by Timothy P. Weber. *Southwestern Journal of Theology* 27 (1985): 63-64.

Butler, Diane Hochstedt. "An Interview with Carl F. H. Henry." *TSF Bulletin,* March/April 1987, 16-19.

Callahan, James. "Reforming Dispensationalism." *Fides et Historia* 28 (1996): 68-83.

Campbell, George Van Pelt. "Religion and Culture: Challenges and Prospects in the Next Generation." *Journal of the Evangelical Theological Society* 43 (2000): 287-301.

Carson, D. A. "God, the Bible and Spiritual Warfare: A Review Article." *Journal of the Evangelical Theological Society* 42 (1999): 251-270.

Chafer, Lewis Sperry. "Dispensational Distinctions Challenged." *Bibliotheca Sacra* 100 (1943): 337-345.

Clapp, Rodney. "Democracy as Heresy." *Christianity Today,* February 20, 1987, 17-23.

———. "Overdosing on the Apocalypse: How End-Times Junkies Can Become Sane and Responsible." *Christianity Today,* October 28, 1991, 26-29.

Clark, Gordon H. "Reply to Roger Nicole." In *The Philosophy of Gordon H. Clark: A Festschrift,* ed. Ronald H. Nash, 468-484. Philadelphia: Presbyterian & Reformed 1968.

Clouse, Robert G. "The Evangelical Christian, Social Concern, and a Theology of Hope." *The Evangelical Quarterly* 44 (1972): 68-75.

———. "The New Christian Right, America, and the Kingdom of God." *Christian Scholar's Review* 12 (1983): 3-16.

Clowney, Edmund P. "The Christian College and the Transformation of Culture." *Christian Scholar's Review* 1 (1970): 5-18.

———. "The Politics of the Kingdom." *Westminster Theological Journal* 41 (1972): 291-310.

Clutter, Ronald T. "Dispensational Study Group: An Introduction." *Grace Theological Journal* 10 (1989): 123-124.

Craycraft, Kenneth R., Jr. "Christ's Counter-Kingdom." *Regeneration Quarterly* (Winter 1995): 19-21.

"Dabru Emet: A Jewish Statement on Christians and Christianity." *New York Times,* September 10, 2000, 23.

Daniels, Tom D., Richard J. Jensen, and Allen Lichtenstein. "Resolving the Paradox in Politicized Christian Fundamentalism." *Western Journal of Speech Communication* 29 (1985): 248-266.

Davis, John Jefferson. "Ecological 'Blind Spots' in the Structure and Content of Recent Evangelical Systematic Theologies." *Journal of the Evangelical Theological Society* 43 (2000): 273-286.

Dayton, Donald W. "The Social and Political Conservatism of Modern American Evangelicalism: A Preliminary Search for the Reasons." *Union Seminary Quarterly Review* 32 (1977): 71-80.

Dennison, William D. "Dutch Neo-Calvinism and the Roots for Transformation: An Introductory Essay." *Journal of the Evangelical Theological Society* 42 (1999): 271-291.

Dilday, Russell H., Jr. "On Higher Ground: 1984 SBC Convention Sermon." In *Going for the Jugular: A Documentary History of the SBC Holy War,* ed. Walter B. Shurden and Randy Shepley, 112-123. Macon, Ga.: Mercer, 1996.

Dorman, Ted. "The Joint Declaration on the Doctrine of Justification: Retrospect and Prospects." *Journal of the Evangelical Theological Society* 44 (2001): 421-434.

Edwards, Jonathan. "A History of the Work of Redemption (1773)." In *The Works of Jonathan Edwards,* ed. Edward Hickman, 1:532-619. London: William Ball, 1834; reprint, Edinburgh: Banner of Truth, 1974.

Elwell, Walter A. "Dispensationalisms of the Third Kind." *Christianity Today,* September 12, 1994, 28.

Epp, Eldon Jay. "Mediating Approaches to the Kingdom: Werner George Kümmel and George Eldon Ladd." In *The Kingdom of God in Twentieth-Century Interpretation,* ed. Wendell Willis, 35-52. Peabody, Mass.: Hendrickson, 1987.

Eskridge, Larry. "And, the Most Influential Evangelical of the Last 25 Years Is . . ." *Evangelical Studies Bulletin* 17 (2001): 1-4.

Falwell, Jerry. "An Agenda for the 1980s." In *Piety and Politics: Evangelicals and Fundamentalists Confront the World,* ed. Richard John Neuhaus and Michael Cromartie, 109-124. Washington, D.C.: Ethics and Public Policy Center, 1987.

Fea, John. "Fundamentalism, Neo-Evangelicalism, and the American Dispensationalist Establishment in the 1950s." *Michigan Theological Journal* 4 (1993): 115-132.

Ferguson, Sinclair. "The Whole Counsel of God: Fifty Years of Theological Studies." *Westminster Theological Journal* 50 (1988): 257-281.

Fosdick, Harry Emerson. "Shall the Fundamentalists Win? A Sermon Preached at the First Presbyterian Church, New York, May 21, 1922." In *The Fundamentalist-Modernist Conflict: Opposing Views on Three Major Issues,* ed. Joel A. Carpenter, 2-15. New York: Garland, 1988.

Frame, John M. "In Defense of Something Close to Biblicism: Reflections on *Sola Scriptura* and History in Theological Method." *Westminster Theological Journal* 59 (1997): 269-291.

Gaffin, Richard B., Jr. "A Cessationist View." In *Are Miraculous Gifts for Today? Four Views,* ed. Wayne A. Grudem, 25-64. Grand Rapids, Mich.: Zondervan, 1996.

———. "The Holy Spirit." *Westminster Theological Journal* 43 (1980): 58-78.

———. "'Life-Giving Spirit': Probing the Center of Paul's Pneumatology." *Journal of the Evangelical Theological Society* 41 (1998): 573-589.

———. "The Usefulness of the Cross." *Westminster Theological Journal* 41 (1979): 228-246.

Gaffin, Richard B., Jr., ed. "A New Paradigm in Theology?" *Westminster Theological Journal* 56 (1994): 379-390.

Geisler, Norman. "A Premillennial View of Law and Government." *Bibliotheca Sacra* 142 (1985): 250-266.

George, Timothy. "Peacemaker Preface." *Baptist Peacemaker,* April 1983, 2.

———. "The Priesthood of All Believers." In *The People of God: Essays on the Believers' Church,* ed. Paul Basden and David S. Dockery, 85-95. Nashville: Broadman, 1991.

———. "What I'd Like to Tell the Pope About the Church." *Christianity Today,* June 15, 1998, 41-44.

Granberg-Michaelson, Wesley. "The Promise of God's Reign: The Church's Role in the World's Future." *Sojourners* 13 (1984): 16-19.

Grenz, Stanley J. "An Agenda for Evangelical Theology in the Postmodern Context." *Didaskalia* 9 (1998): 1-16.

———. "Articulating the Christian Belief-Mosaic: Theological Method After the Demise of Foundationalism." In *Evangelical Futures: A Conversation on Theological Method,* ed. John G. Stackhouse, Jr., 107-138. Grand Rapids, Mich.: Baker, 2000.

———. "The Deeper Significance of the Millennium Debate." *Southwestern Journal of Theology* 36 (1994): 14-21.

———. "An Evangelical Response to Ferguson, Holloway, and Lowery: Restoring a Trinitarian Understanding of the Church in Practice." In *Evangelicalism and the Stone-Campbell Movement,* ed. William R. Baker, 228-234. Downers Grove, Ill.: InterVarsity Press, 2002.

———. "'Fideistic Revelationalism': Donald Bloesch's Antirationalist Theological Method." In *Evangelical Theology in Transition: Theologians in Dialogue with Donald Bloesch,* ed. Elmer M. Colyer, 35-60. Downers Grove, Ill.: InterVarsity Press, 1999.

———. "Systematics Nouveau." *The Reformed Journal,* October 1990, 27-29.

———. "Toward an Evangelical Theology of the Religions." *Journal of Ecumenical Studies* 31 (1994): 49-65.

———. "What Does Hollywood Have to Do with Wheaton? The Place of (Pop) Culture in Theological Reflection." *Journal of the Evangelical Theological Society* 43 (2000): 303-314.

Hafemann, Scott. "Seminary, Subjectivity, and the Centrality of Scripture: Reflections on the Current Crisis in Evangelical Seminary Education." *Journal of the Evangelical Theological Society* 31 (1988): 129-143.

Harper, Brad. "The Kingdom of God in George Eldon Ladd as a Theological Foundation for the Role of the Church in Society." In *God and Caesar: Selected Essays from the Evangelical Theological Society's Convention in Washington D.C.,* ed. Michael Bauman and David Hall, 187-200. Camp Hill, Pa.: Christian Publications, 1994.

Hart, D. G. "Christian Scholars, Secular Universities, and the Problem with the Antithesis." *Christian Scholar's Review* 30 (2001): 383-402.

———. "Christianity and Liberalism in a Postliberal Age." *Westminster Theological Journal* 56 (1994): 329-344.

———. "Christianity, Modern Liberalism, and J. Gresham Machen." *Modern Age* 39 (1997): 234-245.

———. "Machen, Confessional Presbyterianism, and Twentieth-Century Protestantism." In *Reforming the Center: American Protestantism, 1900 to the Present,* ed. Douglas Jacobsen and William Vance Trollinger, Jr., 129-149. Grand Rapids, Mich.: Eerdmans, 1998.

———. "What Can Presbyterians Learn from Lutherans?" *Logia* 8 (1999): 3-8.

Hauerwas, Stanley. "Christian Ethics in America: A Promising Obituary." In *Introduction to Christian Theology: Contemporary North American Perspectives,* ed. Roger A. Badham, 103-120. Louisville: Westminster/John Knox, 1998.

————. "How 'Christian Ethics' Came to Be." In *The Hauerwas Reader,* ed. John Berkman and Michael Cartwright, 37-50. Durham, N.C.: Duke University Press, 2001.

————. "Why Clinton Is Incapable of Lying: A Christian Analysis." In *Judgment Day at the White House: A Critical Declaration Exploring Moral Issues and the Political Use and Abuse of Religion,* ed. Gabriel Fackre, 28-31. Grand Rapids, Mich.: Eerdmans, 1999.

Henry, Carl F. H. "American Evangelicals in a Turning Time." *Christian Century,* November 5, 1980, 1058-1062.

————. "Christianity and the Economic Crisis." *Eternity,* June 1955, 14-15, 43-45.

————. "The Church in the World or the World in the Church? A Review Article." *Journal of the Evangelical Theological Society* 34 (1991): 381-383.

————. "Crepe-Hangers in the Church." *Christianity Today,* March 29, 1968, 23-24.

————. "Crisis in the Pulpit." *Christianity Today,* June 4, 1965, 24-25.

————. "Dare We Renew the Controversy? Part II: The Fundamentalist Reduction." *Christianity Today,* June 24, 1957, 23-26.

————. "Evangelicals in the Social Struggle." In *Salt and Light: Evangelical Political Thought in Modern America,* ed. Augustus Cerillo, Jr., and Murray W. Dempster, 26-40. Grand Rapids, Mich.: Baker, 1989.

————. "Feature Interview: The Debate Over Divine Election." *Christianity Today,* October 12, 1959, 3-18.

————. "Fifty Years a Baptist." In *Why I Am a Baptist,* ed. Tom J. Nettles and Russell D. Moore, 209-217. Nashville: Broadman & Holman, 2001.

————. "Fortunes of the Christian Worldview." *Trinity Journal* 19 (1998): 163-176.

————. "Getting Down to Business." *Southern Baptist Watchman,* June 1992, 1-2.

————. "A Hard Look at American Worship." *Christianity Today,* December 8, 1967, 27-29.

————. "Isolated from the Church?" *Christianity Today,* September 16, 1966, 31-32.

————. "Jesus Christ and the Last Days." In *Prophecy in the Making: Messages Prepared for the Jerusalem Conference on Biblical Prophecy,* 169-186. Carol Stream, Ill.: Creation House, 1971.

————. "Martyn Lloyd-Jones: From Buckingham to Westminster." *Christianity Today,* February 8, 1980, 27-34.

————. "Natural Law and a Nihilistic Culture." *First Things* 49 (1995): 55-60.

————. "The New Coalitions." *Christianity Today,* November 17, 1989, 26-28.

————. "Pulpit and Pew: A New Appraisal." *Christianity Today,* October 29, 1956, 20-24.

————. "Reflections on the Kingdom of God." *Journal of the Evangelical Theological Society* 35 (1992): 39-50.

————. "Response." In *No Longer Exiles: The Religious New Right in American Politics,* ed. Michael Cromartie, 75-77. Washington, D.C.: Ethics and Public Policy Center, 1993.

————. "State." In *Baker's Dictionary of Theology,* ed. Everett F. Harrison, Geoffrey W. Bromiley, and Carl F. H. Henry, 501-502. Grand Rapids, Mich.: Baker, 1960.

————. "A Summons to Justice." *Christianity Today,* July 20, 1992, 40.

———. "Theology and Biblical Authority: A Review Article." *Journal of the Evangelical Theological Society* 19 (1976): 315-323.

———. "Twenty Years a Baptist." *Foundations* 1 (1958): 46-54.

———. "The Undoing of the Modern Mind." In *Evangelical Roots: A Tribute to Wilbur Smith*, ed. Kenneth S. Kantzer, 101-122. Nashville: Thomas Nelson, 1978.

———. "The Vigor of the New Evangelicalism," Part 1. *Christian Life*, January 1948, 30-34.

———. "The Vigor of the New Evangelicalism," Part 2. *Christian Life*, March 1948, 35-85.

———. "Will Christianity Outlive Its Critics?" *Modern Age* 33 (1990): 122-132.

Himmelfarb, Gertrude. "The Election and the Culture Wars." *Commentary*, May 2000, 23-25.

———. "On the Future of Conservatism: A Symposium." *Commentary*, February 1997, 29-32.

Hittinger, Russell. "How Now Shall We Bear Witness?" *Touchstone*, March 2000, 31-34.

Hodges, Zane. "Calvinism Ex Cathedra: A Review of John H. Gerstner's *Wrongly Dividing the Word of Truth: A Critique of Dispensationalism*." *Journal of the Grace Evangelical Society* 4 (1991): 59-70.

———. "A Dispensational Understanding of Acts 2." In *Issues in Dispensationalism*, ed. Wesley R. Willis and John R. Master, 167-182. Chicago: Moody, 1994.

House, H. Wayne. "Creation and Redemption: A Study of Kingdom Interplay." *Journal of the Evangelical Theological Society* 35 (1992): 3-17.

Hunter, James Davison. "Religion and Political Civility: The Coming Generation of American Evangelicals." *Journal for the Scientific Study of Religion* 23 (1984): 364-380.

Johnson, Elliott. "Hermeneutical Principles and the Interpretation of Psalm 110." *Bibliotheca Sacra* 149 (1992): 428-437.

———. "Prophetic Fulfillment: The Already and Not Yet." In *Issues in Dispensationalism*, ed. Wesley R. Willis and John R. Master, 183-202. Chicago: Moody, 1994.

Johnston, Robert K. "American Evangelicalism: An Extended Family." In *The Variety of American Evangelicalism*, ed. Donald W. Dayton and Robert K. Johnston, 252-272. Downers Grove, Ill.: InterVarsity Press, 1991.

Jones, Larry, and Gerald T. Sheppard. "The Politics of Biblical Eschatology: Ronald Reagan and the Impending Nuclear Armageddon." *TSF Bulletin*, September/October 1984, 16-18.

Karlberg, Mark W. Review of *The Holy Spirit*, by Sinclair B. Ferguson. *Journal of the Evangelical Theological Society* 42 (1999): 529-531.

Kirk, Russell. "Civilization Without Religion?" *Modern Age* 33 (1990): 151-156.

Kline, Meredith G. "Comments on an Old-New Error." *Westminster Theological Journal* 40 (1978): 172-189.

———. "The First Resurrection." *Westminster Theological Journal* 37 (1974): 366-375.

———. "The First Resurrection: A Reaffirmation." *Westminster Theological Journal* 39 (1976): 110-119.

Kuschke, Arthur W., Jr. Review of *Crucial Questions About the Kingdom of God,* by George Eldon Ladd. *Westminster Theological Journal* 15 (1953): 156-159.

Ladd, George Eldon. "Dispensational Theology." *Christianity Today,* October 12, 1959, 38-41.

―――. "Eschatology and the Unity of New Testament Theology." *Expository Times* 68 (1957): 268-273.

―――. "Historic Premillennialism." In *The Meaning of the Millennium: Four Views,* ed. Robert G. Clouse, 17-40. Downers Grove, Ill.: InterVarsity Press, 1977.

―――. "Israel and the Church." *Evangelical Quarterly* 36 (1964): 206-213.

―――. "Kingdom of Christ, God, Heaven." In *The Evangelical Dictionary of Theology,* ed. Walter Elwell, 607-611. Grand Rapids, Mich.: Baker, 1984.

―――. "Kingdom of God." In *The International Standard Bible Encyclopedia,* ed. Geoffrey W. Bromiley. Rev. ed. Grand Rapids, Mich.: Eerdmans, 1986.

―――. "The Kingdom of God and the Church." *Foundations* 4 (1961): 164-171.

―――. "Kingdom of God—Reign or Realm?" *Journal of Biblical Literature* 81 (1962): 230-238.

―――. "The Revelation of Christ's Glory." *Christianity Today,* September 1, 1958, 13-14.

―――. "Revelation 20 and the Millennium." *Review and Expositor* 57 (1960): 167-175.

―――. "Why Not Prophetic-Apocalyptic?" *Journal of Biblical Literature* 76 (1957): 192-200.

Land, Richard D. "Southern Baptists and the Fundamentalist Tradition in Biblical Interpretation, 1845–1945." *Baptist History and Heritage* 19 (1984): 29-31.

Lawler, Peter Augustine. "Democratic Therapy and the End of Community." *Intercollegiate Review* 32 (1997): 27-33.

Letham, Robert. "Is Evangelicalism Christian?" *Evangelical Quarterly* 67 (1995): 3-16.

―――. Review of *A New Systematic Theology of the Christian Faith* by Robert L. Reymond. *Westminster Theological Journal* 62 (2000): 314-319.

Lightner, Robert P. "Nondispensational Responses to Theonomy." *Bibliotheca Sacra* 143 (1986): 134-145.

―――. "Theonomy and Dispensationalism." *Bibliotheca Sacra* 143 (1986): 26-36.

Linker, Damon. "Richard Rorty: Liberal Absolutist." *Policy Review* 100 (April/May 2000): 81-86.

Lints, Richard. "Two Theologies or One? Warfield and Vos on the Nature of Theology." *Westminster Theological Journal* 54 (1992): 235-253.

Lucas, Sean Michael. "Fundamentalisms Revived and Still Standing: A Review Essay." *Westminster Theological Journal* 60 (1998): 327-337.

Luther, Martin. "Admonition to Peace: A Reply to the Twelve Articles of the Peasants in Swabia." In *Luther's Works.* Vol. 46, *The Christian in Society,* part 3, 5-43. Edited by Robert C. Schultz. Translated by Charles M. Jacobs. Philadelphia: Fortress, 1967.

―――. "Against the Robbing and Murdering Hordes of Peasants." In *Luther's Works.* Vol. 46, *The Christian in Society,* part 3, 47-55. Edited by Robert C. Schultz. Translated by Charles M. Jacobs. Philadelphia: Fortress, 1967.

Macchia, Frank D. "Justification and the Spirit: A Pentecostal Reflection on the Doctrine by Which the Church Stands or Falls." *Pneuma* 22 (2000): 3-21.

———. "Justification Through New Creation: The Holy Spirit and the Doctrine by Which the Church Stands or Falls." *Theology Today* 58 (2001): 202-217.

MacLeod, David J. "The Exaltation of Christ: An Exposition of Philippians 2:9-11." *Bibliotheca Sacra* 158 (2001): 437-450.

Marsden, George M. "Defining Fundamentalism." *Christian Scholar's Review* 1 (1971): 141-151.

———. "Does Evangelicalism Have a Future?" *Reformed Journal*, April 1989, 2-3.

———. "The Incoherent University." *Hedgehog Review* 2 (2000): 92-105.

———. "Introduction: Reformed and American." In *Reformed Theology in America: A History of Its Modern Development*, ed. David F. Wells, 1-12. Grand Rapids, Mich.: Baker, 1997.

———. "Unity and Diversity in the Evangelical Resurgence." In *Altered Landscapes: Christianity in America, 1935–1985*, 61-76. Grand Rapids, Mich.: Eerdmans, 1989.

Marshall-Green, Molly. "George Eldon Ladd." In *Baptist Theologians*, ed. Timothy George and David S. Dockery, 480-495. Nashville: Broadman, 1990.

Marty, Martin E. "Reformed America and America Reformed." *Reformed Journal*, March 1989, 8-11.

———. "Will Success Spoil Evangelicalism?" *Christian Century*, July 19-26, 2000, 757-761.

———. "The Years of the Evangelicals." *Christian Century*, February 15, 1989, 171-174.

McCartney, Dan G. "Ecce Homo: The Coming of the Kingdom as the Restoration of Human Vicegerency." *Westminster Theological Journal* 56 (1994): 1-21.

McClay, Wilfred M. "Individualism and Its Discontents." *Virginia Quarterly Review* 77 (2001): 391-405.

McDermott, Gerald R. "Jonathan Edwards and the Culture Wars: A New Resource for Public Theology and Philosophy." *Pro Ecclesia* 4 (1995): 268-280.

McLean, John A. "Did Jesus Correct the Disciples' View of the Kingdom?" *Bibliotheca Sacra* 151 (April/June 1994): 215-227.

Mohler, R. Albert, Jr. "A Call for Baptist Evangelicals and Evangelical Baptists: Communities of Faith and a Common Quest for Identity." In *Southern Baptists and American Evangelicals: The Conversation Continues*, ed. David S. Dockery, 224-239. Nashville: Broadman & Holman, 1993.

———. "Church Discipline: The Missing Mark." In *The Compromised Church: The Present Evangelical Crisis*, ed. John H. Armstrong, 171-188. Wheaton, Ill.: Crossway, 1998.

———. "Contending for Truth in an Age of Anti-Truth." In *Here We Stand: A Call from Confessing Evangelicals*, ed. James Montgomery Boice and Benjamin E. Sasse, 59-76. Grand Rapids, Mich.: Baker, 1996.

———. "The Eclipse of God at Century's End: Evangelicals Attempt Theology Without Theism." *Southern Baptist Journal of Theology* 1 (1997): 6-15.

———. "'Evangelical': What's in a Name?" In *The Coming Evangelical Crisis*, ed. John H. Armstrong, 29-44. Chicago: Moody, 1996.

———. "The Integrity of the Evangelical Tradition and the Challenge of the Postmodern Paradigm." In *The Challenge of Postmodernism,* ed. David S. Dockery, 67-88. Wheaton, Ill.: Victor, 1995.

———. "Reformist Evangelicalism: A Center Without a Circumference." In *A Confessing Theology for Postmodern Times,* ed. Michael S. Horton, 131-150. Wheaton, Ill.: Crossway, 2000.

Moore, Russell D. "Baptist After All: Resurgent Conservatives Face the Future." In *Why I Am a Baptist,* ed. Tom J. Nettles and Russell D. Moore, 233-246. Nashville: Broadman & Holman, 2001.

———. "The Gospel According to Jane Roe: Abortion Rights and the Reshaping of Evangelical Theology." *Southern Baptist Journal of Theology* 7 (2003): 40-53.

———. "In Search of an Evangelical Identity." *SBC Life,* January 2001, 7.

———. "Of Sacraments and Sawdust: ECT, the Culture Wars, and the Quandary of Evangelical Identity." *Southern Baptist Journal of Theology* 5 (2001): 36-48.

———. "Resurgence vs. McWorld? American Culture and the Future of Baptist Conservatism." *Southern Baptist Journal of Theology* 7 (2003): 32-49.

———. Review of *Across the Spectrum: Understanding Issues in Evangelical Theology,* by Gregory A. Boyd and Paul R. Eddy. *Journal of the Evangelical Theological Society* 46 (2003): 157-158.

———. Review of *Honky-Tonk Gospel: Sin and Salvation in Country Music,* by Gene Edward Veith and Thomas L. Wilmeth. *Southern Baptist Journal of Theology* 6 (2002): 108-109.

———. Review of *Mother Kirk: The Case for Liturgy in the Reformed Tradition,* by D. G. Hart. *Southern Baptist Journal of Theology* 7 (2003): 100-102.

———. Review of *Separation of Church and State* by Philip Hamburger. *Southern Baptist Journal of Theology* 7 (2003): 84-85.

———. Review of *The Mosaic of Christian Belief: Twenty Centuries of Unity and Diversity,* by Roger E. Olson. *Southern Baptist Journal of Theology* 7 (2003): 98-99.

———. Review of *The Race Set Before Us: A Biblical Theology of Perseverance and Assurance,* by Thomas R. Schreiner and Ardel B. Caneday. *Southern Baptist Journal of Theology* 6 (2002): 80-81.

———. "Till Every Foe Is Vanquished: Emerging Sociopolitical Implications of Progressive Dispensational Eschatology." In *Looking into the Future: Evangelical Essays in Eschatology,* ed. David W. Baker, 342-361. Grand Rapids, Mich.: Baker, 2001.

Moorhead, James H. "Engineering the Millennium: Kingdom Building in American Protestantism, 1880–1920." *Princeton Seminary Bulletin* 3 (1994): 104-128.

Mouw, Richard J. "Another Look at the Infra/Supralapsarian Debate." *Calvin Theological Journal* 35 (2000): 136-151.

———. "The Call to Holy Worldliness." *Reformed Journal,* January 1989, 8-14.

———. "A Kinder, Gentler Calvinism." *Reformed Journal,* October 1990, 11-13.

———. "Public Religion: Through Thick and Thin." *Christian Century,* June 7-14, 2000, 648-651.

Muether, John R. "Contemporary Evangelicalism and the Triumph of the New School." *Westminster Theological Journal* 50 (1988): 339-347.

Nebeker, Gary L. "The Theme of Hope in Dispensationalism." *Bibliotheca Sacra* 158 (2001): 3-20.

Neuhaus, Richard John. "The End of Democracy? The Judicial Usurpation of Politics." *First Things*, November 1996, 18-20.

Nichols, Stephen J. "The Dispensational View of the Davidic Kingdom: A Response to Progressive Dispensationalism." *The Master's Seminary Journal* 7 (1996): 213-239.

———. Review of *Progressive Dispensationalism*, by Craig A. Blaising and Darrell L. Bock. *Trinity Journal* 15 (1994): 253-255.

Noll, Mark A. "Survey Among Biblical Scholars." Appendix in *Between Faith and Criticism: Evangelicals, Scholarship and the Bible in America*, 199-214. San Francisco: Harper & Row, 1986.

Nuechterlein, James. "Conservative Confusions." *First Things*, May 2000, 7-8.

Ockenga, Harold John. "Introduction." In Carl F. H. Henry, *The Uneasy Conscience of Modern Fundamentalism*, 13-14. Grand Rapids, Mich.: Eerdmans, 1947.

———. "The Unvoiced Multitudes." In *Evangelical Action! A Report on the Organization of the National Association of Evangelicals for United Action*, 19-39. Boston: United Action Press, 1942.

O'Donovan, Oliver, and Joan Lockwood O'Donovan. "The Patristic Age." In *From Irenaeus to Grotius: A Sourcebook in Christian Political Thought*, ed. Oliver O'Donovan and Joan Lockwood O'Donovan, 1-7. Grand Rapids, Mich.: Eerdmans, 1999.

O'Leary, Stephen, and Michael McFarland. "The Political Use of Mythic Discourse: Prophetic Interpretation in Pat Robertson's Presidential Campaign." *The Quarterly Journal of Speech* 75 (1989): 433-452.

Olson, Roger E. "The Future of Evangelical Theology." *Christianity Today*, February 9, 1998, 40-48.

———. "Postconservative Evangelicals Greet the Postmodern Age." *Christian Century*, May 3, 1995, 480-483.

———. "Reforming Evangelical Theology." In *Evangelical Futures: A Conversation on Theological Method*, ed. John G. Stackhouse, Jr., 201-208. Grand Rapids, Mich.: Baker, 2000.

———. Review of *Most Moved Mover: A Theology of God's Openness* by Clark H. Pinnock and *Searching for an Adequate God: A Dialogue Between Process and Free Will Theists*, ed. by John B. Cobb, Jr., and Clark H. Pinnock. *Christian Century*, January 30/February 6, 2002, 37-39.

———. "Whales and Elephants: Both God's Creatures but Can They Meet?" *Pro Ecclesia* 4 (1995): 165-189.

Ostling, Richard N. "America's Ever-Changing Religious Landscape." In *What's God Got to Do With the American Experiment?*, ed. E. J. Dionne, Jr., and John J. DiIulio, Jr., 17-24. Washington, D.C.: Brookings Institution Press, 2000.

Pate, C. Marvin. "The Church." In *The Evangelical Dictionary of Biblical Theology*, ed. Walter A. Elwell. Grand Rapids, Mich.: Baker, 1996.

———. "A Progressive Dispensationalist View of Revelation." In *Four Views on the Book of Revelation*, ed. C. Marvin Pate, 133-176. Grand Rapids, Mich.: Zondervan, 1998.

Paulien, Jonathan K. "The End of Time? The Effect of Prophecy on American Politics." *Liberty,* January/February 2000, 8-10.

Pierard, Richard. "The New Religious Right in American Politics." In *Evangelicalism and Modern America,* ed. George Marsden, 161-174. Grand Rapids, Mich.: Eerdmans, 1984.

Pinnock, Clark H. "Erickson's Three-Volume *Magnum Opus.*" *TSF Bulletin,* January/February 1986, 29-30.

———. "Evangelical Theologians Facing the Future: An Ancient and a Future Paradigm." *Wesleyan Theological Journal* 33 (1998): 7-28.

———. "Fuller Theological Seminary and the Nature of Evangelicalism." *Christian Scholar's Review* 23 (1993): 44-47.

———. "In Response to Dr. Daniel Fuller." *Christian Scholar's Review* 2 (1973): 333-335.

———. "Toward a More Inclusive Eschatology." In *Looking into the Future: Evangelical Studies in Eschatology,* ed. David W. Baker, 249-262. Grand Rapids, Mich.: Baker, 2001.

Plant, Robert. "Community." In *The Blackwell Encyclopedia of Political Thought,* ed. David Miller, 88-90. Oxford: Blackwell, 1987.

Podhoretz, Norman. "The Christian Right and Its Demonizers." *National Review,* April 3, 2000, 30-32.

Ponnuru, Ramesh. "This We Must Do." *National Review,* January 22, 2001, 31-34.

Poythress, Vern S. "The Church as Family: Why Male Leadership in the Family Requires Male Leadership in the Church." In *Recovering Biblical Manhood and Womanhood: A Response to Evangelical Feminism,* 233-247. Wheaton, Ill.: Crossway, 1991.

———. "Currents Within Amillennialism." *Presbyterion* 26 (2000): 21-25.

———. "Response to Paul S. Karleen's Paper 'Understanding Covenant Theologians.'" *Grace Theological Journal* 10 (1989): 147-155.

———. "Response to Robert L. Saucy's Paper." *Grace Theological Journal* 10 (1989): 157-159.

Pratt, Raymond. "The Social Emphasis of New Evangelicalism." *Central Bible Quarterly* 21 (1978): 18-47.

Pyne, Robert A. "The New Man and Immoral Society." *Bibliotheca Sacra* 154 (1997): 259-274.

———. "The 'Seed,' the Spirit, and the Blessing of Abraham." *Westminster Theological Journal* 152 (1995): 211-222.

Radmacher, Earl D. "The Current Status of Dispensationalism and Its Eschatology." In *Perspectives on Evangelical Theology,* ed. Kenneth S. Kantzer and Stanley N. Gundry, 163-176. Grand Rapids, Mich.: Baker, 1979.

Ramos, Norma. "Pornography Is a Social Justice Issue." In *Feminism and Pornography: Oxford Readings in Feminism,* 45-47. New York: Oxford University Press, 2000.

Richard, Ramesh P. "Elements of a Biblical Philosophy of History." *Bibliotheca Sacra* 138 (1981): 108-118.

———. "Non-Christian Interpretations of History." *Bibliotheca Sacra* 138 (1981): 13-21.

————. "The Premillennial Interpretation of History." *Bibliotheca Sacra* 138 (1981): 203-212.

Robinson, Anthony. "The Church as Countercultural Enclave." Review of *Resident Aliens: Life in the Christian Colony*, by Stanley Hauerwas and William H. Willimon. *Christian Century* 107 (1990): 739-741.

Rogers, Adrian. "Response." In *The Proceedings of the Conference on Biblical Inerrancy*, 101-106. Nashville: Broadman, 1987.

Rogers, Cleon. "The Davidic Covenant in Acts-Revelation." *Bibliotheca Sacra* 151 (1994): 71-84.

Rorty, Richard. "The Moral Purposes of the University: An Exchange." *Hedgehog Review* 2 (2000): 106-117.

Sandeen, Ernest R. "Toward a Historical Interpretation of the Origins of Fundamentalism." *Church History* 36 (1967): 66-83.

Saucy, Mark. "Exaltation Christology in Hebrews: What Kind of Reign?" *Trinity Journal* 14 (1993): 41-62.

————. "The Kingdom-of-God Sayings in Matthew." *Bibliotheca Sacra* 151 (1994): 175-197.

Saucy, Robert L. "The Crucial Issue Between Dispensational and Non-Dispensational Systems." *Criswell Theological Review* 1 (1986): 149-165.

————. "Dispensationalism and the Salvation of the Kingdom." *TSF Bulletin*, May/June 1984: 6-7.

————. "The Locus of the Church." *Criswell Theological Review* 1 (1987): 387-399.

————. "The Presence of the Kingdom and the Life of the Church." *Bibliotheca Sacra* 145 (1988): 30-46.

————. "A Rationale for the Future of Israel." *Journal of the Evangelical Theological Society* 28 (1985): 433-442.

————. "Response to *Understanding Dispensationalists*, by Vern S. Poythress." *Grace Theological Journal* 10 (1989): 139-145.

————. "'Sinners' Who Are Forgiven or 'Saints' Who Sin?" *Bibliotheca Sacra* 152 (October/December 1995): 400-412.

Scanlon, Michael J. "Eschatology." In *Augustine Through the Ages: An Encyclopedia*, 316-318. Grand Rapids, Mich.: Eerdmans, 1999.

Schaeffer, Francis A. "Modern Man and the Problem of Authority." *Journal of Faith Theological Seminary* 4 (1951): 3-10.

Schemm, Peter R., Jr. "Galatians 3:28: Prooftext or Context?" *Journal for Biblical Manhood and Womanhood* 8 (2003): 23-30.

Seifrid, Mark A. "The 'New Perspective on Paul' and Its Problems." *Themelios* 25 (2000): 4-18.

Shogren, Gary S. "Presently Entering the Kingdom of Christ: The Background and Purpose of Col. 1:12-14." *Journal of the Evangelical Theological Society* 31 (1988): 173-180.

Shy, Edward Todd. "Clamoring for a King." *Regeneration Quarterly* (Winter 1995): 10-13.

Sidey, Ken. "For the Love of Zion." *Christianity Today*, March 9, 1992, 46-50.

Silk, Mark. "The Rise of the 'New Evangelicalism': Shock and Adjustment." In *Between the Times: The Travail of the Protestant Establishment in America, 1900–1960*, ed. William R. Hutchison, 278-299. New York: Cambridge University Press, 1989.

Simmons, Paul D. "The Pastor as Prophet: How Naked the Public Square?" *Review and Expositor* 86 (1989): 517-531.

Smith, Morton. "The Southern Tradition." In *Reformed Theology in America: A History of Its Modern Development*, 189-207. Grand Rapids, Mich.: Eerdmans, 1985.

Smith, Timothy L. "The Evangelical Kaleidoscope and the Call to Unity." *Christian Scholar's Review* 15 (1986): 125-140.

Spencer, Stephen R. "Reformed Theology, Covenant Theology, and Dispensationalism." In *Integrity of Heart and Skillfulness of Hands: Biblical and Leadership Studies in Honor of Donald K. Campbell*, ed. Charles H. Dyer and Roy B. Zuck, 239-254. Grand Rapids, Mich.: Baker, 1994.

Sproul, R.C., Jr. "Coram Deo." *Tabletalk*, December 1998, 2.

Stackhouse, John G., Jr. "The Perils of Left and Right." *Christianity Today*, August 10, 1998, 58-59.

Stafford, Tim. "Ron Sider's Unsettling Crusade." *Christianity Today*, April 27, 1992, 18-22.

Stinson, Randy. "Our Mother Who Art in Heaven: A Brief Overview and Critique of Evangelical Feminists and the Use of Feminine God-Language." *Journal for Biblical Manhood and Womanhood* 8 (2003): 20-33.

Straton, John Roach. "Do True Believers Need to Keep At It?" *Religious Herald*, March 19, 1925, 3.

Thomas, Cal, and Jay Sekulow. "What Role for Religious Conservatives?" *The American Enterprise*, April/May 2000, 14-15.

Thomas, Robert L. "A Critique of Progressive Dispensational Hermeneutics." In *When the Trumpet Sounds*, ed. Thomas Ice and Timothy Demy, 413-426. Eugene, Ore.: Harvest, 1995.

———. "The Hermeneutics of Progressive Dispensationalism." *Master's Seminary Journal* 6 (Spring 1995): 79-95.

———. "Improving Evangelical Ethics: An Analysis of the Problem and a Proposed Solution." *Journal of the Evangelical Theological Society* 34 (1991): 3-20.

Thorsell, Paul R. "The Spirit in the Present Age: Preliminary Fulfillment of the Predicted New Covenant According to Paul." *Journal of the Evangelical Theological Society* 41 (1998): 397-414.

Toon, Peter. "The Significance of the Ascension for Believers." *Bibliotheca Sacra* 141 (January/March 1984): 16-27.

Toussaint, Stanley D. "The Contingency of the Coming of the Kingdom." In *Integrity of Heart, Skillfulness of Hands*, ed. Charles H. Dyer and Roy B. Zuck, 222-237. Grand Rapids, Mich.: Baker, 1994.

Townsend, Jeffrey L. "Premillennialism Summarized: Conclusion." In *The Coming Millennial Kingdom: A Case for Premillennial Interpretation*, ed. Donald K. Campbell and Jeffrey L. Townsend, 263-271. Grand Rapids, Mich.: Kregel, 1997.

Trueman, Carl R. "Admiring the Sistine Chapel: Reflections on Carl Henry's *God, Revelation, and Authority*." *Themelios* 25 (2000): 48-58.

Turner, David L. "'Dubious Evangelicalism'?—A Response." *Grace Theological Journal* 12 (1992): 263-277.

Turner, Helen Lee, and James L. Guth. "The Politics of Armageddon: Dispensationalism Among Southern Baptist Ministers." In *Religion and Political Behavior in the United States,* ed. Ted G. Jelen, 187-208. New York: Praeger, 1989.

Vos, Geerhardus. "The Eschatological Aspect of the Pauline Conception of the Spirit." In *Biblical and Theological Studies,* by the Members of the Faculty of Princeton Theological Seminary, 209-259. New York: Scribner, 1912.

————. "Our Lord's Doctrine of the Resurrection." In *Redemptive History and Biblical Interpretation: The Shorter Writings of Geerhardus Vos,* 317-323. Phillipsburg, N.J.: Presbyterian & Reformed, 1980.

————. "The Pauline Eschatology and Chiliasm." *Princeton Theological Review* 9 (1911): 26-60.

Wallis, Jim. "What Does Washington Have to Say to Grand Rapids?" *Sojourners,* July 1977, 3-7.

Walsh, Brian J. "Worldviews, Modernity, and the Task of Christian College Education." *Faculty Dialogue: Journal of the Institute for Christian Leadership* 18 (1992): 13-35.

Walvoord, John F. "Biblical Kingdoms Compared and Contrasted." In *Issues in Dispensationalism,* ed. Wesley R. Willis and John R. Master, 75-91. Chicago: Moody, 1994.

————. "The Present Work of Christ on Earth." *Bibliotheca Sacra* 122 (1965): 291-301.

————. Review of *Jesus and the Kingdom,* by George Eldon Ladd. *Bibliotheca Sacra* 122 (1965): 74-76.

————. Review of *The Presence of the Future: The Eschatology of Biblical Realism,* by George Eldon Ladd. *Bibliotheca Sacra* 131 (1974): 273.

Ware, Bruce A. "New Dimensions in Eschatology." In *New Dimensions in Evangelical Thought: Essays in Honor of Millard J. Erickson,* ed. David S. Dockery, 354-365. Downers Grove, Ill.: InterVarsity Press, 1998.

Warfield, Benjamin B. "Resurrection—A Fundamental Doctrine." In *Benjamin B. Warfield: Selected Shorter Writings,* ed. John E. Meeter, 1:193-202. Phillipsburg, N.J.: Presbyterian & Reformed, 1970.

Watson, Nancy. "Faithful Dissenters? Feminist Ecclesiologies and Dissent." *Scottish Journal of Theology* 51 (1998): 464-484.

Weber, Timothy. "How Evangelicals Became Israel's Best Friend." *Christianity Today,* October 5, 1998, 38-49.

Weeks, David L. "Carl F. H. Henry's Moral Arguments for Evangelical Political Activism." *Journal of Church and State* 40 (1998): 83-106.

————. "The Uneasy Politics of Modern Evangelicalism." *Christian Scholar's Review* 30 (2001): 403-418.

Weyrich, Paul. "The Moral Minority." *Christianity Today,* September 6, 1999, 44-45.

White, R. Fowler. "Agony, Irony, and Victory in Inaugurated Eschatology: Reflections on the Current Amillennial-Postmillennial Debate." *Westminster Theological Journal* 62 (2000): 161-176.

Wilcox, Clyde, Sharon Linzey, and Ted G. Jelen. "Reluctant Warriors: Premillennialism and Politics in the Moral Majority." *Journal for the Scientific Study of Religion* 30 (1991): 245-258.

Williams, Michael. "Of Heaven and History: The Verticalist Eschatology of Geerhardus Vos." *Pro Rege* 20 (1992): 9-18.

———. "On Eschatological Discontinuity: The Confession of an Eschatological Reactionary." *Presbyterion* 25 (1999): 13-20.

———. "Rapture or Resurrection?" *Presbyterion* 24 (1998): 9-37.

———. "Regeneration in Cosmic Context." *Evangelical Journal* 7 (1989): 68-80.

———. "A Restorational Alternative to Augustinian Verticalist Eschatology." *Pro Rege* 20 (1992): 11-24.

Williams, Michael D. "Where's the Church? The Church as the Unfinished Business of Dispensational Theology." *Grace Theological Journal* 10 (1989): 165-182.

Wolfe, Alan. "The Opening of the Evangelical Mind." *Atlantic Monthly,* October 2000, 55-76.

Woodbridge, John D., and Randall H. Balmer. "The Princetonians and Biblical Authority: An Assessment of the Ernest Sandeen Proposal." In *Scripture and Truth,* ed. D. A. Carson and John D. Woodbridge, 244-279. Grand Rapids, Mich.: Baker, 1992.

Woodiwiss, Ashley. "Revising Our Pledges of Allegiance: From 'Christian America' to the Gospel of the Resurrection." *Touchstone,* September/October 1998, 28-33.

Woodward, Kenneth. "Sex, Sin, and Salvation." *Newsweek,* November 2, 1998, 37.

Wright, Christopher J. H. "The Use of the Bible in Social Ethics: Paradigms, Types, and Eschatology." *Transformation* 1 (1984): 11-20.

Yong, Amos. "Discerning the Spirit(s) in the World of Religions." In *No Other Gods Before Me? Evangelicals and the Challenge of World Religions,* ed. John G. Stackhouse, Jr., 37-61. Grand Rapids, Mich.: Baker, 2001.

Young, Warren C. "The Christian Hope and the Social Order." *The Mennonite Quarterly Review* 28 (1954): 88-101.

DISSERTATIONS AND THESES

French, Henry Frank. "The Concept of the Church in the Theology of Walter Rauschenbusch." Ph.D. diss., Drew University, 1986.

Lawless, Charles E., Jr. "The Relationship Between Evangelism and Spiritual Warfare in the North American Spiritual Warfare Movement, 1986–1997." Ph.D. diss., The Southern Baptist Theological Seminary, 1997.

Matthews, Douglas K. "Approximating the Millennium: Toward a Coherent Premillennial Theology of Social Transformation." Ph.D. diss., Baylor University, 1992.

Mohler, R. Albert, Jr. "Evangelical Theology and Karl Barth: Representative Models of Response." Ph.D. diss., The Southern Baptist Theological Seminary, 1989.

Moore, Russell D. "Kingdom Theology and the American Evangelical Consensus: Emerging Implications for Sociopolitical Engagement." Ph.D. diss., The Southern Baptist Theological Seminary, 2002.

Richard, Ramesh. "Hermeneutical Prolegomena to Premillennial Social Ethics." Th.D. diss., Dallas Theological Seminary, 1982.

Weeks, David L. "The Political Thought of Carl F. H. Henry." Ph.D. diss., Loyola University of Chicago, 1991.

OTHER MATERIALS

Blaising, Craig A. "The Baptism with the Holy Spirit in the History of Redemption." Paper presented to the Dispensational Study Group at the annual meeting of the Evangelical Theological Society, Lisle, Ill., November 17, 1994.

———. "Law, Gospel, and the Unity of Scripture in Progressive Dispensationalism." Paper presented to the Biblical Theology Study Group at the annual meeting of the Evangelical Theological Society, Colorado Springs, November 15, 2001.

Breshears, Gerry. "New Directions in Dispensationalism." Paper presented at the annual meeting of the Evangelical Theological Society, Kansas City, Mo., November 23, 1991.

Gaffin, Richard B., Jr. "Pentecost: Before and After." Paper presented to the Dispensational Study Group at the annual meeting of the Evangelical Theological Society, Lisle, Ill., November 17, 1994.

Harvey, Paul. "Race, Gender, and Southern Baptist Identity Politics." Address given to the Center for the Study of the Southern Baptist Convention, Louisville, February 27, 2001.

Henry, Carl F. H. "The Character of a Theologian." Paper presented at The Southern Baptist Theological Seminary, Louisville, January 28, 1998.

———. "The Instability of Twentieth-Century Theology." Paper presented at The Southern Baptist Theological Seminary, Louisville, January 28, 1998.

———. "A Troubled Conscience Fifty Years Later." Paper presented at The Southern Baptist Theological Seminary, Louisville, January 28, 1998.

Lemke, Steve W. "Evangelical Theology in the Twenty-First Century." Paper presented at the southwestern regional meeting of the Evangelical Theological Society, Fort Worth, Tex., April 7, 2000.

Master, John. "A Perspective of the Ministry of the Holy Spirit in the Old and New Testaments." Paper presented to the Dispensational Study Group at the annual meeting of the Evangelical Theological Society, Lisle, Ill., November 17, 1994.

Nichols, Stephen J. "Already Ladd—Not Yet Dispensationalism: D. Bock and Progressive Dispensationalism." Paper presented at the eastern regional meeting of the Evangelical Theological Society, Philadelphia, April 2, 1993.

———. "The Dispensational View of the Davidic Kingdom: A Response to Progressive Dispensationalism." Paper presented at the annual meeting of the Evangelical Theological Society, Philadelphia, November 18, 1995.

Pyne, Robert. "The New Man in an Immoral Society." Paper presented at the annual meeting of the Evangelical Theological Society, Santa Clara, Calif., November 20, 1997.

GENERAL INDEX

Israel, 72-73, 95-96, 116, 119-120, 242-243n. 193; culmination of in Jesus Christ, the true Israelite, 117-120; God's promises to, 118-119. *See also* church, continuity with Israel; Zionism

Jacoby, Russell, 79
Jefferson, Thomas, 226n. 8
Jenkins, Jerry, 261n. 157
Jerusalem Conference on Biblical Prophecy, 31
Jesus and the Kingdom (Ladd), 31-32
Jesus Christ, 59, 100, 112, 118, 119, 145; ascension of, 152; messianic work of, 105-106, 113; ministry of, 94-95; redemptive work of, 104-105; resurrection of, 110, 111, 123, 152, 209nn. 143, 146, 148, 235n. 120; as the righteousness of God, 98; as the true Israelite, 119-120. *See also* Davidic King, the
Jesus movement, 133, 166
Jewett, Paul, 269n. 17
John Paul II, 70
Jones, Bob, Jr., 67
Jones, Larry, 221n. 285

kaleidoscope metaphor, 20, 194n. 36
Kant, Immanuel, 226n. 8
Karlberg, Mark W., 214n. 208
Keeping Faith (Carter), 189n. 3
Kennedy, D. James, 190n. 9
Keyes, Alan, 179
King, Martin Luther, Jr., 226n. 13
Kingdom ecclesiology: and covenantal development, 143-146; and dispensational development, 140-143; and the emerging evangelical consensus, 138-140
Kingdom eschatology, 76-80; and dispensational development, 39-52; and the emerging evangelical consensus, 36-39; and evangelical engagement, 52-53
Kingdom of God, the, 20, 21-22, 47, 56-57, 80, 82-83, 85-88, 97-99; "already/not yet" nature of, 66-67, 70-71, 74, 102, 137, 140, 151-152, 154-155, 232n. 87; broad themes of Kingdom and church, 147; as future consummation, 42-44, 49-52; and God's redeeming activity, 94; messianic, 148-149; "not yet" phase of, 70-71, 74, 101
Kingdom soteriology, 112-113; and covenantal development, 96-102, 116-117; and dispensational development, 90-96; and the emerging evangelical consensus, 88-90; and warfare imagery, 106
Kingdom theology, 24, 140; and covenantal development, 44-52; and dispensational development, 39-44; and evangelical engagement, 22-24
Kirk, Russell, 125
Kline, Meredith, 49
Kraynak, Robert, 71, 267n. 225
Kristol, Irving, 177

Kümmel, Werner Georg, 31-32, 202nn. 40, 41
Kuyper, Abraham, 51, 76, 197nn. 57, 62, 198n. 64, 233n. 99, 235n. 124, 244n. 215; on salvation, 96-97
Kyle, Richard, 73, 222n. 288

Ladd, George Eldon, 22, 26, 39, 44, 46, 50, 63, 77, 78, 79, 97, 101, 109, 116, 197nn. 57, 60, 206n. 96, 228n. 37, 229n. 40; Kingdom theology of, 31-36, 86-88, 136-138, 143, 202n. 38, 203nn. 47, 50, 51, 204n. 74, 228nn. 33, 35, 250nn. 36, 38; works on eschatology, 202n. 37
LaHaye, Tim, 42, 261n. 157
Land, Richard D., 160, 194n. 37
Late Great Planet Earth, The (Lindsey), 161
Left Behind novels, 161
Lemke, Steve W., 269n. 21
Letham, Robert, 238n. 142
Lewis, C. S., 52
Lewis, Gordon R., 37
liberalism, 19, 23, 27, 54-55, 74, 97, 103, 109, 124, 132, 135, 226n. 13, 227n. 20
liberation theology, 76, 223n. 300, 240n. 167
Liberty Federation, 16
Lightner, Robert, 198n. 64
Lincoln, Andrew T., 110
Lindsell, Harold, 269-270n. 23
Lindsey, Hal, 37, 42, 43, 161, 221n. 282
Lints, Richard, 160, 197n. 57
Lloyd-Jones, D. Martyn, 68, 74, 218n. 252
Lord's Supper, 163, 262n. 171

Macchia, Frank D., 242n. 188
Machen, J. Gresham, 83, 101, 178, 198n. 64, 215n. 211, 242n. 190, 259n. 138
MacLeod, David J., 237n. 139
Marsden, George, 66-67, 170, 194n. 38, 198n. 2, 218n. 242, 236nn. 129, 131, 247-248n. 2, 252n. 66
Marshall, Molly T., 271n. 42
Martin, William, 127, 190n. 9
Marty, Martin E., 191n. 18, 220n. 275
Martyr, Justin, 119-120
Marx, Karl, 30, 78
Marxism, 20, 74, 171-172, 251n. 52
Master, John, 214n. 206
Mathews, Shailer, 54, 222nn. 289, 293, 227n. 21, 246-247n. 235
McCabe, L. D., 270n. 27
McCarraher, Eugene, 223n. 297
McCartney, Dan G., 99
McClain, Alva, 33, 229n. 40, 232n. 78
McIntire, Carl, 67
Meyer, F. B., 252n. 63
modernism, Protestant, 27, 29, 30, 54, 226n. 8
Mohler, R. Albert, Jr., 160, 194n. 36, 251nn. 56, 57, 260nn. 148, 150
Moltmann, Jürgen, 37, 205n. 79, 221n. 283
Mondale, Walter, 221n. 286
Moody, Dwight L., 90
Moody Monthly, 230n. 60

SCRIPTURE INDEX